Prentice Hall

LITERATURE

Timeless Voices, Timeless Themes

Reader's Companion

BRONZE LEVEL

Upper Saddle River, New Jersey
Glenview, Illinois
Needham, Massachusetts

ISBN 0-13-062377-6

10 08 07 06 05 04

Acknowledgments

Grateful acknowledgment is made to the following for permission to reprint copyrighted material:

Miriam Altschuler Literary Agency
"Treasure of Lemon Brown" by Walter Dean Myers from *Boy's Life Magazine*, March 1983. Copyright © 1983 by Walter Dean Myers.

AMG
"A Christmas Carol: Scrooge and Marley" by Israel Horovitz, an adaptation of Charles Dickens's *A Christmas Carol.* Copyright © 1994 by Fountain Pen, Inc. All rights reserved.

Arte Público Press
"Maestro" by Pat Mora is reprinted with permission from the publisher of *Borders* (Houston: Arte Público Press—University of Houston, 1986).

Susan Bergholz Literary Services, New York
"Four Skinny Trees" from *The House on Mango Street.* Copyright © 1984 by Sandra Cisneros. Published by Vintage Books, a division of Random House, Inc., and in hardcover by Alfred A. Knopf in 1994. All rights reserved.

Curtis Brown Ltd.
"Ribbons" by Laurence Yep, from *American Girl*, Jan/Feb 1992. Copyright © 1992 by Laurence Yep.

Brandt & Hochman Literary Agents, Inc.
"The Third Wish" from *Not What You Expected: A Collection of Short Stories* by Joan Aiken. Copyright © 1974 by Joan Aiken.

Delacorte Press, a division of Random House, Inc.
"The Luckiest Time of All" from *The Lucky Stone* by Lucille Clifton. Copyright © 1979 by Lucille Clifton. All rights reserved.

Don Congdon Associates, Inc.
"All Summer In A Day" by Ray Bradbury, published in *The Magazine of Fantasy and Science Fiction*, March 1, 1954. Copyright © 1954, renewed 1982 by Ray Bradbury.

Farrar, Straus & Giroux, Inc.
"The Cat Who Thought She Was a Dog and the Dog Who Thought He Was a Cat" from *Naftali the Storyteller and His Horse, Sus* by Isaac Bashevis Singer. Copyright © 1973, 1976 by Isaac Bashevis Singer.

M.W. Farrell, executrix for the Estate of Juliet Piggott Wood
"Popocatepetl and Ixtlaccihuatl" from *Mexican Folk Tales* by Juliet Piggott. Copyright © 1973 by Juliet Piggott.

Golden Books Family Entertainment
"The Bride of Pluto" (retitled "Demeter and Persephone") from *Golden Treasury of Myths and Legends* by Anne Terry White. Copyright © 1959 Western Publishing Company, Inc. All rights reserved.

G.P Putnam's Sons, a division of Penguin Putnam, Inc.
"Two Kinds" by Amy Tan from *The Joy Luck Club.* Copyright © 1989 by Amy Tan. "Our Finest Hour" from *The Osgood Files* by Charles Osgood. Copyright © 1986, 1987, 1988, 1989, 1990, 1991 by Charles Osgood.

Harcourt, Inc.
Excerpt from *In Search of Our Mother's Gardens: Womanist Prose*, copyright © 1983 by Alice Walker. "Seventh Grade" from *Baseball in April and Other Stories*, copyright © 1990 by Gary Soto.

HarperCollins Publishers, Inc.
"How the Snake Got Poison" from *Mules and Men* by Zora Neale Hurston. Copyright © 1935 by Zora Neale Hurston. Copyright renewed 1963 by John C. Hurston and Joel Hurston. From *An American Childhood* by Annie Dillard. Copyright © 1987 by Annie Dillard.

John Hawkins & Associates Inc.
"My Furthest-Back Person—The African" by Alex Haley, published July 16, 1972, by *The New York Times Magazine.* Copyright © 1972 by Alex Haley.

Bill Hilgers, Esq., for the Estate of Barbara Jordan
"All Together Now" by Barbara Jordan, originally published in *Sesame Street Parents*, July/August 1994.

(Acknowledgments continue on page 284.)

Contents

Unit 5: Just For Fun

Unit 6: Looking at Literary Forms: Short Story

Unit 7: Nonfiction

Unit 8: Drama

Unit 9: Poetry

Unit 10: Legends, Folk Tales, and Myths

Part 2: Selection Summaries With Alternative Reading Strategies

Unit 1: Independence and Identity

Unit 2: Common Threads

Unit 3: What Matters

Unit 4: Meeting Challenges

Unit 5: Just For Fun

Unit 6: Looking at Literary Forms: Short Story

Unit 7: Nonfiction

Unit 8: Drama

Unit 9: Poetry

Unit 10: Legends, Folk Tales, and Myths

Part 1

Selections With Interactive Reading Support and Practice

Part 1 is a companion for *Prentice Hall Literature: Timeless Voices, Timeless Themes.* It will guide and support you as you interact with the literature from *Prentice Hall Literature: Timeless Voices, Timeless Themes.*

- Start by looking at the **Prepare to Read** pages for the literature selection in *Prentice Hall Literature: Timeless Voices, Timeless Themes.*
- Review the **Literary Analysis** and **Reading Strategy** skills taught on those **Prepare to Read** pages. You will apply those skills as you use the *Reader's Companion.*
- Look at the art for the selection in *Prentice Hall Literature: Timeless Voices, Timeless Themes.*
- Now go to the Preview page in the *Reader's Companion.* Use the written and visual summaries of the selection to direct your reading.
- Then read the selection in the *Reader's Companion.*
- Respond to all the questions as you read. Write in the *Reader's Companion*—really! Circle things that interest you—underline things that puzzle you. Number ideas or events to help you keep track of them. Look for the **Mark the Text** logo for special help with active reading.
- Use the Reader's Response and Thinking About the Skill questions at the end of each selection to relate your reading to your own life.

Interacting With the Text

As you read, use the information and notes to guide you in interacting with the selection. The examples on these pages show you how to use the notes as a companion when you read. They will guide you in applying reading and literary skills and in thinking about the selection. When you read other texts, you can practice the thinking skills and strategies found here.

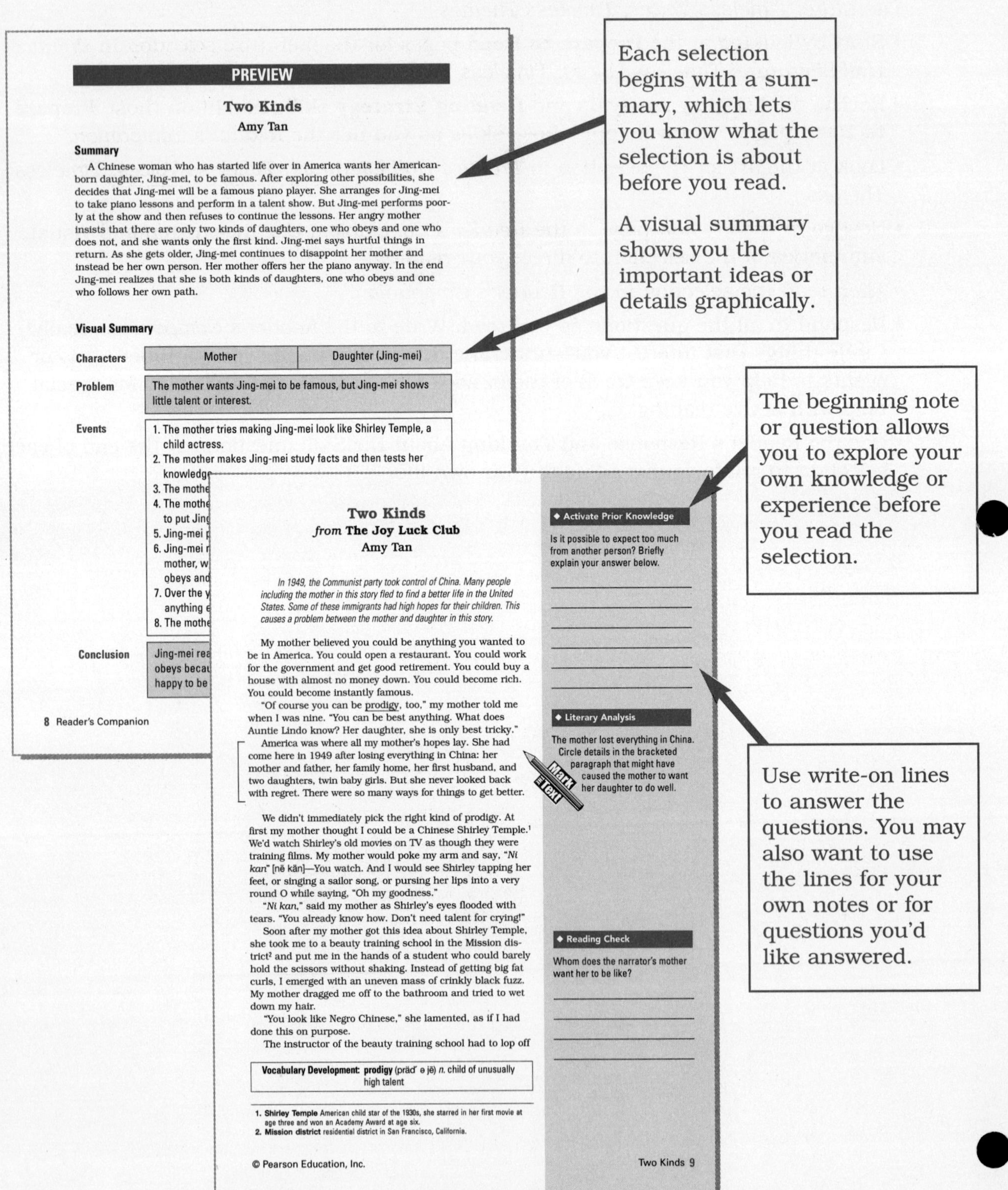

PREVIEW

Two Kinds

Amy Tan

Summary

A Chinese woman who has started life over in America wants her American-born daughter, Jing-mei, to be famous. After exploring other possibilities, she decides that Jing-mei will be a famous piano player. She arranges for Jing-mei to take piano lessons and perform in a talent show. But Jing-mei performs poorly at the show and then refuses to continue the lessons. Her angry mother insists that there are only two kinds of daughters, one who obeys and one who does not, and she wants only the first kind. Jing-mei says hurtful things in return. As she gets older, Jing-mei continues to disappoint her mother and instead be her own person. Her mother offers her the piano anyway. In the end Jing-mei realizes that she is both kinds of daughters, one who obeys and one who follows her own path.

Visual Summary

Characters	Mother	Daughter (Jing-mei)
Problem	The mother wants Jing-mei to be famous, but Jing-mei shows little talent or interest.	
Events	1. The mother tries making Jing-mei look like Shirley Temple, a child actress. 2. The mother makes Jing-mei study facts and then tests her knowledge 3. The mothe 4. The mothe to put Jing 5. Jing-mei p 6. Jing-mei r mother, w obeys and 7. Over the y anything e 8. The mothe	
Conclusion	Jing-mei rea obeys becau happy to be	

8 Reader's Companion

Two Kinds

from **The Joy Luck Club**

Amy Tan

In 1949, the Communist party took control of China. Many people including the mother in this story fled to find a better life in the United States. Some of these immigrants had high hopes for their children. This causes a problem between the mother and daughter in this story.

My mother believed you could be anything you wanted to be in America. You could open a restaurant. You could work for the government and get good retirement. You could buy a house with almost no money down. You could become rich. You could become instantly famous.

"Of course you can be prodigy, too," my mother told me when I was nine. "You can be best anything. What does Auntie Lindo know? Her daughter, she is only best tricky."

America was where all my mother's hopes lay. She had come here in 1949 after losing everything in China: her mother and father, her family home, her first husband, and two daughters, twin baby girls. But she never looked back with regret. There were so many ways for things to get better.

We didn't immediately pick the right kind of prodigy. At first my mother thought I could be a Chinese Shirley Temple.[1] We'd watch Shirley's old movies on TV as though they were training films. My mother would poke my arm and say, "*Ni kan*" [nē kän]—You watch. And I would see Shirley tapping her feet, or singing a sailor song, or pursing her lips into a very round O while saying, "Oh my goodness."

"*Ni kan*," said my mother as Shirley's eyes flooded with tears. "You already know how. Don't need talent for crying!"

Soon after my mother got this idea about Shirley Temple, she took me to a beauty training school in the Mission district[2] and put me in the hands of a student who could barely hold the scissors without shaking. Instead of getting big fat curls, I emerged with an uneven mass of crinkly black fuzz. My mother dragged me off to the bathroom and tried to wet down my hair.

"You look like Negro Chinese," she lamented, as if I had done this on purpose.

The instructor of the beauty training school had to lop off

Vocabulary Development: prodigy (präd´ ə jē) *n.* child of unusually high talent

1. **Shirley Temple** American child star of the 1930s, she starred in her first movie at age three and won an Academy Award at age six.
2. **Mission district** residential district in San Francisco, California.

◆ **Activate Prior Knowledge**

Is it possible to expect too much from another person? Briefly explain your answer below.

◆ **Literary Analysis**

The mother lost everything in China. Circle details in the bracketed paragraph that might have caused the mother to want her daughter to do well.

Mark the Text

◆ **Reading Check**

Whom does the narrator's mother want her to be like?

© Pearson Education, Inc.

Two Kinds 9

Each selection begins with a summary, which lets you know what the selection is about before you read.

A visual summary shows you the important ideas or details graphically.

The beginning note or question allows you to explore your own knowledge or experience before you read the selection.

Use write-on lines to answer the questions. You may also want to use the lines for your own notes or for questions you'd like answered.

◆ Literary Analysis

What is Old Chong's **motive** for being pleased, even though the rest of the room is quiet?

Chong, had seen me go through the right motions and had not heard anything wrong at all. I swept my right foot out, went down on my knee, looked up and smiled. The room was quiet, except for Old Chong, who was beaming and shouting, "Bravo! Bravo! Well done!" But then I saw my mother's face, her stricken face. The audience clapped weakly, and as I walked back to my chair, with my whole face quivering as I tried not to cry, I heard a little boy whisper loudly to his mother, "That was awful," and the mother whispered back, "Well, she certainly tried."

And now I realized how many people were in the audience, the whole world it seemed. I was aware of eyes burning into my back. I felt the shame of my mother and father as they sat stiffly throughout the rest of the show.

We could have escaped during intermission. Pr... and some strange sense of honor must have anch... my parents to their chairs. And so we watched ...: the eighteen-year-old boy with a fake mustache ... did a magic show and juggled flaming hoops wh...ding a unicycle. The breasted girl with white ma... who sang from *Madama Butterfly* and got honorable mention. And the eleven-year-old boy who won first prize playing a tricky violin song that sounded like a busy bee.

...fter the ... , the Jongs, and the St. Clairs ...m the Joy Luck Club came up to my mother and father.

"Lots of talented kids," Auntie Lindo said vaguely, smiling broadly.

"That was somethin' else," said my father, and I wondered if he was referring to me in a humorous way, or whether he even remembered what I had done.

Waverly looked at me and shrugged her shoulders. "You aren't a genius like me," she said matter-of-factly. And if I hadn't felt so bad, I would have pulled her braids and punched her stomach.

But my mother's expression ... quiet, blank look that said she ... same way, and it seemed as if e... up, like gawkers at the scene of... parts were actually missing. Wh... home, my father was humming ... mother was silent. I kept thinki... we got home before shouting at ... unlocked the door to our apartr... and then went to the back, into... tions. No blame. And in a way, ... been waiting for her to start sh... and cry and blame her for all m...

◆ Reading Strategy

Circle the word you find within the underlined word *honorable*. Adding *-able* to that word changes it from a noun to an adjective. Explain why "honorable mention" would be something good.

Mark the Text

◆ Reading Check

Whose response hurts the narrator the most?

Vocabulary Development: devasta... complet...

16 Reader's Companion

Underlined and bracketed text helps you examine and interact with specific passages in the text.

When you see this symbol, you should underline, circle, or mark the text as indicated.

time. I put the jewelry in special silk pouches. The sweaters she had knitted in yellow, pink, bright orange—all the colors I hated—I put those in moth-proof boxes. I found some old Chinese silk dresses, the kind with little slits up the sides. I rubbed the old silk against my skin, then wrapped them in tissue and decided to take them home with me.

After I had the piano tuned, I opened the lid and touched the keys. It sounded even richer than I remembered. Really, it was a very good piano. Inside the bench were the same exercise notes with handwritten scales, the same secondhand music books with their covers held together with yellow tape.

I opened up the Schumann book to the dark little piece I had played at the recital. It was on the left-hand side of the page, "Pleading Child." It looked more difficult than I remembered. I played a few bars, surprised at how easily the notes came back to me.

And for the first time, or so it seemed, I noticed the piece on the right-hand side. It was called "Perfectly Contented." I tried to play this one as well. It had a lighter melody but the same flowing rhythm and turned out to be quite easy. "Pleading Child" was shorter but slower; "Perfectly Contented" was longer, but faster. And after I played them both a few times, I realized they were two halves of the same song.

◆ Stop to Reflect

How have the narrator's feelings toward her mother changed since she was a child?

◆ Literary Analysis

Read the last paragraph of the story carefully. What clues does it contain about the narrator's **motive** in telling the story?

Reader's Response: What advice would you have given the mother and daughter?

Thinking About the Skill: What did you learn about using word roots and word parts?

© Pearson Education, Inc.

Two Kinds **19**

After reading, you can write your thoughts and reactions to the selection.

You can also make notes about the skills and stategies that were most helpful to you. Thinking about the skill will help you apply it to other reading situations.

The Cat Who Thought She Was a Dog and the Dog Who Thought He Was a Cat

Isaac Bashevis Singer

Summary

Jan Skiba lives in a small hut with his wife, his daughters, a dog, and a cat. They are poor, but they don't really notice. Even the dog and cat get along, for they do not realize that they are different from each other. Then one day the Skibas buy a mirror. For the first time, they see what they look like. They notice flaws in their appearance and begin to long for changes in their lives. The dog and cat realize that they are different and begin to fight. Finally, Jan decides that the mirror is no good. He returns it, and the family returns to normal.

Visual Summary

What are things like at first?	What happens after the family buys a mirror?	What happens after Jan gets rid of the mirror?
Skiba family • very poor • live in a small hut	Jan Skiba • dislikes his thick lips and buck teeth	Burek the dog • again thinks he is a cat • plays with Kot
Burek the dog • thinks he is a cat • plays with Kot	Marianna Skiba • thinks missing tooth makes her ugly	Kot the cat • again thinks she is a dog • plays with Burek
Kot the cat • thinks she is a dog • plays with Burek	Skiba daughters • dislike something about their looks	Skiba daughters • make good marriages
	Burek the dog • gets angry at his reflection • fights with Kot	Skiba family • returns to normal
	Kot the cat • becomes confused • fights with Burek	

The Cat Who Thought She Was a Dog and the Dog Who Thought He Was a Cat

Isaac Bashevis Singer

The Skibas only have money for things they really need. When they get a luxury—a mirror—problems arise.

Once there was a poor peasant, Jan Skiba by name. He lived with his wife and three daughters in a one-room hut with a straw roof, far from the village. The house had a bed, a bench bed, and a stove, but no mirror. A mirror was a luxury for a poor peasant. And why would a peasant need a mirror? Peasants aren't curious about their appearance.

But this peasant did have a dog and a cat in his hut. The dog was named Burek and the cat Kot. They had both been born within the same week. As little food as the peasant had for himself and his family, he still wouldn't let his dog and cat go hungry. Since the dog had never seen another dog and the cat had never seen another cat and they saw only each other, the dog thought he was a cat and the cat thought she was a dog. True, they were far from being alike by nature. The dog barked and the cat meowed. The dog chased rabbits and the cat lurked after mice. But must all creatures be exactly like their own kind? The peasant's children weren't exactly alike either. Burek and Kot lived on good terms, often ate from the same dish, and tried to mimic each other. <u>When Burek barked, Kot tried to bark along, and when Kot meowed, Burek tried to meow too. Kot occasionally chased rabbits and Burek made an effort to catch a mouse.</u>

The peddlers who bought groats,[1] chickens, eggs, honey, calves, and whatever was available from the peasants in the village never came to Jan Skiba's poor hut. They knew that Jan was so poor he had nothing to sell. But one day a peddler happened to stray there. When he came inside and began to lay out his wares, Jan Skiba's wife and daughters were bedazzled by all the pretty doodads. From his sack the peddler drew yellow beads, false pearls, tin earrings, rings, brooches, colored kerchiefs, garters, and other such trinkets. But what enthralled the women of the house most was a mirror set in a wooden frame. They asked the peddler its price and he said a half gulden, which was a lot of money for poor peasants. After a while, Jan Skiba's wife, Marianna, made a proposition to the peddler. She would pay him five groshen a month for the mirror. The peddler hesitated a

1. **groats** (grōtz) *n.* coarsely cracked grains, especially wheat, buckwheat, oats, or barley.

◆ Activate Prior Knowledge

Imagine how people might react to seeing themselves in a mirror for the first time. Write your ideas briefly on the lines below.

◆ Reading Strategy

When you **clarify a word's meaning,** look at the words and phrases near the unknown word to find clues to its meaning. To clarify the meaning of *mimic,* look at the underlined sentence following it.
1. What are the animals doing?
2. What is the meaning of *mimic*?
Write your answers on the lines below.

1. _____

2. _____

◆ Reading Check

Which of the peddler's wares interests the women most of all?

◆ **Reading Strategy**

If *groshen* is a word you don't know, the word *pay* will help you **clarify its meaning.** Underline other words in the bracketed section that help you clarify the meaning of *groshen.*

Mark the Text

moment. The mirror took up too much space in his sack and there was always the danger it might break. He, therefore, decided to go along, took the first payment of five groshen from Marianna, and left the mirror with the family. He visited the region often and he knew the Skibas to be honest people. He would gradually get his money back and a profit besides.

The mirror created a commotion in the hut. Until then Marianna and the children had seldom seen themselves. Before they had the mirror, they had only seen their reflections in the barrel of water that stood by the door. Now they could see themselves clearly and they began to find defects in their faces, defects they had never noticed before. Marianna was pretty but she had a tooth missing in front and she felt that this made her ugly. One daughter discovered that her nose was too snub and too broad; a second that her chin was too narrow and too long; a third that her face was sprinkled with freckles. Jan Skiba too caught a glimpse of himself in the mirror and grew displeased by his thick lips and his teeth, which protruded like a buck's. That day, the women of the house became so absorbed in the mirror they didn't cook supper, didn't make up the bed, and neglected all the other household tasks. Marianna had heard of a dentist in the big city who could replace a missing tooth, but such things were expensive. The girls tried to console each other that they were pretty enough and that they would find suitors, but they no longer felt as jolly as before. They had been afflicted with the vanity of city girls. The one with the broad nose kept trying to pinch it together with her fingers to make it narrower; the one with the too-long chin pushed it up with her fist to make it shorter; the one with the freckles wondered if there was a salve[2] in the city that could remove freckles. But where would the money come from for the fare to the city? And what about the money to buy this salve? For the first time the Skiba family deeply felt its poverty and envied the rich.

◆ **Reading Strategy**

To help you **clarify the meaning** of *neglected* in the underlined sentence, look at the rest of the sentence: the women didn't cook and they didn't make the bed. Does *neglected* mean they did or didn't do the rest of the chores?

____

____

____

____

Mark the Text

But the human members of the household were not the only ones affected. The dog and the cat also grew disturbed by the mirror. The hut was low and the mirror had been hung

Vocabulary Development: **protruded** (prō tro͞od´ id) *v.* stuck out; extended
console (kən sōl´) *v.* comfort; make less sad
afflicted (ə flik´ tid) *v.* received pain or suffering
vanity (van´ ə tē) *n.* the quality of being very proud of one's appearance

2. **salve** (sav) *n.* lotion or ointment used to soothe or heal.

just above a bench. The first time the cat sprang up on the bench and saw her image in the mirror, she became terribly perplexed. She had never before seen such a creature. Kot's whiskers bristled, she began to meow at her reflection and raised a paw to it, but the other creature meowed back and raised her paw too. Soon the dog jumped up on the bench, and when he saw the other dog he became wild with rage and shock. He barked at the other dog and showed him his teeth, but the other barked back and bared his fangs too. So great was the distress of Burek and Kot that for the first time in their lives they turned on each other. Burek took a bite out of Kot's throat and Kot hissed and spat at him and clawed his muzzle. They both started to bleed and the sight of blood aroused them so that they nearly killed or crippled each other. The members of the household barely managed to separate them. Because a dog is stronger than a cat, Burek had to be tied outside, and he howled all day and all night. In their anguish, both the dog and the cat stopped eating.

When Jan Skiba saw the disruption the mirror had created in his household, he decided a mirror wasn't what his family needed. "Why look at yourself," he said, "when you can see and admire the sky, the sun, the moon, the stars, and the earth, with all its forests, meadows, rivers, and plants?" He took the mirror down from the wall and put it away in the woodshed. When the peddler came for his monthly installment, Jan Skiba gave him back the mirror and in its stead, bought kerchiefs and slippers for the women. After the mirror disappeared, Burek and Kot returned to normal. Again Burek thought he was a cat and Kot was sure she was a dog. Despite all the defects the girls had found in themselves, they made good marriages. The village priest heard what had happened at Jan Skiba's house and he said, "A glass mirror shows only the skin of the body. The real image of a person is in his willingness to help himself and his family and, as far as possible, all those he comes in contact with. This kind of mirror reveals the very soul of the person."

Vocabulary Development: **anguish** (aŋ´gwish) *n.* great suffering; agony

Reader's Response: How would your life be different without mirrors? List two ways.

1. __________

2. __________

◆ Reading Strategy

Mark the Text: The cat is seeing herself for the first time and this confuses her. Circle clues to the meaning of *perplexed* in the underlined sentences.

◆ Stop to Reflect

Think about what happened when the Skibas got the mirror. In what way was the family better off without it?

◆ Literary Analysis

Mark the Text: Singer ends his tale with a **moral**, a guide for living. Underline the moral that the priest states. Then explain it in your own words below.

Two Kinds

Amy Tan

Summary

A Chinese woman who has started life over in America wants her American-born daughter, Jing-mei, to be famous. After exploring other possibilities, she decides that Jing-mei will be a famous piano player. She arranges for Jing-mei to take piano lessons and perform in a talent show. But Jing-mei performs poorly at the show and then refuses to continue the lessons. Her angry mother insists that there are only two kinds of daughters, one who obeys and one who does not, and she wants only the first kind. Jing-mei says hurtful things in return. As she gets older, Jing-mei continues to disappoint her mother and instead be her own person. Her mother offers her the piano anyway. In the end Jing-mei realizes that she is both kinds of daughters, one who obeys and one who follows her own path.

Visual Summary

Characters	Mother	Daughter (Jing-mei)
Problem	The mother wants Jing-mei to be famous, but Jing-mei shows little talent or interest.	
Events	1. The mother tries making Jing-mei look like Shirley Temple, a child actress. 2. The mother makes Jing-mei study facts and then tests her knowledge. 3. The mother makes Jing-mei take piano lessons with Mr. Chong. 4. The mother wants to show off her daughter and gets Mr. Chong to put Jing-mei in a talent show. 5. Jing-mei plays badly in the talent show. 6. Jing-mei refuses to continue piano lessons and fights with her mother, who says there are two kinds of daughter, one who obeys and one who does not. 7. Over the years, Jing-mei is true to herself but does not do anything especially well. 8. The mother offers her the piano for her thirtieth birthday.	
Conclusion	Jing-mei realizes that she is both kinds of daughter, one who obeys because she needs the approval of others and one who is happy to be herself.	

Two Kinds

from The Joy Luck Club

Amy Tan

In 1949, the Communist party took control of China. Many people including the mother in this story fled to find a better life in the United States. Some of these immigrants had high hopes for their children. This causes a problem between the mother and daughter in this story.

My mother believed you could be anything you wanted to be in America. You could open a restaurant. You could work for the government and get good retirement. You could buy a house with almost no money down. You could become rich. You could become instantly famous.

"Of course you can be prodigy, too," my mother told me when I was nine. "You can be best anything. What does Auntie Lindo know? Her daughter, she is only best tricky."

America was where all my mother's hopes lay. She had come here in 1949 after losing everything in China: her mother and father, her family home, her first husband, and two daughters, twin baby girls. But she never looked back with regret. There were so many ways for things to get better.

We didn't immediately pick the right kind of prodigy. At first my mother thought I could be a Chinese Shirley Temple.[1] We'd watch Shirley's old movies on TV as though they were training films. My mother would poke my arm and say, "*Ni kan*" [nē kän]—You watch. And I would see Shirley tapping her feet, or singing a sailor song, or pursing her lips into a very round O while saying, "Oh my goodness."

"*Ni kan*," said my mother as Shirley's eyes flooded with tears. "You already know how. Don't need talent for crying!"

Soon after my mother got this idea about Shirley Temple, she took me to a beauty training school in the Mission district[2] and put me in the hands of a student who could barely hold the scissors without shaking. Instead of getting big fat curls, I emerged with an uneven mass of crinkly black fuzz. My mother dragged me off to the bathroom and tried to wet down my hair.

"You look like Negro Chinese," she lamented, as if I had done this on purpose.

The instructor of the beauty training school had to lop off

Vocabulary Development: prodigy (präd′ ə jē) *n.* child of unusually high talent

1. **Shirley Temple** American child star of the 1930s, she starred in her first movie at age three and won an Academy Award at age six.
2. **Mission district** residential district in San Francisco, California.

◆ Activate Prior Knowledge

Is it possible to expect too much from another person? Briefly explain your answer below.

____

____

____

____

____

____

◆ Literary Analysis

Mark the Text

The mother lost everything in China. Circle details in the bracketed paragraph that might have caused the mother to want her daughter to do well.

◆ Reading Check

Whom does the narrator's mother want her to be like?

____

____

____

____

these soggy clumps to make my hair even again. "Peter Pan is very popular these days," the instructor assured my mother. I now had hair the length of a boy's, with straight-across bangs that hung at a slant two inches above my eyebrows. I liked the haircut and it made me actually look forward to my future fame.

In fact, in the beginning, I was just as excited as my mother, maybe even more so. I pictured this prodigy part of me as many different images, trying each one on for size. I was a dainty ballerina girl standing by the curtains, waiting to hear the right music that would send me floating on my tiptoes. I was like the Christ child lifted out of the straw manger, crying with holy indignity. I was Cinderella stepping from her pumpkin carriage with sparkly cartoon music filling the air.

In all of my imaginings, I was filled with a sense that I would soon become *perfect*. My mother and father would adore me. I would be beyond reproach. I would never feel the need to sulk for anything.

But sometimes the prodigy in me became impatient. "If you don't hurry up and get me out of here, I'm disappearing for good," it warned. "And then you'll always be nothing."

Every night after dinner, my mother and I would sit at the Formica kitchen table. She would present new tests, taking her examples from stories of amazing children she had read in *Ripley's Believe It or Not*, or *Good Housekeeping*, *Reader's Digest*, and a dozen other magazines she kept in a pile in our bathroom. My mother got these magazines from people whose houses she cleaned. And since she cleaned many houses each week, we had a great assortment. She would look through them all, searching for stories about remarkable children.

The first night she brought out a story about a three-year-old boy who knew the capitals of all the states and even most of the European countries. A teacher was quoted as saying the little boy could also pronounce the names of the foreign cities correctly.

"What's the capital of Finland?" my mother asked me, looking at the magazine story.

All I knew was the capital of California, because Sacramento was the name of the street we lived on in Chinatown. "Nairobi!"[3] I guessed, saying the most foreign word I could think of. She checked to see if that was possibly one way to pronounce "Helsinki" [hel siŋ´ kē] before showing me the answer.

Vocabulary Development: reproach (ri prōch´) *n.* disgrace; blame

3. Nairobi (nī rō´ bē) capital of Kenya, a country in east central Africa.

◆ Reading Strategy

Circle the word you find in the underlined word *impatient.* The **prefix,** or initial word part, *im-* means "not." *Patient* means "able to wait calmly." Write the meaning of *impatient* on the lines.

Mark the Text

____

____

◆ Reading Strategy

What familiar word and common **suffix,** or ending, can you find in the underlined word *assortment*?

____

____

◆ Reading Check

In the beginning, how does the narrator feel about becoming a prodigy?

____

____

____

The tests got harder—multiplying numbers in my head, finding the queen of hearts in a deck of cards, trying to stand on my head without using my hands, predicting the daily temperatures in Los Angeles, New York, and London.

One night I had to look at a page from the Bible for three minutes and then report everything I could remember. "Now Jehoshaphat had riches and honor in abundance and . . . that's all I remember, Ma," I said.

And after seeing my mother's disappointed face once again, something inside of me began to die. I hated the tests, the raised hopes and failed expectations. Before going to bed that night, I looked in the mirror above the bathroom sink and when I saw only my face staring back—and that it would always be this ordinary face—I began to cry. Such a sad, ugly girl! I made high-pitched noises like a crazed animal, trying to scratch out the face in the mirror.

And then I saw what seemed to be the prodigy side of me—because I had never seen that face before. I looked at my reflection, blinking so I could see more clearly. The girl staring back at me was angry, powerful. This girl and I were the same. I had new thoughts, willful thoughts, or rather thoughts filled with lots of won'ts. I won't let her change me, I promised myself. I won't be what I'm not.

So now on nights when my mother presented her tests, I performed listlessly, my head propped on one arm. I pretended to be bored. And I was. I got so bored I started counting the bellows of the foghorns out on the bay while my mother drilled me in other areas. The sound was comforting and reminded me of the cow jumping over the moon. And the next day, I played a game with myself, seeing if my mother would give up on me before eight bellows. After a while I usually counted only one, maybe two bellows at most. At last she was beginning to give up hope.

Two or three months had gone by without any mention of my being a prodigy again. And then one day my mother was watching *The Ed Sullivan Show*[4] on TV. The TV was old and the sound kept shorting out. Every time my mother got halfway up from the sofa to adjust the set, the sound would go back on and Ed would be talking. As soon as she sat down, Ed would go silent again. She got up, the TV broke into loud piano music. She sat down. Silence. Up and down, back and forth, quiet and loud. It was like a stiff embraceless dance between her and the TV set. Finally she stood by the set with her hand on the sound dial.

◆ Reading Strategy

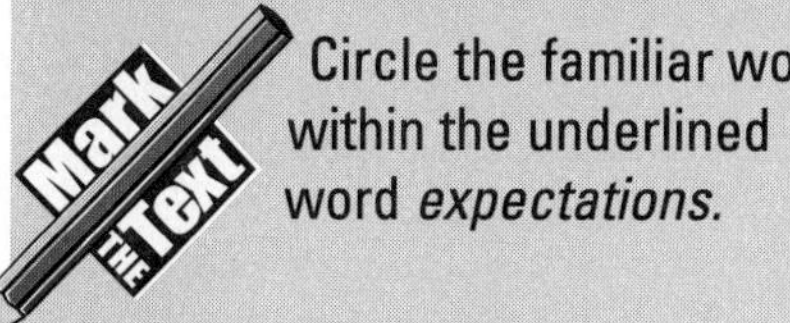

Circle the familiar word within the underlined word *expectations.*

◆ Literary Analysis

Characters' motives are the emotions and goals that drive characters to act in one way or another. Some powerful motives are love, anger, hope, and ambition. This moment marks a turning point for the narrator. What new motive is she reacting to?

◆ Reading Check

The narrator is tired of failing tests. She has a new sense of her own power. What decision does she make?

4. **The Ed Sullivan Show** popular variety show, hosted by Ed Sullivan, that ran from 1955 to 1971.

◆ **Reading Check**

How does the mother react to the girl on television?

____

____

____

____

____

____

◆ **Literary Analysis**

What is the narrator's **motive** for speaking kindly about the girl on *The Ed Sullivan Show* after her mother has criticized the girl's performance?

____

____

____

____

____

____

◆ **Literary Analysis**

The narrator's mother and Mr. Chong trade services. 1. What does the mother gain from the exchange? 2. What do you learn about her **motives**?

1. ______________________________

____

2. ______________________________

____

She seemed entranced by the music, a little frenzied piano piece with this mesmerizing quality, sort of quick passages and then teasing lilting ones before it returned to the quick playful parts.

"*Ni kan*," my mother said, calling me over with hurried hand gestures. "Look here."

I could see why my mother was fascinated by the music. It was being pounded out by a little Chinese girl, about nine years old, with a Peter Pan haircut. The girl had the sauciness of a Shirley Temple. She was proudly modest like a proper Chinese child. And she also did this fancy sweep of a curtsy, so that the fluffy skirt of her white dress cascaded slowly to the floor like the petals of a large carnation.

In spite of these warning signs, I wasn't worried. Our family had no piano and we couldn't afford to buy one, let alone reams of sheet music and piano lessons. So I could be generous in my comments when my mother bad-mouthed the little girl on TV.

"Play note right, but doesn't sound good! No singing sound," complained my mother.

"What are you picking on her for?" I said carelessly. "She's pretty good. Maybe she's not the best, but she's trying hard." I knew almost immediately I would be sorry I said that.

"Just like you," she said. "Not the best. Because you not trying." She gave a little huff as she let go of the sound dial and sat down on the sofa.

The little Chinese girl sat down also to play an encore of "Anitra's Dance" by Grieg.[5] I remember the song, because later on I had to learn how to play it.

Three days after watching *The Ed Sullivan Show*, my mother told me what my schedule would be for piano lessons and piano practice. She had talked to Mr. Chong, who lived on the first floor of our apartment building. Mr. Chong was a retired piano teacher and my mother had traded housecleaning services for weekly lessons and a piano for me to practice on every day, two hours a day, from four until six.

When my mother told me this, I felt as though I had been sent to hell. I whined and then kicked my foot a little when I couldn't stand it anymore.

"Why don't you like me the way I am? I'm *not* a genius! I

Vocabulary Development: **mesmerizing** (mez´ mər īz´ iŋ) *adj.* hypnotizing
sauciness (sô´ sē nes) *n.* liveliness; boldness; spirit

5. **Grieg** (grēg) Edvard Grieg (1843–1907), Norwegian composer.

can't play the piano. And even if I could, I wouldn't go on TV if you paid me a million dollars!" I cried.

My mother slapped me. "Who ask you be genius?" she shouted. "Only ask you be your best. For you sake. You think I want you be genius? Hnnh! What for! Who ask you!"

"So ungrateful," I heard her mutter in Chinese. "If she had as much talent as she has temper, she would be famous now."

Mr. Chong, whom I secretly nicknamed Old Chong, was very strange, always tapping his fingers to the silent music of an invisible orchestra. He looked ancient in my eyes. He had lost most of the hair on top of his head and he wore thick glasses and had eyes that always looked tired and sleepy. But he must have been younger than I thought, since he lived with his mother and was not yet married.

I met Old Lady Chong once and that was enough. She had this peculiar smell like a baby that had done something in its pants. And her fingers felt like a dead person's, like an old peach I once found in the back of the refrigerator; the skin just slid off the meat when I picked it up.

I soon found out why Old Chong had retired from teaching piano. He was deaf. "Like Beethoven!"[6] he shouted to me. "We're both listening only in our head!" And he would start to conduct his frantic silent sonatas.

Our lessons went like this. He would open the book and point to different things, explaining their purpose: "Key! Treble! Bass! No sharps or flats! So this is C major! Listen now and play after me!"

And then he would play the C scale a few times, a simple chord, and then, as if inspired by an old, unreachable itch, he gradually added more notes and running trills and a pounding bass until the music was really something quite grand.

I would play after him, the simple scale, the simple chord, and then I just played some nonsense that sounded like a cat running up and down on top of garbage cans. Old Chong smiled and applauded and then said, "Very good! But now you must learn to keep time!"

So that's how I discovered that Old Chong's eyes were too slow to keep up with the wrong notes I was playing. He went through the motions in half-time. To help me keep rhythm, he stood behind me, pushing down on my right shoulder for every beat. He balanced pennies on top of my wrists so I would keep them still as I slowly played scales and arpeggios.[7] He had me curve my hand around an apple and keep that shape when playing chords. He marched stiffly to show

6. **Beethoven** (bā´ tō´ vən) Ludwig van Beethoven (1770–1827), German composer who began to lose his hearing in 1801. By 1817 he was completely deaf. Some of his greatest pieces were written when he was deaf.

7. **arpeggios** (är pej´ ē ōz) *n.* notes in a chord played in quick succession instead of at the same time.

◆ Reading Strategy

Mark the Text

Circle the word you find within the underlined word *ungrateful*. The word part *un-* means "not." Write the definition of *ungrateful* below.

____

____

____

◆ Reading Strategy

The underlined word *unreachable* has a familiar word sandwiched between two word parts. What word is it?

____

____

____

◆ Reading Check

What important information has the narrator learned about Old Chong?

____

____

____

me how to make each finger dance up and down, staccato[8] like an obedient little soldier.

He taught me all these things, and that was how I also learned I could be lazy and get away with mistakes, lots of mistakes. If I hit the wrong notes because I hadn't practiced enough, I never corrected myself. I just kept playing in rhythm. And Old Chong kept conducting his own private reverie.

So maybe I never really gave myself a fair chance. I did pick up the basics pretty quickly, and I might have become a good pianist at that young age. But I was so determined not to try, not to be anybody different that I learned to play only the most ear-splitting preludes, the most discordant hymns.

Over the next year, I practiced like this, dutifully in my own way. And then one day I heard my mother and her friend Lindo Jong both talking in a loud bragging tone of voice so others could hear. It was after church, and I was leaning against the brick wall wearing a dress with stiff white petticoats. Auntie Lindo's daughter, Waverly, who was about my age, was standing farther down the wall about five feet away. We had grown up together and shared all the closeness of two sisters squabbling over crayons and dolls. In other words, for the most part, we hated each other. I thought she was snotty. Waverly Jong had gained a certain amount of fame as "Chinatown's Littlest Chinese Chess Champion."

"She bring home too many trophy," lamented Auntie Lindo that Sunday. "All day she play chess. All day I have no time do nothing but dust off her winnings." She threw a scolding look at Waverly, who pretended not to see her.

"You lucky you don't have this problem," said Auntie Lindo with a sigh to my mother.

And my mother squared her shoulders and bragged: "Our problem worser than yours. If we ask Jing-mei wash dish, she hear nothing but music. It's like you can't stop this natural talent."

And right then, I was determined to put a stop to her foolish pride.

A few weeks later, Old Chong and my mother conspired to have me play in a talent show which would be held in the church hall. By then, my parents had saved up enough to buy me a secondhand piano, a black Wurlitzer spinet[9] with a scarred bench. It was the showpiece of our living room.

For the talent show, I was to play a piece called "Pleading

◆ Literary Analysis

What do you think **motivates** the narrator to be "determined not to try"?

____

____

____

____

____

____

◆ Literary Analysis

What do you think **motivates** Auntie Lindo to talk this way about her daughter?

____

____

____

____

____

____

Vocabulary Development: conspired (kən spīrd′) *v.* planned together secretly

8. **staccato** (stə kät′ ō) *adv.* played crisply, with distinct breaks between notes.
9. **spinet** (spin′ it) *n.* small, upright piano.

Child" from Schumann's[10] *Scenes from Childhood.* It was a simple, moody piece that sounded more difficult than it was. I was supposed to memorize the whole thing, playing the repeat parts twice to make the piece sound longer. But I dawdled over it, playing a few bars and then cheating, looking up to see what notes followed. I never really listened to what I was playing. I daydreamed about being somewhere else, about being someone else.

The part I liked to practice best was the fancy curtsy: right foot out, touch the rose on the carpet with a pointed foot, sweep to the side, left leg bends, look up and smile.

My parents invited all the couples from the Joy Luck Club[11] to witness my debut. Auntie Lindo and Uncle Tin were there. Waverly and her two older brothers had also come. The first two rows were filled with children both younger and older than I was. The littlest ones got to go first. They recited simple nursery rhymes, squawked out tunes on miniature violins, twirled Hula Hoops, pranced in pink ballet tutus, and when they bowed or curtsied, the audience would sigh in unison, "Awww," and then clap enthusiastically.

When my turn came, I was very confident. I remember my childish excitement. It was as if I knew, without a doubt, that the prodigy side of me really did exist. I had no fear whatsoever, no nervousness. I remember thinking to myself, This is it! This is it! I looked out over the audience, at my mother's blank face, my father's yawn, Auntie Lindo's stiff-lipped smile, Waverly's sulky expression. I had on a white dress layered with sheets of lace, and a pink bow in my Peter Pan haircut. As I sat down I envisioned people jumping to their feet and Ed Sullivan rushing up to introduce me to everyone on TV.

And I started to play. It was so beautiful. I was so caught up in how lovely I looked that at first I didn't worry how I would sound. So it was a surprise to me when I hit the first wrong note and I realized something didn't sound quite right. And then I hit another and another followed that. A chill started at the top of my head and began to trickle down. Yet I couldn't stop playing, as though my hands were bewitched. I kept thinking my fingers would adjust themselves back, like a train switching to the right track. I played this strange jumble through two repeats, the sour notes staying with me all the way to the end.

When I stood up, I discovered my legs were shaking. Maybe I had just been nervous and the audience, like Old

Vocabulary Development: debut (dā byo͞o′) *n.* first performance in public

10. Schumann (sho͞o′ män) Robert Alexander Schumann (1810–1856), German composer.
11. Joy Luck Club four Chinese women who have been meeting for years to socialize, play games, and tell stories from the past.

◆ Reading Check

Circle the name of the composer of the piece the narrator will play in the talent show.

◆ Reading Strategy

Look at the parts of the underlined word *nervousness.* Circle the smaller word within it and underline the **suffix.**

◆ Reading Strategy

The underlined word *envisioned* can be separated into a **prefix,** a smaller word, and a **suffix.** The word *vision* tells you that *envisioned* has something to do with seeing. The prefix *en-* intensifies or makes the word *vision* stronger. Write your definition of *envisioned.*

____

____

◆ Reading Check

What happens when the girl begins to play at the recital?

____

____

____

____

◆ **Literary Analysis**

What is Old Chong's **motive** for being pleased, even though the rest of the room is quiet?

◆ **Reading Strategy**

Circle the word you find within the underlined word *honorable.* Adding *-able* to that word changes it from a noun to an adjective. Explain why "honorable mention" would be something good.

Mark THE Text

◆ **Reading Check**

Whose response hurts the narrator the most?

Chong, had seen me go through the right motions and had not heard anything wrong at all. I swept my right foot out, went down on my knee, looked up and smiled. The room was quiet, except for Old Chong, who was beaming and shouting, "Bravo! Bravo! Well done!" But then I saw my mother's face, her stricken face. The audience clapped weakly, and as I walked back to my chair, with my whole face quivering as I tried not to cry, I heard a little boy whisper loudly to his mother, "That was awful," and the mother whispered back, "Well, she certainly tried."

And now I realized how many people were in the audience, the whole world it seemed. I was aware of eyes burning into my back. I felt the shame of my mother and father as they sat stiffly throughout the rest of the show.

We could have escaped during intermission. Pride and some strange sense of honor must have anchored my parents to their chairs. And so we watched it all: the eighteen-year-old boy with a fake mustache who did a magic show and juggled flaming hoops while riding a unicycle. The breasted girl with white makeup who sang from *Madama Butterfly* and got honorable mention. And the eleven-year-old boy who won first prize playing a tricky violin song that sounded like a busy bee.

After the show, the Hsus, the Jongs, and the St. Clairs from the Joy Luck Club came up to my mother and father.

"Lots of talented kids," Auntie Lindo said vaguely, smiling broadly.

"That was somethin' else," said my father, and I wondered if he was referring to me in a humorous way, or whether he even remembered what I had done.

Waverly looked at me and shrugged her shoulders. "You aren't a genius like me," she said matter-of-factly. And if I hadn't felt so bad, I would have pulled her braids and punched her stomach.

But my mother's expression was what devastated me: a quiet, blank look that said she had lost everything. I felt the same way, and it seemed as if everybody were now coming up, like gawkers at the scene of an accident, to see what parts were actually missing. When we got on the bus to go home, my father was humming the busy-bee tune and my mother was silent. I kept thinking she wanted to wait until we got home before shouting at me. But when my father unlocked the door to our apartment, my mother walked in and then went to the back, into the bedroom. No accusations. No blame. And in a way, I felt disappointed. I had been waiting for her to start shouting, so I could shout back and cry and blame her for all my misery.

Vocabulary Development: devastated (dev´ ə stā tid) *v.* destroyed; completely upset

I assumed my talent-show fiasco meant I never had to play the piano again. But two days later, after school, my mother came out of the kitchen and saw me watching TV.

"Four clock," she reminded me as if it were any other day. I was stunned, as though she were asking me to go through the talent-show torture again. I wedged myself more tightly in front of the TV.

"Turn off TV," she called from the kitchen five minutes later.

I didn't budge. And then I decided. I didn't have to do what my mother said anymore. I wasn't her slave. This wasn't China. I had listened to her before and look what happened. She was the stupid one.

She came out from the kitchen and stood in the arched entryway of the living room. "Four clock," she said once again, louder.

"I'm not going to play anymore," I said nonchalantly. "Why should I? I'm not a genius."

[She walked over and stood in front of the TV. I saw her chest was heaving up and down in an angry way.]

"No!" I said, and I now felt stronger, as if my true self had finally emerged. So this was what had been inside me all along.

"No! I won't!" I screamed.

She yanked me by the arm, pulled me off the floor, snapped off the TV. She was frighteningly strong, half pulling, half carrying me toward the piano as I kicked the throw rugs under my feet. She lifted me up and onto the hard bench. I was sobbing by now, looking at her bitterly. Her chest was heaving even more and her mouth was open, smiling crazily as if she were pleased I was crying.

"You want me to be someone that I'm not!" I sobbed. "I'll never be the kind of daughter you want me to be!"

"Only two kinds of daughters," she shouted in Chinese. "Those who are obedient and those who follow their own mind! Only one kind of daughter can live in this house. Obedient daughter!"

"Then I wish I wasn't your daughter. I wish you weren't my mother," I shouted. As I said these things I got scared. It felt like worms and toads and slimy things crawling out of my chest, but it also felt good, as if this awful side of me had surfaced, at last.

"Too late change this," said my mother shrilly.

And I could sense her anger rising to its breaking point. I wanted to see it spill over. And that's when I remembered the babies she had lost in China, the ones we never talked about. "Then I wish I'd never been born!" I shouted. "I wish I were dead! Like them."

Vocabulary Development: fiasco (fē as´ cō) *n.* complete failure

◆ Literary Analysis

Mark the Text Circle the word in the bracketed paragraph that gives you a clue to the mother's **motive.**

◆ Reading Strategy

What word can you find within *frighteningly*?

____

Use a form of *frighten* to complete this sentence: My mother was so strong she __________ me.

____

____

____

◆ Reading Check

What does the mother do after the recital?

____

____

____

____

It was as if I had said the magic words. Alakazam!—and her face went blank, her mouth closed, her arms went slack, and she backed out of the room, stunned, as if she were blowing away like a small brown leaf, thin, brittle, lifeless.

It was not the only disappointment my mother felt in me. In the years that followed, I failed her so many times, each time asserting my own will, my right to fall short of expectations. I didn't get straight As. I didn't become class president. I didn't get into Stanford. I dropped out of college.

For unlike my mother, I did not believe I could be anything I wanted to be. I could only be me.

And for all those years, we never talked about the disaster at the recital or my terrible accusations afterward at the piano bench. All that remained unchecked, like a betrayal that was now unspeakable. So I never found a way to ask her why she had hoped for something so large that failure was inevitable.

And even worse, I never asked her what frightened me the most: Why had she given up hope?

For after our struggle at the piano, she never mentioned my playing again. The lessons stopped. The lid to the piano was closed, shutting out the dust, my misery, and her dreams.

So she surprised me. A few years ago, she offered to give me the piano, for my thirtieth birthday. I had not played in all those years. I saw the offer as a sign of forgiveness, a tremendous burden removed.

"Are you sure?" I asked shyly. "I mean, won't you and Dad miss it?"

"No, this your piano," she said firmly. "Always your piano. You only one can play."

"Well, I probably can't play anymore," I said. "It's been years."

"You pick up fast," said my mother, as if she knew this was certain. "You have natural talent. You could been genius if you want to."

"No I couldn't."

"You just not trying," said my mother. And she was neither angry nor sad. She said it as if to announce a fact that could never be disproved. "Take it," she said.

But I didn't at first. It was enough that she had offered it to me. And after that, every time I saw it in my parents' living room, standing in front of the bay windows, it made me feel proud, as if it were a shiny trophy I had won back.

Last week I sent a tuner over to my parents' apartment and had the piano reconditioned, for purely sentimental reasons. My mother had died a few months before and I had been getting things in order for my father, a little bit at a

◆ Reading Strategy

Circle the smaller word within the underlined word *unspeakable* and underline the **prefix** and **suffix.** Think about how each part contributes to the meaning of the word. What does *unspeakable* mean?

Mark the Text

___

___

___

___

___

◆ Reading Check

Why does the narrator believe her mother has forgiven her?

___

___

___

___

time. I put the jewelry in special silk pouches. The sweaters she had knitted in yellow, pink, bright orange—all the colors I hated—I put those in moth-proof boxes. I found some old Chinese silk dresses, the kind with little slits up the sides. I rubbed the old silk against my skin, then wrapped them in tissue and decided to take them home with me.

After I had the piano tuned, I opened the lid and touched the keys. It sounded even richer than I remembered. Really, it was a very good piano. Inside the bench were the same exercise notes with handwritten scales, the same secondhand music books with their covers held together with yellow tape.

I opened up the Schumann book to the dark little piece I had played at the recital. It was on the left-hand side of the page, "Pleading Child." It looked more difficult than I remembered. I played a few bars, surprised at how easily the notes came back to me.

And for the first time, or so it seemed, I noticed the piece on the right-hand side. It was called "Perfectly Contented." I tried to play this one as well. It had a lighter melody but the same flowing rhythm and turned out to be quite easy. "Pleading Child" was shorter but slower; "Perfectly Contented" was longer, but faster. And after I played them both a few times, I realized they were two halves of the same song.

Reader's Response: What advice would you have given the mother and daughter?

____

____

Thinking About the Skill: What did you learn about using word roots and word parts?

____

____

◆ Stop to Reflect

How have the narrator's feelings toward her mother changed since she was a child?

____

____

____

____

____

____

____

◆ Literary Analysis

Read the last paragraph of the story carefully. What clues does it contain about the narrator's **motive** in telling the story?

____

____

____

____

____

____

____

____

____

____

My Furthest-Back Person (The Inspiration for *Roots*)

Alex Haley

Summary

Alex Haley tells how he traced his family's roots to Africa. Checking government records from just after the Civil War, he was excited to find that relatives he'd heard about had actually lived. He then began checking his grandmother's story of the family's "furthest-back person" in America. Some of the strange words she had used turned out to be from an African language. Also *Kin-tay*, the name she called the "furthest-back person," turned out to be the old West African family name *Kinte*. Traveling to Africa, Haley found his distant Kinte relatives and heard the family history from a traditional oral historian. Piecing together all his research, he confirmed his grandmother's story: His "furthest-back person" in America was Kunta Kinte, a 16-year-old African kidnapped near the Gambia River in 1767, shipped to Annapolis, Maryland, and sold into slavery.

Visual Summary

Starting Point: Grandmother's stories of relatives include the family's "furthest-back person" in America, a man named Kin-tay, who was kidnapped in Africa, brought to 'Naplis, and sold into slavery.

Research in America	Research in Africa	Research in England
1. Census records confirm 1800s relatives 2. Cousin Georgia repeats story of furthest-back relative Kin-tay 3. Professor identifies strange African words; one is Gambia River 4. Dr. Curtin identifies Kin-tay as old African family name Kinte 9. Records in Maryland show arrival and sale of 98 slaves Sept./Oct. 1767	5. Gambians confirm terms are Gambia River and Kinte 6. Traditional storyteller tells of Kinte family history and disappearance of 16-year-old Kunta in time of "king's soldiers"	7. Records show soldiers sent mid-1767 to protect Britain's James Fort on Gambia River 8. Shipping records show British ship with 140 slaves left Gambia for Annapolis on July 5, 1767

Conclusion: Research confirms that Haley's family's "furthest-back person" in America was Kunta Kinte, a kidnapped Gambian brought to Annapolis, Maryland, in 1767, and sold into slavery.

My Furthest-Back Person (The Inspiration for *Roots*)

Alex Haley

Alex Haley had a difficult time finding out about his ancestors. His search was challenging because few records were kept in the 1800s, especially for enslaved Africans.

One Saturday in 1965 I happened to be walking past the National Archives building in Washington. Across the interim years I had thought of Grandma's old stories—otherwise I can't think what diverted me up the Archives' steps. And when a main reading room desk attendant asked if he could help me, I wouldn't have dreamed of admitting to him some curiosity hanging on from boyhood about my slave forebears. I kind of bumbled that I was interested in census records of Alamance County, North Carolina, just after the Civil War.

The microfilm rolls were delivered, and I turned them through the machine with a building sense of intrigue, viewing in different census takers' penmanship an endless parade of names. After about a dozen microfilmed rolls, I was beginning to tire, when in utter astonishment I looked upon the names of Grandma's parents: Tom Murray, Irene Murray . . . older sisters of Grandma's as well—every one of them a name that I'd heard countless times on her front porch.

It wasn't that I hadn't believed Grandma. You just *didn't* not believe my Grandma. It was simply so uncanny actually seeing those names in print and in official U.S. Government records.

During the next several months I was back in Washington whenever possible, in the Archives, the Library of Congress, the Daughters of the American Revolution Library. (Whenever black attendants understood the idea of my search, documents I requested reached me with miraculous speed.) In one source or another during 1966 I was able to document at least the highlights of the cherished family story. I would have given anything to have told Grandma, but, sadly, in 1949 she had gone. So I went and told the only survivor of those Henning front-porch storytellers: Cousin Georgia Anderson, now in her 80's in Kansas City, Kan. Wrinkled, bent, not well herself, she was so overjoyed, repeating to me the old stories and sounds; they were like Henning echoes: "Yeah, boy, that African say his name was *'Kin-tay'*; he say the

Vocabulary Development: **intrigue** (in′ trēg) *n.* curiosity and interest
uncanny (un kan′ ē) *adj.* strange; eerie
cherished (cher′ ishd) *adj.* beloved; valued

◆ Activate Prior Knowledge

What is one thing you would like to know about your ancestors?

___

___

◆ Literary Analysis

Mark the Text

In a **personal essay,** the writer shares his or her thoughts and reactions. The writer uses the pronoun *I*. The style is conversational, as if the writer is speaking to you. In the bracketed section underline words that show that this is a personal essay—the pronoun *I*, and anything known only to the narrator.

◆ Reading Strategy

You can **break down long sentences** to figure out what they mean. To find who the underlined sentence is about, look after the first comma. The word *I* shows that this sentence is about the author, Alex Haley. Keep reading until you come to what seems most important. Write that part of the sentence below.

___

___

___

◆ Reading Check

What does Haley find in the census records?

___

___

___

___

___

◆ **Reading Strategy**

Who is this underlined sentence about? Circle the word that tells you, then write the person's name.

Mark the Text

The main action in this sentence comes after the dash (—). Circle the words that describe how Haley felt when he saw historical treasures.

◆ **Reading Check**

At first, Haley was interested in finding out about his ancestors. What does he want to find out about now?

◆ **Stop to Reflect**

Why is it important for Haley to learn what language his ancestors spoke?

banjo was *'ko,'* an' the river *'Kamby Bolong,'* an' he was off choppin' some wood to make his drum when they grabbed 'im!" Cousin Georgia grew so excited we had to stop her, calm her down, "You go 'head, boy! Your grandma an' all of 'em—they up there watching what you do!"

That week I flew to London on a magazine assignment. Since by now I was steeped in the old, in the past, scarcely a tour guide missed me—I was awed at so many historical places and treasures I'd heard of and read of. I came upon the Rosetta stone in the British Museum, marveling anew at how Jean Champollion, the French archaeologist, had miraculously deciphered its ancient demotic and hieroglyphic texts[1] . . .

The thrill of that just kept hanging around in my head. I was on a jet returning to New York when a thought hit me. Those strange, unknown-tongue sounds, always part of our family's old story . . . they were obviously bits of our original African *"Kin-tay's"* native tongue. What specific tongue? Could I somehow find out?

Back in New York, I began making visits to the United Nations Headquarters lobby; it wasn't hard to spot Africans. I'd stop any I could, asking if my bits of phonetic sounds held any meaning for them. A couple of dozen Africans quickly looked at me, listened, and took off—understandably dubious about some Tennesseean's accent alleging "African" sounds.

My research assistant, George Sims (we grew up together in Henning), brought me some names of ranking scholars of African linguistics. One was particularly intriguing: a Belgian- and English-educated Dr. Jan Vansina; he had spent his early career living in West African villages, studying and tape-recording countless oral histories that were narrated by certain very old African men; he had written a standard textbook, "The Oral Tradition."

So I flew to the University of Wisconsin to see Dr. Vansina. In his living room I told him every bit of the family story in the fullest detail that I could remember it. Then, intensely, he queried me about the story's relay across the generations, about the gibberish of "*k*" sounds Grandma had fiercely muttered to herself while doing her housework, with my brothers and me giggling beyond her hearing at what we had dubbed "Grandma's noises."

Vocabulary Development: queried (kwir´ ēd) *v.* asked

1. **demotic and hieroglyphic texts** (dē mät´ ik and hī´ ər ō´ glif´ ik) *adj.* ancient Egyptian writing, using symbols and pictures to represent words.

Dr. Vansina, his manner very serious, finally said, "These sounds your family has kept sound very probably of the tongue called 'Mandinka.'"

I'd never heard of any "Mandinka." Grandma just told of the African saying "*ko*" for banjo, or "*Kamby Bolong*" for a Virginia river.

Among Mandinka stringed instruments, Dr. Vansina said, one of the oldest was the "*kora.*"

"*Bolong,*" he said, was clearly Mandinka for "river." Preceded by "*Kamby,*" it very likely meant "Gambia River."

Dr. Vansina telephoned an eminent Africanist colleague, Dr. Philip Curtin. He said that the phonetic "*Kin-tay*" was correctly spelled "*Kinte,*" a very old clan that had originated in Old Mali. The Kinte men traditionally were blacksmiths, and the women were potters and weavers.

I knew I must get to the Gambia River.

The first native Gambian I could locate in the U.S. was named Ebou Manga, then a junior attending Hamilton College in upstate Clinton, N.Y. He and I flew to Dakar, Senegal, then took a smaller plane to Yundum Airport, and rode in a van to Gambia's capital, Bathurst. Ebou and his father assembled eight Gambia government officials. I told them Grandma's stories, every detail I could remember, as they listened intently, then reacted. "'*Kamby Bolong*' of course is Gambia River!" I heard. "But more clue is your forefather's saying his name was '*Kinte.*'" Then they told me something I would never ever have fantasized—that in places in the back country lived very old men, commonly called *griots*, who could tell centuries of the histories of certain very old family clans. As for *Kintes*, they pointed out to me on a map some family villages, Kinte-Kundah, and Kinte-Kundah Janneh-Ya, for instance.

The Gambian officials said they would try to help me. I returned to New York dazed. It is embarrassing to me now, but despite Grandma's stories, I'd never been concerned much with Africa, and I had the routine images of African people living mostly in exotic jungles. But a compulsion now laid hold of me to learn all I could, and I began devouring books about Africa, especially about the slave trade. Then one Thursday's mail contained a letter from one of the Gambian officials, inviting me to return there.

Monday I was back in Bathurst. It galvanized me when the officials said that a *griot* had been located who told the *Kinte*

Vocabulary Development: **eminent** (em′ ə nənt) *adj.* distinguished or outstanding

◆ Stop to Reflect

Why do you think Haley says that he must get to the Gambia River?

◆ Reading Strategy

The subject of the underlined sentence is "they" and the action is "told." However, the most important information is what was told. Circle the most important part of the sentence.

Mark the Text

◆ Reading Check

How does Haley learn that his ancestors were probably from the Gambia River region?

◆ **Reading Check**

Why is Haley eager to meet the *griot*?

◆ **Reading Strategy**

The main part of the underlined sentence is "I sensed him." What does the sentence say about "him"?

◆ **Reading Check**

What does *toubob kolong* mean?

clan history—his name was Kebba Kanga Fofana. To reach him, I discovered, required a modified safari: renting a launch to get upriver, two land vehicles to carry supplies by a roundabout land route, and employing finally 14 people, including three interpreters and four musicians, since a *griot* would not speak the revered clan histories without background music.

The boat Baddibu vibrated upriver, with me acutely tense: Were these Africans maybe viewing me as but another of the pith-helmets?[2] After about two hours, we put in at James Island, for me to see the ruins of the once British-operated James Fort. Here two centuries of slave ships had loaded thousands of cargoes of Gambian tribespeople. The crumbling stones, the deeply oxidized swivel cannon, even some remnant links of chain seemed all but impossible to believe. Then we continued upriver to the left-bank village of Albreda, and there put ashore to continue on foot to Juffure [jo͞o′ fo͞o rā], village of the *griot*. Once more we stopped, for me to see *toubob kolong*, the "white man's well," now almost filled in, in a swampy area with abundant, tall, saw-toothed grass. It was dug two centuries ago to "17 men's height deep" to insure survival drinking water for long-driven, famishing coffles[3] of slaves.

Walking on, I kept wishing that Grandma could hear how her stories had led me to the "*Kamby Bolong*." (Our surviving storyteller Cousin Georgia died in a Kansas City hospital during this same morning, I would learn later.) Finally, Juffure village's playing children, sighting us, flashed an alert. The 70-odd people came rushing from their circular, thatch-roofed, mud-walled huts, with goats bounding up and about, and parrots squawking from up in the palms. I sensed him in advance somehow, the small man amid them, wearing a pillbox cap and an off-white robe—the *griot*. Then the interpreters went to him, as the villagers thronged around me.

And it hit me like a gale wind: every one of them, the whole crowd, was *jet black*. An enormous sense of guilt swept me—a sense of being some kind of hybrid . . . a sense of being impure among the pure. It was an awful sensation.

The old *griot* stepped away from my interpreters and the crowd quickly swarmed around him—all of them buzzing. An interpreter named A.B.C. Salla came to me; he whispered: "Why they stare at you so, they have never seen here a black American." And that hit me: I was symbolizing for them twenty-five millions of us they had never seen. What did they think of me—of us?

Then abruptly the old *griot* was briskly walking toward me. His eyes boring into mine, he spoke in Mandinka, as if in-

2. **pith-helmets** *n.* here, tourists or hunters on safari, who traditionally wore this type of fabric-covered hard hat.
3. **coffles** (kôf′ əlz) *n.* groups of animals or slaves chained or tied together in a line.

stinctively I should understand—and A.B.C. Salla translated:

"Yes . . . we have been told by the forefathers . . . that many of us from this place are in exile . . . in that place called America . . . and in other places."

I suppose I physically wavered, and they thought it was the heat; rustling whispers went through the crowd, and a man brought me a low stool. Now the whispering hushed—the musicians had softly begun playing *kora* and *balafon*, and a canvas sling lawn seat was taken by the *griot*, Kebba Kanga Fofana, aged 73 "rains" (one rainy season each year). He seemed to gather himself into a physical rigidity, and he began speaking the *Kinte* clan's ancestral oral history; it came rolling from his mouth across the next hours . . . 17th- and 18th-century *Kinte* lineage details, predominantly what men took wives; the children they "begot," in the order of their births; those children's mates and children.

Events frequently were dated by some proximate[4] singular physical occurrence. It was as if some ancient scroll were printed indelibly within the *griot's* brain. Each few sentences or so, he would pause for an interpreter's translation to me. I distill here the essence:

The *Kinte* clan began in Old Mali, the men generally blacksmiths ". . . who conquered fire," and the women potters and weavers. One large branch of the clan moved to Mauretania from where one son of the clan, Kairaba Kunta Kinte, a Moslem Marabout holy man, entered Gambia. He lived first in the village of Pakali N'Ding; he moved next to Jiffarong village; ". . . and then he came here, into our own village of Juffure."

In Juffure, Kairaba Kunta Kinte took his first wife, ". . . a Mandinka maiden, whose name was Sireng. By her, he begot two sons, whose names were Janneh and Saloum. Then he got a second wife, Yaisa. By her, he begot a son, Omoro."

The three sons became men in Juffure. Janneh and Saloum went off and found a new village, Kinte-Kundah Janneh-Ya. "And then Omoro, the youngest son, when he had 30 rains, took as a wife a maiden, Binta Kebba.

"And by her, he begot four sons—Kunta, Lamin, Suwadu, and Madi . . ."

Sometimes, a "begotten," after his naming, would be accompanied by some later-occurring detail, perhaps as ". . . in time of big water (flood), he slew a water buffalo." Having named those four sons, now the *griot* stated such a detail.

"About the time the king's soldiers came, the eldest of these four sons, Kunta, when he had about 16 rains, went away from his village, to chop wood to make a drum . . . and he was never seen again . . ."

4. **proximate** (präks´ ə mət) *adj.* near in time.

◆ Literary Analysis

The groups of three periods in the underlined section (. . .) are called ellipsis marks. They show a pause. How do they help you understand how the words sounded when Haley heard them?

______

______

______

◆ Stop to Reflect

Why do you think Haley "physically wavered" when the *griot* talks about exiles?

______

______

______

______

______

______

◆ Reading Check

What does Haley symbolize for the Africans who see him?

______

______

______

Goose-pimples the size of lemons seemed to pop all over me. In my knapsack were my cumulative notebooks, the first of them including how in my boyhood, my Grandma, Cousin Georgia and the others told of the African "*Kin-tay*" who always said he was kidnapped near his village—while chopping wood to make a drum . . .

◆ **Reading Check**

Why does Haley get goose pimples?

I showed the interpreter, he showed and told the *griot*, who excitedly told the people; they grew very agitated. Abruptly then they formed a human ring, encircling me, dancing and chanting. Perhaps a dozen of the women carrying their infant babies rushed in toward me, thrusting the infants into my arms conveying, I would later learn, "the laying on of hands . . . through this flesh which is us, we are you, and you are us." The men hurried me into their mosque, their Arabic praying later being translated outside: "Thanks be to Allah for returning the long lost from among us." Direct descendants of Kunta Kinte's blood brothers were hastened, some of them from nearby villages, for a family portrait to be taken with me, surrounded by actual ancestral sixth cousins. More symbolic acts filled the remaining day.

When they would let me leave, for some reason I wanted to go away over the African land. Dazed, silent in the bumping Land Rover, I heard the cutting staccato of talking drums. Then when we sighted the next village, its people came thronging to meet us. They were all—little naked ones to wizened elders—waving, beaming; amid a cacophony of crying out; and then my ears identified their words: "*Meester Kinte! Meester Kinte!*"

◆ **Literary Analysis**

What response does Haley have to the crowds that gather to greet him?

Let me tell you something: I am a man. But I remember the sob surging up from my feet, flinging up my hands before my face and bawling as I had not done since I was a baby . . . the jet-black Africans were jostling,[5] staring . . . I didn't care, with the feelings surging. If you really knew the odyssey of us millions of black Americans, if you really knew how we came in the seeds of our forefathers, captured, driven, beaten, inspected, bought, branded, chained in foul ships, if you really knew, you needed weeping . . .

Back home, I knew that what I must write, really, was our black saga, where any individual's past is the essence of the millions'. Now flat broke, I went to some editors I knew, describing the Gambian miracle, and my desire to pursue the research; Doubleday contracted to publish, and Reader's Digest to condense the projected book; then I had advances to travel further.

What ship brought Kinte to Grandma's "'Naplis" (Annapolis, Md., obviously)? The old *griot's* time reference to "king's

5. **jostling** (jäs´ ling) *v.* bumping and pushing, as in a crowd.

soldiers" sent me flying to London. Feverish searching at last identified, in British Parliament records, "Colonel O'Hare's Forces," dispatched in mid-1767 to protect the then British-held James Fort whose ruins I'd visited. So Kunta Kinte was down in some ship probably sailing later that summer from the Gambia River to Annapolis.

Now I feel it was fated that I had taught myself to write in the U.S. Coast Guard. For the sea dramas I had concentrated on had given me years of experience searching among yellowing old U.S. maritime records. So now in English 18th Century marine records I finally tracked ships reporting themselves in and out to the Commandant of the Gambia River's James Fort. And then early one afternoon I found that a Lord Ligonier under a Captain Thomas Davies had sailed on the Sabbath of July 5, 1767. Her cargo: 3,265 elephants' teeth, 3,700 pounds of beeswax, 800 pounds of cotton, 32 ounces of Gambian gold and 140 slaves; her destination: "Annapolis."

That night I recrossed the Atlantic. In the Library of Congress the Lord Ligonier's arrival was one brief line in "Shipping In The Port Of Annapolis—1748–1775." I located the author, Vaughan W. Brown, in his Baltimore brokerage office. He drove to Historic Annapolis, the city's historical society, and found me further documentation of her arrival on Sept. 29, 1767. (Exactly two centuries later, Sept. 29, 1967, standing, staring seaward from an Annapolis pier, again I knew tears.) More help came in the Maryland Hall of Records. Archivist Phebe Jacobsen found the Lord Ligonier's arriving customs declaration listing, "98 Negroes"—so in her 86-day crossing, 42 Gambians had died, one among the survivors being 16-year-old Kunta Kinte. Then the microfilmed Oct. 1, 1767, Maryland Gazette contained, on page two, an announcement to prospective buyers from the ship's agents, Daniel of St. Thos. Jenifer and John Ridout (the Governor's secretary): "from the River GAMBIA, in AFRICA . . . a cargo of choice, healthy SLAVES . . ."

Vocabulary Development: destination (des´ tə nā´ shən) *n.* the place to which something is being sent

Reader's Response: What question would you like to ask Haley about his experiences?

____

____

Thinking About the Skill: Describe the process of breaking down a long sentence.

____

____

◆ **Reading Check**

What is Haley searching for?

____

____

What information does he find?

____

____

____

◆ **Stop to Reflect**

What does this essay tell you about Alex Haley? List three qualities he shows.

1. ______________________________

____

2. ______________________________

____

3. ______________________________

____

PREVIEW

A Day's Wait

Ernest Hemingway

Summary

When Schatz has the flu, his father calls the doctor. The doctor says that Schatz's temperature is 102 degrees. Later that day, Schatz asks about his temperature. He is very quiet and worried, and his father cannot understand why. Finally, Schatz asks when he is going to die. His father says he is not that ill and will not die. Schatz says that boys at school in France told him a person could not live with a temperature of 44 degrees. His father then realizes that Schatz has been waiting to die all day, ever since he heard the doctor. The father explains that in France they use a different kind of thermometer. On that thermometer a normal temperature is 37 degrees. On the thermometer the doctor used, normal is 98 degrees. Schatz is very relieved by the explanation.

Visual Summary

A Day's Wait: The story takes place in one day

Early Morning to 11 AM

Schatz comes down with flu. → Father calls doctor. → Doctor says temperature is 102 degrees. → Father tries to read to Schatz.

11 AM to Late Afternoon

Schatz sends father away. → Father goes hunting. → Father returns to house. → Father learns Schatz wouldn't see anyone all day.

Late Afternoon to Early Evening

When Schatz asks about dying, father says Schatz won't die. → Schatz says in France such high temperature meant certain death. → Father explains that Schatz confused two types of thermometers. → Father realizes Schatz has spent all day in bed expecting to die.

A Day's Wait

Ernest Hemingway

In this story, confusion arises from the fact that there are different ways of measuring temperature. In the United States, we use degrees Fahrenheit (°F). On this scale, water freezes at 32°F and boils at 212°F. Many other countries use the Celsius scale. On this scale, water freezes at 0°C and boils at 100°C.

He came into the room to shut the windows while we were still in bed and I saw he looked ill. He was shivering, his face was white, and he walked slowly as though it ached to move.

"What's the matter, Schatz?"[1]

"I've got a headache."

"You better go back to bed."

"No. I'm all right."

"You go to bed. I'll see you when I'm dressed."

But when I came downstairs he was dressed, sitting by the fire, looking a very sick and miserable boy of nine years. When I put my hand on his forehead I knew he had a fever.

"You go up to bed," I said, "you're sick."

"I'm all right," he said.

When the doctor came he took the boy's temperature.

"What is it?" I asked him.

"One hundred and two."

Downstairs, the doctor left three different medicines in different colored capsules with instructions for giving them. One was to bring down the fever, another a purgative, the third to overcome an acid condition. The germs of influenza can only exist in an acid condition, he explained. He seemed to know all about influenza and said there was nothing to worry about if the fever did not go above one hundred and four degrees. This was a light epidemic of flu and there was no danger if you avoided pneumonia.

Back in the room I wrote the boy's temperature down and made a note of the time to give the various capsules.

"Do you want me to read to you?"

"All right. If you want to," said the boy. His face was very white and there were dark areas under his eyes. He lay still in the bed and seemed very detached from what was going on.

I read aloud from Howard Pyle's *Book of Pirates;* but I could see he was not following what I was reading.

"How do you feel, Schatz?" I asked him.

Vocabulary Development: epidemic (ep´ ə dem´ ik) *n.* outbreak of a contagious disease

1. **Schatz** (shäts) German term of affection, used here as a loving nickname.

◆ Activate Prior Knowledge

Have you ever been very sick? What was it like to lie in bed all day?

◆ Reading Strategy

A **word's root** is the main part of the word. It is the part that is left when suffixes and prefixes are removed. The underlined word *miserable* contains the root *mis-*, meaning "wrong or bad." The suffix *-able* means "in a state of." Knowing the meaning of the root, the suffix, and that the boy had a headache, what do you think *miserable* means?

◆ Reading Check

What is wrong with the boy?

"Just the same, so far," he said.

I sat at the foot of the bed and read to myself while I waited for it to be time to give another capsule. It would have been natural for him to go to sleep, but when I looked up he was looking at the foot of the bed, looking very strangely.

"Why don't you try to go to sleep? I'll wake you up for the medicine."

"I'd rather stay awake."

After a while he said to me, "You don't have to stay in here with me, Papa, if it bothers you."

"It doesn't bother me."

"No. I mean you don't have to stay if it's going to bother you."

I thought perhaps he was a little lightheaded and after giving him the prescribed capsules at eleven o'clock I went out for a while. It was a bright, cold day, the ground covered with a sleet that had frozen so that it seemed as if all the bare trees, the bushes, the cut brush and all the grass and the bare ground had been varnished with ice. I took the young Irish setter for a little walk up the road and along a frozen creek, but it was difficult to stand or walk on the glassy surface and the red dog slipped and slithered and I fell twice, hard, once dropping my gun and having it slide away over the ice.

We flushed a covey of quail under a high clay bank with overhanging brush and I killed two as they went out of sight over the top of the bank. Some of the covey lit in trees but most of them scattered into brush piles and it was necessary to jump on the ice-coated mounds of brush several times before they would flush. Coming out while you were poised unsteadily on the icy, springy brush they made difficult shooting, and I killed two, missed five, and started back pleased to have found a covey close to the house and happy there were so many left to find on another day.

At the house they said the boy had refused to let anyone come into the room.

"You can't come in," he said. "You mustn't get what I have."

I went up to him and found him in exactly the position I had left him, white-faced, but with the tops of his cheeks flushed by the fever, staring still, as he had stared at the foot of the bed.

I took his temperature.

"What is it?"

"Something like a hundred," I said. It was one hundred and two and four tenths.

"It was a hundred and two," he said.

"Who said so?"

"The doctor."

"Your temperature is all right," I said. "It's nothing to worry about."

Vocabulary Development: **flushed** (flusht) *v.* drove from hiding
covey (kuv´ ē) *n.* small flock of birds

◆ **Reading Strategy**

The **root** of *prescribed* is *scrib. Prescribed* means "to order as medicine or treatment." Other words with the same root include *scribe,* which means "a person paid to write," and *scribble,* meaning "to write carelessly." What do these words have in common? Write your answer on the lines below.

____

____

____

____

◆ **Literary Analysis**

Mark the Text

Most stories center on a **conflict,** or a struggle. An **internal conflict** takes place within one character. The person may be trying to overcome fear, control anger, or make a choice. Circle signs of the boy's internal conflict in the bracketed passage.

"I don't worry," he said, "but I can't keep from thinking."

"Don't think," I said. "Just take it easy."

"I'm taking it easy," he said and looked straight ahead. He was evidently holding tight on to himself about something.

"Take this with water."

"Do you think it will do any good?"

"Of course it will."

I sat down and opened the *Pirate* book and commenced to read, but I could see he was not following, so I stopped.

"About what time do you think I'm going to die?" he asked.

"What?"

"About how long will it be before I die?"

"You aren't going to die. What's the matter with you?"

"Oh, yes, I am. I heard him say a hundred and two."

"People don't die with a fever of one hundred and two. That's a silly way to talk."

"I know they do. At school in France the boys told me you can't live with forty-four degrees. I've got a hundred and two."

He had been waiting to die all day, ever since nine o'clock in the morning.

"You poor Schatz," I said. "Poor old Schatz. It's like miles and kilometers. You aren't going to die. That's a different thermometer. On that thermometer thirty-seven is normal. On this kind it's ninety-eight."

"Are you sure?"

"Absolutely," I said. "It's like miles and kilometers. You know, like how many kilometers we make when we do seventy miles in the car?"

"Oh," he said.

But his gaze at the foot of the bed relaxed slowly. The hold over himself relaxed too, finally, and the next day it was very slack and he cried very easily at little things that were of no importance.

Vocabulary Development: evidently (ev′ ə dent′ lē) *adv.* clearly; obviously

Reader's Response: Do you think the boy was brave or foolish? Explain.

____

____

Thinking About the Skill: How does knowing the meaning of word roots help you understand the meaning of words you do not know?

____

____

◆ Literary Analysis

The underlined question marks the **climax**—the turning point, or moment of greatest suspense. The boy's question reveals something about what he believes. What does his question reveal?

____

____

____

____

◆ Reading Strategy

The word *kilometer* is made up of two parts: *kilo-*, meaning "thousand," and the **root** *meter*, a measure of distance. (A meter is approximately equal to three feet.) What is the meaning of *kilometer*?

____

____

____

Was Tarzan a Three-Bandage Man?

Bill Cosby

Summary

When Bill Cosby was young, he and his friends tried to act cool by imitating their sports heroes. Bill's mother pokes fun at him for walking funny to copy famous ball players. She scolds him for putting bandages on his face to imitate champion boxers. Cosby now realizes it might have been better to imitate the boxers who gave injuries rather than those who received them.

Visual Summary

Cosby and Friends' Actions	Cosby's Mother's Reaction	Adult Cosby's Reaction
• Copy walk of Jackie Robinson, fastest man in baseball • Copy walk of football player Buddy Helm • Imitate boxers like Sugar Ray Robinson by wearing a bandage above an eye	• Pokes fun by questioning Robinson's shoes and whether walk slows speed • Pokes fun at how son twists his legs to copy these men's walks • Suggests son is being stupid and needs better role models; makes him remove his bandage	• Pokes fun by saying walk was painful • Pokes fun by suggesting the behavior made little sense

Was Tarzan a Three-Bandage Man?

Bill Cosby

In this piece, Bill Cosby tells of his admiration for two famous African American sports figures—baseball star Jackie Robinson and boxer Sugar Ray Robinson. Jackie Robinson was the first African American to play in the major leagues. Sugar Ray Robinson won six world championships between 1946 and 1958.

In the days before athletes had learned how to incorporate themselves, they were shining heroes to American kids. In fact, they were such heroes to me and my friends that we even imitated their walks. When Jackie Robinson, a pigeon-toed[1] walker, became famous, we walked pigeon-toed, a painful form of locomotion unless you were Robinson or a pigeon.

"Why you walkin' like that?" said my mother one day.

"This is Jackie *Robinson's* walk," I proudly replied.

"There's somethin' wrong with his shoes?"

"He's the fastest man in baseball."

"He'd be faster if he didn't walk like that. His mother should make him walk right."

A few months later, when football season began, I stopped imitating Robinson and began to walk bowlegged[2] like a player named Buddy Helm.

"Why you always tryin' to change the shape of your legs?" said my mother. "You keep doin' that an' they'll fall off—an' I'm not gettin' you new ones."

Although baseball and football stars inspired us, our real heroes were the famous prize fighters, and the way to emulate a fighter was to walk around with a Band-Aid over one eye. People with acne walked around that way too, but we hoped it was clear that we were worshipping good fists and not bad skin.

The first time my mother saw me being Sugar Ray, not Jackie Robinson, she said, "What's that bandage for?"

"Oh, nuthin'," I replied.

"Now that's a new kinda stupid answer. That bandage gotta be coverin' somethin'—besides your entire brain."

"Well, it's just for show. I wanna look like Sugar Ray Robinson."

"The fastest man in baseball."

Vocabulary Development: **incorporate** (in kôr´ pôr āt) *v.* form into a legal business

1. **pigeon-toed** (pij´ ən tōd) *adj.* having the feet turned in toward each other.
2. **bowlegged** (bō´ leg ed) *adj.* having legs that are curved outward.

◆ Activate Prior Knowledge

Have you ever admired someone so much that you imitated something about him or her? Describe your experience. If you've never done so, describe a person you admire.

______

______

______

______

______

______

◆ Reading Strategy

When you do not know the meaning of a word, you can sometimes use **context clues**—the words and phrases nearby—to help you understand the unfamiliar word. In the underlined sentence, Bill Cosby says that he admired prize fighters most of all, and that he and his friends would walk around with a Band-Aid over one eye. Since prize fighters might also wear a Band-Aid, what do you think *emulate* might mean?

______

______

◆ Reading Check

What does Cosby do when he admires someone?

______

______

______

◆ Literary Analysis

This piece is an **anecdote**, a short, personal story. Cosby's heroes are sports figures. His mother's hero is Booker T. Washington, a leading black educator from an earlier time. What do these different types of heroes tell you about the difference between Cosby and his mother?

____

____

____

____

____

◆ Reading Strategy

To find the meaning of the underlined word *attire*, look at the sentence before it. The words "the toughest guys of all *wore* tourniquets" give you a clue to its meaning. What do you think the meaning of *attire* is? Write it on the lines.

____

____

____

"No, that's a different one."

"You doin' Swiss Family Robinson[3] next?"

"Swiss Family Robinson? They live in the projects?"

"You'd know who they are if you read more books instead of makin' yourself look like an accident. Why can't you try to imitate someone like Booker T. Washington?"[4]

"Who does he play for?"

"Bill, let's put it this way: you take off that bandage right now or I'll have your father move you up to stitches."

The following morning on the street, I dejectedly told the boys, "My mother says I gotta stop wearin' a bandage. She wants my whole head to show."

"What's wrong with that woman?" said Fat Albert. "She won't let you do *nuthin'*."

"It's okay, Cos," said Junior, "'cause one bandage ain't enough anyway. My brother says the really tough guys wear two."

"One over each eye?" I asked him.

"Or one eye and one nose," he said.

"Man, I wouldn't want to mess with no two-bandage man," said Eddie.

And perhaps the toughest guys of all wore tourniquets around their necks. We were capable of such attire, for we were never more ridiculous than when we were trying to be tough and cool. Most ridiculous, of course, was that our hero worshipping was backwards: we should have been emulating the men who had *caused* the need for bandages.

Vocabulary Development: **dejectedly** (dē jek′ tid lē) *adv.* sadly; showing discouragement
tourniquets (tur′ ni kits) *n.* devices used to stop bleeding in an emergency, as a bandage tightly twisted to stop the flow of blood

3. **Swiss Family Robinson** fictional family stranded on a desert island.
4. **Booker T. Washington** (1856–1915) African American educator and author.

Reader's Response: If you had been Bill Cosby's friend, do you think you would have imitated sports heroes in the same way? Why or why not?

____

____

Thinking About the Skill: How do context clues help you understand the meanings of words?

____

____

from In Search of Our Mothers' Gardens

Alice Walker

Summary

Alice Walker praises her mother and other African American women like her. Walker sees her mother as an artist whose talents helped make Walker the writer she is today. Her mother revealed her artistic talent in the stories she told and in the flower gardens she grew. Being poor and working hard all her life did not stop her from taking time to grow these lovely gardens. Walker admires how black women of her mother's generation managed to "hold on" despite the difficulty of their lives. From these women, Walker has inherited a respect for strength as well as a love of beauty.

Visual Summary

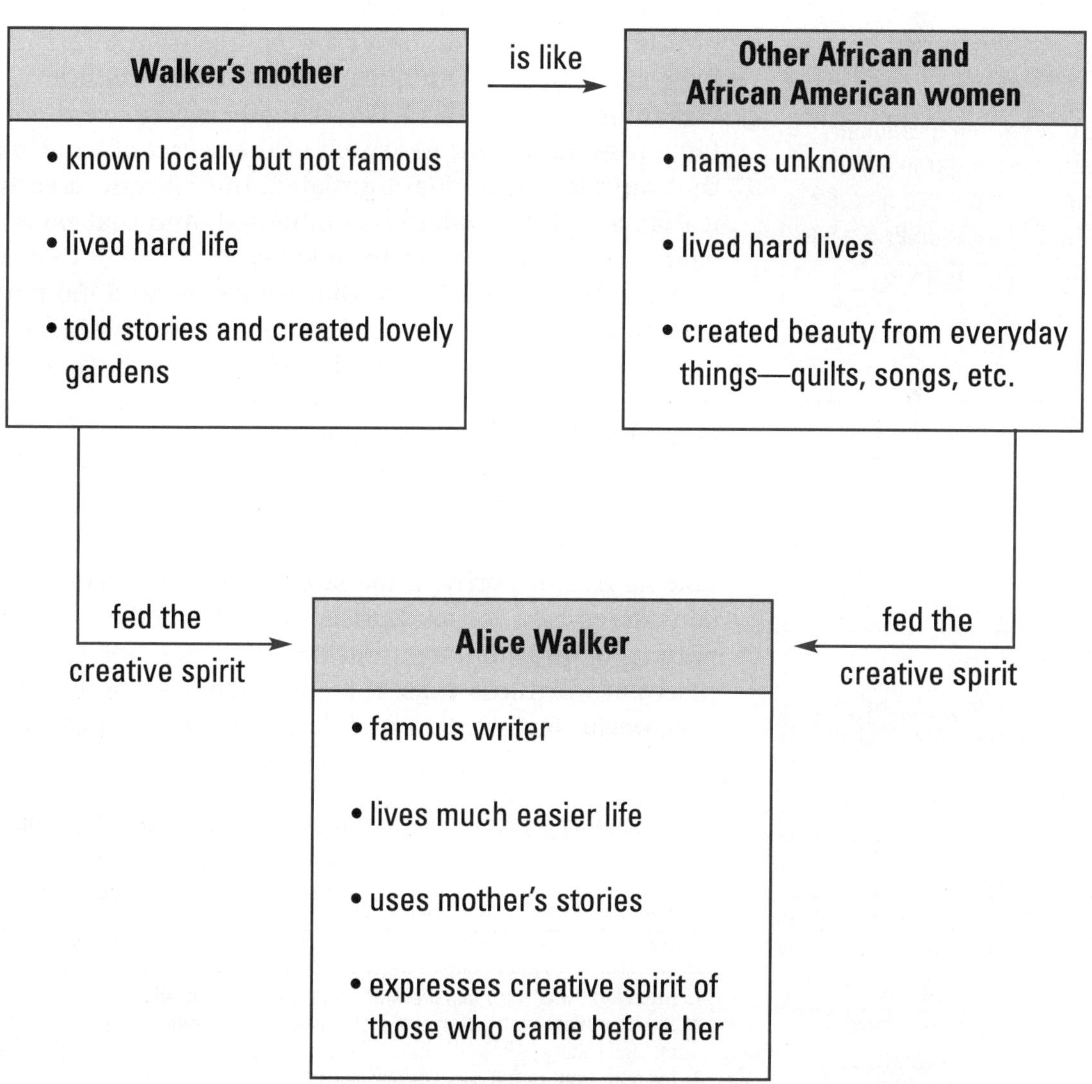

◆ Activate Prior Knowledge

Have you ever been inspired by someone you've known or read about? Describe this person and explain why you find him or her inspiring.

____

____

____

____

____

____

____

____

◆ Literary Analysis

A **tribute** is a written or spoken work that honors a person. Write three things from the bracketed passage that Alice Walker uses as reasons to honor her mother.

1. ________________________________

____

2. ________________________________

____

3. ________________________________

____

◆ Stop to Reflect

Why do you think the quilt is so valuable?

____

____

____

____

from In Search of Our Mothers' Gardens

Alice Walker

Alice Walker's parents were sharecroppers—farmers who did not own the land they worked on. The landowner would give the farmers seed and tools and would receive in return a percentage of the farmers' crops. Sharecroppers had to work very hard to make a living, which is why it is all the more amazing that Walker's mother did so much in addition to her field work.

My mother made all the clothes we wore, even my brothers' overalls. She made all the towels and sheets we used. She spent the summers canning vegetables and fruits. She spent the winter evenings making quilts enough to cover all our beds.

During the "working" day, she labored beside—not behind—my father in the fields. Her day began before sunup, and did not end until late at night. There was never a moment for her to sit down, undisturbed, to unravel her own private thoughts; never a time free from interruption—by work or the noisy inquiries of her many children. And yet, it is to my mother—and all our mothers who were not famous—that I went in search of the secret of what has fed that muzzled[1] and often mutilated, but vibrant, creative spirit that the black woman has inherited, and that pops out in wild and unlikely places to this day.

But when, you will ask, did my overworked mother have time to know or care about feeding the creative spirit?

The answer is so simple that many of us have spent years discovering it. We have constantly looked high, when we should have looked high—and low.

For example: in the Smithsonian Institution[2] in Washington, D.C., there hangs a quilt unlike any other in the world. In fanciful,[3] inspired, and yet simple and identifiable figures, it portrays the story of the Crucifixion.[4] It is considered rare, beyond price. Though it follows no known pattern of quilt-making, and though it is made of bits and pieces of worthless rags, it is obviously the work of a person of powerful imagination and deep spiritual feeling. Below this

Vocabulary Development: **mutilated** (myo͞ot´ əl āt´ id) *adj.* damaged or injured
vibrant (vī´ brənt) *adj.* lively and energetic

1. **muzzled** (muz´ əld) *adj.* prevented from expressing itself.
2. **Smithsonian Institution** group of museums with exhibits in the fields of science, art, and history.
3. **fanciful** (fan´ si fəl) *adj.* playfully imaginative.
4. **the Crucifixion** (kro͞o´ sə fik´ shən) Jesus Christ's suffering and death on the cross.

quilt I saw a note that says it was made by "an anonymous Black woman in Alabama, a hundred years ago."

If we could locate this "anonymous" black woman from Alabama, she would turn out to be one of our grandmothers—an artist who left her mark in the only materials she could afford, and in the only medium her position in society allowed her to use.

And so our mothers and grandmothers have, more often than not anonymously, handed on the creative spark, the seed of the flower they themselves never hoped to see: or like a sealed letter they could not plainly read.

And so it is, certainly, with my own mother. Unlike "Ma" Rainey's songs,[5] which retained their creator's name even while blasting forth from Bessie Smith's mouth,[6] no song or poem will bear my mother's name. Yet so many of the stories that I write, that we all write, are my mother's stories. Only recently did I fully realize this: that through years of listening to my mother's stories of her life, I have absorbed not only the stories themselves, but something of the manner in which she spoke, something of the urgency that involves the knowledge that her stories—like her life—must be recorded. It is probably for this reason that so much of what I have written is about characters whose counterparts in real life are so much older than I am.

But the telling of these stories, which came from my mother's lips as naturally as breathing, was not the only way my mother showed herself as an artist. For stories, too, were subject to being distracted, to dying without conclusion. Dinners must be started, and cotton must be gathered before the big rains. The artist that was and is my mother showed itself to me only after many years. This is what I finally noticed:

Like Mem, a character in *The Third Life of Grange Copeland*,[7] my mother adorned with flowers whatever shabby house we were forced to live in. And not just your typical straggly[8] country stand of zinnias, either. She planted ambitious gardens—and still does—with over fifty different varieties of plants that bloom profusely from early March until late November. Before she left home for the fields, she watered her flowers, chopped up the grass, and laid out new beds. When she returned from the fields she might divide

Vocabulary Development: **anonymous** (ə nän′ ə məs) *adj.* with no name known
profusely (prō fyo͞os′ lē) *adv.* freely or plentifully

5. **"Ma" Rainey's songs** Gertrude ("Ma") Rainey, one of America's first blues singers, lived during the early years of the twentieth century.
6. **Bessie Smith's mouth** Bessie Smith was a well-known blues singer (1898?–1937), who knew and learned from "Ma" Rainey.
7. ***The Third Life of Grange Copeland*** the title of a novel by Alice Walker.
8. **straggly** (strag′ lē) *adj.* spread out in an irregular way.

◆ **Reading Strategy**

The English word *anonymous*, found in the bracketed passage, contains the Greek **root** *-nym*, which means "name." The prefix *ano-* means "without." Knowing what the **word root** and the prefix mean, what do you think *anonymous* means?

____

____

◆ **Literary Analysis**

Mark the Text

Underline ideas in this paragraph that indicate that this essay is a **tribute**.

◆ **Reading Check**

Mark the Text

Underline the answer to this question: Why does Walker's mother not finish all of her stories?

◆ **Reading Strategy**

The underlined word *spirea* has a Greek **word root**. Look it up in a dictionary. Write down the **word root** and its meaning. Then write down the definition of the word.

____

____

____

◆ **Literary Analysis**

In the bracketed passage, underline two sentences that answer this question: How do people pay **tribute** to Walker's mother's garden?

Mark the Text

◆ **Reading Check**

Who is this poem about?

____

____

Who wrote it?

____

____

clumps of bulbs, dig a cold pit,[9] uproot and replant roses, or prune branches from her taller bushes or trees—until night came and it was too dark to see.

Whatever she planted grew as if by magic, and her fame as a grower of flowers spread over three counties. Because of her creativity with her flowers, even my memories of poverty are seen through a screen of blooms—sunflowers, petunias, roses, dahlias, forsythia, spirea, delphiniums, verbena . . . and on and on.

And I remember people coming to my mother's yard to be given cuttings from her flowers; I hear again the praise showered on her because whatever rocky soil she landed on, she turned into a garden. A garden so brilliant with colors, so original in its design, so magnificent with life and creativity, that to this day people drive by our house in Georgia—perfect strangers and imperfect strangers—and ask to stand or walk among my mother's art.

I notice that it is only when my mother is working in her flowers that she is radiant, almost to the point of being invisible—except as Creator: hand and eye. She is involved in work her soul must have. Ordering the universe in the image of her personal conception of Beauty.

Her face, as she prepares the Art that is her gift, is a legacy[10] of respect she leaves to me, for all that illuminates and cherishes life. She has handed down respect for the possibilities—and the will to grasp them.

For her, so hindered and intruded upon in so many ways, being an artist has still been a daily part of her life. This ability to hold on, even in very simple ways, is work black women have done for a very long time.

This poem is not enough, but it is something, for the woman who literally covered the holes in our walls with sunflowers:

They were women then
My mama's generation
Husky of voice—Stout of
Step
With fists as well as
Hands
How they battered down
Doors

Vocabulary Development: **radiant** (rā´ dē ənt) *adj.* filled with light; shining brightly
illuminates (i lo͞o´ mə nāts´) *v.* brightens; sheds light on
hindered (hin´ dərd) *adj.* held back

9. **cold pit** hole in which seedlings are planted at the beginning of the spring.
10. **legacy** (leg´ ə sē) *n.* something handed down by a parent or an ancestor.

And ironed
Starched white
Shirts
How they led
Armies
Headragged[11] *Generals*
Across mined[12]
Fields
Booby-trapped[13]
Kitchens
To discover books
Desks
A place for us
How they knew what we
Must know
Without knowing a page
Of it
Themselves.

Guided by my heritage of a love of beauty and a respect for strength—in search of my mother's garden, I found my own.

And perhaps in Africa over two hundred years ago, there was just such a mother; perhaps she painted vivid and daring decorations in oranges and yellows and greens on the walls of her hut; perhaps she sang—in a voice like Roberta Flack's[14]—*sweetly* over the compounds of her village; perhaps she wove the most stunning mats or told the most ingenious[15] stories of all the village storytellers. Perhaps she was herself a poet—though only her daughter's name is signed to the poems that we know.

Perhaps Phillis Wheatley's[16] mother was also an artist.

Perhaps in more than Phillis Wheatley's biological life is her mother's signature made clear.

---

11. **headragged** (hed′ ragd) *adj.* with head wrapped around by a rag or kerchief.
12. **mined** (mīnd) *adj.* filled with buried explosives that are set to go off when stepped on.
13. **booby-trapped** (bo͞o′ bē trapt) *adj.* filled with hidden bombs or mines set to go off when someone touches or lifts an object.
14. **Roberta Flack's** Roberta Flack is a contemporary African American singer.
15. **ingenious** (in jēn′ yəs) *adj.* clever and inventive.
16. **Phillis Wheatley's** Phillis Wheatley (1753?–1784), a poet, considered the first important black writer in America.

Reader's Response: Think about creative skills that your mother or another female relative has passed on to you. How would life be different for you or that person without that skill?

____

____

____

◆ Reading Check

In the poem, what is the mission of "the generals"?

____

____

____

◆ Literary Analysis

In the bracketed passage, to whom does Walker pay **tribute**?

____

____

____

◆ Reading Strategy

From your prior knowledge of what people learn about when they study biology, what do you think the Greek **word root** *bio-* in the underlined sentence means? Look in the dictionary if you need help.

____

____

____

Seventh Grade

Gary Soto

Summary

On his first day of seventh grade, Victor signs up for French because Teresa is taking it. He hopes Teresa will be his girlfriend this year. In the hallway, he runs into his friend Michael, who is also trying to attract girls. Teresa is in Victor's homeroom but not in his other classes except for French. In their first French class, Victor embarrasses himself by pretending to speak the language. The French teacher is not fooled, but Teresa is. Impressed, she asks Victor to help her with French during the year. Victor happily heads for the library to take out some French textbooks.

Visual Summary

Setting

Place: a school in Fresno, California
Time: the first day of seventh grade

Problem

Teresa doesn't notice Victor.

Goal

Victor wants Teresa to be his girlfriend this year.

Events

- Victor knows Spanish but signs up for French because Teresa is taking it.
- In homeroom, Victor makes sure Teresa notices him but is awkward when she says "Hi."
- When his English teacher asks for a noun that names a person, Victor says "Teresa."
- In French class, Victor pretends to know French, though the teacher soon realizes he doesn't.
- Victor is embarrassed and runs off quickly when the bell rings but then must return for a book.

Climax

Teresa is impressed that Victor knows French and asks if he can sometimes help her study.
The teacher hears them talking but does not give away Victor's secret.

Conclusion

Victor agrees to help Teresa with French and heads for the library to take out some French books.

Seventh Grade

Gary Soto

Victor, the main character in "Seventh Grade," is most likely a descendant of immigrants from Mexico. To show Victor and his friend Michael's heritage, Soto has them use many Spanish words and expressions.

On the first day of school, Victor stood in line half an hour before he came to a wobbly card table. He was handed a packet of papers and a computer card on which he listed his one elective, French. He already spoke Spanish and English, but he thought some day he might travel to France, where it was cool; not like Fresno, where summer days reached 110 degrees in the shade. There were rivers in France, and huge churches, and fair-skinned people everywhere, the way there were brown people all around Victor.

Besides, Teresa, a girl he had liked since they were in catechism classes at Saint Theresa's, was taking French, too. With any luck they would be in the same class. Teresa is going to be my girl this year, he promised himself as he left the gym full of students in their new fall clothes. She was cute. And good in math, too, Victor thought as he walked down the hall to his homeroom. He ran into his friend, Michael Torres, by the water fountain that never turned off.

They shook hands, *raza*-style, and jerked their heads at one another in a *saludo de vato.*[1] "How come you're making a face?" asked Victor.

"I ain't making a face, *ese.*[2] This *is* my face." Michael said his face had changed during the summer. He had read a *GQ* magazine that his older brother had borrowed from the Book Mobile and noticed that the male models all had the same look on their faces. They would stand, one arm around a beautiful woman, and *scowl.* They would sit at a pool, their rippled stomachs dark with shadow, and *scowl.* They would sit at dinner tables, cool drinks in their hands, and *scowl.*

"I think it works," Michael said. He scowled and let his upper lip quiver. His teeth showed along with the ferocity of

Vocabulary Development: **elective** (ē lek′ tiv) *n.* optional course or subject in a school or college curriculum
scowl (skoul) *v.* to lower the eyebrows and corners of the mouth; to look angry or irritated
ferocity (fə räs′ ə tē) *n.* fierceness

1. ***raza*-style . . . *saludo de vato*** (säl o͞o′ dō dā bä′ tō) Spanish gestures of greeting between friends.
2. ***ese*** (es′ ā) Spanish word for "man."

◆ Activate Prior Knowledge

Think back to your first day of seventh grade. Were you excited or worried about being in seventh grade? Write your thoughts about that first day.

◆ Reading Strategy

An **idiom** is an expression that has a meaning different from its literal, or word-for-word, meaning.

1. Write the idiom found in the underlined sentence.
2. Then, write its word-for-word meaning.
3. Finally, write what you think the expression means.

1.

2.

3.

◆ Reading Check

Why does Victor choose to study French?

◆ Literary Analysis

The **tone** of a short story—the writer's attitude toward his subject and his characters—can be serious, lighthearted, humorous, suspenseful, and so forth. The tone is determined by the writer's choice of words (slang, everyday or formal language) and by the writer's style (use of imagery, length of sentences). In the bracketed passage, circle two examples that contribute to the story's tone.

Mark the Text

◆ Reading Check

What does Victor think about Michael's scowling?

____

____

What happens when he tries it?

____

____

◆ Reading Strategy

Identify the **idiom** in the underlined sentence. What does Victor actually try to do?

____

____

____

____

his soul. "Belinda Reyes walked by a while ago and looked at me," he said.

Victor didn't say anything, though he thought his friend looked pretty strange. They talked about recent movies, baseball, their parents, and the horrors of picking grapes in order to buy their fall clothes. Picking grapes was like living in Siberia,[3] except hot and more boring.

"What classes are you taking?" Michael said, scowling.

"French. How 'bout you?"

"Spanish. I ain't so good at it, even if I'm Mexican."

"I'm not either, but I'm better at it than math, that's for sure."

A tinny, three-beat bell propelled students to their homerooms. The two friends socked each other in the arm and went their ways, Victor thinking, man, that's weird. Michael thinks making a face makes him handsome.

On the way to his homeroom, Victor tried a scowl. He felt foolish, until out of the corner of his eye he saw a girl looking at him. Umm, he thought, maybe it does work. He scowled with greater conviction.

In homeroom, roll was taken, emergency cards were passed out, and they were given a bulletin to take home to their parents. The principal, Mr. Belton, spoke over the crackling loudspeaker, welcoming the students to a new year, new experiences, and new friendships. The students squirmed in their chairs and ignored him. They were anxious to go to first period. Victor sat calmly, thinking of Teresa, who sat two rows away, reading a paperback novel. This would be his lucky year. She was in his homeroom, and would probably be in his English and math classes. And, of course, French.

The bell rang for first period, and the students herded noisily through the door. Only Teresa lingered, talking with the homeroom teacher.

"So you think I should talk to Mrs. Gaines?" she asked the teacher. "She would know about ballet?"

"She would be a good bet," the teacher said. Then added, "Or the gym teacher, Mrs. Garza."

Victor lingered, keeping his head down and staring at his desk. He wanted to leave when she did so he could bump into her and say something clever.

He watched her on the sly. As she turned to leave, he stood up and hurried to the door, where he managed to catch her eye. She smiled and said, "Hi, Victor."

Vocabulary development: conviction (kən vik′ shən) *n.* belief

3. **Siberia** (sī bir′ ē ə) region in northern Asia known for its harsh winters.

He smiled back and said, "Yeah, that's me." His brown face blushed. Why hadn't he said, "Hi, Teresa," or "How was your summer?" or something nice?

As Teresa walked down the hall, Victor walked the other way, looking back, admiring how gracefully she walked, one foot in front of the other. So much for being in the same class, he thought. As he trudged to English, he practiced scowling.

In English they reviewed the parts of speech. Mr. Lucas, a portly man, waddled down the aisle, asking, "What is a noun?"

"A person, place, or thing," said the class in unison.

"Yes, now somebody give me an example of a person—you, Victor Rodriguez."

"Teresa," Victor said automatically. Some of the girls giggled. They knew he had a crush on Teresa. He felt himself blushing again.

"Correct," Mr. Lucas said. "Now provide me with a place."

Mr. Lucas called on a freckled kid who answered, "Teresa's house with a kitchen full of big brothers."

After English, Victor had math, his weakest subject. He sat in the back by the window, hoping that he would not be called on. Victor understood most of the problems, but some of the stuff looked like the teacher made it up as she went along. It was confusing, like the inside of a watch.

After math he had a fifteen-minute break, then social studies, and, finally, lunch. He bought a tuna casserole with buttered rolls, some fruit cocktail, and milk. He sat with Michael, who practiced scowling between bites.

Girls walked by and looked at him.

"See what I mean, Vic?" Michael scowled. "They love it."

"Yeah, I guess so."

They ate slowly, Victor scanning the horizon for a glimpse of Teresa. He didn't see her. She must have brought lunch, he thought, and is eating outside. Victor scraped his plate and left Michael, who was busy scowling at a girl two tables away.

The small, triangle-shaped campus bustled with students talking about their new classes. Everyone was in a sunny mood. Victor hurried to the bag lunch area, where he sat down and opened his math book. He moved his lips as if he were reading, but his mind was somewhere else. He raised his eyes slowly and looked around. No Teresa.

He lowered his eyes, pretending to study, then looked slowly to the left. No Teresa. He turned a page in the book and stared at some math problems that scared him because he knew he would have to do them eventually. He looked to the right. Still no sign of her. He stretched out lazily in an attempt to disguise his snooping.

Then he saw her. She was sitting with a girlfriend under a

◆ Literary Analysis

Mark the Text

In the **first-person point of view**—the perspective from which a story is written—the narrator is a character in the story and refers to himself or herself as *I*. In the **third-person point of view**, the narrator is not a character in the story, knows the characters' thoughts, and refers to them as *he*, *she* and *them*.

In the bracketed passage, underline two details that indicate what the point of view of this story is.

◆ Stop to Reflect

How does the use of idioms affect the **tone** of this story?

____

____

____

____

◆ Reading Check

In the underlined passage, why does Victor pretend to be studying?

____

____

____

____

plum tree. Victor moved to a table near her and daydreamed about taking her to a movie. When the bell sounded, Teresa looked up, and their eyes met. She smiled sweetly and gathered her books. Her next class was French, same as Victor's.

They were among the last students to arrive in class, so all the good desks in the back had already been taken. Victor was forced to sit near the front, a few desks away from Teresa, while Mr. Bueller wrote French words on the chalkboard. The bell rang, and Mr. Bueller wiped his hands, turned to the class, and said, "*Bonjour.*"[4]

"*Bonjour*," braved a few students.

"*Bonjour*," Victor whispered. He wondered if Teresa heard him.

Mr. Bueller said that if the students studied hard, at the end of the year they could go to France and be understood by the populace.

One kid raised his hand and asked, "What's 'populace'?"

"The people, the people of France."

Mr. Bueller asked if anyone knew French. Victor raised his hand, wanting to impress Teresa. The teacher beamed and said, "*Trés bien. Parlez-vous français*?"[5]

Victor didn't know what to say. The teacher wet his lips and asked something else in French. The room grew silent. Victor felt all eyes staring at him. He tried to bluff his way out by making noises that sounded French.

"La me vave me con le grandma," he said uncertainly.

Mr. Bueller, wrinkling his face in curiosity, asked him to speak up.

Great rosebushes of red bloomed on Victor's cheeks. A river of nervous sweat ran down his palms. He felt awful. Teresa sat a few desks away, no doubt thinking he was a fool. Without looking at Mr. Bueller, Victor mumbled, "Frenchie oh wewe gee in September."

Mr. Bueller asked Victor to repeat what he had said.

"Frenchie oh wewe gee in September," Victor repeated.

Mr. Bueller understood that the boy didn't know French and turned away. He walked to the blackboard and pointed to the words on the board with his steel-edged ruler.

"*Le bateau*," he sang.

"*Le bateau*," the students repeated.

"*Le bateau est sur l'eau*,"[6] he sang.

"*Le bateau est sur l'eau*."

Victor was too weak from failure to join the class. He stared at the board and wished he had taken Spanish, not French. Better yet, he wished he could start his life over. He had never been so embarrassed. He bit his thumb until he tore off a sliver of skin.

◆ Literary Analysis

In the bracketed passage, underline a detail that shows the informal **tone** of the story.

◆ Reading Check

Underline Victor's answer when Mr. Bueller asks him if he speaks French. Then write what his answer means.

____

____

____

◆ Reading Check

Why does Victor tell Mr. Bueller that he knows French?

____

____

____

____

4. ***Bonjour*** (bōn zho͞or′) French for "Hello"; "Good day."
5. ***Trés bien. Parlez-vous français?*** (trā byan pär lā′ vo͞o frän sā′) French for "Very well. Do you speak French?"
6. ***Le bateau est sur l'eau.*** (lə bä tō′ ā so͞or lō) French for "The boat is on the water."

The bell sounded for fifth period, and Victor shot out of the room, avoiding the stares of the other kids, but had to return for his math book. He looked sheepishly at the teacher, who was erasing the board, then widened his eyes in terror at Teresa who stood in front of him. "I didn't know you knew French," she said. "That was good."

Mr. Bueller looked at Victor, and Victor looked back. Oh please, don't say anything, Victor pleaded with his eyes. I'll wash your car, mow your lawn, walk your dog—anything! I'll be your best student and I'll clean your erasers after school.

Mr. Bueller shuffled through the papers on his desk. He smiled and hummed as he sat down to work. He remembered his college years when he dated a girlfriend in borrowed cars. She thought he was rich because each time he picked her up he had a different car. It was fun until he had spent all his money on her and had to write home to his parents because he was broke.

Victor couldn't stand to look at Teresa. He was sweaty with shame. "Yeah, well, I picked up a few things from movies and books and stuff like that." They left the class together. Teresa asked him if he would help her with her French.

"Sure, anytime," Victor said.

"I won't be bothering you, will I?"

"Oh no, I like being bothered."

"*Bonjour*," Teresa said, leaving him outside her next class. She smiled and pushed wisps of hair from her face.

"Yeah, right, *bonjour*," Victor said. He turned and headed to his class. The rosebushes of shame on his face became bouquets of love. Teresa is a great girl, he thought. And Mr. Bueller is a good guy.

He raced to metal shop. After metal shop there was biology, and after biology a long sprint to the public library, where he checked out three French textbooks.

He was going to like seventh grade.

Vocabulary Development: sheepishly (shēp′ ish lē) *adv.* in a shy or embarrassed way

Reader's Response: Have you ever said that you knew something when you really did not? Explain why you did it.

Thinking About the Skill: How would the story be different if it were written from the **first-person point of view**?

◆ Literary Analysis

In the bracketed passage, explain what the reader knows that Victor does not due to the use of the **third-person point of view.**

◆ Reading Check

Why doesn't Mr. Bueller tell Victor and Teresa that he knows Victor can't speak French?

◆ Stop to Reflect

Why is Victor going to like seventh grade?

Melting Pot

Anna Quindlen

Summary

The author describes her New York City neighborhood as a mixture of different ethnic and social groups. She sees the idea of the American melting pot existing where she lives, but only on a person-to-person level. In groups, the people often don't get along, but as individuals they usually do.

Visual Summary

Question: Does America's Melting Pot Exist?

Yes	No
• Author's children are friends with family from Ecuador next door.	• Author's mother as a girl is insulted for being Italian American.
• Neighbors of all backgrounds are friendly because their children play together.	• Author's immigrant grandfather was told "No Irish Need Apply."
• Person-to-person, people get along pretty well.	• Old-timers resent the young professionals, whose moving in causes prices to rise.
• Italian-American old-timers accept author, a young professional, because of her Italian roots.	• The young professionals resent being blamed for high prices.
• People join together on issues that affect them all.	• Old immigrants are suspicious of new immigrants.
• Both "them" and "us" attitudes exist.	• New immigrants think old ones are "bigots."
	• Looked at in broad strokes, the neighborhood is a pressure cooker of groups who don't always mix well.

Conclusion: Melting pot exists person to person but not group to group

Melting Pot
Anna Quindlen

Anna Quindlen's essay, "Melting Pot," describes a city neighborhood that is full of immigrants from all different countries and that is constantly changing as new arrivals appear.

My children are upstairs in the house next door, having dinner with the Ecuadorian family that lives on the top floor. The father speaks some English, the mother less than that. The two daughters are fluent in both their native and their adopted languages, but the youngest child, a son, a close friend of my two boys, speaks almost no Spanish. His parents thought it would be better that way. This doesn't surprise me; it was the way my mother was raised, American among Italians. I always suspected, hearing my grandfather talk about the "No Irish Need Apply" signs outside factories, hearing my mother talk about the neighborhood kids, who called her greaseball, that the American fable of the melting pot was a myth. Here in our neighborhood it exists, but like so many other things, it exists only person-to-person.

The letters in the local weekly tabloid[1] suggest that everybody hates everybody else here, and on a macro level they do. The old-timers are angry because they think the new moneyed professionals are taking over their town. The professionals are tired of being blamed for the neighborhood's rising rents, particularly since they are the ones paying them. The old immigrants are suspicious of the new ones. The new ones think the old ones are bigots. Nevertheless, on a micro level most of us get along. We are friendly with the Ecuadorian family, with the Yugoslavs across the street, and with the Italians next door, mainly by virtue of our children's sidewalk friendships. It took awhile. Eight years ago we were the new people on the block, filling dumpsters with old plaster and lath, . . . (sitting) on the stoop with our demolition masks hanging around our necks like goiters.[2] We thought we could feel people staring at us from behind the sheer curtains on their windows. We were right.

My first apartment in New York was in a gritty warehouse district, the kind of place that makes your parents wince. A

Vocabulary Development: **fluent** (flo͞o´ ənt) *adj.* able to write or speak easily and smoothly
bigots (big´ əts) *n.* narrow-minded, prejudiced people

---

1. **tabloid** (tab´ loid´) *n.* small newspaper.
2. **goiters** (goit´ ərz) *n.* swellings in the lower front of the neck caused by an enlarged thyroid gland.

◆ Activate Prior Knowledge

Perhaps you live in or have seen neighborhoods in a large city on television or in a movie. Describe such an urban neighborhood, including the kinds of buildings, stores, people, and animals in such a neighborhood.

◆ Literary Analysis

An author's choice of words indicates what the **tone** of an essay or short story is. In "Seventh Grade," the writer uses slang and everyday language to show its lighthearted tone. A more serious piece has words that are more formal. In the bracketed passage, circle words that indicate that this essay has a more formal tone.

Mark the Text

◆ Reading Check

1. What do the local newspapers indicate that the people in Quindlen's neighborhood feel about each other? 2. How does Quindlen say they get along?

1. ______________________

2. ______________________

◆ **Reading Check**

Underline the answer to this question: Why was Quindlen comfortable in an Italian neighborhood?

Mark the Text

◆ **Literary Analysis**

After reading the bracketed passage, answer these questions to determine its **point of view**: 1. How many people do you know the thoughts of? 2. Does the author refer to herself as *I*? 3. Does the person telling the story take part in the events?

1. ______

2. ______

3. ______

Is the story told in the **first** or **third person?**

4. ______

◆ **Reading Strategy**

Write down the **idiom** in the underlined passage. Then tell what it means.

______

______

______

______

______

lot of old Italians lived around me, which suited me just fine because I was the granddaughter of old Italians. Their own children and grandchildren had moved to Long Island and New Jersey. All they had was me. All I had was them.

I remember sitting on a corner with a group of half a dozen elderly men, men who had known one another since they were boys sitting together on this same corner, watching a glazier install a great spread of tiny glass panes to make one wall of a restaurant in the ground floor of an old building across the street. The men laid bets on how long the panes, and the restaurant, would last. Two years later two of the men were dead, one had moved in with his married daughter in the suburbs, and the three remaining sat and watched dolefully as people waited each night for a table in the restaurant. "Twenty-two dollars for a piece of veal!" one of them would say, apropos of nothing.[3] But when I ate in the restaurant they never blamed me. "You're not one of them," one of the men explained. "You're one of me." It's an argument familiar to members of almost any embattled race or class: I like you, therefore you aren't like the rest of your kind, whom I hate.

Change comes hard in America, but it comes constantly. The butcher whose old shop is now an antiques store sits day after day outside the pizzeria here like a lost child. The old people across the street cluster together and discuss what kind of money they might be offered if the person who bought their building wants to turn it into condominiums. The greengrocer stocks yellow peppers and fresh rosemary for the gourmands, plum tomatoes and broad-leaf parsley for the older Italians, mangoes for the Indians. He doesn't carry plantains, he says, because you can buy them in the bodega.[4]

Sometimes the baby slips out with the bath water. I wanted to throw confetti the day that a family of rough types who propped their speakers on their station wagon and played heavy metal music at 3:00 A.M. moved out. I stood and smiled as the seedy bar at the corner was transformed into a slick Mexican restaurant. But I liked some of the people who moved out at the same time the rough types did. And I'm not sure I have that much in common with the singles who have made the restaurant their second home.

Yet somehow now we seem to have reached a nice mix. About a third of the people in the neighborhood think of squid as calamari, about a third think of it as sushi, and about a third think of it as bait. Lots of the single people who have moved in during the last year or two are easygoing and

---

3. **apropos** (ap′ rə pō′) **of nothing** without connection.
4. **bodega** (bō dā′ gə) *n.* small Hispanic grocery store.

good-tempered about all the kids. The old Italians have become philosophical about the new Hispanics, although they still think more of them should know English. The firebrand community organizer with the storefront on the block, the one who is always talking about people like us as though we stole our houses out of the open purse of a ninety-year-old blind widow, is pleasant to my boys.

Drawn in broad strokes, we live in a pressure cooker: oil and water, us and them. But if you come around at exactly the right time, you'll find members of all these groups gathered around complaining about the condition of the streets, on which everyone can agree. We melt together, then draw apart. I am the granddaughter of immigrants, a young professional—either an interloper or a longtime resident, depending on your concept of time. I am one of them, and one of us.

Vocabulary Development: **interloper** (in´ tər lō´ pər) *n.* person who intrudes on another's rights or territory

Reader's Response: Would you like to live in a neighborhood like Quindlen's? Why or why not?

____

____

____

____

Thinking About the Skill: How do you determine the **tone** of an essay?

____

____

____

____

____

◆ Reading Check

In what way is Quindlen's neighborhood like a pressure cooker?

____

____

____

◆ Stop to Reflect

What are the good things about Quindlen's neighborhood? What are the more negative things?

____

____

____

____

____

____

____

____

PREVIEW

The Hummingbird That Lived Through Winter

William Saroyan

Summary

Old Dikran, an Armenian immigrant to California, is nearly blind. One cold winter day, he finds a hummingbird. Though the bird is near death, he nurses it back to health and lets it go. The narrator is not sure if the bird survives the rest of winter. However, the next summer, the narrator sees many hummingbirds. Old Dikran says that each of them is the hummingbird they saved.

Visual Summary

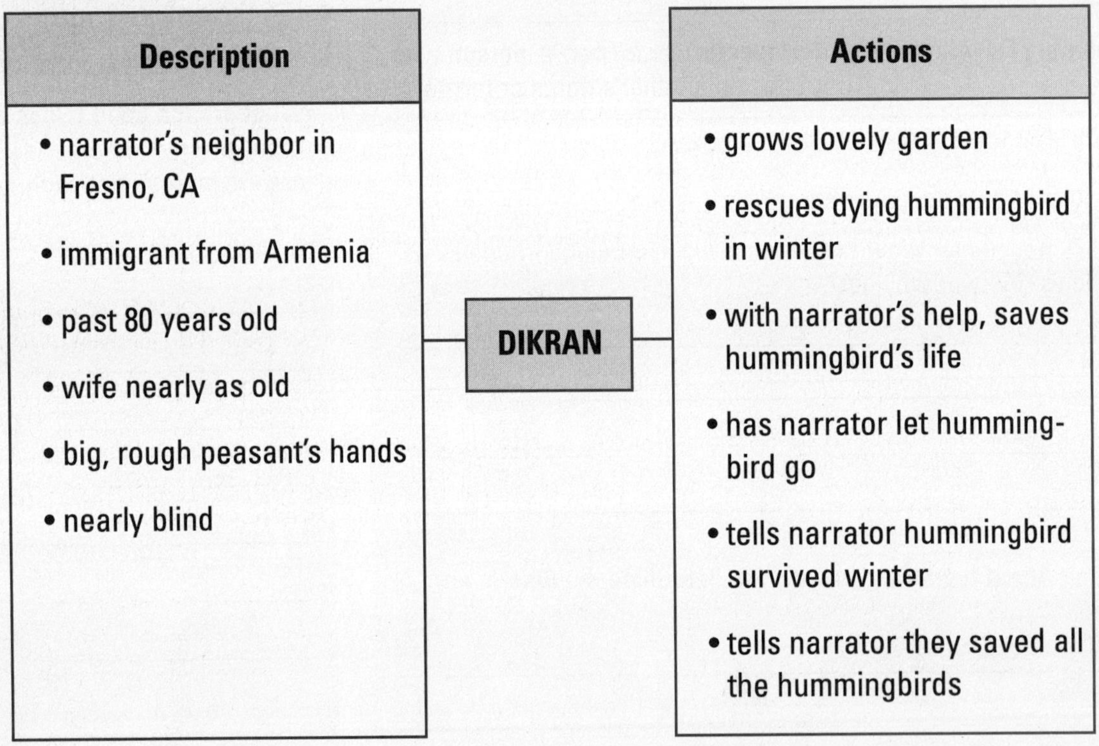

DIKRAN

Description	Actions
• narrator's neighbor in Fresno, CA • immigrant from Armenia • past 80 years old • wife nearly as old • big, rough peasant's hands • nearly blind	• grows lovely garden • rescues dying hummingbird in winter • with narrator's help, saves hummingbird's life • has narrator let hummingbird go • tells narrator hummingbird survived winter • tells narrator they saved all the hummingbirds

The Hummingbird That Lived Through Winter

William Saroyan

Hummingbirds are tiny, jewel-colored birds. Their quick movements and shiny feathers make them a beautiful sight in summer throughout most of the United States. In winter, hummingbirds travel south because their tiny bodies are not strong enough to withstand cold winter temperatures.

There was a hummingbird once which in the wintertime did not leave our neighborhood in Fresno, California.

I'll tell you about it.

Across the street lived old Dikran,[1] who was almost blind. He was past eighty and his wife was only a few years younger. They had a little house that was as neat inside as it was ordinary outside—except for old Dikran's garden, which was the best thing of its kind in the world. Plants, bushes, trees—all strong, in sweet black moist earth whose guardian was old Dikran. All things from the sky loved this spot in our poor neighborhood, and old Dikran loved *them.*

One freezing Sunday, in the dead of winter, as I came home from Sunday School I saw old Dikran standing in the middle of the street trying to distinguish what was in his hand. Instead of going into our house to the fire, as I had wanted to do, I stood on the steps of the front porch and watched the old man. He would turn around and look upward at his trees and then back to the palm of his hand. He stood in the street at least two minutes and then at last he came to me. He held his hand out, and in Armenian[2] he said, "What is this in my hand?"

I looked.

"It is a hummingbird," I said half in English and half in Armenian. Hummingbird I said in English because I didn't know its name in Armenian.

"What is that?" old Dikran asked.

"The little bird," I said. "You know. The one that comes in the summer and stands in the air and then shoots away. The one with the wings that beat so fast you can't see them. It's in your hand. It's dying."

"Come with me," the old man said. "I can't see, and the old lady's at church. I can feel its heart beating. Is it in a bad way? Look again, once."

I looked again. It was a sad thing to behold. This wonderful

1. **Dikran** (dēk´ rän).
2. **Armenian** (är mē´ nē ən) language spoken in Armenia, a country in southwestern Asia, bordering Georgia, Turkey, Iran, and Azerbaijan.

◆ **Activate Prior Knowledge**

Have you or someone you know ever taken care of a sick or hurt pet or a wild animal? Describe the experience.

◆ **Reading Check**

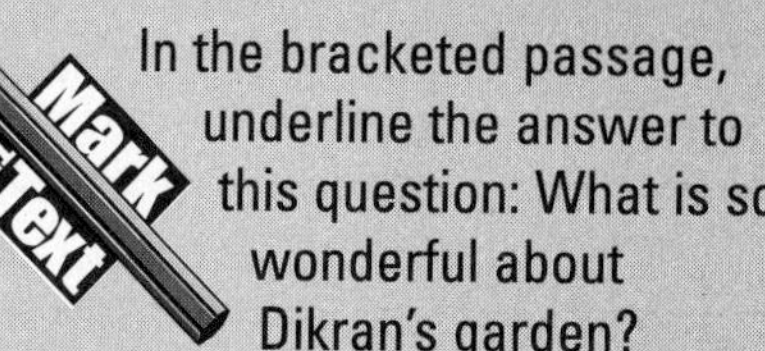

In the bracketed passage, underline the answer to this question: What is so wonderful about Dikran's garden?

◆ **Reading Strategy**

One way to figure out the meaning of an unfamiliar word is to look for a smaller word or **word part** that you recognize within it. What smaller word do you find in the underlined word *guardian*? How does knowing what the smaller word means help you figure out the larger one?

little creature of summertime in the big rough hand of the old peasant. Here it was in the cold of winter, absolutely helpless and pathetic, not suspended in a shaft of summer light, not the most alive thing in the world, but the most helpless and heartbreaking.

"It's dying," I said.

The old man lifted his hand to his mouth and blew warm breath on the little thing in his hand which he could not even see. "Stay now," he said in Armenian. "It is not long till summer. Stay, swift and lovely."

We went into the kitchen of his little house, and while he blew warm breath on the bird he told me what to do.

"Put a tablespoonful of honey over the gas fire and pour it into my hand, but be sure it is not too hot."

This was done.

After a moment the hummingbird began to show signs of fresh life. The warmth of the room, the vapor of the warm honey—and, well, the will and love of the old man. Soon the old man could feel the change in his hand, and after a moment or two the hummingbird began to take little dabs of the honey.

"It will live," the old man announced. "Stay and watch."

The transformation was incredible. The old man kept his hand generously open, and I expected the helpless bird to shoot upward out of his hand, suspend itself in space, and scare the life out of me—which is exactly what happened. The new life of the little bird was magnificent. It spun about in the little kitchen, going to the window, coming back to the heat, suspending, circling as if it were summertime and it had never felt better in its whole life.

The old man sat on the plain chair, blind but attentive. He listened carefully and tried to see, but of course he couldn't. He kept asking about the bird, how it seemed to be, whether it showed signs of weakening again, what its spirit was, and whether or not it appeared to be restless; and I kept describing the bird to him.

When the bird was restless and wanted to go, the old man said, "Open the window and let it go."

"Will it live?" I asked.

"It is alive now and wants to go," he said. "Open the window."

I opened the window, the hummingbird stirred about here and there, feeling the cold from the outside, suspended itself in the area of the open window, stirring this way and that, and then it was gone.

Vocabulary Development: **pathetic** (pə thet′ ik) *adj.* arousing pity, sorrow, and sympathy
transformation (trans′ fər mā′ shən) *n.* change in condition or outward appearance

◆ Reading Strategy

Circle the smaller word that you recognize in the underlined vocabulary word *transformation*. 1. Next, write whether it is a word root, a prefix, or a suffix. 2. Then, write the meaning of the word part. 3. If you know that the prefix *trans-* means "change," what do you think the whole word means?

Mark THE Text

1. ______

2. ______

3. ______

◆ Reading Strategy

In the underlined sentence, circle the prefixes and suffixes and underline the word root in the words *appeared*, *restless*, and *describing*.

Mark THE Text

◆ Reading Check

Why does Dikran let the hummingbird go?

______

"Close the window," the old man said.

We talked a minute or two and then I went home.

The old man claimed the hummingbird lived through that winter, but I never knew for sure. I saw hummingbirds again when summer came, but I couldn't tell one from the other.

One day in the summer I asked the old man.

"Did it live?"

"The little bird?" he said.

"Yes," I said. "That we gave the honey to. You remember. The little bird that was dying in the winter. Did it live?"

"Look about you," the old man said. "Do you see the bird?"

"I see humming*birds*," I said.

"Each of them is our bird," the old man said. "Each of them, each of them," he said swiftly and gently.

Reader's Response: Would you have let the bird go or kept it inside? Explain your answer.

____

____

____

____

____

____

Thinking About the Skill: How might the use of symbols make a literary work meaningful?

____

____

____

____

____

◆ Literary Analysis

A **symbol** is an object that represents an idea larger than itself. For instance, a dove is often used as a **symbol** for peace. What do you think the hummingbird in this story is a **symbol** of?

____

____

____

____

◆ Stop to Reflect

What do you think Dikran thinks our responsibility to animal life is?

____

____

____

____

____

____

PREVIEW

The Third Wish

Joan Aiken

Summary

One evening, while driving through a forest, Mr. Peters discovers a swan tangled in a bush. He frees the swan, who turns into a little man, the King of the Forest. The King agrees to grant Mr. Peters three wishes and gives him three leaves to wish on. He warns that wishes often leave people worse off than before. Mr. Peters wants very little, and he is aware of the trouble wishes often bring. But he is lonely, so he decides to wish for a beautiful wife. His wish is granted with the arrival of Leita, a former swan, whom he then marries. But Leita misses her swan's life and her swan sister Rhea. And in time Mr. Peters realizes that Leita will never be happy as a human being. So he uses his second wish to turn her back into a swan. He and the two swans remain close. Those who know his situation are surprised that he never uses his third wish to ask for another wife. But he says that two wishes are enough for him, and that he prefers to stay true to Leita. One morning he is found dead with a smile on his face and a leaf and white feather in his hands.

Visual Summary

1	2	3	4	5
It is a spring evening. Mr. Peters is driving through the forest.	Mr. Peters hears a noise. He rescues a swan tangled in bushes. The swan turns into the King of the Forest. He gives Mr. Peters three magical leaves that will grant three wishes. Mr. Peters wishes for a wife. The next day he gets a wife who was once a swan. She loves him but desperately misses her old life and swan sister.	Mr. Peters uses his second wish to turn his wife back into a swan.	The wife joins her swan sister. The two stay close with Mr. Peters. He says two wishes are enough and won't wish for another wife.	Mr. Peters is found dead in bed with a smile on his face and the third leaf and a white feather in his hands.

The Third Wish
Joan Aiken

This story is about a man who is granted three wishes. As you read, pay attention to how Mr. Peters uses his wishes. Does he use them wisely or foolishly?

Once there was a man who was driving in his car at dusk on a spring evening through part of the forest of Savernake. His name was Mr. Peters. The primroses were just beginning but the trees were still bare, and it was cold; the birds had stopped singing an hour ago.

As Mr. Peters entered a straight, empty stretch of road he seemed to hear a faint crying, and a struggling and thrashing, as if somebody was in trouble far away in the trees. He left his car and climbed the mossy bank beside the road. Beyond the bank was an open slope of beech trees leading down to thorn bushes through which he saw the gleam of water. He stood a moment waiting to try and discover where the noise was coming from, and presently heard a rustling and some strange cries in a voice which was almost human—and yet there was something too hoarse about it at one time and too clear and sweet at another. Mr. Peters ran down the hill and as he neared the bushes he saw something white among them which was trying to extricate itself; coming closer he found that it was a swan that had become entangled in the thorns growing on the bank of the canal.

The bird struggled all the more frantically as he approached, looking at him with hate in its yellow eyes, and when he took hold of it to free it, hissed at him, pecked him, and thrashed dangerously with its wings which were powerful enough to break his arm. Nevertheless he managed to release it from the thorns, and carrying it tightly with one arm, holding the snaky head well away with the other hand (for he did not wish his eyes pecked out), he took it to the verge of the canal and dropped it in.

The swan instantly assumed great dignity and sailed out to the middle of the water, where it put itself to rights with much dabbling and preening, smoothing its feathers with little showers of drops. Mr. Peters waited, to make sure that it was all right and had suffered no damage in its struggles. Presently the swan, when it was satisfied with its appearance, floated in to the bank once more, and in a moment, instead of the great white bird, there was a little man all in green with a golden crown and long beard, standing by the water. He had fierce glittering eyes and looked by no means friendly.

Vocabulary Development: extricate (eks´ tri kāt´) *v.* to set free

◆ Activate Prior Knowledge

Imagine that you are granted three wishes. What would one of your wishes be?

◆ Reading Strategy

Mark the Text

When you don't understand a word, you can sometimes **clarify its meaning** by looking at the words near it. What words or phrases in the underlined sentence help you find the meaning of *thrashing*? Circle them.

◆ Reading Check

What happens after Mr. Peters frees the swan?

◆ **Literary Analysis**

A writer may describe a character directly or indirectly. In **indirect characterization**, the character's words, thoughts and actions, as well as those of other characters, reveal details about the character. In the bracketed section, circle the word that shows that the King of the Forest is quick to get angry.

Mark the Text

◆ **Reading Check**

What do the three leaves represent?

____

____

____

◆ **Stop to Reflect**

Do you think Mr. Peters has made a wise choice with his first wish? Explain.

____

____

____

____

____

"Well, Sir," he said threateningly, "I see you are presumptuous enough to know some of the laws of magic. You think that because you have rescued—by pure good fortune—the King of the Forest from a difficulty, you should have some fabulous reward."

"I expect three wishes, no more and no less," answered Mr. Peters, looking at him steadily and with composure.

"Three wishes, he wants, the clever man! Well, I have yet to hear of the human being who made any good use of his three wishes—they mostly end up worse off than they started. Take your three wishes then—" he flung three dead leaves in the air "—don't blame me if you spend the last wish in undoing the work of the other two."

Mr. Peters caught the leaves and put two of them carefully in his briefcase. When he looked up the swan was sailing about in the middle of the water again, flicking the drops angrily down its long neck.

Mr. Peters stood for some minutes reflecting on how he should use his reward. He knew very well that the gift of three magic wishes was one which brought trouble more often than not, and he had no intention of being like the forester who first wished by mistake for a sausage, and then in a rage wished it on the end of his wife's nose, and then had to use his last wish in getting it off again. Mr. Peters had most of the things which he wanted and was very content with his life. The only thing that troubled him was that he was a little lonely, and had no companion for his old age. He decided to use his first wish and to keep the other two in case of an emergency. Taking a thorn he pricked his tongue with it, to remind himself not to utter rash wishes aloud. Then holding the third leaf and gazing round him at the dusky undergrowth, the primroses, great beeches and the blue-green water of the canal, he said:

"I wish I had a wife as beautiful as the forest."

A tremendous quacking and splashing broke out on the surface of the water. He thought that it was the swan laughing at him. Taking no notice he made his way through the darkening woods to his car, wrapped himself up in the rug and went to sleep.

When he awoke it was morning and the birds were beginning to call. Coming along the track towards him was the most beautiful creature he had ever seen, with eyes as blue-green as the canal, hair as dusky as the bushes, and skin as white as the feathers of swans.

"Are you the wife that I wished for?" asked Mr. Peters.

Vocabulary Development: **presumptuous** (prē zump´ cho͞o əs) *adj.* overconfident; arrogant
composure (kəm pō´ zhər) *n.* calmness of mind
rash (rash) *adj.* thoughtless

"Yes, I am," she replied. "My name is Leita."

She stepped into the car beside him and they drove off to the church on the outskirts of the forest, where they were married. Then he took her to his house in a remote and lovely valley and showed her all his treasures —the bees in their white hives, the Jersey cows, the hyacinths, the silver candlesticks, the blue cups and the luster bowl for putting primroses in. She admired everything, but what pleased her most was the river which ran by the foot of his garden.

"Do swans come up there?" she asked.

"Yes, I have often seen swans there on the river," he told her, and she smiled.

Leita made him a good wife. She was gentle and friendly, busied herself about the house and garden, polished the bowls, milked the cows and mended his socks. But as time went by Mr. Peters began to feel that she was not happy. She seemed restless, wandered much in the garden, and sometimes when he came back from the fields he would find the house empty and she would return after half an hour or so with no explanation of where she had been. On these occasions she was always especially tender and would put out his slippers to warm and cook his favorite dish—Welsh rarebit[1] with wild strawberries—for supper.

One evening he was returning home along the river path when he saw Leita in front of him, down by the water. A swan had sailed up to the verge and she had her arms round its neck and the swan's head rested against her cheek. She was weeping, and as he came nearer he saw that tears were rolling, too, from the swan's eyes.

"Leita, what is it?" he asked, very troubled.

"This is my sister," she answered. "I can't bear being separated from her."

Now he understood that Leita was really a swan from the forest, and this made him very sad because when a human being marries a bird it always leads to sorrow.

"I could use my second wish to give your sister human shape, so that she could be a companion to you," he suggested.

"No, no," she cried, "I couldn't ask that of her."

"Is it so very hard to be a human being?" asked Mr. Peters sadly.

"Very, very hard," she answered.

"Don't you love me at all, Leita?"

"Yes, I do, I do love you," she said, and there were tears in her eyes again. "But I missed the old life in the forest, the cool

Vocabulary Development: remote (ri mōt′) *adj.* far away from everything else

1. **Welsh rarebit** a dish of melted cheese served on crackers or toast.

◆ Reading Strategy

Leita's actions in the underlined sentence help explain the meaning of *restless*. Circle the phrases describing her actions.

◆ Literary Analysis

Modern fairy tales have some of the same elements as traditional fairy tales, like mysterious events, magic, and animals with unusual abilities. They are different from traditional fairy tales in having details of modern life. What details from the story so far make it a modern fairy tale?

◆ Reading Check

How does Mr. Peters learn what Leita really is?

◆ **Literary Analysis**

Mr. Peters asks Leita if she would like to be turned back into a swan. What does this offer tell you about him?

____

____

____

◆ **Stop to Reflect**

Think about your response to the story. How well do you like Mr. Peters? Leita? How does their situation make you feel?

____

____

____

____

____

____

____

____

◆ **Reading Check**

Underline the sentence that tells Mr. Peters's second wish. Write his wish on the lines below.

____

____

____

grass and the mist rising off the river at sunrise and the feel of the water sliding over my feathers as my sister and I drifted along the stream."

"Then shall I use my second wish to turn you back into a swan again?" he asked, and his tongue pricked to remind him of the old King's words, and his heart swelled with grief inside him.

"Who would clean your socks and cook your meals and see to the hens?"

"I'd do it myself as I did before I married you," he said, trying to sound cheerful.

She shook her head. "No, I could not be as unkind to you as that. I am partly a swan, but I am also partly a human being now. I will stay with you."

Poor Mr. Peters was very distressed on his wife's account and did his best to make her life happier, taking her for drives in the car, finding beautiful music for her to listen to on the radio, buying clothes for her and even suggesting a trip round the world. But she said no to that; she would prefer to stay in their own house near the river.

He noticed that she spent more and more time baking wonderful cakes—jam puffs, petits fours, eclairs and meringues. One day he saw her take a basketful down to the river and he guessed that she was giving them to her sister.

He built a seat for her by the river, and the two sisters spent hours together there, communicating in some wordless manner. For a time he thought that all would be well, but then he saw how thin and pale she was growing.

One night when he had been late doing the account he came up to bed and found her weeping in her sleep and calling:

"Rhea! Rhea! I can't understand what you say! Oh, wait for me, take me with you!"

Then he knew that it was hopeless and she would never be happy as a human. He stooped down and kissed her goodbye, then took another leaf from his notecase, blew it out of the window, and used up his second wish.

Next moment instead of Leita there was a sleeping swan lying across the bed with its head under its wing. He carried it out of the house and down to the brink of the river, and then he said "Leita! Leita!" to waken her, and gently put her into the water. She gazed round her in astonishment for a moment, and then came up to him and rested her head lightly against his hand; next instant she was flying away over the trees towards the heart of the forest.

He heard a harsh laugh behind him, and turning round saw the old King looking at him with a malicious expression.

"Well, my friend! You don't seem to have managed so

Vocabulary Development: malicious (mə lish′ əs) *adj.* spiteful; hateful

wonderfully with your first two wishes, do you? What will you do with the last? Turn yourself into a swan? Or turn Leita back into a girl?"

"I shall do neither," said Mr. Peters calmly. "Human beings and swans are better in their own shapes."

But for all that he looked sadly over towards the forest where Leita had flown, and walked slowly back to his empty house.

Next day he saw two swans swimming at the bottom of the garden, and one of them wore the gold chain he had given Leita after their marriage; she came up and rubbed her head against his hand.

Mr. Peters and his two swans came to be well known in that part of the country; people used to say that he talked to swans and they understood him as well as his neighbours. Many people were a little frightened of him. There was a story that once when thieves tried to break into his house they were set upon by two huge white birds which carried them off bodily and dropped them into the river.

As Mr. Peters grew old everyone wondered at his contentment. Even when he was bent with rheumatism[2] he would not think of moving to a drier spot, but went slowly about his work, milking the cows and collecting the honey and eggs, with the two swans always somewhere close at hand.

Sometimes people who knew his story would say to him: "Mr. Peters, why don't you wish for another wife?"

"Not likely," he would answer serenely. "Two wishes were enough for me, I reckon. I've learned that even if your wishes are granted they don't always better you. I'll stay faithful to Leita."

One autumn night, passers-by along the road heard the mournful sound of two swans singing. All night the song went on, sweet and harsh, sharp and clear. In the morning Mr. Peters was found peacefully dead in his bed with a smile of great happiness on his face. In between his hands, which lay clasped on his breast, were a withered leaf and a white feather.

---

2. **rheumatism** (roo´ mə tiz əm) *n.* pain and stiffness of the joints and muscles.

Reader's Response: Would you have made the same choices as Mr. Peters if you were in his situation? Explain.

____

____

Thinking About the Skill: Describe how nearby words and phrases help you understand unfamiliar words.

____

____

◆ Stop to Reflect

Do you think Mr. Peters used his second wish well? Did his decision surprise you, or did you have a different response?

____

____

____

____

◆ Reading Strategy

Mark the Text

Circle the words or phrases in the underlined sentence that help you figure out the meaning of *set upon.* Write its meaning on the lines below.

____

____

____

____

The Charge of the Light Brigade

Alfred, Lord Tennyson

Summary

Six hundred lightly armed British troops on horseback attack an enemy position. Since the enemy are heavily armed with cannon, the British soldiers know that something was wrong with their orders. Still, they follow their orders bravely, as good soldiers do. Many are killed, but their courage will be honored always.

Visual Summary

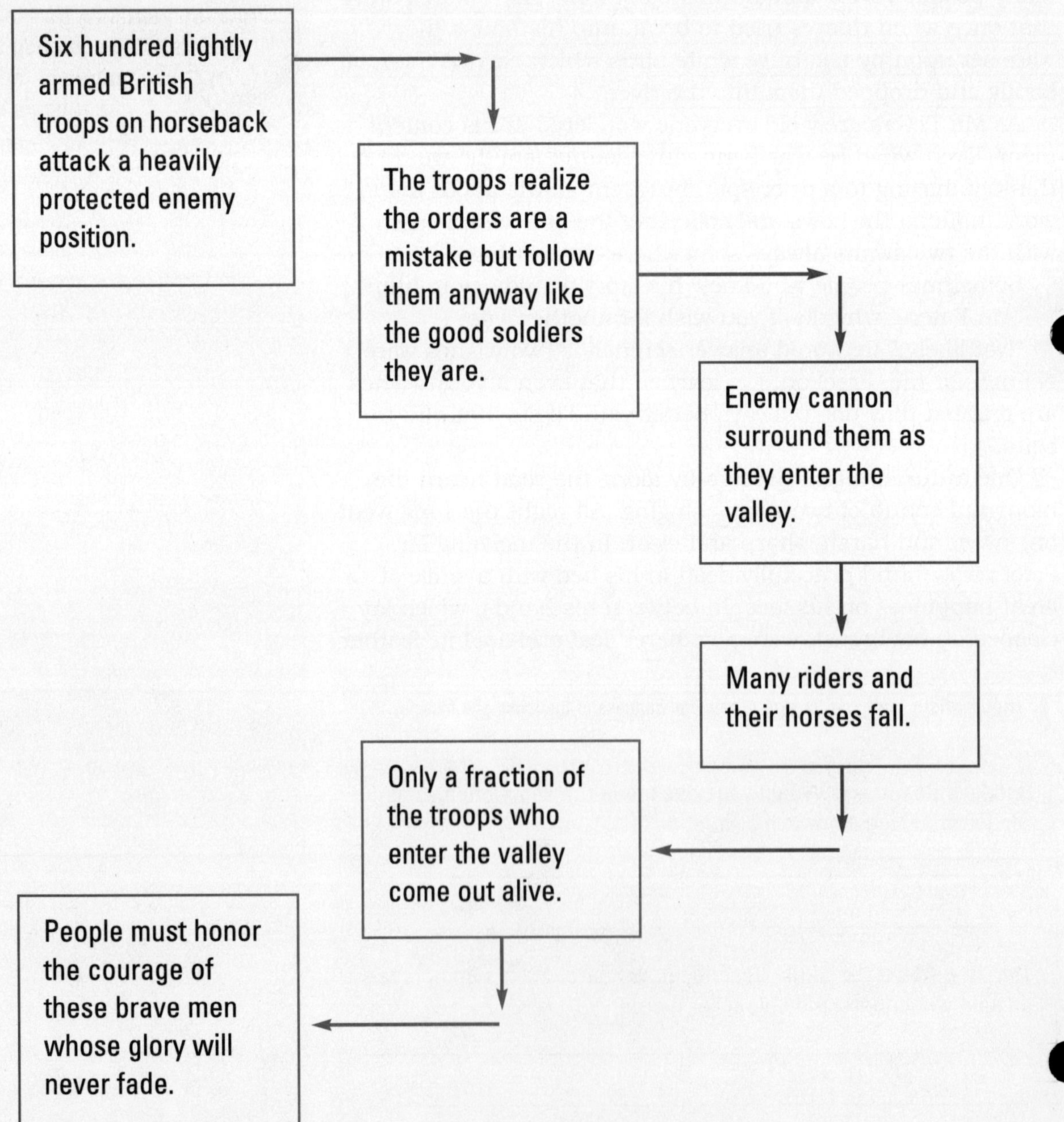

The Charge of the Light Brigade

Alfred, Lord Tennyson

The Crimean War was fought between 1853 and 1856. It pitted British, French, and Turkish soldiers against Russians. As you read, notice details that capture the moments before, during, and after a battle.

1

Half a league,[1] half a league,
Half a league onward,
All in the valley of Death
   Rode the six hundred.
"Forward, the Light Brigade!
Charge for the guns!" he said:
Into the valley of Death
   Rode the six hundred.

2

"Forward, the Light Brigade!"
Was there a man dismayed?
Not though the soldier knew
   Someone had blundered:
Theirs not to make reply,
Theirs not to reason why,
Theirs but to do and die,
Into the valley of Death
   Rode the six hundred.

3

Cannon to right of them,
Cannon to left of them,
Cannon in front of them
   Volleyed and thundered;
Stormed at with shot and shell,
Boldly they rode and well,
Into the jaws of Death,
Into the mouth of Hell
   Rode the six hundred.

Vocabulary Development: **dismayed** (dis mād′) *adj.* afraid; without confidence
blundered (blun′ dərd) *v.* made a foolish mistake
volleyed (väl′ ēd) *v.* fired together

1. **league** (lēg) *n.* three miles.

◆ Activate Prior Knowledge

What images of war do you have? Write two on the lines below.

1. ______________________________

____

2. ______________________________

____

◆ Literary Analysis

Mark the Text

Repetition is the repeated use of words, phrases, or rhythms. Poets use repetition to make their poetry more musical, to emphasize ideas, and to help establish a mood or atmosphere. Circle the repeated words in lines 13–15. Who is being referred to in those lines?

____

____

____

◆ Reading Check

What is the Light Brigade?

____

____

____

◆ **Reading Strategy**

Sometimes familiar **parts** of unfamiliar words can help you understand a word's meaning. They can also help you understand the relationships between words. Circle the familiar word in *gunners*.

Mark the Text

◆ **Literary Analysis**

The poet repeats the word *canon* several times. What effect does this have?

___

___

___

◆ **Reading Check**

Is the poet proud of the soldiers? Explain.

___

___

___

___

___

4

Flashed all their sabers bare,
Flashed as they turned in air,
Sab'ring the gunners there,
Charging an army, while
  All the world wondered:
Plunged in the battery[2] smoke
Right through the line they broke:
Cossack[3] and Russian
Reeled from the saber stroke
  Shattered and sundered.
Then they rode back, but not,
  Not the six hundred.

5

Cannon to right of them,
Cannon to left of them,
Cannon behind them
  Volleyed and thundered;
Stormed at with shot and shell,
While horse and hero fell,
They that had fought so well
Came through the jaws of Death,
Back from the mouth of Hell,
All that was left of them,
  Left of six hundred.

6

When can their glory fade?
O the wild charge they made!
  All the world wondered.
Honor the charge they made!
Honor the Light Brigade,
  Noble six hundred!

Vocabulary Development: **reeled** (rēld) *v.* fell back from a blow
sundered (sun´ dərd) *adj.* broken apart

2. **battery** fortification equipped with heavy guns.
3. **Cossack** (käs´ ak´) people of southern Russia famous as horsemen and cavalrymen.

Reader's Response: How does this poem make you feel about war?

___

___

The Californian's Tale

Mark Twain

Summary

A man hunting for gold in California comes to the attractive, well-kept cabin of a miner named Henry. Henry invites the man in. He credits the loveliness of his home to his young wife who is away until Saturday night. He urges the visitor to stay until she returns. Henry's friends come over on Saturday and give Henry a drug that puts him to sleep. They explain that Henry's wife has been dead for 19 years. Every year, at the time of her death, they go through the act of pretending she's returning. They do this so that Henry doesn't go wild with anger and grief.

Visual Summary

Wednesday	Thursday	Friday	Saturday
• Narrator (storyteller) is hunting for gold. • He meets Henry outside a miner's cabin much nicer than others. • Henry explains that the pretty, comfortable home is the work of his wife, who is visiting relatives. • He insists that the narrator stay until Saturday, when his wife will return.	• Tom, a miner from three miles away, comes to visit that evening. • Henry reads him part of his wife's letter. • Tom promises to return to celebrate her homecoming on Saturday.	• Joe, another miner from nearby, comes to visit. • Henry reads him part of his wife's letter. • Joe too promises to return for the homecoming.	• The narrator checks his watch several times, eager for the wife's arrival. • Charley, Joe and Tom arrive. • Joe serves a drink to toast the wife before she arrives. • Henry is drugged by the drink and falls asleep. • Joe explains that Henry's wife has been dead for 19 years but that they pretend she is alive to keep Henry from going wild with grief.

◆ **Activate Prior Knowledge**

By looking at a house, what can you tell about the people who live there? Briefly describe a house that is familiar to you and explain what its appearance reveals about the people who live in it.

____

____

____

____

____

____

◆ **Literary Analysis**

Local color, the use of detail specific to a region, can add authenticity to a story. In the opening paragraph, underline details that help you see the nearly deserted areas that were once booming mine towns.

Mark THE Text

◆ **Reading Check**

How is the narrator trying to make money?

____

____

____

The Californian's Tale

Mark Twain

The California Gold Rush of 1849 brought thousands to California, eager to get rich. Often, men left wives and family behind and lived in terrible conditions as they worked to make their fortunes. With few women around to make life bearable, it is no wonder the prospector in this story saw a woman's presence as a valuable treasure!

Thirty-five years ago I was out prospecting on the Stanislaus,[1] tramping all day long with pick and pan and horn, and washing a hatful of dirt here and there, always expecting to make a rich strike, and never doing it. It was a lovely region, woodsy, balmy, delicious, and had once been populous, long years before, but now the people had vanished and the charming paradise was a solitude. They went away when the surface diggings gave out. In one place, where a busy little city with banks and newspapers and fire companies and a mayor and aldermen had been, was nothing but a wide expanse of emerald turf, with not even the faintest sign that human life had ever been present there. This was down toward Tuttletown. In the country neighborhood thereabouts, along the dusty roads, one found at intervals the prettiest little cottage homes, snug and cozy, and so cobwebbed with vines snowed thick with roses that the doors and windows were wholly hidden from sight—sign that these were deserted homes, forsaken years ago by defeated and disappointed families who could neither sell them nor give them away. Now and then, half an hour apart, one came across solitary log cabins of the earliest mining days, built by the first gold-miners, the predecessors of the cottage-builders. In some few cases these cabins were still occupied; and when this was so, you could depend upon it that the occupant was the very pioneer who had built the cabin; and you could depend on another thing, too—that he was there because he had once had his opportunity to go home to the States rich, and had not done it; had rather lost his wealth, and had then in his humiliation resolved to sever all communication with his home relatives and friends, and be to them thenceforth as one dead. Round about California in that day were

Vocabulary Development: **balmy** (bäm´ ē) *adj.* soothing; mild; pleasant
predecessors (pred´ ə ses´ ərz) *n.* those who came before
humiliation (hyo͞o mil´ ē ā´ shən) *n.* embarrassment; feeling of hurt pride

1. **Stanislaus** (stå´ ni slôws) *n.* county, river, and mountain, all located in California.

scattered a host of these living dead men—pride-smitten poor fellows, grizzled and old at forty, whose secret thoughts were made all of regrets and longings—regrets for their wasted lives, and longings to be out of the struggle and done with it all.

It was a lonesome land! Not a sound in all those peaceful expanses of grass and woods but the drowsy hum of insects; no glimpse of man or beast; nothing to keep up your spirits and make you glad to be alive. And so, at last, in the early part of the afternoon, when I caught sight of a human creature, I felt a most grateful uplift. This person was a man about forty-five years old, and he was standing at the gate of one of those cozy little rose-clad cottages of the sort already referred to. However, this one hadn't a deserted look; it had the look of being lived in and petted and cared for and looked after; and so had its front yard, which was a garden of flowers, abundant, gay, and flourishing. I was invited in, of course, and required to make myself at home—it was the custom of the country.

It was delightful to be in such a place, after long weeks of daily and nightly familiarity with miners' cabins—with all which this implies of dirt floor, never-made beds, tin plates and cups, bacon and beans and black coffee, and nothing of ornament but war pictures from the Eastern illustrated papers tacked to the log walls. That was all hard, cheerless, materialistic desolation, but here was a nest which had aspects to rest the tired eye and refresh that something in one's nature which, after long fasting, recognizes, when confronted by the belongings of art, howsoever cheap and modest they may be, that it has unconsciously been famishing and now has found nourishment. I could not have believed that a rag carpet could feast me so, and so content me; or that there could be such solace to the soul in wall-paper and framed lithographs,[2] and bright-colored tidies[3] and lamp-mats, and Windsor chairs,[4] and varnished what-nots, with sea-shells and books and china vases on them, and the score of little unclassifiable tricks and touches that a woman's hand distributes about a home, which one sees without knowing he sees them, yet would miss in a moment if they were taken away. The delight that was in my heart showed in my face, and the man saw it and was pleased; saw it so plainly that he answered it as if it had been spoken.

Vocabulary Development: **abundant** (ə bun′ dənt) *adj.* plentiful
desolation (des′ ə lā′ shən) *n.* loneliness; emptiness; misery

2. **lithographs** (lith′ ə grafs′) *n.* type of print.
3. **tidies** (tī′ dēz) *n.* ornamental chair coverings that protect the back, armrests, and headrest.
4. **Windsor** (win′ zər) **chairs** *n.* wooden chairs popular in the 18th century. They had spreading legs, a back of spindles, and usually a saddle seat.

◆ **Reading Strategy**

Briefly **summarize** the narrator's main reasons for liking the cottage so much.

◆ **Reading Check**

In what way is this cottage different from other miners' cabins?

◆ **Stop to Reflect**

What do you think of the owner of the cottage at this point?

◆ **Literary Analysis**

Circle details in the bracketed paragraph that develop the **local color.**

THE Mark Text

◆ **Reading Check**

What is the cabin owner waiting for?

"All her work," he said, caressingly; "she did it all herself—every bit," and he took the room in with a glance which was full of affectionate worship. One of those soft Japanese fabrics with which woman drape with careful negligence the upper part of a picture-frame was out of adjustment. He noticed it, and rearranged it with cautious pains, stepping back several times to gauge the effect before he got it to suit him. Then he gave it a light finishing pat or two with his hand, and said: "She always does that. You can't tell just what it lacks, but it does lack something until you've done that—you can see it yourself after it's done, but that is all you know; you can't find out the law of it. It's like the finishing pats a mother gives the child's hair after she's got it combed and brushed, I reckon. I've seen her fix all these things so much that I can do them all just her way, though I don't know the law of any of them. But she knows the law. She knows the why and the how both; but I don't know the why; I only know the how."

He took me into a bedroom so that I might wash my hands; such a bedroom as I had not seen for years: white counterpane, white pillows, carpeted floor, papered walls, pictures, dressing-table, with mirror and pin-cushion and dainty toilet things; and in the corner a wash-stand, with real china-ware bowl and pitcher,[5] and with soap in a china dish, and on a rack more than a dozen towels—towels too clean and white for one out of practice to use without some vague sense of profanation. So my face spoke again, and he answered with gratified words:

"All her work; she did it all herself—every bit. Nothing here that hasn't felt the touch of her hand. Now you would think—But I mustn't talk so much."

By this time I was wiping my hands and glancing from detail to detail of the room's belongings, as one is apt to do when he is in a new place, where everything he sees is a comfort to his eye and his spirit; and I became conscious, in one of those unaccountable ways, you know, that there was something there somewhere that the man wanted me to discover for myself. I knew it perfectly, and I knew he was trying to help me by furtive indications with his eye, so I tried hard to get on the right track, being eager to gratify him. I failed several times, as I could see out of the corner of my eye without being told; but at last I know I must be looking straight at the thing—knew it from the pleasure issuing in

Vocabulary Development: **furtive** (fur´ tiv) *adj.* sneaky
gratify (grat´ i fī´) *v.* to please

5. **wash-stand, with real china-ware bowl and pitcher** items used for washing before sinks and indoor plumbing were available.

invisible waves from him. He broke into a happy laugh, and rubbed his hands together, and cried out:

"That's it! You've found it. I knew you would. It's her picture."

I went to the little black-walnut bracket on the farther wall, and did find there what I had not yet noticed—a daguerreotype-case. It contained the sweetest girlish face, and the most beautiful, as it seemed to me, that I had ever seen. The man drank the admiration from my face, and was fully satisfied.

"Nineteen her last birthday," he said, as he put the picture back; "and that was the day we were married. When you see her—ah, just wait till you see her!"

"Where is she? When will she be in?"

"Oh, she's away now. She's gone to see her people. They live forty or fifty miles from here. She's been gone two weeks to-day."

"When do you expect her back?"

"This is Wednesday. She'll be back Saturday, in the evening—about nine o'clock, likely."

I felt a sharp sense of disappointment.

"I'm sorry, because I'll be gone by then," I said, regretfully.

"Gone? No—why should you go? Don't go. She'll be so disappointed."

She would be disappointed—that beautiful creature! If she had said the words herself they could hardly have blessed me more. I was feeling a deep, strong longing to see her—a longing so supplicating, so insistent, that it made me afraid. I said to myself: "I will go straight away from this place, for my peace of mind's sake."

"You see, she likes to have people come and stop with us—people who know things, and can talk—people like you. She delights in it; for she knows—oh, she knows nearly everything herself, and can talk, oh, like a bird—and the books she reads, why, you would be astonished. Don't go; it's only a little while, you know, and she'll be so disappointed."

I heard the words, but hardly noticed them, I was so deep in my thinkings and strugglings. He left me, but I didn't know. Presently he was back, with the picture-case in his hand, and he held it open before me and said:

"There, now, tell her to her face you could have stayed to see her, and you wouldn't."

That second glimpse broke down my good resolution. I would stay and take the risk. That night we smoked the tranquil pipe, and talked till late about various things, but mainly about her; and certainly I had had no such pleasant and restful time for many a day. The Thursday followed and slipped comfortably away. Toward twilight a big miner from three miles away came—one of the grizzled, stranded pioneers—and gave us warm salutation, clothed in grave and sober speech. Then he said:

"I only just dropped over to ask about the little madam,

◆ **Stop to Reflect**

How does the man feel about his wife?

____

____

____

____

____

◆ **Reading Check**

Whom does the narrator want to meet?

____

____

____

◆ **Reading Strategy**

Briefly **summarize** what happens in the bracketed paragraph.

____

____

____

____

____

____

____

____

and when is she coming home. Any news from her?"

"Oh yes, a letter. Would you like to hear it, Tom?"

"Well, I should think I would, if you don't mind, Henry!"

Henry got the letter out of his wallet, and said he would skip some of the private phrases, if we were willing; then he went on and read the bulk of it—a loving, sedate, and altogether charming and gracious piece of handiwork, with a postscript full of affectionate regards and messages to Tom, and Joe, and Charley, and other close friends and neighbors.

As the reader finished, he glanced at Tom, and cried out:

"Oho, you're at it again! Take your hands away, and let me see your eyes. You always do that when I read a letter from her. I will write and tell her."

"Oh no, you mustn't, Henry. I am getting old, you know, and any little disappointment makes me want to cry. I thought she'd be here herself, and now you've got only a letter."

"Well, now, what put that in your head? I thought everybody knew she wasn't coming till Saturday."

"Saturday! Why, come to think, I did know it. I wonder what's the matter with me lately? Certainly I knew it. Ain't we all getting ready for her? Well, I must be going now. But I'll be on hand when she comes, old man!"

Late Friday afternoon another gray veteran tramped over from his cabin a mile or so away, and said the boys wanted to have a little gaiety and a good time Saturday night, if Henry thought she wouldn't be too tired after her long journey to be kept up.

"Tired? She tired! Oh, hear the man! Joe, *you* know she'd sit up six weeks to please any one of you!"

When Joe heard that there was a letter, he asked to have it read, and the loving messages in it for him broke the old fellow all up; but he said he was such an old wreck that that would happen to him if she only just mentioned his name. "Lord, we miss her so!" he said.

Saturday afternoon I found I was taking out my watch pretty often. Henry noticed it, and said, with a startled look:

"You don't think she ought to be here so soon, do you?"

I felt caught, and a little embarrassed; but I laughed, and said it was a habit of mine when I was in a state of expectancy. But he didn't seem quite satisfied; and from that time on he began to show uneasiness. Four times he walked me up the road to a point whence we could see a long distance; and there he would stand, shading his eyes with his hand, and looking. Several times he said:

"I'm getting worried, I'm getting right down worried. I know she's not due till about nine o'clock, and yet something seems to be trying to warn me that something's happened. You don't think anything has happened, do you?"

I began to get pretty thoroughly ashamed of him for his

◆ **Stop to Reflect**

What do you think about Tom's response to hearing the letter from Henry's wife?

◆ **Reading Check**

Why does Henry become uneasy? Circle the event that starts him worrying.

Mark the Text

childishness; and at last, when he repeated that imploring question still another time, I lost my patience for the moment, and spoke pretty brutally to him. It seemed to shrivel him up and cow him; and he looked so wounded and so humble after that, that I detested myself for having done the cruel and unnecessary thing. And so I was glad when Charley, another veteran, arrived toward the edge of the evening, and nestled up to Henry to hear the letter read, and talked over the preparations for the welcome. Charley fetched out one hearty speech after another, and did his best to drive away his friend's bodings and apprehensions.

"Anything *happened* to her? Henry, that's pure nonsense. There isn't anything going to happen to her; just make your mind easy as to that. What did the letter say? Said she was well, didn't it? And said she'd be here by nine o'clock, didn't it? Did you ever know her to fail of her word? Why, you know you never did. Well, then, don't you fret; she'll *be* here, and that's absolutely certain, and as sure as you are born. Come, now, let's get to decorating—not much time left."

Pretty soon Tom and Joe arrived, and then all hands set about adorning the house with flowers. Toward nine the three miners said that as they had brought their instruments they might as well tune up, for the boys and girls would soon be arriving now, and hungry for a good, old-fashioned break-down. A fiddle, a banjo, and a clarinet—these were the instruments. The trio took their places side by side, and began to play some rattling dance-music, and beat time with their big boots.

It was getting very close to nine. Henry was standing in the door with his eyes directed up the road, his body swaying to the torture of his mental distress. He had been made to drink his wife's health and safety several times, and now Tom shouted:

"All hands stand by! One more drink, and she's here!"

Joe brought the glasses on a waiter, and served the party. I reached for one of the two remaining glasses, but Joe growled, under his breath:

"Drop that! Take the other."

Which I did. Henry was served last. He had hardly swallowed his drink when the clock began to strike. He listened till it finished, his face growing pale and paler; then he said:

"Boys, I am sick with fear. Help me—I want to lie down!"

They helped him to the sofa. He began to nestle and drowse, but presently spoke like one talking in his sleep, and said: "Did I hear horses' feet? Have they come?"

One of the veterans answered, close to his ear: "It was

Vocabulary Development: apprehensions (ap′ rē hen′ shənz) *n.* fears; anxious feelings

◆ Reading Strategy

Summarize the situation at this point in the story, including the narrator's feelings, Henry's mood, and the impact of Charley's arrival.

◆ Literary Analysis

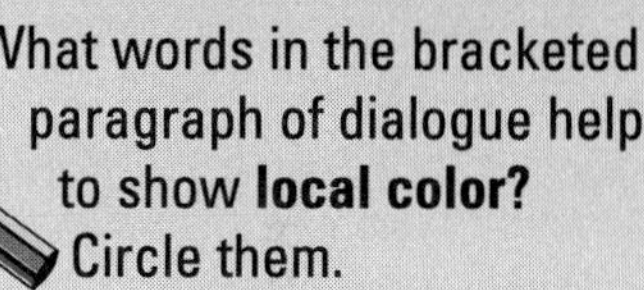

What words in the bracketed paragraph of dialogue help to show **local color?** Circle them.

◆ Reading Check

What happens when the narrator reaches for a glass?

Jimmy Parrish come to say the party got delayed, but they're right up the road a piece, and coming along. Her horse is lame, but she'll be here in half an hour."

"Oh, I'm *so* thankful nothing has happened!"

He was asleep almost before the words were out of his mouth. In a moment those handy men had his clothes off, and had tucked him into his bed in the chamber where I had washed my hands. They closed the door and came back. Then they seemed preparing to leave; but I said: "Please don't go, gentlemen. She won't know me; I am a stranger."

They glanced at each other. Then Joe said:

"She? Poor thing, she's been dead nineteen years!"

"Dead?"

"That or worse. She went to see her folks half a year after she was married, and on her way back, on a Saturday evening, the Indians captured her within five miles of this place, and she's never been heard of since."

"And he lost his mind in consequence?"

"Never has been sane an hour since. But he only gets bad when that time of the year comes round. Then we begin to drop in here, three days before she's due, to encourage him up, and ask if he's heard from her, and Saturday we all come and fix up the house with flowers, and get everything ready for a dance. We've done it every year for nineteen years. The first Saturday there was twenty-seven of us, without counting the girls; there's only three of us now, and the girls are all gone. We drug him to sleep, or he would go wild; then he's all right for another year—thinks she's with him till the last three or four days come round; then he begins to look for her, and gets out his poor old letter, and we come and ask him to read it to us. Lord, she was a darling!"

◆ **Reading Strategy**

Summarize what you have learned about Henry's wife.

____

____

____

____

____

____

◆ **Reading Check**

Why doesn't Henry's wife appear?

____

____

____

____

Reader's Response: Were you surprised by the ending of the story? Explain your response.

____

____

Thinking About the Skill: How did summarizing help you understand the story?

____

____

PREVIEW

Four Skinny Trees

Sandra Cisneros

Summary

The speaker admires four skinny trees that grow outside the window of her city apartment. They possess a secret strength and keep surviving in spite of their surroundings. The trees inspire the speaker to keep going too.

Visual Summary

How Trees Are Similar to Speaker	How Speaker Is Similar to Trees
• Are only ones who understand speaker • Have skinny necks and pointy elbows • Do not belong in surroundings	• Is only one who understands the four trees • Has skinny neck and pointy elbows • Does not belong in her surroundings

Speaker will try to be like the four trees in other ways.

What Trees May Teach Speaker
• Have secret strength in hidden roots • Grab the earth with hairy toes • Bite sky with violent teeth • Stay angry and survive • How to survive • Grow despite concrete • Never forget to reach

◆ Activate Prior Knowledge

Do you have a special tree or river, or a place you go when you feel sad? Write a brief description of that place and how it makes you feel.

◆ Reading Strategy

Writers sometimes use **figurative language**—language not meant to be taken literally—to compare one thing to something else. In the underlined sentence, circle what the trees are being compared to.

Mark the Text

◆ Literary Analysis

This piece is about trees, but it has many **levels of meaning.** Can you think of a deeper meaning to the text?

◆ Reading Check

Cisneros thinks trees have a secret. What is it?

Four Skinny Trees

Sandra Cisneros

Where you live probably has a big influence on the way you see the world. In this piece, Sandra Cisneros describes the setting that surrounds her and how it shapes her thoughts and feelings.

They are the only ones who understand me. I am the only one who understands them. Four skinny trees with skinny necks and pointy elbows like mine. Four who do not belong here but are here. Four raggedy excuses planted by the city. From our room we can hear them, but Nenny just sleeps and doesn't appreciate these things.

Their strength is secret. They send ferocious roots beneath the ground. They grow up and they grow down and grab the earth between their hairy toes and bite the sky with violent teeth and never quit their anger. This is how they keep.

Let one forget his reason for being, they'd all droop like tulips in a glass, each with their arms around the other. Keep, keep, keep, trees say when I sleep. They teach.

When I am too sad and too skinny to keep keeping, when I am a tiny thing against so many bricks, then it is I look at trees. When there is nothing left to look at on this street. Four who grew despite concrete. Four who reach and do not forget to reach. Four whose only reason is to be and be.

Vocabulary Development: **ferocious** (fə rō´ shəs) *adj.* fierce; savage

Reader's Response: Do you feel the same way about trees? Explain.

Thinking About the Skill: How does figurative language affect a piece of writing?

The Night the Bed Fell

James Thurber

Summary

James Thurber recalls the chain of events that led to confusion one night when he was a boy. His father went to sleep in the attic to do some thinking. His mother was afraid the wobbly attic bed would collapse. During the night, young James accidentally tipped over his cot. The noises caused his mother to scream. This woke his brother Herman, who yelled at the mother to calm herself. This woke Briggs, a visiting cousin, who spilled on himself because he thought he had stopped breathing. By this time James's other brother, Roy, and the dog Rex were also awake, with Rex barking and attacking Briggs. All the noise woke the father, who came down from the attic and asked what was going on.

Visual Summary

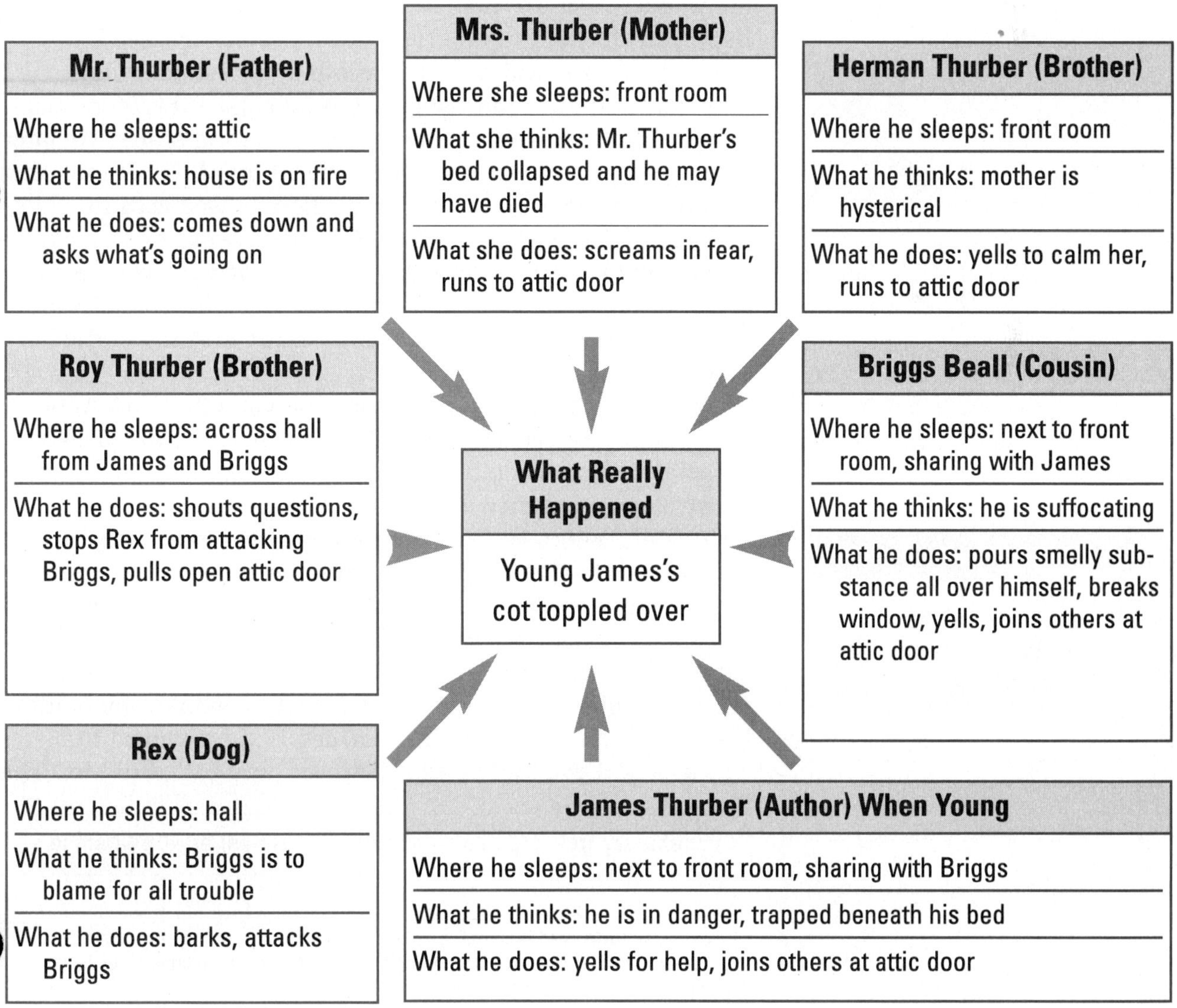

Mr. Thurber (Father)
- Where he sleeps: attic
- What he thinks: house is on fire
- What he does: comes down and asks what's going on

Mrs. Thurber (Mother)
- Where she sleeps: front room
- What she thinks: Mr. Thurber's bed collapsed and he may have died
- What she does: screams in fear, runs to attic door

Herman Thurber (Brother)
- Where he sleeps: front room
- What he thinks: mother is hysterical
- What he does: yells to calm her, runs to attic door

Roy Thurber (Brother)
- Where he sleeps: across hall from James and Briggs
- What he does: shouts questions, stops Rex from attacking Briggs, pulls open attic door

What Really Happened

Young James's cot toppled over

Briggs Beall (Cousin)
- Where he sleeps: next to front room, sharing with James
- What he thinks: he is suffocating
- What he does: pours smelly substance all over himself, breaks window, yells, joins others at attic door

Rex (Dog)
- Where he sleeps: hall
- What he thinks: Briggs is to blame for all trouble
- What he does: barks, attacks Briggs

James Thurber (Author) When Young
- Where he sleeps: next to front room, sharing with Briggs
- What he thinks: he is in danger, trapped beneath his bed
- What he does: yells for help, joins others at attic door

◆ Activate Prior Knowledge

Relate an event (with family, at school, or with friends) that seems funny now but that caused a commotion when it happened.

____

____

____

____

____

____

◆ Reading Check

Underline the sentence that tells what the narrator's father decides to do.

Mark the Text

____

◆ Reading Strategy

Significant events are the important events that move a story forward. What significant event does the title mention?

____

____

____

The Night the Bed Fell

James Thurber

To Thurber, life's humor came from looking back calmly on moments of chaos. In this essay, Thurber calmly recounts an example of the total, but humorous, confusion that he always described as being typical of his childhood.

I suppose that the high-water mark of my youth in Columbus, Ohio, was the night the bed fell on my father. It makes a better recitation (unless, as some friends of mine have said, one has heard it five or six times) than it does a piece of writing, for it is almost necessary to throw furniture around, shake doors, and bark like a dog, to lend the proper atmosphere and verisimilitude[1] to what is admittedly a somewhat incredible tale. Still, it did take place.

It happened, then, that my father had decided to sleep in the attic one night, to be away where he could think. My mother opposed the notion strongly because, she said, the old wooden bed up there was unsafe: it was wobbly and the heavy headboard would crash down on father's head in case the bed fell, and kill him. There was no dissuading him, however, and at a quarter past ten he closed the attic door behind him and went up the narrow twisting stairs. We later heard ominous creakings as he crawled into bed. Grandfather, who usually slept in the attic bed when he was with us, had disappeared some days before. On these occasions he was usually gone six or eight days and returned growling and out of temper, with the news that the Federal Union[2] was run by a passel of blockheads and that the Army of the Potomac[3] didn't have a chance.

We had visiting us at this time a nervous first cousin of mine named Briggs Beall, who believed that he was likely to cease breathing when he was asleep. It was his feeling that if he were not awakened every hour during the night, he might die of suffocation. He had been accustomed to setting an alarm clock to ring at intervals until morning, but I persuaded him to abandon this. He slept in my room and I told him that I was such a light sleeper that if anybody quit breathing in the same room with me, I would wake instantly. He tested me the first night—which I had suspected he would—by holding his breath after my regular breathing had convinced him I was asleep. I was not asleep, however, and called to him. This

Vocabulary Development: ominous (äm′ ə nəs) *adj.* threatening

1. **verisimilitude** (ver′ ə si mil′ ə to͞od′) *n.* appearance of being true or real.
2. **Federal Union** Northern side during the Civil War. His grandfather is under the illusion that the Civil War has not yet ended.
3. **Army of the Potomac** one of the Northern armies during the Civil War.

seemed to allay his fears a little, but he took the precaution of putting a glass of spirits of camphor[4] on a little table at the head of his bed. In case I didn't arouse him until he was almost gone, he said, he would sniff the camphor, a powerful reviver. Briggs was not the only member of his family who had his crotchets.[5] Old Aunt Melissa Beall (who could whistle like a man, with two fingers in her mouth) suffered under the premonition that she was destined to die on South High Street, because she had been born on South High Street and married on South High Street. Then there was Aunt Sarah Shoaf, who never went to bed at night without the fear that a burglar was going to get in and blow chloroform[6] under her door through a tube. To avert this calamity—for she was in greater dread of anesthetics than of losing her household goods—she always piled her money, silverware, and other valuables in a neat stack just outside her bedroom, with a note reading: "This is all I have. Please take it and do not use your chloroform, as this is all I have." Aunt Gracie Shoaf also had a burglar phobia, but she met it with more fortitude. She was confident that burglars had been getting into her house every night for forty years. The fact that she never missed any thing was to her no proof to the contrary. She always claimed that she scared them off before they could take anything, by throwing shoes down the hallway. When she went to bed she piled, where she could get at them handily, all the shoes there were about her house. Five minutes after she had turned off the light, she would sit up in bed and say "Hark!" Her husband, who had learned to ignore the whole situation as long ago as 1903, would either be sound asleep or pretend to be sound asleep. In either case he would not respond to her tugging and pulling, so that presently she would arise, tiptoe to the door, open it slightly and heave a shoe down the hall in one direction, and its mate down the hall in the other direction. Some nights she threw them all, some nights only a couple of pair.

But I am straying from the remarkable incidents that took place during the night that the bed fell on father. By midnight we were all in bed. The layout of the rooms and the disposition[7] of their occupants is important to an understanding of what later occurred. In the front room upstairs (just under father's attic bedroom) were my mother and my brother Herman, who sometimes sang in his sleep, usually "Marching Through Georgia" or "Onward, Christian

Vocabulary Development: **allay** (a lā́) *v.* put to rest; calm
fortitude (fôrt́ ə to͞od́) *n.* firm courage

4. **spirits of camphor** liquid with a powerful odor.
5. **crotchets** (kräch́ əts) *n.* peculiar or stubborn ideas.
6. **chloroform** (klôŕ ə fôrḿ) *n.* substance used at one time as an anesthetic, or painkiller, during operations because it can cause a person to pass out.
7. **disposition** (diś pə zish́ ən) *n.* arrangement.

◆ Reading Strategy

These descriptions of Thurber's relatives are not part of the action on the evening Thurber's father decides to sleep in the attic. Explain why they are not **significant events.**

◆ Reading Check

Circle the names of each of Thurber's three aunts and underline each one's surprising belief or habit.

Mark the Text

◆ Literary Analysis

A **humorous essay** is a short, true story meant to amuse the reader. How does the description of the relatives that leads up to this point contribute to making this a humorous essay?

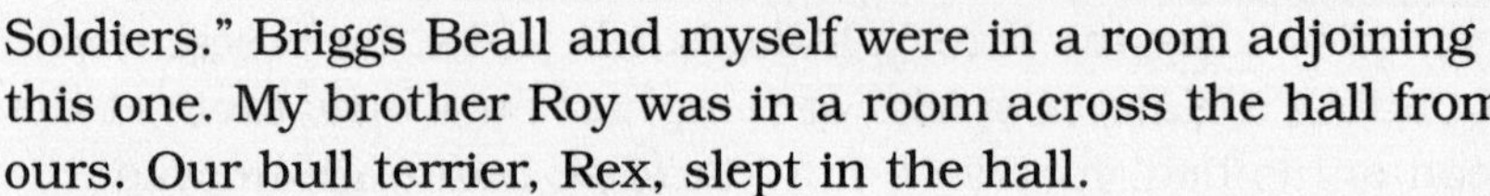

Soldiers." Briggs Beall and myself were in a room adjoining this one. My brother Roy was in a room across the hall from ours. Our bull terrier, Rex, slept in the hall.

My bed was an army cot, one of those affairs which are made wide enough to sleep on comfortably only by putting up, flat with the middle section, the two sides which ordinarily hang down like the sideboards of a drop-leaf table. When these sides are up, it is perilous to roll too far toward the edge, for then the cot is likely to tip completely over, bringing the whole bed down on top of one, with a tremendous banging crash. This, in fact, is precisely what happened about two o'clock in the morning. (It was my mother who, in recalling the scene later, first referred to it as "the night the bed fell on your father.")

Always a deep sleeper, slow to arouse (I had lied to Briggs), I was at first unconscious of what had happened when the iron cot rolled me onto the floor and toppled over on me. It left me still warmly bundled up and unhurt, for the bed rested above me like a canopy. Hence I did not wake up, only reached the edge of consciousness and went back. The racket, however, instantly awakened my mother, in the next room, who came to the immediate conclusion that her worst dread was realized: the big wooden bed upstairs had fallen on father. She therefore screamed, "Let's go to your poor father!" It was this shout, rather than the noise of my cot falling, that awakened Herman, in the same room with her. He thought that mother had become, for no apparent reason, hysterical. "You're all right, Mamma!" he shouted, trying to calm her. They exchanged shout for shout for perhaps ten seconds: "Let's go to your poor father!" and "You're all right!" That woke up Briggs. By this time I was conscious of what was going on, in a vague way, but did not yet realize that I was under my bed instead of on it. Briggs, awakening in the midst of loud shouts of fear and apprehension, came to the quick conclusion that he was suffocating and that we were all trying to "bring him out." With a low moan, he grasped the glass of camphor at the head of his bed and instead of sniffing it poured it over himself. The room reeked of camphor. "Ugf, ahfg," choked Briggs, like a drowning man, for he had almost succeeded in stopping his breath under the deluge of pungent spirits. He leaped out of bed and groped toward the open window, but he came up against one that was closed. With his hand, he beat out the glass, and I could hear it crash and tinkle on the alleyway below. It was at this juncture that I, in trying to get up, had the uncanny sensation of feeling my bed above me! Foggy with sleep, I now suspected, in my turn, that the whole

◆ **Reading Strategy**

How do you know that this crash will be a **significant event** in the story?

◆ **Literary Analysis**

In the bracketed section, what is funny about how Briggs responds to the commotion?

◆ **Reading Check**

What incorrect ideas are behind the chaos in the scene described in this paragraph? Underline three.

Mark the Text

Vocabulary Development: **perilous** (per´ ə ləs) *adj.* dangerous
deluge (del´ yo͞oj´) *n.* great flood or rush of anything
pungent (pun´ jənt) *adj.* sharp-smelling

uproar was being made in a frantic endeavor to extricate me from what must be an unheard-of and perilous situation. "Get me out of this!" I bawled. "Get me out!" I think I had the nightmarish belief that I was entombed in a mine. "Gugh," gasped Briggs, floundering in his camphor.

By this time my mother, still shouting, pursued by Herman, still shouting, was trying to open the door to the attic, in order to go up and get my father's body out of the wreckage. The door was stuck, however, and wouldn't yield. Her frantic pulls on it only added to the general banging and confusion. Roy and the dog were now up, the one shouting questions, the other barking.

Father, farthest away and soundest sleeper of all, had by this time been awakened by the battering on the attic door. He decided that the house was on fire. "I'm coming, I'm coming!" he wailed in a slow, sleepy voice—it took him many minutes to regain full consciousness. My mother, still believing he was caught under the bed, detected in his "I'm coming!" the mournful, resigned note of one who is preparing to meet his Maker. "He's dying!" she shouted.

"I'm all right!" Briggs yelled to reassure her. "I'm all right!" He still believed that it was his own closeness to death that was worrying mother. I found at last the light switch in my room, unlocked the door, and Briggs and I joined the others at the attic door. The dog, who never did like Briggs, jumped for him—assuming that he was the culprit in whatever was going on—and Roy had to throw Rex and hold him. We could hear father crawling out of bed upstairs. Roy pulled the attic door open, with a mighty jerk, and father came down the stairs, sleepy and irritable but safe and sound. My mother began to weep when she saw him. Rex began to howl. "What in the name of heaven is going on here?" asked father.

The situation was finally put together like a gigantic jigsaw puzzle. Father caught a cold from prowling around in his bare feet but there were no other bad results. "I'm glad," said mother, who always looked on the bright side of things, "that your grandfather wasn't here."

Vocabulary Development: **extricate** (eks´ trə kāt´) *v.* set free; disentangle
culprit (kul´ prit) *n.* guilty person

Reader's Response: Which part of the story did you think was the funniest?

____

____

Thinking About the Skill: In what way might identifying significant events also be useful for reading fiction?

____

____

◆ Literary Analysis

Things keep getting more chaotic. Underline some of the sounds in the bracketed passage that contribute to making this **humorous essay** increasingly funny.

Mark the Text

◆ Reading Check

Picture in your mind the action in the hallway at this point. List who is there and what they are doing.

____

____

____

____

____

____

____

◆ Stop to Reflect

How do you think the family members figured out what had happened?

____

____

____

____

____

____

____

____

____

PREVIEW

All Summer in a Day

Ray Bradbury

Summary

On the planet Venus, seven years of rain is about to stop for a short while. The other students in Margot's class have forgotten what the sun is like. They look forward to seeing it. They tease Margot, who came from Earth and remembers what the sun is like. Margot is an outsider who does not join in most of their games. As a cruel joke, they lock her in a closet before going out to play in the only hour of sunshine they will see in seven years. When the rain starts up again, the children sadly return indoors. They realize they made Margot miss the sunshine. Knowing how cruel they have been, they slowly go to the closet to let her out.

Visual Summary

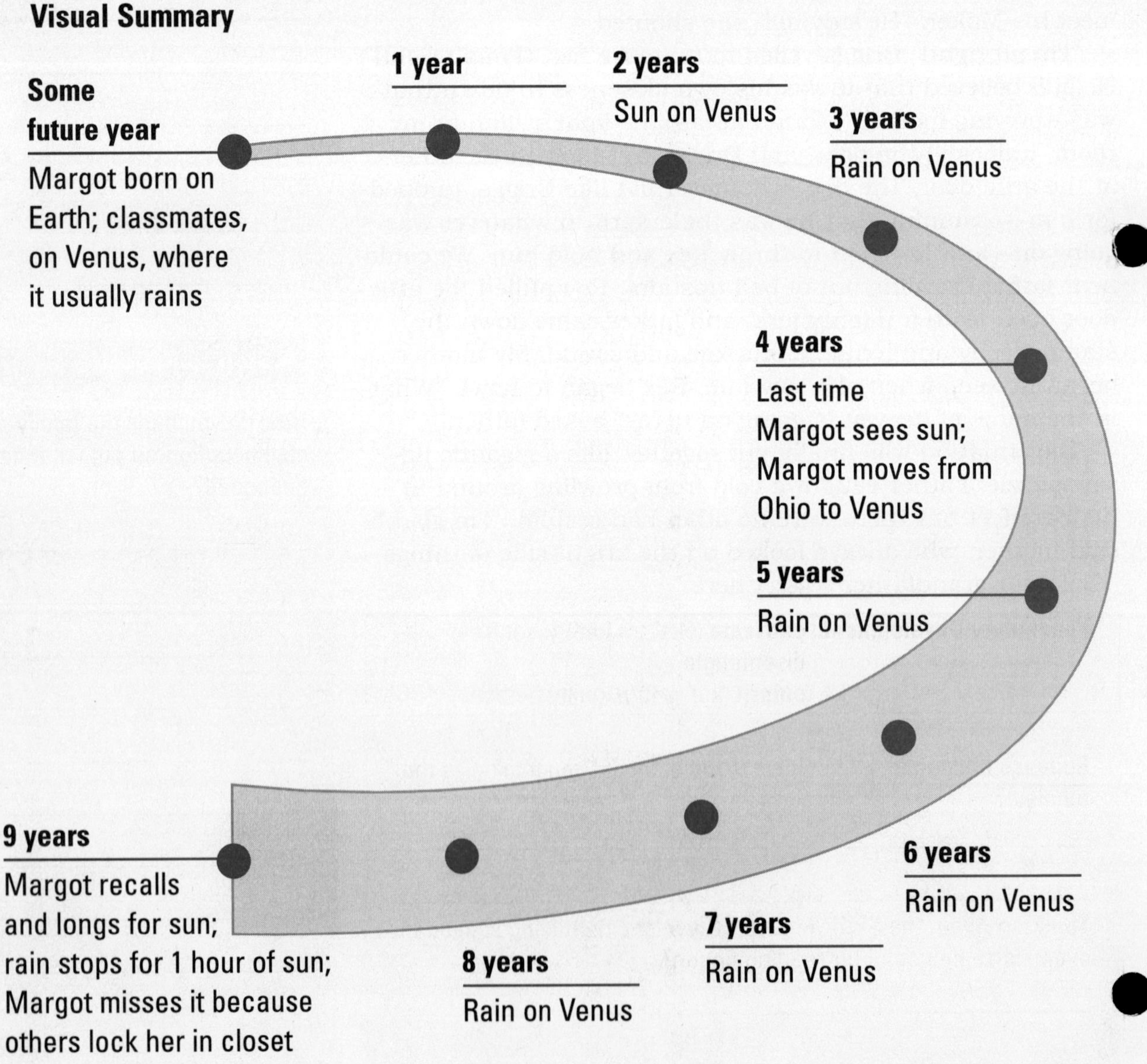

All Summer in a Day
Ray Bradbury

The planet Venus has a very high surface temperature. When this story was written, some scientists believed that the clouds of Venus hid a watery world. That information may have led Bradbury to create a setting of soggy jungles and constant rain.

"Ready?"

"Ready."

"Now?"

"Soon."

"Do the scientists really know? Will it happen today, will it?"

"Look, look; see for yourself!"

The children pressed to each other like so many roses, so many weeds, intermixed, peering out for a look at the hidden sun.

It rained.

It had been raining for seven years; thousands upon thousands of days compounded and filled from one end to the other with rain, with the drum and gush of water, with the sweet crystal fall of showers and the concussion of storms so heavy they were tidal waves come over the islands. A thousand forests had been crushed under the rain and grown up a thousand times to be crushed again. And this was the way life was forever on the planet Venus and this was the schoolroom of the children of the rocket men and women who had come to a raining world to set up civilization and live out their lives.

"It's stopping, it's stopping!"

"Yes, yes!"

Margot stood apart from them, from these children who could never remember a time when there wasn't rain and rain and rain. They were all nine years old, and if there had been a day, seven years ago, when the sun came out for an hour and showed its face to the stunned world, they could not recall. Sometimes, at night, she heard them stir, in remembrance, and she knew they were dreaming and remembering gold or a yellow crayon or a coin large enough to buy the world with. She knew they thought they remembered a warmness, like a blushing in the face, in the body, in the arms and legs and trembling hands. But then they always awoke to the tatting drum, the endless shaking down of clear bead necklaces upon the roof, the walk, the gardens,

Vocabulary Development: concussion (kən kush′ ən) *n.* violent shock or blow

◆ Activate Prior Knowledge

Have you ever been excluded from a group or taken part in excluding someone else? Write about what happened and how it made you feel.

◆ Literary Analysis

The **setting** of a story is the time and place in which the story's action takes place. Circle the name of where the story takes place. Then underline two details about the weather and plant growth.

Mark the Text

◆ Reading Check

What do the children hope will happen today?

the forests, and their dreams were gone.

All day yesterday they had read in class about the sun. About how like a lemon it was, and how hot. And they had written small stories or essays or poems about it:

I think the sun is a flower,
That blooms for just one hour.

That was Margot's poem, read in a quiet voice in the still classroom while the rain was falling outside.

"Aw, you didn't write that!" protested one of the boys.

"I did," said Margot. "I *did.*"

"William!" said the teacher.

But that was yesterday. Now the rain was slackening, and the children were crushed in the great thick windows.

"Where's teacher?"

"She'll be back."

"She'd better hurry, we'll miss it!"

They turned on themselves, like a feverish wheel, all fumbling spokes.

Margot stood alone. She was a very frail girl who looked as if she had been lost in the rain for years and the rain had washed out the blue from her eyes and the red from her mouth and the yellow from her hair. She was an old photograph dusted from an album, whitened away, and if she spoke at all her voice would be a ghost. Now she stood, separate, staring at the rain and the loud wet world beyond the huge glass.

"What're *you* looking at?" said William.

Margot said nothing.

"Speak when you're spoken to." He gave her a shove. But she did not move; rather she let herself be moved only by him and nothing else.

They edged away from her, they would not look at her. She felt them go away. And this was because she would play no games with them in the echoing tunnels of the underground city. If they tagged her and ran, she stood blinking after them and did not follow. When the class sang songs about happiness and life and games her lips barely moved. Only when they sang about the sun and the summer did her lips move as she watched the drenched windows.

And then, of course, the biggest crime of all was that she had come here only five years ago from Earth, and she remembered the sun and the way the sun was and the sky was when she was four in Ohio. And they, they had been on Venus all their lives, and they had been only two years old when last the sun came out and had long since forgotten the

Vocabulary Development: slackening (slak′ ən iŋ) *v.* easing; becoming less active

◆ **Reading Strategy**

Compare and contrast characters to find out how they are alike and how they are different. Answer the following questions based on the underlined section.
1. What does William do and say?
2. How does Margot respond?
3. Are they alike or different?
Answer on the lines below.

1. ______________________________
____
____

2. ______________________________
____
____

3. ______________________________
____
____

◆ **Reading Strategy**

In the bracketed passage, underline two ways in which Margot is different from the other children.

Mark the Text

◆ **Literary Analysis**

A **conflict** is a struggle between the characters in a story. Underline the sentence that explains the main reason for the struggle between Margot and her classmates.

Mark the Text

color and heat of it and the way it really was. But Margot remembered.

"It's like a penny," she said once, eyes closed.

"No, it's not!" the children cried.

"It's like a fire," she said, "in the stove."

"You're lying, you don't remember!" cried the children.

But she remembered and stood quietly apart from all of them and watched the patterning windows. And once, a month ago, she had refused to shower in the school shower rooms, had clutched her hands to her ears and over her head, screaming the water mustn't touch her head. So after that, dimly, dimly, she sensed it, she was different and they knew her difference and kept away.

There was talk that her father and mother were taking her back to Earth next year; it seemed vital to her that they do so, though it would mean the loss of thousands of dollars to her family. And so, the children hated her for all these reasons of big and little consequence. They hated her pale snow face, her waiting silence, her thinness, and her possible future.

"Get away!" The boy gave her another push. "What're you waiting for?"

Then, for the first time, she turned and looked at him. And what she was waiting for was in her eyes.

"Well, don't wait around here!" cried the boy savagely. "You won't see nothing!"

Her lips moved.

"Nothing!" he cried. "It was all a joke, wasn't it?" He turned to the other children. "Nothing's happening today. *Is* it?"

They all blinked at him and then, understanding, laughed and shook their heads. "Nothing, nothing!"

"Oh, but," Margot whispered, her eyes helpless. "But this is the day, the scientists predict, they say, they *know*, the sun . . ."

"All a joke!" said the boy, and seized her roughly. "Hey, everyone, let's put her in a closet before teacher comes!"

"No," said Margot, falling back.

They surged about her, caught her up and bore her, protesting, and then pleading, and then crying, back into a tunnel, a room, a closet, where they slammed and locked the door. They stood looking at the door and saw it tremble from her beating and throwing herself against it. They heard her muffled cries. Then, smiling, they turned and went out

Vocabulary Development: **vital** (vīt´ əl) *adj.* necessary to life; critically important
surged (surjd) *v.* moved in a violent swelling motion

◆ Stop to Reflect

Why doesn't Margot want to take a shower?

◆ Literary Analysis

Explain how the **setting** adds to the **conflict**.

◆ Reading Check

In the underlined sentence, what is Margot waiting for?

◆ Reading Check

Underline the passage that tells what the children did to Margot.

◆ **Stop to Reflect**

How would you feel if you had never seen the sun and it finally came out?

◆ **Reading Check**

Why are the children so excited about the sunshine?

◆ **Literary Analysis**

In the bracketed passage, contrast the **setting** now with the setting described on the first page of the story.

and back down the tunnel, just as the teacher arrived.

"Ready, children?" She glanced at her watch.

"Yes!" said everyone.

"Are we all here?"

"Yes!"

The rain slackened still more.

They crowded to the huge door.

The rain stopped.

It was as if, in the midst of a film concerning an avalanche, a tornado, a hurricane, a volcanic eruption, something had, first, gone wrong with the sound apparatus, thus muffling and finally cutting off all noise, all of the blasts and repercussions and thunders, and then, second, ripped the film from the projector and inserted in its place a peaceful tropical slide which did not move or tremor. The world ground to a standstill. The silence was so immense and unbelievable that you felt your ears had been stuffed or you had lost your hearing altogether. The children put their hands to their ears. They stood apart. The door slid back and the smell of the silent, waiting world came in to them.

The sun came out.

It was the color of flaming bronze and it was very large. And the sky around it was a blazing blue tile color. And the jungle burned with sunlight as the children, released from their spell, rushed out, yelling, into the springtime.

"Now, don't go too far," called the teacher after them. "You've only two hours, you know. You wouldn't want to get caught out!"

But they were running and turning their faces up to the sky and feeling the sun on their cheeks like a warm iron; they were taking off their jackets and letting the sun burn their arms.

"Oh, it's better than the sun lamps, isn't it?"

"Much, much better!"

They stopped running and stood in the great jungle that covered Venus, that grew and never stopped growing, tumultuously, even as you watched it. It was a nest of octopi, clustering up great arms of fleshlike weed, wavering, flowering in this brief spring. It was the color of rubber and ash, this jungle, from the many years without sun. It was the color of stones and white cheeses and ink, and it was the color of the moon.

Vocabulary Development: tumultuously (to͞o mulʹ cho͞o əs lē) *adv.* noisily and violently

The children lay out, laughing, on the jungle mattress, and heard it sigh and squeak under them, resilient and alive. They ran among the trees, they slipped and fell, they pushed each other, they played hide-and-seek and tag, but most of all they squinted at the sun until tears ran down their faces, they put their hands up to that yellowness and that amazing blueness and they breathed of the fresh, fresh air and listened and listened to the silence which suspended them in a blessed sea of no sound and no motion. They looked at everything and savored everything. Then, wildly, like animals escaped from their caves, they ran and ran in shouting circles. They ran for an hour and did not stop running.

And then—

In the midst of their running one of the girls wailed.

Everyone stopped.

The girl, standing in the open, held out her hand.

"Oh, look, look," she said, trembling.

They came slowly to look at her opened palm.

In the center of it, cupped and huge, was a single raindrop.

She began to cry, looking at it.

They glanced quietly at the sky.

"Oh, Oh."

A few cold drops fell on their noses and their cheeks and their mouths. The sun faded behind a stir of mist. A wind blew cool around them. They turned and started to walk back toward the underground house, their hands at their sides, their smiles vanishing away.

A boom of thunder startled them and like leaves before a new hurricane, they tumbled upon each other and ran. Lightning struck ten miles away, five miles away, a mile, a half mile. The sky darkened into midnight in a flash.

They stood in the doorway of the underground for a moment until it was raining hard. Then they closed the door and heard the gigantic sound of the rain falling in tons and avalanches, everywhere and forever.

"Will it be seven more years?"

"Yes. Seven."

Then one of them gave a little cry.

"Margot!"

"What?"

"She's still in the closet where we locked her."

"Margot."

They stood as if someone had driven them, like so many

Vocabulary Development: **resilient** (ri zil′ yənt) *adj.* springing back into shape
savored (sā′ vərd) *v.* enjoyed

◆ Reading Check

Underline three things the children did in the sunlight.

◆ Literary Analysis

How do you think seeing the sun will affect the **conflict** between Margot and her classmates?

____

____

____

____

◆ Reading Check

Circle the sentence that shows the moment one of the students remembers Margot.

◆ **Stop to Reflect**

How do you think Margot is feeling right now?

____

____

____

____

◆ **Reading Strategy**

Contrast Margot's feelings with those of the other children.

____

____

____

____

____

stakes, into the floor. They looked at each other and then looked away. They glanced out at the world that was raining now and raining and raining steadily. They could not meet each other's glances. Their faces were solemn and pale. They looked at their hands and feet, their faces down.

"Margot."

One of the girls said, "Well . . .?"

No one moved.

"Go on," whispered the girl.

They walked slowly down the hall in the sound of cold rain. They turned through the doorway to the room in the sound of the storm and thunder, lightning on their faces, blue and terrible. They walked over to the closet door slowly and stood by it.

Behind the closet door was only silence.

They unlocked the door, even more slowly, and let Margot out.

Reader's Response: What is your reaction to the way the other children treat Margot?

____

____

Thinking About the Skill: In what way did comparing and contrasting characters help you understand the story?

____

____

The Highwayman

Alfred Noyes

Summary

A dashing highwayman, or thief of the road, rides to an inn to see his love, the innkeeper's beautiful daughter Bess. He promises to return by the next night. The stable worker Tim, in love with Bess himself, overhears the couple. The next day soldiers hunting for the highwayman arrive at the inn. They gag and tie up Bess, tying a gun to her body, and tell her to keep watch. She hears her love riding closer. With no other way to warn him, she pulls the trigger of the gun, killing herself. The highwayman hears the shot and flees. The next day, when he learns what happened, he returns and is shot and killed. The ghosts of the highwayman and Bess are said to haunt the inn.

Visual Summary

1	2	3	4	5
The story takes place on a winter night in England of the 1700s.	The highwayman rides to the inn to visit Bess, the innkeeper's daughter. He promises to return by the next night at the latest. Tim, a stable worker in love with Bess, overhears. The next day soldiers hunt down the highwayman. They tie and gag Bess with a gun tied to her body. Bess hears her love approaching.	As the highwayman nears, Bess warns him of danger by pulling the trigger and killing herself.	The highwayman flees when he hears the shot. The next day he learns what happened to Bess and returns, only to be shot and killed.	The ghosts of the highwayman and Bess haunt the inn.

◆ Activate Prior Knowledge

Have you ever chosen to do something difficult to help someone you cared about? Describe the experience.

____

____

____

____

____

____

____

____

◆ Reading Check

Underline three details that describe the highwayman's appearance.

◆ Reading Check

Who is waiting for the highwayman?

____

____

____

The Highwayman

Alfred Noyes

A highwayman is a robber on horseback. The story told in this poem is set in the past, when travel was slow and people stayed at inns to avoid the dangers of traveling at night.

Part One

The wind was a <u>torrent</u> of darkness among the gusty trees.
The moon was a ghostly galleon[1] tossed upon cloudy seas.
The road was a ribbon of moonlight over the purple moor,[2]
And the highwayman came riding—
Riding—riding—
The highwayman came riding, up to the old inn door.

He'd a French cocked-hat on his forehead, a bunch of lace at his chin,
A coat of the claret velvet, and breeches of brown doe-skin.
They fitted with never a wrinkle. His boots were up to the thigh.
And he rode with a jewelled twinkle,
His pistol butts a-twinkle,
His rapier hilt[3] a-twinkle, under the jewelled sky.

Over the cobbles he clattered and clashed in the dark innyard.
He tapped with his whip on the shutters, but all was locked and barred.
He whistled a tune to the window, and who should be waiting there
But the <u>landlord's</u> black-eyed daughter,
Bess, the landlord's daughter,
Plaiting a dark red love knot into her long black hair.

Vocabulary Development: **torrent** (tôr´ ənt) *n.* flood
landlord (land´ lôrd) *n.* person who keeps a rooming house, inn, etc.

1. **galleon** (gal´ ē ən) *n.* large Spanish sailing ship.
2. **moor** (moor) *n.* open, rolling land with swamps.
3. **rapier** (rā´ pē ər) **hilt** large cup-shaped handle of a rapier, which is a type of sword.

And dark in the dark old innyard a stable wicket creaked
Where Tim the ostler[4] listened. His face was white and peaked.
His eyes were hollows of madness, his hair like moldy hay,
But he loved the landlord's daughter,
The landlord's red-lipped daughter.
Dumb as a dog he listened, and he heard the robber say—
"One kiss, my bonny[5] sweetheart, I'm after a prize to-night,
But I shall be back with the yellow gold before the morning light;
Yet, if they press me sharply, and harry[6] me through the day,
Then look for me by moonlight,
Watch for me by moonlight,
I'll come to thee by moonlight, though hell should bar the way."

He rose upright in the stirrups. He scarce could reach her hand,
But she loosened her hair in the casement.[7] His face burnt like a brand[8]
As the black cascade of perfume came tumbling over his breast;
And he kissed its waves in the moonlight,
(O, sweet black waves in the moonlight!)
Then he tugged at his rein in the moonlight, and galloped away to the west.

◆ **Literary Analysis**

Suspense is the nervous uncertainty about the outcome of events. Underline the part of Tim's description that adds to the **suspense.**

Mark the Text

◆ **Reading Strategy**

Story events usually fit together in a **cause-and-effect** relationship. One event (the **cause**) makes another happen (the **effect**). Tim overhears the highwayman's plans. What might happen because of his overhearing?

____
____
____
____
____

◆ **Literary Analysis**

How does the bracketed passage build the **suspense** in the poem?

____
____
____
____
____

Vocabulary Development: cascade (kas kād′) *n.* waterfall or anything tumbling like water

4. **ostler** (äs′lər) *n.* person who takes care of horses at an inn or a stable.
5. **bonny** (bän′ ē) *adj.* Scottish for "pretty."
6. **harry** (har′ ē) *v.* to disturb by constant attacks.
7. **casement** (kās′ mənt) *n.* window frame that opens on hinges.
8. **brand** (brand) *n.* piece of burning wood.

◆ Reading Strategy

What **causes** the troops to set a trap for the highwayman?

◆ Literary Analysis

Circle the word in the underlined passage that helps create **suspense.**

Mark THE Text

◆ Reading Check

Why have the soldiers tied up the woman?

Part Two

He did not come in the dawning. He did not come at noon;
And out of the tawny sunset, before the rise of the moon,
When the road was a gypsy's ribbon, looping the purple moor,
A redcoat troop came marching—
Marching—marching—
King George's men[9] came marching, up to the old inn door.

They said no word to the landlord. They drank his ale instead
But they gagged his daughter, and bound her, to the foot of her narrow bed.
Two of them knelt at her casement, with muskets at their side!
There was death at every window;
And hell at one dark window;
For Bess could see, through her casement, the road that *he* would ride.

They had tied her up to attention, with many a sniggering jest.[10]
They had bound a musket beside her, with the muzzle beneath her breast!
"Now, keep good watch!" and they kissed her. She heard the doomed man say—
Look for me by moonlight;
Watch for me by moonlight;
I'll come to thee by moonlight, though hell should bar the way!

She twisted her hands behind her; but all the knots held good!
She writhed her hands till her fingers were wet with sweat or blood!
They stretched and strained in the darkness, and the hours crawled by like years,

Vocabulary Development: tawny (tô´ nē) *adj.* tan; yellowish brown
bound (bound) *v.* tied

9. **King George's men** soldiers serving King George of England.
10. **sniggering** (snig´ ər iŋ) **jest** sly joke.

Till, now, on the stroke of midnight,
Cold, on the stroke of midnight,
The tip of one finger touched it! The trigger at least was hers!

The tip of one finger touched it. She strove no more for the rest.
Up, she stood up to attention, with the muzzle beneath her breast.
She would not risk their hearing; she would not strive again;
For the road lay bare in the moonlight;
Blank and bare in the moonlight;
And the blood of her veins, in the moonlight, throbbed to her love's refrain.

Tlot-tlot; tlot-tlot! Had they heard it? The horsehoofs ringing clear;
Tlot-tlot, tlot-tlot, in the distance? Were they deaf that they did not hear?
Down the ribbon of moonlight, over the brow of the hill,
The highwayman came riding—
Riding—riding—
The redcoats looked to their priming![11] She stood up, straight and still.

Tlot-tlot, in the frosty silence! *Tlot-tlot,* in the echoing night!
Nearer he came and nearer. Her face was like a light.
Her eyes grew wide for a moment; she drew one last deep breath,
Then her finger moved in the moonlight,
Her musket shattered the moonlight,
Shattered her breast in the moonlight and warned him—with her death.

He turned. He spurred to the west; he did not know who stood
Bowed, with her head o'er the musket, drenched with her own blood!
Not till the dawn he heard it, and his face grew grey to hear
How Bess, the landlord's daughter,
The landlord's black-eyed daughter,

Vocabulary Development: strive (strīv) *v.* struggle

11. **priming** (prī′ miŋ) *n.* explosive used to set off the charge in a gun.

◆ Literary Analysis

What is **suspenseful** about the fact that Bess is able to reach the gun's trigger?

◆ Stop to Reflect

Why do you think Bess struggles to reach the gun's trigger?

◆ Reading Check

Why does Bess shoot herself?

◆ Reading Check

What does the highwayman do when he hears the shot?

◆ **Reading Strategy**

Underline the detail that explains what **causes** the highwayman to return to the inn.

Had watched for her love in the moonlight, and died in
the darkness there.

Back, he spurred like a madman, shouting a curse to
the sky,
With the white road smoking behind him and his rapier
brandished high.
Blood-red were his spurs in the golden noon; wine-red
was his velvet coat;
When they shot him down on the highway,
Down like a dog on the highway,
And he lay in his blood on the highway, with a bunch
of lace at his throat.

. . . .

And still of a winter's night, they say, when the wind
is in the trees,
When the moon is a ghostly galleon tossed upon cloudy
seas,
When the road is a ribbon of moonlight over the purple
moor,
A highwayman comes riding—
Riding—riding—
A highwayman comes riding, up to the old inn door.

Over the cobbles he clatters and clangs in the dark inn
yard.
He taps with his whip on the shutters, but all is locked
and barred.
He whistles a tune to the window, and who should be
waiting there
But the landlord's black-eyed daughter,
Bess, the landlord's daughter,
Plaiting a dark red love knot into her long black hair.

◆ **Reading Check**

What happens to the highwayman when he returns?

____

____

____

◆ **Stop to Reflect**

What is different about the last two stanzas of the poem?

____

____

____

____

____

____

Vocabulary Development: brandished (bran´ dishd) *adj.* waved in a threatening way

Reader's Response: Who do you think was braver—Bess or the highwayman? Why?

____

____

Thinking About the Skill: Describe a cause/effect relationship.

____

____

Amigo Brothers

Piri Thomas

Summary

The "Amigo Brothers" are close friends of seventeen. They grew up in the same building in a poor neighborhood of New York City. They are very different in appearance, but they share a common passion: boxing. For years they have trained together, but now they must fight each other in the very important division finals. They train separately and worry about hurting each other. Yet, in the end, they throw their toughest punches. They realize that their friendship will endure no matter who wins. When the time comes to announce the winner of the match, the two friends have already embraced and left the ring.

Visual Summary

Setting	Place: poor neighborhood of New York City Time: July and August
Main Characters	Antonio Cruz and Felix Vargas, two 17-year-old boys
Background	Grew up in the same building. Are as close as brothers.
Goal	To be champion lightweight boxers
Problem	Must fight each other in important boxing match
Complications	• Don't want to hurt each other • Must do their best • Only one winner possible
Actions/Reactions	• Find it awkward to discuss upcoming fight • Agree to stop training together in last week • Fight with all they have, pulling no punches • Even have trouble stopping at final bell
Resolution	• Leave ring together before winner is announced • Realize friendship is more important than winning

◆ Activate Prior Knowledge

Have you ever watched a boxing match? What kind of training do you think would help prepare a boxer for a big match?

____

____

____

◆ Reading Strategy

An **inference** is a guess based on information that is given. Felix and Antonio both live in a tenement, a rundown, low-rent apartment building. What can you **infer** about them from this detail?

____

____

____

____

____

◆ Literary Analysis

Point of view refers to the angle or position from which a writer tells a story. A story in the **first person point of view** is told from the viewpoint of a person within the story and uses the pronoun *I* to refer to him- or herself. A story in the **third person point of view** is told by a narrator outside the story and uses the pronouns *he* or *she* to refer to the characters. The narrator knows the characters' thoughts. From what **point of view** is this story told?

____

____

Amigo[1] Brothers

Piri Thomas

The two teens in this story both want to represent their boxing club in the annual Golden Gloves tournament, the most famous amateur boxing event in the United States. However, only one of the two can win the qualifying match.

Antonio Cruz and Felix Vargas were both seventeen years old. They were so together in friendship that they felt themselves to be brothers. They had known each other since childhood, growing up on the lower east side of Manhattan in the same tenement building on Fifth Street between Avenue A and Avenue B.

Antonio was fair, lean, and lanky, while Felix was dark, short, and husky. Antonio's hair was always falling over his eyes, while Felix wore his black hair in a natural Afro style.

Each youngster had a dream of someday becoming lightweight champion of the world. Every chance they had the boys worked out, sometimes at the Boys Club on 10th Street and Avenue A and sometimes at the pro's gym on 14th Street. Early morning sunrises would find them running along the East River Drive, wrapped in sweat shirts, short towels around their necks, and handkerchiefs Apache style around their foreheads.

While some youngsters were into street negatives, Antonio and Felix slept, ate, rapped, and dreamt positive. Between them, they had a collection of *Fight* magazines second to none, plus a scrapbook filled with torn tickets to every boxing match they had ever attended, and some clippings of their own. If asked a question about any given fighter, they would immediately zip out from their memory banks divisions, weights, records of fights, knock-outs, technical knock-outs,[2] and draws or losses.

Each had fought many bouts representing their community and had won two gold-plated medals plus a silver and bronze medallion. The difference was in their style. Antonio's lean form and long reach made him the better boxer, while Felix's short and muscular frame made him the better slugger. Whenever they had met in the ring for sparring sessions, it had always been hot and heavy.

Now, after a series of elimination bouts,[3] they had been informed that they were to meet each other in the division finals that were scheduled for the seventh of August, two weeks away—the winner to represent the Boys Club in the Golden Gloves Championship Tournament.

1. **amigo** (ə mē´ gō) *adj.* Spanish for "friend" (usually a noun).
2. **technical knock-outs** occasions when a fight is stopped because one of the fighters is too hurt to continue, even though he is still on his feet.
3. **elimination bouts** matches in which only the winners go on to fight in other matches.

The two boys continued to run together along the East River Drive. But even when joking with each other, they both sensed a wall rising between them.

One morning less than a week before their bout, they met as usual for their daily work-out. They fooled around with a few jabs at the air, slapped skin, and then took off, running lightly along the dirty East River's edge.

Antonio glanced at Felix who kept his eyes purposely straight ahead, pausing from time to time to do some fancy leg work while throwing one-twos followed by upper cuts to an imaginary jaw. Antonio then beat the air with a barrage of body blows and short devastating lefts with an overhand jaw-breaking right.

After a mile or so, Felix puffed and said, "Let's stop a while, bro. I think we both got something to say to each other." Antonio nodded. It was not natural to be acting as though nothing unusual was happening when two ace-boon buddies were going to be blasting each other within a few short days.

They rested their elbows on the railing separating them from the river. Antonio wiped his face with his short towel. The sunrise was now creating day.

Felix leaned heavily on the river's railing and stared across to the shores of Brooklyn. Finally, he broke the silence.

"Man, I don't know how to come out with it."

Antonio helped. "It's about our fight, right?"

"Yeah, right." Felix's eyes squinted at the rising orange sun.

"I've been thinking about it too, *panín.*[4] In fact, since we found out it was going to be me and you, I've been awake at night, pulling punches on you, trying not to hurt you."

"Same here. It ain't natural not to think about the fight. I mean, we both are *cheverote*[5] fighters and we both want to win. But only one of us can win. There ain't no draws in the eliminations."

Felix tapped Antonio gently on the shoulder. "I don't mean to sound like I'm bragging, bro. But I wanna win, fair and square."

Antonio nodded quietly. "Yeah. We both know that in the ring the better man wins. Friend or no friend, brother or no . . ."

Felix finished it for him. "Brother. Tony, let's promise something right here. Okay?"

Vocabulary Development: devastating (dev′ əs tāt′ iŋ) *adj.* destructive; overwhelming

4. **panín** (pä nēn′) *n.* Spanish for "pal."
5. **cheverote** (che bē rō′ te) *adj.* Spanish for "great."

◆ Literary Analysis

After reading the bracketed passage, write two ways you know this story is written from the third person **point of view.**

1. ______________________________

____

2. ______________________________

____

◆ Stop to Reflect

How would you feel if you and your best friend were competing against each other in an important competition?

____

____

____

____

◆ Reading Check

Why is this fight so important to both Felix and Antonio?

____

____

____

____

____

____

◆ Reading Strategy

What can you **infer** about Felix and Antonio's relationship from the bracketed conversation?

◆ Stop to Reflect

Why don't the friends want to see each other before the fight?

◆ Reading Check

Underline the sentence that tells the boys' plan for their relationship after the fight.

Mark the Text

"If it's fair, *hermano*,[6] I'm for it." Antonio admired the courage of a tugboat pulling a barge five times its welterweight size.

"It's fair, Tony. When we get into the ring, it's gotta be like we never met. We gotta be like two heavy strangers that want the same thing and only one can have it. You understand, don'tcha?"

"*Sí*, I know." Tony smiled. "No pulling punches. We go all the way."

"Yeah, that's right. Listen, Tony. Don't you think it's a good idea if we don't see each other until the day of the fight? I'm going to stay with my Aunt Lucy in the Bronx. I can use Gleason's Gym for working out. My manager says he got some sparring partners with more or less your style."

Tony scratched his nose pensively. "Yeah, it would be better for our heads." He held out his hand, palm upward. "Deal?"

"Deal." Felix lightly slapped open skin.

"Ready for some more running?" Tony asked lamely.

"Naw, bro. Let's cut it here. You go on. I kinda like to get things together in my head."

"You ain't worried, are you?" Tony asked.

"No way, man." Felix laughed out loud. "I got too much smarts for that. I just think it's cooler if we split right here. After the fight, we can get it together again like nothing ever happened."

The amigo brothers were not ashamed to hug each other tightly.

"Guess you're right. Watch yourself, Felix. I hear there's some pretty heavy dudes up in the Bronx. *Suavecito*,[7] okay?"

"Okay. You watch yourself too, *sabe*?"[8]

Tony jogged away. Felix watched his friend disappear from view, throwing rights and lefts. Both fighters had a lot of psyching up to do before the big fight.

The days in training passed much too slowly. Although they kept out of each other's way, they were aware of each other's progress via the ghetto grapevine.

The evening before the big fight, Tony made his way to the roof of his tenement. In the quiet early dark, he peered over the ledge. Six stories below the lights of the city blinked and the sounds of cars mingled with the curses and the laughter of children in the street. He tried not to think of Felix, feeling he had succeeded in psyching his mind. But only in the ring would he really know. To spare Felix hurt, he would have to knock him out, early and quick.

Up in the South Bronx, Felix decided to take in a movie

---

6. **hermano** (ar mä´ no) *n.* Spanish for "brother."
7. **suavecito** (swä ve sē´ tō) Spanish for "take it easy."
8. **sabe** (sä bā´) *v.* Spanish for "understand?"

in an effort to keep Antonio's face away from his fists. The flick was *The Champion* with Kirk Douglas, the third time Felix was seeing it.

The champion was getting hit hard. He was saved only by the sound of the bell.

Felix became the champ and Tony the challenger.

The movie audience was going out of its head. The challenger, confident that he had the championship in the bag, threw a left. The champ countered with a dynamite right.

Felix's right arm felt the shock. Antonio's face, superimposed on the screen, was hit by the awesome blow. Felix saw himself in the ring, blasting Antonio against the ropes. The challenger fell to the canvas.

When Felix finally left the theatre, he had figured out how to psyche himself for tomorrow's fight. It was Felix the Champion vs. Antonio the Challenger.

He walked up some dark streets, deserted except for small pockets of wary-looking kids wearing gang colors. Despite the fact that he was Puerto Rican like them, they eyed him as a stranger to their turf. Felix did a fast shuffle, bobbing and weaving, while letting loose a torrent of blows that would demolish whatever got in its way. It seemed to impress the brothers, who went about their own business.

Finding no takers, Felix decided to split to his aunt's. Walking the streets had not relaxed him, neither had the fight flick. All it had done was to stir him up. He let himself quietly into his Aunt Lucy's apartment and went straight to bed, falling into a fitful sleep with sounds of the gong for Round One.

Antonio was passing some heavy time on his rooftop. How would the fight tomorrow affect his relationship with Felix? After all, fighting was like any other profession. Friendship had nothing to do with it. A gnawing doubt crept in. He cut negative thinking real quick by doing some speedy fancy dance steps, bobbing and weaving like mercury.[9] The night air was blurred with perpetual motions of left hooks and right crosses. Felix, his *amigo* brother, was not going to be Felix at all in the ring. Just an opponent with another face. Antonio went to sleep, hearing the opening bell for the first round. Like his friend in the South Bronx, he prayed for victory, via a quick clean knock-out in the first round.

Large posters plastered all over the walls of local shops

Vocabulary Development: **superimposed** (so͞o′ pər im pōzd′) *adj.* put or stacked on top of something else
perpetual (pər pech′ o͞o əl) *adj.* unending

9. **mercury** (mʉr′ kyo͞o rē) *n.* the element mercury, also known as quicksilver because it is so quick and fluid.

◆ Reading Check

Underline the phrase that tells Felix's strategy for the fight. Then, from the previous page, write what Tony's strategy is.

Mark the Text

◆ Reading Strategy

Make an inference about why the neighborhood boys leave Felix alone.

◆ Literary Analysis

In the underlined sentence, the third-person narrator tells something that neither boy knows about the other. What is it? What effect does their not knowing have on the reader?

◆ **Reading Strategy**

Circle details in the text that help you **make an inference** about why the fight between Antonio and Felix had created so much interest.

Mark the Text

◆ **Literary Analysis**

If this story were being told by Antonio, he would not know what Felix was thinking. Circle the detail in the underlined sentence that Antonio would not know.

Mark the Text

◆ **Reading Check**

Why was the bout moved from the Boys Club gymnasium to Tompkins Square Park?

____

____

____

announced the fight between Antonio Cruz and Felix Vargas as the main bout.

The fight had created great interest in the neighborhood. Antonio and Felix were well liked and respected. Each had his own loyal following. Antonio's fans counted on his boxing skills. On the other side, Felix's admirers trusted in his dynamite-packed fists.

Felix had returned to his apartment early in the morning of August 7th and stayed there, hoping to avoid seeing Antonio. He turned the radio on to *salsa* music[10] sounds and then tried to read while waiting for word from his manager.

The fight was scheduled to take place in Tompkins Square Park. It had been decided that the gymnasium of the Boys Club was not large enough to hold all the people who were sure to attend. In Tompkins Square Park, everyone who wanted could view the fight, whether from ringside or window fire escapes or tenement rooftops.

The morning of the fight Tompkins Square was a beehive of activity with numerous workers setting up the ring, the seats, and the guest speakers' stand. The scheduled bouts began shortly after noon and the park had begun filling up even earlier.

The local junior high school across from Tompkins Square Park served as the dressing room for all the fighters. Each was given a separate classroom with desk tops, covered with mats, serving as resting tables. Antonio thought he caught a glimpse of Felix waving to him from a room at the far end of the corridor. He waved back just in case it had been him.

The fighters changed from their street clothes into fighting gear. Antonio wore white trunks, black socks, and black shoes. Felix wore sky blue trunks, red socks, and white boxing shoes. Each had dressing gowns to match their fighting trunks with their names neatly stitched on the back.

The loudspeakers blared into the open windows of the school. There were speeches by dignitaries, community leaders, and great boxers of yesteryear. Some were well prepared, some improvised on the spot. They all carried the same message of great pleasure and honor at being part of such a historic event. This great day was in the tradition of champions emerging from the streets of the lower east side.

Interwoven with the speeches were the sounds of the

10. **salsa** (säl′ sä) **music** *n.* Latin American dance music.

other boxing events. After the sixth bout, Felix was much relieved when his trainer Charlie said, "Time change. Quick knock-out. This is it. We're on."

Waiting time was over. Felix was escorted from the classroom by a dozen fans in white T-shirts with the word FELIX across their fronts.

Antonio was escorted down a different stairwell and guided through a roped-off path.

As the two climbed into the ring, the crowd exploded with a roar. Antonio and Felix both bowed gracefully and then raised their arms in acknowledgment.

Antonio tried to be cool, but even as the roar was in its first birth, he turned slowly to meet Felix's eyes looking directly into his. Felix nodded his head and Antonio responded. And both as one, just as quickly, turned away to face his own corner.

Bong—bong—bong. The roar turned to stillness.

"Ladies and Gentlemen. *Señores y Señoras.*"[11]

The announcer spoke slowly, pleased at his bilingual efforts.

"Now the moment we have all been waiting for—the main event between two fine young Puerto Rican fighters, products of our lower east side. In this corner, weighing 134 pounds, Felix Vargas. And in this corner, weighing 133 pounds, Antonio Cruz. The winner will represent the Boys Club in the tournament of champions, the Golden Gloves. There will be no draw. May the best man win."

The cheering of the crowd shook the window panes of the old buildings surrounding Tompkins Square Park. At the center of the ring, the referee was giving instructions to the youngsters.

"Keep your punches up. No low blows. No punching on the back of the head. Keep your heads up. Understand. Let's have a clean fight. Now shake hands and come out fighting."

Both youngsters touched gloves and nodded. They turned and danced quickly to their corners. Their head towels and dressing gowns were lifted neatly from their shoulders by their trainers' nimble fingers. Antonio crossed himself. Felix did the same.

BONG! BONG! ROUND ONE.

Felix and Antonio turned and faced each other squarely in a fighting pose. Felix wasted no time. He came in fast, head low, half hunched toward his right shoulder, and lashed out with a straight left. He missed a right cross as Antonio slipped the punch and countered with one-two-three lefts that snapped Felix's head back, sending a mild shock

11. **señores y señoras** (se nyoˊ res ē se nyoˊ räs) Spanish for "Gentlemen and Ladies."

◆ Stop to Reflect

Why does Felix feel relieved?

◆ Reading Strategy

Make an inference about how the fighters are feeling. Circle details in the text that helped you make your inference.

Mark the Text

◆ Literary Analysis

In what way does the narrator's **third person point of view** help you learn about the announcer?

◆ Reading Check

Why can't the fight end in a tie?

coursing through him. If Felix had any small doubt about their friendship affecting their fight, it was being neatly dispelled.

Antonio danced, a joy to behold. His left hand was like a piston pumping jabs one right after another with seeming ease. Felix bobbed and weaved and never stopped boring in. He knew that at long range he was at a disadvantage. Antonio had too much reach on him. Only by coming in close could Felix hope to achieve the dreamed-of knockout.

Antonio knew the dynamite that was stored in his *amigo* brother's fist. He ducked a short right and missed a left hook. Felix trapped him against the ropes just long enough to pour some punishing rights and lefts to Antonio's hard midsection. Antonio slipped away from Felix, crashing two lefts to his head, which set Felix's right ear to ringing.

Bong! Both *amigos* froze a punch well on its way, sending up a roar of approval for good sportsmanship.

Felix walked briskly back to his corner. His right ear had not stopped ringing. Antonio gracefully danced his way toward his stool none the worse, except for glowing glove burns, showing angry red against the whiteness of his midribs.

"Watch that right, Tony." His trainer talked into his ear. "Remember Felix always goes to the body. He'll want you to drop your hands for his overhand left or right. Got it?"

Antonio nodded, spraying water out between his teeth. He felt better as his sore midsection was being firmly rubbed.

Felix's corner was also busy.

"You gotta get in there, fella." Felix's trainer poured water over his curly Afro locks. "Get in there or he's gonna chop you up from way back."

Bong! Bong! Round two. Felix was off his stool and rushed Antonio like a bull, sending a hard right to his head. Beads of water exploded from Antonio's long hair.

Antonio, hurt, sent back a blurring barrage of lefts and rights that only meant pain to Felix, who returned with a short left to the head followed by a looping right to the body. Antonio countered with his own flurry, forcing Felix to give ground. But not for long.

Felix bobbed and weaved, bobbed and weaved, occasionally punching his two gloves together.

Antonio waited for the rush that was sure to come. Felix closed in and feinted with his left shoulder and threw his right instead. Lights suddenly exploded inside Felix's head

◆ Reading Strategy

From the bracketed passage, what can you **infer** about the boys as athletes?

____

____

____

◆ Stop to Reflect

Think about the narrative of round one and what Tony's trainer says and draw a conclusion about how well the fight is going for Tony.

____

____

____

____

____

____

◆ Reading Check

What are Antonio and Felix's strengths?

____

____

____

____

Vocabulary Development: dispelled (dis peld′) *v.* driven away; made to disappear

as Antonio slipped the blow and hit him with a pistonlike left catching him flush on the point of his chin.

Bedlam broke loose as Felix's legs momentarily buckled. He fought off a series of rights and lefts and came back with a strong right that taught Antonio respect.

Antonio danced in carefully. He knew Felix had the habit of playing possum when hurt, to sucker an opponent within reach of the powerful bombs he carried in each fist.

A right to the head slowed Antonio's pretty dancing. He answered with his own left at Felix's right eye that began puffing up within three seconds.

Antonio, a bit too eager, moved in too close and Felix had him entangled into a rip-roaring, punching toe-to-toe slugfest that brought the whole Tompkins Square Park screaming to its feet.

Rights to the body. Lefts to the head. Neither fighter was giving an inch. Suddenly a short right caught Antonio squarely on the chin. His long legs turned to jelly and his arms flailed out desperately. Felix, grunting like a bull, threw wild punches from every direction. Antonio, groggy, bobbed and weaved, evading most of the blows. Suddenly his head cleared. His left flashed out hard and straight catching Felix on the bridge of his nose.

Felix lashed back with a haymaker, right off the ghetto streets. At the same instant, his eye caught another left hook from Antonio. Felix swung out trying to clear the pain. Only the frenzied screaming of those along ringside let him know that he had dropped Antonio. Fighting off the growing haze, Antonio struggled to his feet, got up, ducked, and threw a smashing right that dropped Felix flat on his back.

Felix got up as fast as he could in his own corner, groggy but still game. He didn't even hear the count. In a fog, he heard the roaring of the crowd, who seemed to have gone insane. His head cleared to hear the bell sound at the end of the round. He was very glad. His trainer sat him down on the stool.

In his corner, Antonio was doing what all fighters do when they are hurt. They sit and smile at everyone.

The referee signaled the ring doctor to check the fighters out. He did so and then gave his okay. The cold water sponges brought clarity to both *amigo* brothers. They were rubbed until their circulation ran free.

Bong! Round three—the final round. Up to now it had been tic-tac-toe; pretty much even. But everyone knew there

Vocabulary Development: evading (ē vād′ iŋ) *adj.* keeping away from or avoiding

◆ Literary Analysis

After reading the passage, write two examples that show the story's third person **point of view.**

1. ______________________

____

2. ______________________

____

◆ Reading Strategy

What do the fierce fighting efforts of Antonio and Felix lead you to **infer** about their feelings?

____

____

◆ Reading Check

Describe the condition of the fighters at this point in the fight.

____

____

____

____

◆ Reading Strategy

Circle details that help you infer that both boys still want to win the fight.

Mark the Text

◆ Reading Check

Describe what happens after the final bell signaling the end of the fight.

could be no draw and this round would decide the winner.

This time, to Felix's surprise, it was Antonio who came out fast, charging across the ring. Felix braced himself but couldn't ward off the barrage of punches. Antonio drove Felix hard against the ropes.

The crowd ate it up. Thus far the two had fought with *mucho corazón.*[12] Felix tapped his gloves and commenced his attack anew. Antonio, throwing boxer's caution to the winds, jumped in to meet him.

Both pounded away. Neither gave an inch and neither fell to the canvas. Felix's left eye was tightly closed. Claret red blood poured from Antonio's nose. They fought toe-to-toe.

The sounds of their blows were loud in contrast to the silence of a crowd gone completely mute. The referee was stunned by their savagery.

Bong! Bong! Bong! The bell sounded over and over again. Felix and Antonio were past hearing. Their blows continued to pound on each other like hailstones.

Finally the referee and the two trainers pried Felix and Antonio apart. Cold water was poured over them to bring them back to their senses.

They looked around and then rushed toward each other. A cry of alarm surged through Tompkins Square Park. Was this a fight to the death instead of a boxing match?

The fear soon gave way to wave upon wave of cheering as the two *amigos* embraced.

No matter what the decision, they knew they would always be champions to each other.

BONG! BONG! BONG! "Ladies and Gentlemen. *Señores* and *Señoras.* The winner and representative to the Golden Gloves Tournament of Champions is . . ."

The announcer turned to point to the winner and found himself alone. Arm in arm the champions had already left the ring.

---

12. mucho corazón (mo͞o´ chō cô rä sôn´) Spanish for "much courage."

Reader's Response: Were you surprised by the ending? Explain your reaction.

Thinking About the Skill: What information did you learn by making inferences?

PREVIEW

Our Finest Hour

Charles Osgood

Summary

TV reporter Charles Osgood describes a series of mistakes on the night he was the substitute anchor on the *CBS Evening News*. First the lead story he introduced did not appear on the monitor—a different story ran instead. Then the next report didn't appear either. Then there was no commercial when there was supposed to be. Later a peculiar news story that no one had checked in advance showed up on the monitor and had to be cut in the middle. Then the executive producer's angry scream in the studio was picked up by a microphone and broadcast on the air. To top it all off, journalists from China were visiting the studio that night to observe the news.

Visual Summary

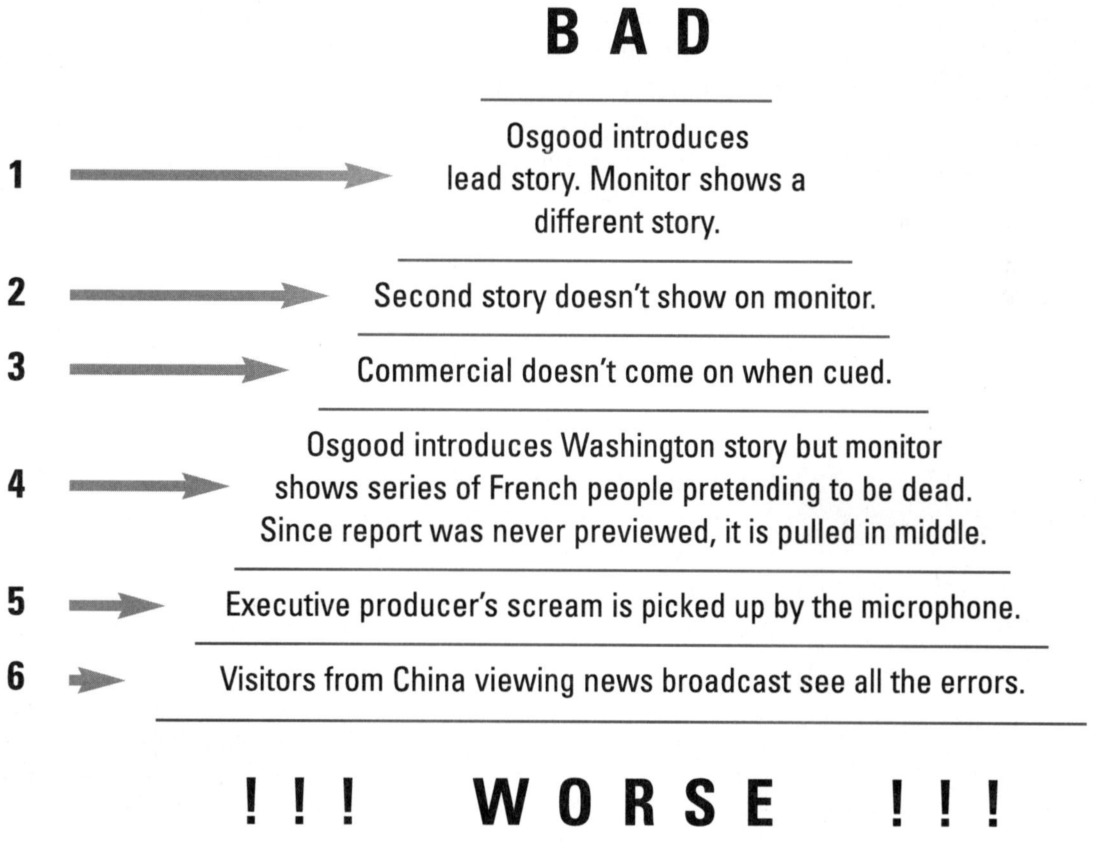

B A D

1 → Osgood introduces lead story. Monitor shows a different story.

2 → Second story doesn't show on monitor.

3 → Commercial doesn't come on when cued.

4 → Osgood introduces Washington story but monitor shows series of French people pretending to be dead. Since report was never previewed, it is pulled in middle.

5 → Executive producer's scream is picked up by the microphone.

6 → Visitors from China viewing news broadcast see all the errors.

! ! ! W O R S E ! ! !

◆ Activate Prior Knowledge

Think of a movie, television show, or story in which humor arises from a series of mistakes. Write down one or two such mistakes that you found funny.

◆ Reading Strategy

Authors usually write to achieve a **purpose**—to persuade, entertain, inform, or reflect on an experience. What is the author's purpose in retelling the humorous events in the bracketed passage?

◆ Reading Check

Why is this an unusual night for the *CBS Evening News*?

Our Finest Hour

Charles Osgood

Although people who report the news look relaxed, they are actually under a lot of pressure. Because the news is broadcast live, any mistake made by the anchor, reporters, or crew will be seen on TV. Anchors (the main announcers) must handle any mistakes—mispronunciations, technical difficulties, incorrect graphics—as they occur.

Only occasionally do most reporters or correspondents get to "anchor" a news broadcast. Anchoring, you understand, means sitting there in the studio and telling some stories into the camera and introducing the reports and pieces that other reporters do. It looks easy enough. It is easy enough, most of the time . . .

It was back when I was relatively new at CBS News. I'd been in the business a while, but only recently had moved over to CBS News. I was old, but I was new. It was a Saturday night and I was filling in for Roger Mudd[1] on the *CBS Evening News*. Roger was on vacation. The regular executive producer[2] of the broadcast, Paul Greenberg, was on vacation, too. And so was the regular cameraman and the regular editor and the regular director. Somewhere along the line we had one too many substitutes that night.

I said "Good evening" and introduced the first report and turned to the monitor to watch it. What I saw was myself looking at the monitor. Many seconds passed. Finally there was something on the screen. A reporter was beginning a story. It was not the story I had introduced. Instead, it was a different story by a different reporter. This was supposed to be the second item in the newscast. So I shuffled my script around and made the first piece second and the second piece first. When I came back on camera, I explained what it was we had seen and reintroduced the first piece. Again there was a long, awkward pause. I shuffled my papers. I scribbled on the script. I turned to the monitor. Finally, the floor director, who was filling in for the regular floor director, cued me to go on. So I introduced the next report. It didn't come up either, so I said we'd continue in just a moment. Obvious cue for a commercial, I thought, but it took a while to register in the control room. When a commercial did come

Vocabulary Development: correspondents (kôr´ ə spän´ dəntz) *n.* persons hired by a news organization to provide news from a distant place

1. **Roger Mudd** *CBS News* reporter from 1961 to 1980. He was a backup anchorperson for Walter Cronkite during the time of this story.
2. **executive producer** person responsible for the quality of the newscast.

up, there was a frantic scramble in the studio to reorganize what was left of the broadcast. But by now everything had come undone.

When the commercial was over, I introduced a piece from Washington. What came up was a series of pictures of people who seemed to be dead. One man was slumped over a car wheel. Two or three people were lying in the middle of the street. Another man was propped up against the wall of the building, his eyes staring vacantly into space. Then came the voice of Peter Kalisher. "This was the town where everyone died," he said. I knew nothing whatsoever about this piece. It was not scheduled for the broadcast. Peter Kalisher was in Paris as far as I knew. But there had been nothing on the news wires about everybody in Paris having died. In the "fishbowl," the glassed-in office where the executive producer sits, there were at least three people yelling into telephones. Nobody in there knew anything about this piece either. The story was about some little town in France that was demonstrating the evils of cigarette smoking. Seems the population of the town was the same number as smoking-related deaths in France in a given year. It was a nice story well told, but since nobody in authority at CBS News, New York, had seen it or knew what was coming next, they decided to dump out of it and come back to me. I, of course, was sitting there looking at the piece with bewilderment written all over my face, when suddenly, in the midst of all these French people pretending to be dead, I saw myself, bewilderment and all.

All in all, it was not the finest broadcast CBS News has ever done. But the worst part came when I introduced the "end piece," a feature story that Hughes Rudd had done about raft racing on the Chatahoochie River.[3] Again, when I finished the introduction, I turned to the monitor and, again, nothing happened. Then, through the glass window of the "fishbowl," I heard a loud and plaintive wail. "What is going on?" screamed the fill-in executive producer. I could hear him perfectly clearly, and so could half of America. The microphone on my tie-clip was open. Standing in the control room watching this, with what I'm sure must have been great interest, was a delegation of visiting journalists from the People's Republic of China.[4] They must have had a really great impression of American electronic journalism.

Vocabulary Development: bewilderment (bē wil′ dər mənt) *n.* state of confusion

3. **Chatahoochie** (cha tə hü′ chē) **River** river running south through Georgia and forming part of the borders of Georgia, Alabama, and Florida.
4. **People's Republic of China** official name of China.

◆ **Reading Strategy**

Humor is writing that aims to make the reader laugh. Underline the visual details that add humor to the bracketed section.

Mark the Text

◆ **Reading Strategy**

Is the underlined statement understated (less than the truth) or exaggerated (greater than the truth)?

____

____

How do you know?

____

____

____

____

____

◆ **Reading Check**

According to the author, what is the worst part of the broadcast?

____

____

____

____

____

____

◆ Stop to Reflect

What do you think is Charles Osgood's message? Do you think he successfully conveys his message to his readers? Explain.

The next Monday morning, sitting back at the radio desk where I belonged, I became aware of a presence standing quietly next to my desk. It was Richard Salant, the wise and gentle man who was then president of CBS News. He'd been waiting until I finished typing a sentence before bending over and inquiring softly: "What *was* going on?"

Reader's Response: What part of the essay did you think was the funniest?

Thinking About the Skill: How can recognizing the author's purpose help you when you read?

PREVIEW

Cat on the Go

James Herriot

Summary

Animal doctor James Herriot and his assistant Tristan save the life of a badly injured stray cat brought to their office. Herriot's wife Helen then cares for the cat in their home and names it Oscar. The cat is unusually friendly. After he recovers, he disappears one evening and shows up at a church meeting. Another night, he sits in on a darts championship. After the third such incident, the Herriots realize that Oscar enjoys large gatherings of people. One day the cat's previous owners, who live some distance away, show up after a long search to claim him. The Herriots sadly give him up. Then they decide to visit him. Oscar is out when they arrive but greets them warmly when he returns—from sitting in on a local yoga class.

Visual Summary

Oscar the Stray	Oscar the Herriot Pet	Oscar Back with His Owners
• Found by Marjorie Simpson, postman's teenaged daughter • Is badly injured and near death • Brought to animal doctor James Herriot and his assistant Tristan • Saved by unusual surgery • Nursed to health by Helen Herriot, who calls him Oscar	• Becomes one of the family • Visited often by Tristan • Vanishes one night and is brought back from a church meeting • Disappears again and is brought back from a darts championship • Goes off again, this time to a Women's Institute meeting • Continues to appear at neighborhood gatherings	• Was pet of a Gibbons family, who finally locate and claim him • Leaves the Herriots, who miss him a lot • Is not home at first when the Herriots pay a visit • Recognizes them and seems happy to see them • Had been sitting in on a local yoga class when they arrived

◆ Activate Prior Knowledge

Have you ever lost a pet or known someone who has? Briefly tell what happened.

____

____

____

____

____

____

____

____

____

____

____

____

Cat on the Go

James Herriot

Veterinarians must complete years of training before they can be licensed. Usually veterinarians specialize in small animals, such as house pets, or large animals, such as horses and cows. Like doctors, they sometimes perform surgery. Today's veterinarians have access to far more sophisticated equipment than Herriot did.

One winter evening Tristan shouted up the stairs from the passage far below.

"Jim! Jim!"

I went out and stuck my head over the bannisters. "What is it, Triss?"

"Sorry to bother you, Jim, but could you come down for a minute?" The upturned face had an anxious look.

I went down the long flights of steps two at a time and when I arrived slightly breathless on the ground floor Tristan beckoned me through to the consulting room at the back of the house. A teenage girl was standing by the table, her hand resting on a stained roll of blanket.

"It's a cat," Tristan said. He pulled back a fold of the blanket and I looked down at a large, deeply striped tabby. At least he would have been large if he had had any flesh on his bones, but ribs and pelvis stood out painfully through the fur and as I passed my hand over the motionless body I could feel only a thin covering of skin.

Tristan cleared his throat. "There's something else, Jim."

I looked at him curiously. For once he didn't seem to have a joke in him. I watched as he gently lifted one of the cat's hind legs and rolled the abdomen into view. There was a gash on the ventral surface[1] through which a coiled cluster of intestines spilled grotesquely onto the cloth. I was still shocked and staring when the girl spoke.

"I saw this cat sittin' in the dark, down Brown's yard. I thought 'e looked skinny, like, and a bit quiet and I bent down to give 'im a pat. Then I saw 'e was badly hurt and I went home for a blanket and brought 'im round to you."

"That was kind of you," I said. "Have you any idea who he belongs to?"

The girl shook her head. "No, he looks like a stray to me."

"He does indeed." I dragged my eyes away from the terrible wound. "You're Marjorie Simpson, aren't you?"

◆ Reading Check

What is wrong with the cat?

____

____

____

____

Vocabulary Development: grotesquely (grō tesk´ lē) *adv.* in a strange or distorted way

1. **ventral** (ven´ trəl) **surface** surface near or on the belly.

"Yes."

"I know your Dad well. He's our postman."

"That's right." She gave a half smile then her lips trembled.

"Well, I reckon I'd better leave 'im with you. You'll be goin' to put him out of his misery. There's nothing anybody can do about . . . about that?"

I shrugged and shook my head. The girl's eyes filled with tears, she stretched out a hand and touched the emaciated animal then turned and walked quickly to the door.

"Thanks again, Marjorie," I called after the retreating back. "And don't worry—we'll look after him."

In the silence that followed, Tristan and I looked down at the shattered animal. Under the surgery lamp it was all too easy to see. He had almost been disemboweled[2] and the pile of intestines was covered in dirt and mud.

"What d'you think did this?" Tristan said at length. "Has he been run over?"

"Maybe," I replied. "Could be anything. An attack by a big dog or somebody could have kicked him or struck him." All things were possible with cats because some people seemed to regard them as fair game for any cruelty.

Tristan nodded. "Anyway, whatever happened, he must have been on the verge of starvation. He's a skeleton. I bet he's wandered miles from home."

"Ah well," I sighed. "There's only one thing to do. Those guts are perforated in several places. It's hopeless."

Tristan didn't say anything but he whistled under his breath and drew the tip of his forefinger again and again across the furry cheek. And, unbelievably, from somewhere in the scraggy chest a gentle purring arose.

The young man looked at me, round eyed. "My God, do you hear that?"

"Yes . . . amazing in that condition. He's a good-natured cat."

Tristan, head bowed, continued his stroking. I knew how he felt because, although he preserved a cheerfully hard-boiled attitude to our patients he couldn't kid me about one thing: he had a soft spot for cats. Even now, when we are both around the sixty mark, he often talks to me about the cat he has had for many years. It is a typical relationship—they tease each other unmercifully—but it is based on real affection.

"It's no good, Triss," I said gently. "It's got to be done." I reached for the syringe but something in me rebelled against

Vocabulary Development: emaciated (ē mā′ shē āt′ id) *adj.* extremely thin; starving

2. **disemboweled** (dis′ im bou′ əld) *v.* lost its intestines.

◆ Literary Analysis

Mark the Text

The qualities that make a person or animal special are called **character traits.** Underline Tristan's actions in the bracketed paragraph. What character traits does he show?

____

____

____

____

____

____

◆ Reading Check

What problem does Herriot face?

____

____

____

____

____

plunging a needle into that mutilated body. Instead I pulled a fold of the blanket over the cat's head.

"Pour a little ether onto the cloth," I said. "He'll just sleep away."

Wordlessly, Tristan unscrewed the cap of the ether bottle and poised it above the head. Then from under the shapeless heap of blanket we heard it again: the deep purring which increased in volume till it boomed in our ears like a distant motorcycle.

Tristan was like a man turned to stone, hand gripping the bottle rigidly, eyes staring down at the mound of cloth from which the purring rose in waves of warm friendly sound.

At last he looked up at me and gulped. "I don't fancy this much, Jim. Can't we do something?"

"You mean, put that lot back?"

"Yes."

"But the bowels are damaged—they're like a sieve in parts."

"We could stitch them, couldn't we?"

I lifted the blanket and looked again. "Honestly, Triss, I wouldn't know where to start. And the whole thing is filthy."

He didn't say anything, but continued to look at me steadily. And I didn't need much persuading. I had no more desire to pour ether onto that comradely purring than he had.

"Come on, then," I said. "We'll have a go."

With the oxygen bubbling and the cat's head in the anesthetic mask we washed the whole prolapse[3] with warm saline.[4] We did it again and again but it was impossible to remove every fragment of caked dirt. Then we started the painfully slow business of stitching the many holes in the tiny intestines, and here I was glad of Tristan's nimble fingers which seemed better able to manipulate the small round-bodied needles than mine.

Two hours and yards of catgut[5] later, we dusted the patched up peritoneal[6] surface with sulfanilamide[7] and pushed the entire mass back into the abdomen. When I had sutured muscle layers and skin everything looked tidy but I had a nasty feeling of sweeping undesirable things under the carpet. The extensive damage, all that contamination—peritonitis[8] was inevitable.

Vocabulary Development: inevitable (in ev′ ə tə bəl) *adj.* certain to happen

◆ **Reading Strategy**

An **idiom** is a word or expression used in a certain language or region. Its meaning is likely to differ from the meanings of the individual words. What is meant by the expression "that lot" in the underlined sentence?

____

____

____

◆ **Literary Analysis**

Both men believe the cat's injuries are incurable, yet they are reluctant to put the animal out of its misery. What **character trait** does this reveal?

____

____

◆ **Reading Check**

What do Tristan and Jim do to the cat?

____

____

____

____

3. **prolapse** (prō′ laps) *n.* internal organ—here, the intestines—that has fallen out of place.
4. **saline** (sā′ lēn) *n.* salt solution.
5. **catgut** (kat′ gut′) *n.* tough string or thread used in surgery.
6. **peritoneal** (per′ i tō nē′ əl) *adj.* having to do with the membrane that lines the abdomen.
7. **sulfanilamide** (sul′ fə nil′ ə mīd) *n.* sulfa drugs used to treat infections before penicillin and other antibiotics were discovered.
8. **peritonitis** (per′ i tō nīt′ is) *n.* inflammation of the abdominal lining.

"He's alive, anyway, Triss," I said as we began to wash the instruments. "We'll put him onto sulfapyridine and keep our fingers crossed." There were still no antibiotics at that time but the new drug was a big advance.

The door opened and Helen came in. "You've been a long time, Jim." She walked over to the table and looked down at the sleeping cat. "What a poor skinny little thing. He's all bones."

"You should have seen him when he came in." Tristan switched off the sterilizer and screwed shut the valve on the anesthetic machine. "He looks a lot better now."

She stroked the little animal for a moment. "Is he badly injured?"

"I'm afraid so, Helen," I said. "We've done our best for him but I honestly don't think he has much chance."

"What a shame. And he's pretty, too. Four white feet and all those unusual colors." With her finger she traced the faint bands of auburn and copper-gold among the gray and black.

Tristan laughed. "Yes, I think that chap has a ginger Tom somewhere in his ancestry."

Helen smiled, too, but absently, and I noticed a broody look about her. She hurried out to the stock room and returned with an empty box.

"Yes . . . yes . . ." she said thoughtfully. "I can make a bed in this box for him and he'll sleep in our room, Jim."

"He will?"

"Yes, he must be warm, mustn't he?"

"Of course."

Later, in the darkness of our bed-sitter,[9] I looked from my pillow at a cozy scene. Sam in his basket on one side of the flickering fire and the cat cushioned and blanketed in his box on the other.

As I floated off into sleep it was good to know that my patient was so comfortable, but I wondered if he would be alive in the morning. . . .

I knew he was alive at 7:30 a.m. because my wife was already up and talking to him. I trailed across the room in my pajamas and the cat and I looked at each other. I rubbed him under the chin and he opened his mouth in a rusty miaow. But he didn't try to move.

"Helen," I said. "This little thing is tied together inside with catgut. He'll have to live on fluids for a week and even then he probably won't make it. If he stays up here you'll be spooning milk into him umpteen times a day."

"Okay, okay." She had that broody look again.

It wasn't only milk she spooned into him over the next few days. Beef essence, strained broth and a succession of

9. **bed-sitter** (bed′sit′ter) *n.* British term for a one-room apartment.

◆ Literary Analysis

Mark the Text

Underline Helen's words and actions in the bracketed section. What do they tell you about her **character traits**?

____

____

____

◆ Literary Analysis

The word *broody* can mean "ready to hover over and protect offspring" or "inclined to dwell moodily on one's thoughts." How might each of those meanings apply to Helen's **character traits**?

____

____

____

____

____

____

____

◆ Reading Check

How does Jim know the cat is still alive in the morning?

____

____

____

◆ Stop to Reflect

Jim knows they are keeping the cat when Helen tells him its name. How does he know that?

◆ Reading Strategy

Underline the section that tells why Jim doesn't worry about Oscar eating solid food.

Mark THE Text

◆ Literary Analysis

In the underlined sentences, what **traits** are revealed by Tristan and Oscar?

sophisticated baby foods found their way down his throat at regular intervals. One lunch time I found Helen kneeling by the box.

"We shall call him Oscar," she said.

"You mean we're keeping him?"

"Yes."

I am fond of cats but we already had a dog in our cramped quarters and I could see difficulties. Still I decided to let it go.

"Why Oscar?"

"I don't know." Helen tipped a few drops of chop gravy onto the little red tongue and watched intently as he swallowed.

One of the things I like about women is their mystery, the unfathomable part of them, and I didn't press the matter further. But I was pleased at the way things were going. I had been giving the sulfapyridine every six hours and taking the temperature night and morning, expecting all the time to encounter the roaring fever, the vomiting and the tense abdomen of peritonitis. But it never happened.

It was as though Oscar's animal instinct told him he had to move as little as possible because he lay absolutely still day after day and looked up at us—and purred.

His purr became part of our lives and when he eventually left his bed, sauntered through to our kitchen and began to sample Sam's dinner of meat and biscuit it was a moment of triumph. And I didn't spoil it by wondering if he was ready for solid food; I felt he knew.

From then on it was sheer joy to watch the furry scarecrow fill out and grow strong, and as he ate and ate and the flesh spread over his bones the true beauty of his coat showed in the glossy medley of auburn, black and gold. We had a handsome cat on our hands.

Once Oscar had fully recovered, Tristan was a regular visitor.

He probably felt, and rightly, that he, more than I, had saved Oscar's life in the first place and he used to play with him for long periods. His favorite ploy was to push his leg round the corner of the table and withdraw it repeatedly just as the cat pawed at it.

Oscar was justifiably irritated by this teasing but showed his character by lying in wait for Tristan one night and biting him smartly[10] in the ankle before he could start his tricks.

Vocabulary Development: sauntered (sôn´ tərd) *v.* strolled

10. **smartly** (smart´ lē) *adv.* sharply.

From my own point of view Oscar added many things to our menage.[11] Sam was delighted with him and the two soon became firm friends. Helen adored him and each evening I thought afresh that a nice cat washing his face by the hearth gave extra comfort to a room.

Oscar had been established as one of the family for several weeks when I came in from a late call to find Helen waiting for me with a stricken face.

"What's happened?" I asked.

"It's Oscar—he's gone!"

"Gone? What do you mean?"

"Oh, Jim, I think he's run away."

I stared at her. "He wouldn't do that. He often goes down to the garden at night. Are you sure he isn't there?"

"Absolutely. I've searched right into the yard. I've even had a walk round the town. And remember." Her chin quivered. "He . . . he ran away from somewhere before."

I looked at my watch. "Ten o'clock. Yes, that is strange. He shouldn't be out at this time."

As I spoke the front door bell jangled. I galloped down the stairs and as I rounded the corner in the passage I could see Mrs. Heslington, the vicar's[12] wife, through the glass. I threw open the door. She was holding Oscar in her arms.

"I believe this is your cat, Mr. Herriot," she said.

"It is indeed, Mrs. Heslington. Where did you find him?"

She smiled. "Well it was rather odd. We were having a meeting of the Mothers' Union at the church house and we noticed the cat sitting there in the room."

"Just sitting . . .?"

"Yes, as though he were listening to what we were saying and enjoying it all. It was unusual. When the meeting ended I thought I'd better bring him along to you."

"I'm most grateful, Mrs. Heslington." I snatched Oscar and tucked him under my arm. "My wife is distraught—she thought he was lost."

It was a little mystery. Why should he suddenly take off like that? But since he showed no change in his manner over the ensuing week we put it out of our minds.

Then one evening a man brought in a dog for a distemper[13] inoculation and left the front door open. When I went up to our flat I found that Oscar had disappeared again. This time Helen and I scoured the marketplace and side alleys in vain and when we returned at half past nine we

Vocabulary Development: distraught (dis trôt′) *adj.* extremely upset

11. **menage** (mā näzh′) *n.* household.
12. **vicar** (vik′ ər) *n.* parish priest.
13. **distemper** (dis tem′ pər) *adj.* infectious viral disease of young dogs.

◆ Literary Analysis

To look *stricken* is to look deeply distressed. What **character traits** are revealed in the bracketed passage by Helen's stricken face and quivering chin?

____

____

____

____

____

◆ Reading Check

Mark the Text

Underline the sentence that tells where Oscar went.

◆ Stop to Reflect

Why do you think Oscar ran away?

____

____

____

____

____

◆ Literary Analysis

Underline clues in the bracketed passage that tell you about Jack Newbould's **character traits.**

Mark the Text

◆ Literary Analysis

Remember that Oscar is also a character in this story. As you read, make notes on what you can tell about Oscar's **character traits** from his actions.

____

____

____

____

____

____

____

____

◆ Reading Check

What does Oscar do every few nights?

____

____

____

were both despondent. It was nearly eleven and we were thinking of bed when the doorbell rang.

It was Oscar again, this time resting on the ample stomach of Jack Newbould. Jack was a gardener at one of the big houses. He hiccuped gently and gave me a huge benevolent smile. "Brought your cat, Mr. Herriot."

"Gosh, thanks, Jack!" I said, scooping up Oscar gratefully. "Where the devil did you find him?"

"Well, s'matter o' fact 'e sort of found me."

"What do you mean?"

Jack closed his eyes for a few moments before articulating carefully. "Thish is a big night, tha knows, Mr. Herriot. Darts championship. Lots of t'lads round at t'Dog and Gun—lotsh and lotsh of 'em. Big gatherin'."

"And our cat was there?"

"Aye, he were there, all right. Sitting among t'lads. Shpent t'whole evenin' with us."

"Just sat there, eh?"

"That 'e did." Jack giggled reminiscently. "By gaw 'e enjoyed 'isself. Ah gave 'em a drop out of me own glass and once or twice ah thought 'e was goin' to have a go at chuckin' a dart. He's some cat." He laughed again.

As I bore Oscar upstairs I was deep in thought. What was going on here? These sudden desertions were upsetting Helen and I felt they could get on my nerves in time.

I didn't have long to wait till the next one. Three nights later he was missing again. This time Helen and I didn't bother to search—we just waited.

He was back earlier than usual. I heard the door bell at nine o'clock. It was the elderly Miss Simpson peering through the glass. And she wasn't holding Oscar—he was prowling on the mat waiting to come in.

Miss Simpson watched with interest as the cat stalked inside and made for the stairs. "Ah, good, I'm so glad he's come home safely. I knew he was your cat and I've been intrigued by his behavior all evening."

"Where . . . may I ask?"

"Oh, at the Women's Institute. He came in shortly after we started and stayed there till the end."

"Really? What exactly was your program, Miss Simpson?"

"Well, there was a bit of committee stuff, then a short talk with lantern slides by Mr. Walters from the water company and we finished with a cake-making competition."

"Yes . . . yes . . . and what did Oscar do?"

She laughed. "Mixed with the company, apparently enjoyed the slides and showed great interest in the cakes."

Vocabulary Development: despondent (di spän′ dənt) *adj.* lacking hope; depressed
intrigued (in trēgd′) *v.* fascinated

"I see. And you didn't bring him home?"

"No, he made his own way here. As you know, I have to pass your house and I merely rang your bell to make sure you knew he had arrived."

"I'm obliged to you, Miss Simpson. We were a little worried."

I mounted the stairs in record time. Helen was sitting with the cat on her knee and she looked up as I burst in.

"I know about Oscar now," I said.

"Know what?"

"Why he goes on these nightly outings. He's not running away—he's visiting."

"Visiting?"

"Yes," I said. "Don't you see? He likes getting around, he loves people, especially in groups, and he's interested in what they do. He's a natural mixer."

Helen looked down at the attractive mound of fur curled on her lap. "Of course . . . that's it . . . he's a socialite!"

"Exactly, a high stepper!"

"A cat-about-town!"

It all afforded us some innocent laughter and Oscar sat up and looked at us with evident pleasure, adding his own throbbing purr to the merriment. But for Helen and me there was a lot of relief behind it; ever since our cat had started his excursions there had been the gnawing fear that we would lose him, and now we felt secure.

From that night our delight in him increased. There was endless joy in watching this facet of his character unfolding. He did the social round meticulously, taking in most of the activities of the town. He became a familiar figure at whist drives,[14] jumble sales,[15] school concerts and scout bazaars. Most of the time he was made welcome, but was twice ejected from meetings of the Rural District Council who did not seem to relish the idea of a cat sitting in on their deliberations.

At first I was apprehensive about his making his way through the streets but I watched him once or twice and saw that he looked both ways before tripping daintily across. Clearly he had excellent traffic sense and this made me feel that his original injury had not been caused by a car.

Taking it all in all, Helen and I felt that it was a kind stroke of fortune which had brought Oscar to us. He was a warm and cherished part of our home life. He added to our happiness.

When the blow fell it was totally unexpected.

I was finishing the evening surgery.[16] I looked round the door and saw only a man and two little boys.

---

14. **whist** (hwist) **drives** attempts to raise money for charities and other purposes by playing the card game whist.
15. **jumble sales** British term for sales of contributed articles to raise money for charity.
16. **surgery** (sur´ jər ē) *n.* British term for "office hours."

◆ Stop to Reflect

Do you think Oscar is trying to run away? Explain your answer.

____

____

____

____

____

◆ Reading Strategy

Mark the Text

Circle the expressions describing Oscar's socializing habits. What expressions would you use to describe Oscar? List two.

1. ______________________________

____

2. ______________________________

____

◆ Reading Check

How do Jim and Helen now feel about Oscar's evening trips?

____

____

____

____

____

____

____

◆ **Stop to Reflect**

The narrator says, "When the blow fell, it was totally unexpected." What blow do you think is going to fall?

◆ **Literary Analysis**

Circle six words in the bracketed passage that show that this character has an unusual way of speaking. What word does he use in place of *I*?

Mark THE Text

◆ **Reading Check**

When they see Oscar, they call him Tiger. Why?

"Next, please," I said.

The man stood up. He had no animal with him. He was middle-aged, with the rough weathered face of a farm worker. He twirled a cloth cap nervously in his hands.

"Mr. Herriot?" he said.

"Yes, what can I do for you?"

He swallowed and looked me straight in the eyes. "Ah think you've got ma cat."

"What?"

"Ah lost ma cat a bit since." He cleared his throat. "We used to live at Missdon but ah got a job as plowman to Mr. Horne of Wederly. It was after we moved to Wederly that t'cat went missin'. Ah reckon he was tryin' to find 'is way back to his old home."

"Wederly? That's on the other side of Brawton—over thirty miles away."

"Aye, ah knaw, but cats is funny things."

"But what makes you think I've got him?"

He twisted the cap around a bit more. "There's a cousin o' mine lives in Darrowby and ah heard tell from 'im about this cat that goes around to meetin's. I 'ad to come. We've been huntin' everywhere."

"Tell me," I said. "This cat you lost. What did he look like?"

"Gray and black and sort o' gingery. Right bonny[17] 'e was. And 'e was allus goin' out to gatherin's."

A cold hand clutched at my heart. "You'd better come upstairs. Bring the boys with you."

Helen was putting some coal on the fire of the bed-sitter.

"Helen," I said. "This is Mr.—er—I'm sorry, I don't know your name."

"Gibbons, Sep Gibbons. They called me Septimus because ah was the seventh in family and it looks like ah'm goin' t'same way 'cause we've got six already. These are our two youngest." The two boys, obvious twins of about eight, looked up at us solemnly.

I wished my heart would stop hammering. "Mr. Gibbons thinks Oscar is his. He lost his cat some time ago."

My wife put down her little shovel. "Oh . . . oh . . . I see." She stood very still for a moment then smiled faintly. "Do sit down. Oscar's in the kitchen, I'll bring him through."

She went out and reappeared with the cat in her arms. She hadn't got through the door before the little boys gave tongue.

"Tiger!" they cried. "Oh, Tiger, Tiger!"

17. **bonny** (bän′ ē) *adj.* pretty.

The man's face seemed lit from within. He walked quickly across the floor and ran his big work-roughened hand along the fur.

"Hullo, awd lad," he said, and turned to me with a radiant smile. "It's 'im, Mr. Herriot. It's 'im awright, and don't 'e look well!"

"You call him Tiger, eh?" I said.

"Aye," he replied happily. "It's them gingery stripes. The kids called 'im that. They were brokenhearted when we lost 'im."

As the two little boys rolled on the floor our Oscar rolled with them, pawing playfully, purring with delight.

Sep Gibbons sat down again. "That's the way 'e allus went on wi' the family. They used to play with 'im for hours. By gaw we did miss 'im. He were a right favorite."

I looked at the broken nails on the edge of the cap, at the decent, honest, uncomplicated Yorkshire[18] face so like the many I had grown to like and respect. Farm men like him got thirty shillings a week in those days and it was reflected in the threadbare jacket, the cracked, shiny boots and the obvious hand-me-downs of the boys.

But all three were scrubbed and tidy, the man's face like a red beacon, the children's knees gleaming and their hair carefully slicked across their foreheads. They looked like nice people to me. I didn't know what to say.

Helen said it for me. "Well, Mr. Gibbons." Her tone had an unnatural brightness. "You'd better take him."

The man hesitated. "Now then, are ye sure, Missis Herriot?"

"Yes . . . yes, I'm sure. He was your cat first."

"Aye, but some folks 'ud say finders keepers or summat like that. Ah didn't come 'ere to demand 'im back or owt of t'sort."

"I know you didn't, Mr. Gibbons, but you've had him all those years and you've searched for him so hard. We couldn't possibly keep him from you."

He nodded quickly. "Well, that's right good of ye." He paused for a moment, his face serious, then he stooped and picked Oscar up. "We'll have to be off if we're goin' to catch the eight o'clock bus."

Helen reached forward, cupped the cat's head in her hands and looked at him steadily for a few seconds. Then she patted the boys' heads. "You'll take good care of him, won't you?"

"Aye, missis, thank ye, we will that." The two small faces looked up at her and smiled.

18. **Yorkshire** region of northern England.

◆ Literary Analysis

What kind of person do you think Sep Gibbons is, based on the details of his appearance, speech, and actions? Underline three clues in the text that reveal his **character traits.** Then write a sentence about him.

Mark the Text

____

____

____

____

____

____

◆ Stop to Reflect

Do you think it was difficult for Helen to decide to give Oscar back? Explain.

____

____

____

____

◆ Reading Check

What happens to Oscar?

____

____

____

"I'll see you down the stairs, Mr. Gibbons," I said.

On the descent I tickled the furry cheek resting on the man's shoulder and heard for the last time the rich purring. On the front door step we shook hands and they set off down the street. As they rounded the corner of Trengate they stopped and waved, and I waved back at the man, the two children and the cat's head looking back at me over the shoulder.

It was my habit at that time in my life to mount the stairs two or three at a time but on this occasion I trailed upwards like an old man, slightly breathless, throat tight, eyes prickling.

I cursed myself for a sentimental fool but as I reached our door I found a flash of consolation. Helen had taken it remarkably well. She had nursed that cat and grown deeply attached to him, and I'd have thought an unforeseen calamity like this would have upset her terribly. But no, she had behaved calmly and rationally.

It was up to me to do as well. I adjusted my features into the semblance of a cheerful smile and marched into the room.

Helen had pulled a chair close to the table and was slumped face down against the wood. One arm cradled her head while the other was stretched in front of her as her body shook with an utterly abandoned weeping.

I had never seen her like this and I was appalled. I tried to say something comforting but nothing stemmed the flow of racking sobs.

Feeling helpless and inadequate I could only sit close to her and stroke the back of her head. Maybe I could have said something if I hadn't felt just about as bad myself.

You get over these things in time. After all, we told ourselves, it wasn't as though Oscar had died or got lost again—he had gone to a good family who would look after him. In fact he had really gone home.

And of course, we still had our much-loved Sam, although he didn't help in the early stages by sniffing disconsolately where Oscar's bed used to lie then collapsing on the rug with a long lugubrious sigh.

There was one other thing, too. I had a little notion forming in my mind, an idea which I would spring on Helen when the time was right. It was about a month after that shattering night and we were coming out of the cinema at Brawton at the end of our half day. I looked at my watch.

"Only eight o'clock," I said. "How about going to see Oscar?"

Helen looked at me in surprise. "You mean—drive on to Wederly?"

"Yes, it's only about five miles."

A smile crept slowly across her face. "That would be lovely. But do you think they would mind?"

◆ Literary Analysis

What does Herriot's walking up the stairs "like an old man" tell the reader about his **character**?

____

____

____

____

◆ Literary Analysis

Compare Helen's actions in the bracketed section to how she behaved when the Gibbonses were present. What **character traits** do these different actions show?

____

____

____

____

____

____

◆ Reading Check

How did Sam feel about Oscar's leaving?

____

____

____

____

"The Gibbons? No, I'm sure they wouldn't. Let's go."

Wederly was a big village and the plowman's cottage was at the far end a few yards beyond the Methodist chapel. I pushed open the garden gate and we walked down the path.

A busy-looking little woman answered my knock. She was drying her hands on a striped towel.

"Mrs. Gibbons?" I said.

"Aye, that's me."

"I'm James Herriot—and this is my wife."

Her eyes widened uncomprehendingly. Clearly the name meant nothing to her.

"We had your cat for a while," I added.

Suddenly she grinned and waved her towel at us. "Oh aye, ah remember now. Sep told me about you. Come in, come in!"

The big kitchen-living room was a tableau[19] of life with six children and thirty shillings a week. Battered furniture, rows of much-mended washing on a pulley, black cooking range and a general air of chaos.

Sep got up from his place by the fire, put down his newspaper, took off a pair of steel-rimmed spectacles and shook hands.

He waved Helen to a sagging armchair. "Well, it's right nice to see you. Ah've often spoke of ye to t'missis."

His wife hung up her towel. "Yes, and I'm glad to meet ye both. I'll get some tea in a minnit."

She laughed and dragged a bucket of muddy water into a corner. "I've been washin' football jerseys. Them lads just handed them to me tonight—as if I haven't enough to do."

As she ran the water into the kettle I peeped surreptitiously around me and I noticed Helen doing the same. But we searched in vain. There was no sign of a cat. Surely he couldn't have run away again? With a growing feeling of dismay I realized that my little scheme could backfire devastatingly.

It wasn't until the tea had been made and poured that I dared to raise the subject.

"How—" I asked diffidently. "How is—er—Tiger?"

"Oh, he's grand," the little woman replied briskly. She glanced up at the clock on the mantelpiece. "He should be back any time now, then you'll be able to see 'im."

As she spoke, Sep raised a finger. "Ah think ah can hear 'im now."

Vocabulary Development: surreptitiously (sʉr´ əp tish´ əs lē) *adv.* secretly

19. **tableau** (tab´ lō) *n.* dramatic scene or picture.

◆ Reading Check

What are Jim and Helen going to do?

____

____

____

◆ Literary Analysis

Mark the Text

As you read this description of the Gibbons's home, what **character traits** of the family do you see? Underline clues in the text.

◆ Literary Analysis

Describe two **character traits** of Mrs. Gibbons.

____

____

____

____

◆ Reading Check

Why isn't Oscar at home when the Herriots arrive for their visit?

____

____

____

____

◆ **Literary Analysis**

Circle two **traits** of Oscar's mentioned in the under-lined sentence.

◆ **Literary Analysis**

Find the two words in the bracketed section that show Mrs. Gibbons is from Yorkshire. Write them and the words they stand for.

____

____

____

____

He walked over and opened the door and our Oscar strode in with all his old grace and majesty. He took one look at Helen and leaped onto her lap. With a cry of delight she put down her cup and stroked the beautiful fur as the cat arched himself against her hand and the familiar purr echoed round the room.

"He knows me," she murmured. "He knows me."

Sep nodded and smiled. "He does that. You were good to 'im. He'll never forget ye, and we won't either, will we mother?"

"No, we won't, Mrs. Herriot," his wife said as she applied butter to a slice of gingerbread. "That was a kind thing ye did for us and I 'ope you'll come and see us all whenever you're near."

"Well, thank you," I said. "We'd love to—we're often in Brawton."

I went over and tickled Oscar's chin, then I turned again to Mrs. Gibbons. "By the way, it's after nine o'clock. Where has he been till now?"

She poised her butter knife and looked into space.

"Let's see, now," she said. "It's Thursday, isn't it? Ah yes, it's 'is night for the Yoga class."

Reader's Response: Would you like to have a cat like Oscar? Explain.

____

____

Thinking About the Skill: What is the definition of an idiom?

____

____

The Luckiest Time of All

Lucille Clifton

Summary

Elzie tells her great-granddaughter Tee the story of how she and her friend Ovella ran off to see the Silas Greene show, a kind of traveling circus, when they were young. On the show grounds, a cute dancing dog amused the crowd. Seeing people toss coins at the dog, Elzie threw her "lucky stone." But the stone hit the dog on the nose, and he began chasing Elzie. She was then rescued by a boy named Amos Pickens. Meeting Amos changed her life, since he would later become her husband. So the stone proved very lucky indeed!

Visual Summary

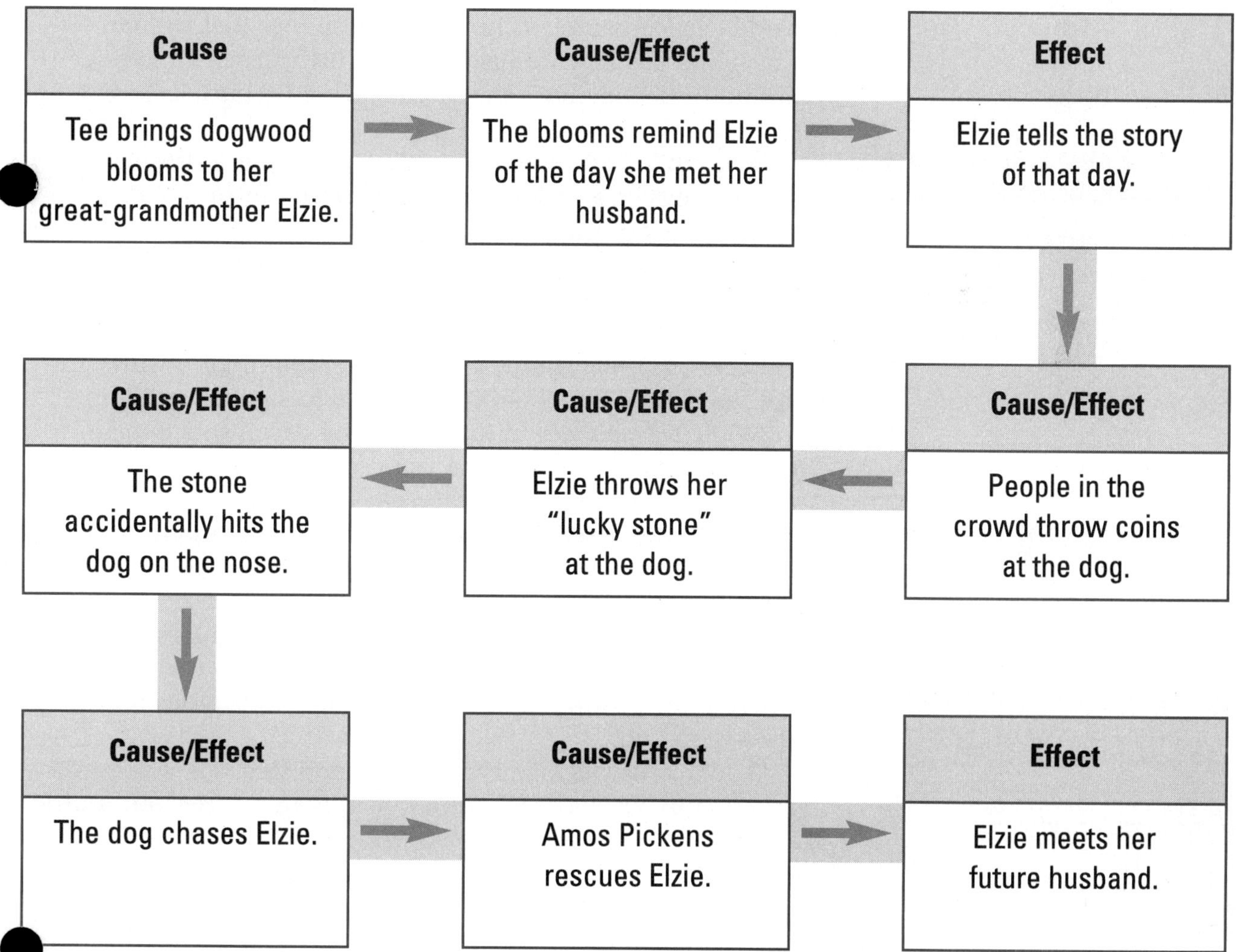

◆ Activate Prior Knowledge

Have you ever met someone by chance, then become friends? Describe what happened.

The Luckiest Time of All

Lucille Clifton

Dialect is a special form of language. Dialects differ from standard language in pronunciation, grammar, and word choice. The author of this story uses a dialect from the rural South, including words such as usta *for "used to," and* nothin *for "nothing." Dialect gives a story the sound of actual speech.*

Mrs. Elzie F. Pickens was rocking slowly on the porch one afternoon when her Great-granddaughter, Tee, brought her a big bunch of dogwood blooms, and that was the beginning of a story.

"Ahhh, now that dogwood reminds me of the day I met your Great-granddaddy, Mr. Pickens, Sweet Tee.

"It was just this time, spring of the year, and me and my best friend Ovella Wilson, who is now gone, was goin to join the Silas Greene. Usta be a kinda show went all through the South, called it the Silas Greene show. Somethin like the circus. Me and Ovella wanted to join that thing and see the world. Nothin wrong at home or nothin, we just wanted to travel and see new things and have high times. Didn't say nothin to nobody but one another. Just up and decided to do it.

"Well, this day we plaited our hair and put a dress and some things in a crokasack[1] and started out to the show. Spring day like this.

◆ Literary Analysis

Hyperbole is exaggeration or overstatement for effect. What does Clifton mean by calling the circus show "the world" in the underlined sentence?

"We got there after a good little walk and it was the world, Baby, such music and wonders as we never had seen! They had everything there, or seemed like it.

"Me and Ovella thought we'd walk around for a while and see the show before goin to the office to sign up and join.

"While we was viewin it all we come up on this dancin dog. Cutest one thing in the world next to you, Sweet Tee, dippin and movin and head bowin to that music. Had a little ruffly skirt on itself and up on two back legs twistin and movin to the music. Dancin dancin dancin till people started throwin pennies out of they pockets.

◆ Reading Check

What is the Silas Greene?

"Me and Ovella was caught up too and laughin so. She took a penny out of her pocket and threw it to the ground where that dog was dancin, and I took two pennies and threw 'em both.

"The music was faster and faster and that dog was turnin and turnin. Ovella reached in her sack and threw out a little

1. **crokasack** (krō´ kər sak) *n.* bag made of burlap or similar material, usually spelled croker sack.

pin she had won from never being late at Sunday school. And me, laughin and all excited, reached in my bag and threw out my lucky stone!

"Well, I knew right off what I had done. Soon as it left my hand it seemed like I reached back out for it to take it back. But the stone was gone from my hand and Lord, it hit that dancin dog right on his nose!

"Well, he lit out after me, poor thing. He lit out after me and I flew! Round and round the Silas Greene we run, through every place me and Ovella had walked before, but now that dancin dog was a runnin dog and all the people was laughin at the new show, which was us!

"I felt myself slowin down after a while and I thought I would turn around a little bit to see how much gain that cute little dog was makin on me. When I did I got such a surprise! Right behind me was the dancin dog and right behind him was the finest fast runnin hero in the bottoms of Virginia.

"And that was Mr. Pickens when he was still a boy! He had a length of twine in his hand and he was twirlin it around in the air just like the cowboy at the Silas Greene and grinnin fit to bust.

"While I was watchin how the sun shined on him and made him look like an angel come to help a poor sinner girl, why, he twirled that twine one extra fancy twirl and looped it right around one hind leg of that dancin dog and brought him low.

"I stopped then and walked slow and shy to where he had picked up that poor dog to see if he was hurt, cradlin him and talkin to him soft and sweet. That showed me how kind and gentle he was, and when we walked back to the dancin dog's place in the show he let the dog loose and helped me to find my stone. I told him how shiny black it was and how it had the letter A scratched on one side. We searched and searched and at last he spied it!

"Ovella and me lost heart for shows then and we walked on home. And a good little way, the one who was gonna be your Great-granddaddy was walkin on behind. Seein us safe. Us walkin kind of slow. Him seein us safe. Yes." Mrs. Pickens' voice trailed off softly and Tee noticed she had a little smile on her face.

"Grandmama, that stone almost got you bit by a dog that time. It wasn't so lucky that time, was it?"

Tee's Great-grandmother shook her head and laughed out loud.

"That was the luckiest time of all, Tee Baby. It got me acquainted with Mr. Amos Pickens, and if that ain't luck, what could it be! Yes, it was luckier for me than for anybody, I think. Least mostly I think it."

◆ Reading Strategy

Sometimes you can **clarify a word's meaning** by looking at the words around it. After the dog got hit with the stone, he "lit out" after the girl who threw the stone. Underline the words that help you understand the meaning of "lit out" in the bracketed paragraph.

Mark the Text

◆ Reading Check

Who saves Mrs. Pickens from the dog?

____

____

____

◆ Stop to Reflect

Why do you think Ovella and Mrs. Pickens lose interest in being in the show?

____

____

____

____

◆ **Reading Check**

Why was the black stone lucky?

Tee laughed with her Great-grandmother though she didn't exactly know why.

"I hope I have that kind of good stone luck one day," she said.

"Maybe you will someday," her Great-grandmother said.

And they rocked a little longer and smiled together.

Reader's Response: Were you surprised to learn that Mr. Pickens and Elzie got married? Why or why not?

Thinking About the Skill: How can nearby words help you understand an unfamiliar word?

How the Snake Got Poison

Zora Neale Hurston

Summary

The snake went up to God and explained how dangerous it was crawling around on his belly in the dust. So God gave him poison to protect himself. But then he bit and killed so many small animals that they complained to God. So God sent for the snake and asked why he was biting everything instead of using the poison only to protect himself. The snake explained that he could not tell who was friend and who was foe and had to bite everything to protect himself. So God gave the snake a kind of bell to tie on his tail. That way, those who weren't out to harm the snake would avoid him when they heard the warning sound. And that is how the snake got his poison and his rattles.

Visual Summary

Problem		Solution
• Snake complains that because he crawls on his belly in the dust, everyone stamps on and kills him.	→	• God gives him poison for protection.
• Snake still does not know who is friend and who is foe.	→	• Snake bites and kills everything with his poison.
• Small animals complain snake is killing them off.	→	• God gives snake bells, or rattles, to warn away those not trying to harm him. Snake will then bite only those who come near.

◆ Activate Prior Knowledge

Do you know any stories about how something began? Briefly retell one.

◆ Literary Analysis

A **character's perspective** is the viewpoint from which he or she observes events. The snake views events from the ground. Circle the problem he complains about in the underlined sentences.

◆ Literary Analysis

Circle the problem the varmints complain about.

◆ Reading Check

What has happened in the story so far?

How the Snake Got Poison

Zora Neale Hurston

Folk tales are stories that are told aloud from one generation to the next. Some folk tales tell how something began, like this African American tale about how the snake got poison. Most cultures have tales that were invented to explain various aspects of nature.

Well, when God made de snake he put him in de bushes to ornament de ground. But things didn't suit de snake so one day he got on de ladder and went up to see God.

"Good mawnin', God."

"How do you do, Snake?"

"Ah[1] ain't so many, God, you put me down here on my belly in de dust and everything trods upon me and kills off my generations. Ah ain't got no kind of protection at all."

God looked off towards immensity and thought about de subject for awhile, then he said, "Ah didn't mean for nothin' to be stompin' you snakes lak dat. You got to have some kind of a protection. Here, take dis poison and put it in yo' mouf and when they tromps on you, protect yo'self."

So de snake took de poison in his mouf and went on back.

So after awhile all de other varmints went up to God.

"Good evenin', God."

"How you makin' it, varmints?"

"God, please do somethin' 'bout dat snake. He' layin' in de bushes there wid poison in his mouf and he's strikin' everything dat shakes de bushes. He's killin' up our generations. Wese skeered to walk de earth."

So God sent for de snake and tole him:

"Snake, when Ah give you dat poison, Ah didn't mean for you to be hittin' and killin' everything dat shake de bush. I give you dat poison and tole you to protect yo'self when they tromples on you. But you killin' everything dat moves. Ah didn't mean for you to do dat."

De snake say, "Lawd, you know Ah'm down here in de dust. Ah ain't got no claws to fight wid, and Ah ain't got no feets to git me out de way. All Ah kin see is feets comin' to tromple me. Ah can't tell who my enemy is and who is my friend. You gimme dis protection in my mouf and Ah uses it."

Vocabulary Development: immensity (i men′ si tē) *n.* something extremely large or immeasurably vast

1. **Ah** dialect for "I."

God thought it over for a while then he says:

"Well, snake, I don't want yo' generations all stomped out and I don't want you killin' everything else dat moves. Here take dis bell and tie it to yo' tail. When you hear feets comin' you ring yo' bell and if it's yo' friend, he'll be keerful. If it's yo' enemy, it's you and him."

So dat's how de snake got his poison and dat's how come he got rattles.

Reader's Response: How would you have solved the problems in this folk tale?

____

____

Thinking About the Skill: How did the snake's perspective influence his view of the situation?

____

____

◆ **Reading Check**

What does the snake get besides poison?

____

____

____

____

____

____

PREVIEW

After Twenty Years

O. Henry

Summary

One night a police officer walks the nearly empty streets of a New York business area. In a dark store doorway is a man named Bob waiting to meet his friend Jimmy Wells. Bob explains that he hasn't seen Jimmy since leaving New York twenty years ago to make his fortune out west. The two promised to meet in twenty years at Big Joe Brady's restaurant, now this store. Bob is sure Jimmy will show up. After the officer leaves, another man arrives and greets Bob by name. Bob soon realizes this man is not Jimmy. In fact he is a plainclothes officer who arrests "Silky Bob" for crimes in Chicago. He hands Bob a note from Jimmy, who actually was the first officer. Jimmy came to meet his old friend but recognized Bob as a wanted man. He didn't have the heart to arrest Bob himself, so he sent a fellow officer.

Visual Summary

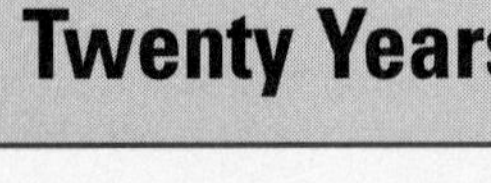

Parting friends Jimmy Wells and Bob agree to meet again at Big Joe Brady's New York restaurant in twenty years

What Happens to Jimmy Wells	What Happens to Bob
• remains in New York City	• leaves New York to seek his fortune out west
• unknown to Bob and reader, becomes a New York City police officer	• unknown to Jimmy and reader, becomes "Silky Bob," gangster wanted in Chicago
• unknown to Bob and reader, keeps appointment outside closed store that was once Big Joe's	• keeps appointment outside closed store that was once Big Joe's
• recognizes Bob as a wanted man	• fails to recognize Jimmy in uniform
• doesn't have the heart to arrest his old friend	• is sure loyal friend Jimmy will keep appointment
• sends another officer to arrest Bob	• recognizes second arrival is not Jimmy
• sends note with second officer, explaining situation to Bob (and reader)	• learns the truth (as reader does) when he is arrested and reads Jimmy's note

After Twenty Years

O. Henry

You have probably had the experience of seeing a friend after a long absence. During your time apart, you and your friend's looks, interests, or taste in clothing may have changed. Imagine how different someone might look and act if you had not seen him or her for twenty years.

The policeman on the beat moved up the avenue impressively. The impressiveness was habitual and not for show, for spectators were few. The time was barely 10 o'clock at night, but chilly gusts of wind with a taste of rain in them had well nigh[1] depeopled the streets.

Trying doors as he went, twirling his club with many intricate and artful movements, turning now and then to cast his watchful eye adown the pacific thoroughfare,[2] the officer, with his stalwart form and slight swagger, made a fine picture of a guardian of the peace. The vicinity was one that kept early hours. Now and then you might see the lights of a cigar store or of an all-night lunch counter; but the majority of the doors belonged to business places that had long since been closed.

When about midway of a certain block the policeman suddenly slowed his walk. In the doorway of a darkened hardware store a man leaned, with an unlighted cigar in his mouth. As the policeman walked up to him the man spoke up quickly.

"It's all right, officer," he said, reassuringly. "I'm just waiting for a friend. It's an appointment made twenty years ago. Sounds a little funny to you, doesn't it? Well, I'll explain if you'd like to make certain it's all straight. About that long ago there used to be a restaurant where this store stands—'Big Joe' Brady's restaurant."

"Until five years ago," said the policeman. "It was torn down then."

The man in the doorway struck a match and lit his cigar. The light showed a pale, square-jawed face with keen eyes, and a little white scar near his right eyebrow. His scarfpin was a large diamond, oddly set.

Vocabulary Development: **spectators** (spek´ tāt´ ərz) *n.* people who watch something without taking part; onlookers
intricate (in´ tri kit) *adj.* complex; full of complicated detail

1. **well nigh** (nī) very nearly.
2. **pacific thoroughfare** calm street.

◆ Activate Prior Knowledge

How is police work today different from that of one hundred years ago? Give two examples.

1. __________
2. __________

◆ Reading Strategy

Mark the Text

To understand a long, complex sentence, **break it** into groups of words, using the punctuation as a guide where possible. Find the *subject* of the sentence (who or what it is about) and the *predicate* (the action word that says what happens).

In the first bracketed passage, underline the subject of the sentence once and the predicate twice. Then draw vertical (up and down) lines to divide the sentence into readable chunks.

◆ Reading Strategy

Mark the Text

Foreshadowing is the use of clues to hint at later events in the story. These clues create curiosity and anticipation about what will happen as the story unfolds. In the second bracketed paragraph, underline the sentence that hints that the officer has seen something suspicious. Then explain why it is foreshadowing.

____

____

____

____

◆ Literary Analysis

Some short stories have a **surprise ending**—an ending different from what the events of the story lead you to believe will happen. A successful surprise ending is clever and startling but really does make sense. In the first bracketed passage, underline one hint that **foreshadows** the fact that the story might have a surprise ending.

Mark THE Text

◆ Reading Strategy

What part of the underlined sentence describes Jimmy?

____

____

____

____

____

◆ Reading Check

What do comments such as "kind of a plodder," "compete with some of the sharpest wits," and "razor-edge" in the second bracketed passage tell you about the man's opinion of his friend and of himself?

____

____

____

____

____

____

Twenty years ago tonight," said the man, "I dined here at 'Big Joe' Brady's with Jimmy Wells, my best chum, and the finest chap in the world. He and I were raised here in New York, just like two brothers, together. I was eighteen and Jimmy was twenty. The next morning I was to start for the West to make my fortune. You couldn't have dragged Jimmy out of New York; he thought it was the only place on earth. Well, we agreed that night that we would meet here again exactly twenty years from that date and time, no matter what our conditions might be or from what distance we might have to come. We figured that in twenty years each of us ought to have our destiny worked out and our fortunes made, whatever they were going to be."

"It sounds pretty interesting," said the policeman. "Rather a long time between meets, though, it seems to me. Haven't you heard from your friend since you left?"

"Well, yes, for a time we corresponded," said the other. "But after a year or two we lost track of each other. You see, the West is a pretty big proposition, and I kept hustling around over it pretty lively. But I know Jimmy will meet me here if he's alive, for he always was the truest, stanchest old chap in the world. He'll never forget. I came a thousand miles to stand in this door tonight, and it's worth it if my old partner turns up."

The waiting man pulled out a handsome watch, the lids of it set with small diamonds.

"Three minutes to ten," he announced. "It was exactly ten o'clock when we parted here at the restaurant door."

"Did pretty well out West, didn't you?" asked the policeman.

"You bet! I hope Jimmy has done half as well. He was a kind of plodder, though, good fellow as he was. I've had to compete with some of the sharpest wits going to get my pile. A man gets in a groove in New York. It takes the West to put a razor-edge on him."

The policeman twirled his club and took a step or two.

"I'll be on my way. Hope your friend comes around all right. Going to call time on him sharp?"

"I should say not!" said the other. "I'll give him half an hour at least. If Jimmy is alive on earth he'll be here by that time. So long, officer."

"Good-night, sir," said the policeman, passing on along his beat, trying doors as he went.

There was now a fine, cold drizzle falling, and the wind had risen from its uncertain puffs into a steady blow. The few foot passengers astir in that quarter hurried dismally

Vocabulary Development: **destiny** (des´ tə nē) *n.* what will necessarily happen to any person or thing; fate
dismally (diz´ məl lē) *adv.* gloomily; miserably

and silently along with coat collars turned high and pocketed hands. And in the door of the hardware store the man who had come a thousand miles to fill an appointment, uncertain almost to absurdity, with the friend of his youth, smoked his cigar and waited.

About twenty minutes he waited, and then a tall man in a long overcoat, with collar turned up to his ears, hurried across from the opposite side of the street. He went directly to the waiting man.

"Is that you, Bob?" he asked, doubtfully.

"Is that you, Jimmy Wells?" cried the man in the door.

"Bless my heart!" exclaimed the new arrival, grasping both the other's hands with his own. "It's Bob, sure as fate. I was certain I'd find you here if you were still in existence. Well, well, well!—twenty years is a long time. The old restaurant's gone, Bob; I wish it had lasted, so we could have had another dinner there. How has the West treated you, old man?"

"Bully;[3] it has given me everything I asked it for. You've changed lots, Jimmy. I never thought you were so tall by two or three inches."

"Oh, I grew a bit after I was twenty."

"Doing well in New York, Jimmy?"

"Moderately. I have a position in one of the city departments. Come on, Bob; we'll go around to a place I know of, and have a good long talk about old times."

The two men started up the street, arm in arm. The man from the West, his egotism enlarged by success, was beginning to outline the history of his career. The other, submerged in his overcoat, listened with interest.

At the corner stood a drug store, brilliant with electric lights. When they came into this glare each of them turned simultaneously to gaze upon the other's face.

The man from the West stopped suddenly and released his arm.

"You're not Jimmy Wells," he snapped. "Twenty years is a long time, but not long enough to change a man's nose from a Roman to a pug."[4]

"It sometimes changes a good man into a bad one," said the tall man. "You've been under arrest for ten minutes, 'Silky' Bob. Chicago thinks you may have dropped over our

◆ **Reading Strategy**

Mark the Text

In the first bracketed passage, underline the subject of the sentence and circle the predicate. How do the commas help your understanding of the sentence?

____

____

____

____

◆ **Literary Analysis**

Mark the Text

Underline two hints in the second bracketed passage that **foreshadow** the fact that the man in the overcoat may not be Jimmy Wells.

◆ **Literary Analysis**

In the underlined passage, what has changed about the expected course of the story?

____

____

____

____

____

Vocabulary Development: absurdity (ab sʉr´ də tē) *n.* nonsense; foolishness

simultaneously (sī´ məl tā´ nē əs lē) *adv.* at the same time

3. **Bully** very well.
4. **change a man's nose from a Roman to a pug** A Roman nose has a high, prominent bridge; a pug nose is short, thick, and turned up at the end.

◆ Literary Analysis

Explain the story's **surprise ending.** Who is the man in the doorway, and who is the tall man in the long overcoat?

◆ Literary Analysis

Read the bracketed passage. What is **surprising** about the note from Jimmy?

◆ Stop to Reflect

Why do you think Jimmy Wells sent another patrolman to arrest Bob? Were his motivations positive or negative? Explain.

way and wires us she wants to have a chat with you. Going quietly are you? That's sensible. Now, before we go to the station here's a note I was asked to hand to you. You may read it here at the window. It's from Patrolman Wells."

The man from the West unfolded the little piece of paper handed him. His hand was steady when he began to read, but it trembled a little by the time he had finished. The note was rather short.

Bob: I was at the appointed place on time. When you struck the match to light your cigar I saw it was the face of the man wanted in Chicago. Somehow I couldn't do it myself, so I went around and got a plain clothes man to do the job. Jimmy.

Reader's Response: Do you think Patrolman Wells did the right thing? Why or why not?

Thinking About the Skill: How does **foreshadowing** prepare readers for a **surprise ending**? Use the story "After Twenty Years" to give examples.

Rikki-tikki-tavi

Rudyard Kipling

Summary

In this story set in India, Rikki-tikki-tavi is a mongoose, a small furry animal that eats snakes. When a flood washes him from his underground home, he is adopted by the family of a young boy named Teddy. Exploring the garden, he meets Nag and Nagaina, two deadly cobras. Later he rescues Teddy by killing a smaller poisonous snake. That night he overhears the cobras' plot to enter the house and kill Teddy's family. Rikki attacks Nag in the bathroom, fighting until Teddy's father shoots the cobra. The next day Rikki finds Nagaina's eggs and begins crushing them. When she threatens to kill Teddy, Rikki draws her away by threatening to destroy her last egg. Rikki then chases her into her hole and kills her. Teddy's family and the garden animals hail Rikki as a hero.

Visual Summary

Who?	Rikki-tikki-tavi, a small furry animal called a mongoose
Where?	house and grounds of a British family in India
When?	late 1800s, when India was a British colony
What?	saves the lives of Teddy and the rest of the family
How?	fights with and kills several poisonous snakes
Why?	likes the family who adopted him; is natural enemy of snakes

◆ **Activate Prior Knowledge**

Some animals appear to be natural enemies, which is certainly true of the mongoose and the cobra. Name one other pair of natural enemies and describe how they act when together.

____

____

____

____

◆ **Literary Analysis**

A story's **plot** is the arrangement of events—the action—in a story. In the **exposition**, the first part of the plot, the characters and situation are introduced. How does the exposition, found in the first three paragraphs of this story, describe the mongoose?

____

____

____

____

____

____

◆ **Literary Analysis**

A **character** is a person or animal who takes part in a story. Most of the action of the plot revolves around **the major character(s)**. From your reading of the story so far, who do you think the major character of this story is? Why?

____

____

____

Rikki-tikki-tavi

Rudyard Kipling

In this story, you will meet two animals that you probably have not encountered: the cobra and the mongoose. The Indian cobra can reach six feet in length and six inches around. Very poisonous, this snake lifts its body in the air just before striking and forms a hood from ribs near its head. The mongoose is a brown, furry animal about fifteen inches long—the perfect size for a cobra's meal. Despite its size, the mongoose usually wins any battle with a cobra.

This is the story of the great war that Rikki-tikki-tavi fought single-handed, through the bathrooms of the big bungalow in Segowlee cantonment.[1] Darzee, the tailorbird bird, helped him, and Chuchundra,[2] the muskrat, who never comes out into the middle of the floor, but always creeps round by the wall, gave him advice; but Rikki-tikki did the real fighting.

He was a mongoose, rather like a little cat in his fur and his tail, but quite like a weasel in his head and his habits. His eyes and the end of his restless nose were pink; he could scratch himself anywhere he pleased, with any leg, front or back, that he chose to use; he could fluff up his tail till it looked like a bottle brush, and his war cry as he scuttled through the long grass, was: "*Rikk-tikk-tikki-tikki-tchk!*"

One day, a high summer flood washed him out of the burrow where he lived with his father and mother, and carried him, kicking and clucking, down a roadside ditch. He found a little wisp of grass floating there, and clung to it till he lost his senses. When he revived, he was lying in the hot sun on the middle of a garden path, very draggled indeed, and a small boy was saying: "Here's a dead mongoose. Let's have a funeral."

"No," said his mother; "let's take him in and dry him. Perhaps he isn't really dead."

They took him into the house, and a big man picked him up between his finger and thumb and said he was not dead but half choked; so they wrapped him in cotton wool, and warmed him, and he opened his eyes and sneezed.

"Now," said the big man (he was an Englishman who had just moved into the bungalow); "don't frighten him, and we'll see what he'll do."

Vocabulary Development: revived (ri vīvd′) *v.* came back to consciousness
draggled (drag′ əld) *adj.* wet and dirty

1. **Segowlee cantonment** (sē gou′ lē kan tän′ mənt) *n.* living quarters for British troops in Segowlee, India.
2. **Chuchundra** (cho͞o chun′ drə)

It is the hardest thing in the world to frighten a mongoose, because he is eaten up from nose to tail with curiosity. The motto of all the mongoose family is, "Run and find out"; and Rikki-tikki was a true mongoose. He looked at the cotton wool, decided that it was not good to eat, ran all round the table, sat up and put his fur in order, scratched himself, and jumped on the small boy's shoulder.

"Don't be frightened, Teddy," said his father. "That's his way of making friends."

"Ouch! He's tickling under my chin," said Teddy.

Rikki-tikki looked down between the boy's collar and neck, snuffed at his ear, and climbed down to the floor, where he sat rubbing his nose.

"Good gracious," said Teddy's mother, "and that's a wild creature! I suppose he's so tame because we've been kind to him."

"All mongooses are like that," said her husband. "If Teddy doesn't pick him up by the tail, or try to put him in a cage, he'll run in and out of the house all day long. Let's give him something to eat."

They gave him a little piece of raw meat. Rikki-tikki liked it immensely, and when it was finished he went out into the veranda and sat in the sunshine and fluffed up his fur to make it dry to the roots. Then he felt better.

"There are more things to find out about in this house," he said to himself, "than all my family could find out in all their lives. I shall certainly stay and find out."

He spent all that day roaming over the house. He nearly drowned himself in the bathtubs, put his nose into the ink on a writing table, and burned it on the end of the big man's cigar, for he climbed up in the big man's lap to see how writing was done. At nightfall he ran into Teddy's nursery to watch how kerosene lamps were lighted, and when Teddy went to bed Rikki-tikki climbed up too; but he was a restless companion, because he had to get up and attend to every noise all through the night, and find out what made it. Teddy's mother and father came in, the last thing, to look at their boy, and Rikki-tikki was awake on the pillow. "I don't like that," said Teddy's mother; "he may bite the child." "He'll do no such thing," said the father. "Teddy's safer with that little beast than if he had a bloodhound to watch him. If a snake came into the nursery now—"

But Teddy's mother wouldn't think of anything so awful.

Early in the morning Rikki-tikki came to early breakfast in the veranda riding on Teddy's shoulder, and they gave

◆ Reading Strategy

To help you understand a story, you can **predict**—make an educated guess about—what will happen next. In this paragraph, underline the "motto" of the mongoose family and explain what it means. Then predict how this motto might cause trouble for Rikki.

Mark the Text

______

______

______

______

◆ Literary Analysis

While a story usually has only one or two **major characters**, it often has several **minor characters**, who are not the focus of the story but help move the plot forward. Who are the minor characters in the bracketed passage?

______

______

______

◆ Reading Check

Name three things in this bracketed paragraph that show how Rikki lives up to his family motto.

1. ______

2. ______

3. ______

◆ Reading Strategy

Predict what might happen based on the father's statement, which is underlined.

______

______

◆ **Stop to Reflect**

Why do you think Kipling talks about Rikki's mother and the importance of being a house mongoose?

◆ **Literary Analysis**

The **conflict** in a story is the struggle between two opposing characters. How does Rikki's encounter with Darzee help to establish the conflict of the story?

◆ **Reading Check**

After reading the bracketed passage, write three details about the cobra Nag. Then underline which of his characteristics momentarily frightens Rikki.

Mark THE Text

1.

2.

3.

him banana and some boiled egg; and he sat on all their laps one after the other, because every well-brought-up mongoose always hopes to be a house mongoose some day and have rooms to run about in, and Rikki-tikki's mother (she used to live in the General's house at Segowlee) had carefully told Rikki what to do if ever he came across Englishmen.

Then Rikki-tikki went out into the garden to see what was to be seen. It was a large garden, only half cultivated, with bushes as big as summer houses of Marshal Niel roses, lime and orange trees, clumps of bamboos, and thickets of high grass. Rikki-tikki licked his lips. "This is a splendid hunting ground," he said, and his tail grew bottlebrushy at the thought of it, and he scuttled up and down the garden, snuffing here and there till he heard very sorrowful voices in a thornbush.

It was Darzee, the tailorbird, and his wife. They had made a beautiful nest by pulling two big leaves together and stitching them up the edges with fibers, and had filled the hollow with cotton and downy fluff. The nest swayed to and fro, as they sat on the rim and cried.

"What is the matter?" asked Rikki-tikki.

"We are very miserable," said Darzee.

"One of our babies fell out of the nest yesterday and Nag[3] ate him."

"H'm!" said Rikki-tikki, "that is very sad—but I am a stranger here. Who is Nag?"

Darzee and his wife only cowered down in the nest without answering, for from the thick grass at the foot of the bush there came a low hiss—a horrid cold sound that made Rikki-tikki jump back two clear feet. Then inch by inch out of the grass rose up the head and spread hood of Nag, the big black cobra, and he was five feet long from tongue to tail. When he had lifted one third of himself clear of the ground, he stayed balancing to and fro exactly as a dandelion tuft balances in the wind, and he looked at Rikki-tikki with the wicked snake's eyes that never change their expression, whatever the snake may be thinking of.

"Who is Nag?" he said. "*I* am Nag. The great god Brahm[4] put his mark upon all our people when the first cobra spread his hood to keep the sun off Brahm as he slept. Look, and be afraid!"

He spread out his hood more than ever, and Rikki-tikki saw the spectacle mark on the back of it that looks exactly like the eye part of a hook-and-eye fastening. He was afraid for the minute; but it is impossible for a mongoose to stay frightened for any length of time, and though Rikki-tikki had

3. **Nag** (Näg)
4. **Brahm** (bräm) abbreviation of Brahma, the name of the chief god in the Hindu religion.

never met a live cobra before, his mother had fed him on dead ones, and he knew that all a grown mongoose's business in life was to fight and eat snakes. Nag knew that too, and at the bottom of his cold heart he was afraid.

"Well," said Rikki-tikki, and his tail began to fluff up again, "marks or no marks, do you think it is right for you to eat fledglings out of a nest?"

Nag was thinking to himself, and watching the least little movement in the grass behind Rikki-tikki. He knew that mongooses in the garden meant death sooner or later for him and his family; but he wanted to get Rikki-tikki off his guard. So he dropped his head a little, and put it on one side.

"Let us talk," he said. "You eat eggs. Why should not I eat birds?"

"Behind you! Look behind you!" sang Darzee.

Rikki-tikki knew better than to waste time in staring. He jumped up in the air as high as he could go, and just under him whizzed by the head of Nagaina,[5] Nag's wicked wife. She had crept up behind him as he was talking, to make an end of him; and he heard her savage hiss as the stroke missed. He came down almost across her back, and if he had been an old mongoose he would have known that then was the time to break her back with one bite; but he was afraid of the terrible lashing return stroke of the cobra. He bit, indeed, but did not bite long enough, and he jumped clear of the whisking tail, leaving Nagaina torn and angry.

"Wicked, wicked Darzee!" said Nag, lashing up high as he could reach toward the nest in the thornbush; but Darzee had built it out of reach of snakes; and it only swayed to and fro.

Rikki-tikki felt his eyes growing red and hot (when a mongoose's eyes grow red, he is angry), and he sat back on his tail and hind legs like a little kangaroo, and looked all around him, and chattered with rage. But Nag and Nagaina had disappeared into the grass. When a snake misses its stroke, it never says anything or gives any sign of what it means to do next. Rikki-tikki did not care to follow them, for he did not feel sure that he could manage two snakes at once. So he trotted off to the gravel path near the house, and sat down to think. It was a serious matter for him.

If you read the old books of natural history, you will find they say that when the mongoose fights the snake and happens to get bitten, he runs off and eats some herb that cures him. That is not true. The victory is only a matter of quickness of eye and quickness of foot—snake's blow against mongoose's jump—and as no eye can follow the motion of a

---

5. **Nagaina** (nə gī´ nə)

◆ Reading Check

Mark the Text

Underline the phrase that explains why Nag and Nagaina are so eager to kill Rikki.

◆ Reading Strategy

Based on the bracketed passage, what do you **predict** might happen between Rikki and Nag?

◆ Stop to Reflect

Do you think there is a difference between Rikki's eating eggs and Nag's eating birds? Explain.

◆ **Literary Analysis**

The **conflict** of a story increases during the **rising action,** or build-up to the high point of the story. How is Rikki's first tangle with Nag and Nagaina part of the rising action of the story? In other words, how does it intensify the conflict?

◆ **Reading Check**

Underline the evidence in the bracketed passage that tells you that Rikki is a young, inexperienced fighter.

Mark the Text

◆ **Reading Strategy**

How does reading about Rikki's encounter with Karait help you **predict** what might happen next?

snake's head when it strikes, that makes things much more wonderful than any magic herb. Rikki-tikki knew he was a young mongoose, and it made him all the more pleased to think that he had managed to escape a blow from behind. It gave him confidence in himself, and when Teddy came running down the path, Rikki-tikki was ready to be petted.

But just as Teddy was stooping, something flinched a little in the dust, and a tiny voice said: "Be careful. I am death!" It was Karait,[6] the dusty brown snakeling that lies for choice on the dusty earth; and his bite is as dangerous as the cobra's. But he is so small that nobody thinks of him, and so he does the more harm to people.

Rikki-tikki's eyes grew red again, and he danced up to Karait with the peculiar rocking, swaying motion that he had inherited from his family. It looks very funny, but it is so perfectly balanced a gait that you can fly off from it at any angle you please; and in dealing with snakes this is an advantage. If Rikki-tikki had only known, he was doing a much more dangerous thing than fighting Nag, for Karait is so small, and can turn so quickly, that unless Rikki bit him close to the back of the head, he would get the return stroke in his eye or lip. But Rikki did not know: his eyes were all red, and he rocked back and forth, looking for a good place to hold. Karait struck out. Rikki jumped sideways and tried to run in, but the wicked little dusty gray head lashed within a fraction of his shoulder, and he had to jump over the body, and the head followed his heels close.

Teddy shouted to the house: "Oh, look here! Our mongoose is killing a snake"; and Rikki-tikki heard a scream from Teddy's mother. His father ran out with a stick, but by the time he came up, Karait had lunged out once too far, and Rikki-tikki had sprung, jumped on the snake's back, dropped his head far between his fore legs, bitten as high up the back as he could get hold, and rolled away. That bite paralyzed Karait, and Rikki-tikki was just going to eat him up from the tail, after the custom of his family at dinner, when he remembered that a full meal makes a slow mongoose, and if he wanted all his strength and quickness ready, he must keep himself thin.

He went away for a dust bath under the castor-oil bushes, while Teddy's father beat the dead Karait. "What is the use of that?" thought Rikki-tikki. "I have settled it all"; and then Teddy's mother picked him up from the dust and hugged him, crying that he had saved Teddy from death, and

Vocabulary Development: flinched (flincht) *v.* moved back, as if away from a blow

6. **Karait** (kə rīt′)

Teddy's father said that he was a providence,[7] and Teddy looked on with big scared eyes. Rikki-tikki was rather amused at all the fuss, which, of course, he did not understand. Teddy's mother might just as well have petted Teddy for playing in the dust. Rikki was thoroughly enjoying himself.

That night, at dinner, walking to and fro among the wine-glasses on the table, he could have stuffed himself three times over with nice things; but he remembered Nag and Nagaina, and though it was very pleasant to be patted and petted by Teddy's mother, and to sit on Teddy's shoulder, his eyes would get red from time to time, and he would go off into his long war cry of "*Rikk-tikk-tikki-tikki-tchk!*"

Teddy carried him off to bed, and insisted on Rikki-tikki sleeping under his chin. Rikki-tikki was too well bred to bite or scratch, but as soon as Teddy was asleep he went off for his nightly walk round the house, and in the dark he ran up against Chuchundra the muskrat, creeping round by the wall. Chuchundra is a brokenhearted little beast. He whimpers and cheeps all the night, trying to make up his mind to run into the middle of the room, but he never gets there.

"Don't kill me," said Chuchundra, almost weeping. "Rikki-tikki don't kill me."

"Do you think a snake-killer kills muskrats?" said Rikki-tikki scornfully.

"Those who kill snakes get killed by snakes," said Chuchundra, more sorrowfully than ever. "And how am I to be sure that Nag won't mistake me for you some dark night?"

"There's not the least danger," said Rikki-tikki; "but Nag is in the garden, and I know you don't go there."

"My cousin Chua, the rat, told me—" said Chuchundra, and then he stopped.

"Told you what?"

"H'sh! Nag is everywhere, Rikki-tikki. You should have talked to Chua in the garden."

"I didn't—so you must tell me. Quick, Chuchundra, or I'll bite you!"

Chuchundra sat down and cried till the tears rolled off his whiskers. "I am a very poor man," he sobbed. "I never had spirit enough to run out into the middle of the room. H'sh! I mustn't tell you anything. Can't you *hear*, Rikki-tikki?"

Rikki-tikki listened. The house was as still as still, but he thought he could just catch the faintest *scratch-scratch* in

7. **a providence** (präv′ ə dəns) a godsend; a valuable gift.

◆ Stop to Reflect

What does Rikki consider his place in the household to be? How does his impression of his place affect his behavior?

◆ Reading Check

Mark the Text

What is Chuchundra's main personality trait? Underline three details in the text that support your answer.

◆ Literary Analysis

How do Chuchundra and the rat, Chua, affect the **plot**? In other words, how do they help to give Rikki an advantage over the snakes?

◆ **Literary Analysis**

Is Chuchundra a **major** or a **minor** character? Give two reasons why.

1.

2.

◆ **Reading Check**

Explain the plot that Nag and Nagaina have in mind. Why do they want to kill Teddy and his family in addition to Rikki?

◆ **Reading Check**

Underline the two sentences that explain why Nag chooses the bathroom to begin his attack on the family.

Mark the Text

the world—a noise as faint as that of a wasp walking on a windowpane—the dry scratch of a snake's scales on brick-work.

"That's Nag or Nagaina," he said to himself; "and he is crawling into the bathroom sluice.[8] You're right, Chuchundra; I should have talked to Chua."

He stole off to Teddy's bathroom, but there was nothing there, and then to Teddy's mother's bathroom. At the bottom of the smooth plaster wall there was a brick pulled out to make a sluice for the bath water, and as Rikki-tikki stole in by the masonry curb where the bath is put, he heard Nag and Nagaina whispering together outside in the moonlight.

"When the house is emptied of people," said Nagaina to her husband, "*he* will have to go away, and then the garden will be our own again. Go in quietly, and remember that the big man who killed Karait is the first one to bite. Then come out and tell me, and we will hunt for Rikki-tikki together."

"But are you sure that there is anything to be gained by killing the people?" said Nag.

"Everything. When there were no people in the bungalow, did we have any mongoose in the garden? So long as the bungalow is empty, we are king and queen of the garden; and remember that as soon as our eggs in the melon bed hatch (as they may tomorrow), our children will need room and quiet."

"I had not thought of that," said Nag. "I will go, but there is no need that we should hunt for Rikki-tikki afterward. I will kill the big man and his wife, and the child if I can, and come away quietly. Then the bungalow will be empty, and Rikki-tikki will go."

Rikki-tikki tingled all over with rage and hatred at this, and then Nag's head came through the sluice, and his five feet of cold body followed it. Angry as he was, Rikki-tikki was very frightened as he saw the size of the big cobra. Nag coiled himself up, raised his head, and looked into the bath-room in the dark, and Rikki could see his eyes glitter.

"Now, if I kill him here, Nagaina will know;—and if I fight him on the open floor, the odds are in his favor. What am I to do?" said Rikki-tikki-tavi.

Nag waved to and fro, and then Rikki-tikki-tikki heard him drinking from the biggest water jar that was used to fill the bath. "That is good," said the snake. "Now, when Karait was killed, the big man had a stick. He may have that stick still, but when he comes in to bathe in the morning he will not have a stick. I shall wait here till he comes. Nagaina—do you hear me?—I shall wait here in the cool till daytime."

8. **sluice** (sloos) drain.

There was no answer from outside, so Rikki-tikki knew Nagaina had gone away. Nag coiled himself down, coil by coil, round the bulge at the bottom of the waterjar, and Rikki-tikki stayed still as death. After an hour he began to move, muscle by muscle, toward the jar. Nag was asleep, and Rikki-tikki looked at his big back, wondering which would be the best place for a good hold. "If I don't break his back at the first jump," said Rikki, "he can still fight; and if he fights—O Rikki!" He looked at the thickness of the neck below the hood, but that was too much for him; and a bite near the tail would only make Nag savage.

"It must be the head," he said at last; "the head above the hood; and, when I am once there, I must not let go."

Then he jumped. The head was lying a little clear of the water jar, under the curve of it; and, as his teeth met, Rikki braced his back against the bulge of the red earthenware to hold down the head. This gave him just one second's purchase,[9] and he made the most of it. Then he was battered to and fro as a rat is shaken by a dog—to and fro on the floor, up and down, and round in great circles: but his eyes were red, and he held on as the body cart-whipped over the floor, upsetting the tin dipper and the soap dish and the flesh-brush, and banged against the tin side of the bath. As he held he closed his jaws tighter and tighter, for he made sure he would be banged to death, and, for the honor of his family, he preferred to be found with his teeth locked. He was dizzy, aching, and felt shaken to pieces when something went off like a thunderclap just behind him; a hot wind knocked him senseless and red fire singed his fur. The big man had been wakened by the noise, and had fired both barrels of a shotgun into Nag just behind the hood.

Rikki-tikki held on with his eyes shut, for now he was quite sure he was dead; but the head did not move, and the big man picked him up and said: "It's the mongoose again, Alice; the little chap has saved *our* lives now." Then Teddy's mother came in with a very white face, and saw what was left of Nag, and Rikki-tikki dragged himself to Teddy's bedroom and spent half the rest of the night shaking himself tenderly to find out whether he really was broken into forty pieces, as he fancied.

When morning came he was very stiff, but well pleased with his doings. "Now I have Nagaina to settle with, and she will be worse than five Nags, and there's no knowing when the eggs she spoke of will hatch. Goodness! I must go and see Darzee," he said.

Without waiting for breakfast, Rikki-tikki ran to the thornbush where Darzee was singing a song of triumph at

9. **purchase** (pʉr´ chəs) in this case, an advantage.

◆ Reading Strategy

Check the **prediction** you made on page 135 about Nag and Rikki. Was your prediction correct? In what way?

____

____

____

____

____

____

____

◆ Literary Analysis

Why is the death of Nag part of the **rising action** of the **plot**?

____

____

____

____

____

____

____

____

◆ Reading Check

Give two reasons that Rikki worries that Nagaina will be "worse than five Nags."

1. ______________________________

____

2. ______________________________

____

◆ **Stop to Reflect**

Famous battles have often been celebrated by poets and musicians. How does Darzee join in this tradition? Underline two details Darzee mentions about the battle and circle two names of praise he gives Rikki.

Mark THE Text

____

____

◆ **Reading Check**

In the bracketed passage, underline the sentence that explains why Rikki is angry at Darzee.

Mark THE Text

◆ **Reading Strategy**

Predict how Rikki will use the information in the underlined passage. Why is he so angry that Darzee did not tell him this information earlier?

____

____

____

____

____

____

____

____

the top of his voice. The news of Nag's death was all over the garden, for the sweeper had thrown the body on the rubbish heap.

"Oh, you stupid tuft of feathers!" said Rikki-tikki, angrily. "Is this the time to sing?"

"Nag is dead—is dead—is dead!" sang Darzee. "The valiant Rikki-tikki caught him by the head and held fast. The big man brought the bang-stick and Nag fell in two pieces! He will never eat my babies again."

"All that's true enough; but where's Nagaina?" said Rikki-tikki, looking carefully round him.

"Nagaina came to the bathroom sluice and called for Nag," Darzee went on; "and Nag came out on the end of a stick—the sweeper picked him up on the end of a stick and threw him upon the rubbish heap. Let us sing about the great, the red-eyed Rikki-tikki!" and Darzee filled his throat and sang.

"If I could get up to your nest, I'd roll all your babies out!" said Rikki-tikki "You don't know when to do the right thing at the right time. You're safe enough in your nest there, but it's war for me down here. Stop singing a minute, Darzee."

"For the great, the beautiful Rikki-tikki's sake, I will stop," said Darzee. "What is it, O Killer of the terrible Nag!"

"Where is Nagaina, for the third time?"

"On the rubbish heap by the stables, mourning for Nag. Great is Rikki-tikki with the white teeth."

"Bother my white teeth! Have you ever heard where she keeps her eggs?"

"In the melon bed, on the end nearest the wall, where the sun strikes nearly all day. She had them there weeks ago."

"And you never thought it worthwhile to tell me? The end nearest the wall, you said?"

"Rikki-tikki, you are not going to eat her eggs?"

"Not eat exactly; no. Darzee, if you have a grain of sense you will fly off to the stables and pretend that your wing is broken, and let Nagaina chase you away to this bush! I must get to the melon bed, and if I went there now she'd see me."

Darzee was a featherbrained little fellow who could never hold more than one idea at a time in his head; and just because he knew that Nagaina's children were born in eggs like his own, he didn't think at first that it was fair to kill them. But his wife was a sensible bird, and she knew that cobra's eggs meant young cobras later on; so she flew off from the nest, and left Darzee to keep the babies warm, and continue his song about the death of Nag. Darzee was very

Vocabulary Development: mourning (môrn′ iŋ) *adj.* feeling sorrow for the death of a loved one

like a man in some ways.

She fluttered in front of Nagaina by the rubbish heap, and cried out, "Oh, my wing is broken! The boy in the house threw a stone at me and broke it." Then she fluttered more desperately than ever.

Nagaina lifted up her head and hissed, "You warned Rikki-tikki when I would have killed him. Indeed and truly, you've chosen a bad place to be lame in." And she moved toward Darzee's wife, slipping along over the dust.

"The boy broke it with a stone!" shrieked Darzee's wife.

"Well! It may be some consolation to you when you're dead to know that I shall settle accounts with the boy. My husband lies on the rubbish heap this morning, but before night the boy in the house will lie very still. What is the use of running away? I am sure to catch you. Little fool, look at me!"

Darzee's wife knew better than to do *that*, for a bird who looks at a snake's eyes gets so frightened that she cannot move. Darzee's wife fluttered on, piping sorrowfully, and never leaving the ground, and Nagaina quickened her pace.

Rikki-tikki heard them going up the path from the stables, and he raced for the end of the melon patch near the wall. There, in the warm litter about the melons, very cunningly hidden, he found twenty-five eggs, about the size of a bantam's eggs,[10] but with whitish skin instead of shell.

"I was not a day too soon," he said; for he could see the baby cobras curled up inside the skin, and he knew that the minute they were hatched they could each kill a man or a mongoose. He bit off the tops of the eggs as fast as he could, taking care to crush the young cobras, and turned over the litter from time to time to see whether he had missed any. At last there were only three eggs left, and Rikki-tikki began to chuckle to himself, when he heard Darzee's wife screaming:

"Rikki-tikki, I led Nagaina toward the house, and she has gone into the veranda, and—oh, come quickly—she means killing!"

Rikki-tikki smashed two eggs, and tumbled backward down the melon bed with the third egg in his mouth, and scuttled to the veranda as hard as he could put foot to the ground. Teddy and his mother and father were there at early breakfast; but Rikki-tikki saw that they were not eating anything. They sat stone-still, and their faces were white. Nagaina was coiled up on the matting by Teddy's chair, within easy striking distance of Teddy's bare leg, and she was

Vocabulary Development: consolation (kän´ səl ā´ shən) *n.* something that makes you feel better
cunningly (kun´ iŋ lē) *adv.* cleverly

10. **bantam's** (ban´ təmz) **eggs** small chicken's eggs.

◆ Reading Check

Why does Darzee's wife pretend to have a broken wing?

◆ Reading Strategy

Predict why Rikki-tikki does not destroy one of the cobra eggs.

◆ Literary Analysis

What twist does the **plot** take that Rikki and Darzee's wife did not foresee?

◆ **Literary Analysis**

Is Nagaina a **major** or a **minor character**? Give two reasons why.

1.

2.

◆ **Literary Analysis**

In the bracketed passage, the story is approaching its **climax,** or the peak of the **rising action**. How can you tell?

◆ **Stop to Reflect**

Why does Rikki boast to Nagaina about his defeat of Nag?

◆ **Reading Strategy**

Check your **prediction** from page 141 about why Rikki-tikki does not destroy one of the cobra eggs. Was your prediction correct? What does Nagaina do when Rikki tells her this is the last egg?

swaying to and fro singing a song of triumph.

"Son of the big man that killed Nag," she hissed, "stay still. I am not ready yet. Wait a little. Keep very still, all you three. If you move I strike, and if you do not move I strike, Oh, foolish people, who killed my Nag!"

Teddy's eyes were fixed on his father, and all his father could do was to whisper, "Sit still, Teddy. You mustn't move. Teddy, keep still."

Then Rikki-tikki came up and cried: "Turn round, Nagaina; turn and fight!"

"All in good time," said she, without moving her eyes. "I will settle my account with *you* presently. Look at your friends, Rikki-tikki. They are still and white; they are afraid. They dare not move, and if you come a step nearer I strike."

"Look at your eggs," said Rikki-tikki, "in the melon bed near the wall. Go and look, Nagaina."

The big snake turned half round, and saw the egg on the veranda. "Ah-h! Give it to me," she said.

Rikki-tikki put his paws one on each side of the egg, and his eyes were blood-red. "What price for a snake's egg? For a young cobra? For a young king cobra? For the last—the very last of the brood? The ants are eating all the others down by the melon bed."

Nagaina spun clear round, forgetting everything for the sake of the one egg; and Rikki-tikki saw Teddy's father shoot out a big hand, catch Teddy by the shoulder, and drag him across the little table with the teacups, safe and out of reach of Nagaina.

"Tricked! Tricked! Tricked! *Rikk-tck-tck*!" chuckled Rikki-tikki. "The boy is safe, and it was I—I—I that caught Nag by the hood last night in the bathroom." Then he began to jump up and down, all four feet together, his head close to the floor. "He threw me to and fro, but he could not shake me off. He was dead before the big man blew him in two. I did it. *Rikki-tikki-tck-tck*! Come then, Nagaina. Come and fight with me. You shall not be a widow long."

Nagaina saw that she had lost her chance of killing Teddy, and the egg lay between Rikki-tikki's paws. "Give me the egg, Rikki-tikki. Give me the last of my eggs, and I will go away and never come back," she said, lowering her hood.

"Yes, you will go away, and you will never come back; for you will go to the rubbish heap with Nag. Fight, widow! The big man has gone for his gun! Fight!"

Rikki-tikki was bounding all round Nagaina, keeping just out of reach of her stroke, his little eyes like hot coals.

Nagaina gathered herself together, and flung out at him. Rikki-tikki jumped up and backward. Again and again and again she struck, and each time her head came with a whack on the matting of the veranda and she gathered herself together like a watchspring. Then Rikki-tikki danced in a circle to get behind her, and Nagaina spun round to keep her head to his head, so that the rustle of her tail on the matting sounded like dry leaves blown along by the wind.

He had forgotten the egg. It still lay on the veranda, and Nagaina came nearer and nearer to it, till at last, while Rikki-tikki was drawing breath, she caught it in her mouth, turned to the veranda steps, and flew like an arrow down the path, with Rikki-tikki behind her. When the cobra runs for her life, she goes like a whiplash flicked across a horse's neck.

Rikki-tikki knew that he must catch her, or all the trouble would begin again. She headed straight for the long grass by the thornbush, and as he was running Rikki-tikki heard Darzee still singing his foolish little song of triumph. But Darzee's wife was wiser. She flew off her nest as Nagaina came along, and flapped her wings about Nagaina's head. If Darzee had helped they might have turned her; but Nagaina only lowered her hood and went on. Still, the instant's delay brought Rikki-tikki up to her, and as she plunged into the rat hole where she and Nag used to live, his little white teeth were clenched on her tail, and he went down with her—and very few mongooses, however wise and old they may be, care to follow a cobra into its hole. It was dark in the hole; and Rikki-tikki never knew when it might open out and give Nagaina room to turn and strike at him. He held on savagely, and struck out his feet to act as brakes on the dark slope of the hot, moist earth.

Then the grass by the mouth of the hole stopped waving, and Darzee said: "It is all over with Rikki-tikki! We must sing his death song. Valiant Rikki-tikki is dead! For Nagaina will surely kill him underground."

So he sang a very mournful song that he made up all on the spur of the minute, and just as he got to the most touching part the grass quivered again, and Rikki-tikki, covered with dirt, dragged himself out of the hole leg by leg, licking his whiskers. Darzee stopped with a little shout. Rikki-tikki shook some of the dust out of his fur and sneezed. "It is all over," he said. "The widow will never come out again." And the red ants that live between the grass stems heard him, and began to troop down one after another to see if he had spoken the truth.

◆ Reading Strategy

After reading the first bracketed passage, **predict** who will win the battle between Rikki and Nagaina, and how.

____

____

____

____

◆ Reading Check

In the second bracketed passage, what is Darzee's wife doing, and why?

____

____

____

____

____

____

◆ Literary Analysis

Mark the Text

Underline the **climax** of the story.

◆ **Literary Analysis**

A story ends with the **falling action** and the **resolution**, which gives the outcome of the **conflict**. Underline three details of the falling action, and then circle the resolution of the conflict. Remember what the central conflict of the story is, and then write why what you have circled is the resolution.

Mark the Text

____

____

____

____

◆ **Stop to Reflect**

Do you think Rikki is too boastful in the underlined passage? Why or why not?

____

____

____

____

Rikki-tikki curled himself up in the grass and slept where he was—slept and slept till it was late in the afternoon, for he had done a hard day's work.

"Now," he said, when he awoke, "I will go back to the house. Tell the Coppersmith, Darzee, and he will tell the garden that Nagaina is dead."

The Coppersmith is a bird who makes a noise exactly like the beating of a little hammer on a copper pot; and the reason he is always making it is because he is the town crier to every Indian garden, and tells all the news to everybody who cares to listen. As Rikki-tikki went up the path, he heard his "attention" notes like a tiny dinner gong; and then the steady "*Ding-dong-tock*! Nag is dead—*dong*! Nagaina is dead! *Ding-dong-tock*!" That set all the birds in the garden singing, and the frogs croaking; for Nag and Nagaina used to eat frogs as well as little birds.

When Rikki got to the house, Teddy and Teddy's mother and Teddy's father came out and almost cried over him; and that night he ate all that was given him till he could eat no more, and went to bed on Teddy's shoulder, where Teddy's mother saw him when she came to look late at night.

"He saved our lives and Teddy's life," she said to her husband. "Just think, he saved all our lives."

Rikki-tikki woke up with a jump, for all the mongooses are light sleepers.

"Oh, it's you," said he. "What are you bothering for? All the cobras are dead; and if they weren't, I'm here."

Rikki-tikki had a right to be proud of himself; but he did not grow too proud, and he kept that garden as a mongoose should keep it, with tooth and jump and spring and bite, till never a cobra dared show its head inside the walls.

Reader's Response: Why do you think Kipling chose not to describe the battle scene and to end the story as he does? Do you like the way it ends?

____

____

____

Thinking About the Skill: A knowledge of which literary skill—**plot, exposition, conflict, rising action, climax, falling action, resolution**—was the most helpful to you in understanding the story? Why?

____

____

____

Papa's Parrot

Cynthia Rylant

Summary

A boy named Harry Tillian once enjoyed visiting his father's candy store. As he grows older, however, he goes there less often. Meanwhile his father gets a talking parrot that he keeps in the store. Because his father talks so much to the parrot, Harry is embarrassed and goes to the store even less often. Then one day, Harry's father falls ills and has to go to the hospital. Harry goes to the store to help out. He is amazed when the parrot keeps saying, "Where's Harry? Miss him." Harry realizes the bird is echoing his father's words. After a long cry, Harry goes to visit his father at the hospital.

Visual Summary

Before Harry Starts Junior High	After Harry Starts Junior High	After Harry's Father Gets Ill
• Harry visits his father's candy and nut shop often.	• Harry stops going to his father's shop.	• Harry goes to his father's shop to take care of things.
• Harry's friends often stop by.	• His father gets a parrot that he names Rocky.	• The parrot keeps saying "Where's Harry?" and "Miss him."
	• Harry is embarrassed to see his father talking with the parrot.	• Harry realizes the parrot is echoing his father's words.
	• Harry's father gets ill and must go to the hospital.	• Harry weeps.
		• Harry goes to visit his father in the hospital.

◆ **Activate Prior Knowledge**

In "Papa's Parrot," a character suffers a heart attack. List three things that often happen when people have heart attacks. Think of people you know who have had them or discussions you have had with your parents or health care specialists.

1. ______________________

____

2. ______________________

____

3. ______________________

____

◆ **Literary Analysis**

Mark the Text

Writers reveal their characters' personalities through **characterization**. In **direct characterization**, the writer tells characters' traits directly. In the first bracketed passage, underline two things that direct characterization tells about Mr. Tillian's feelings.

◆ **Reading Strategy**

When you **identify with a character**, you put yourself in the character's place and think how you would react to the situations he or she is placed in. After reading the second bracketed passage, write how you would feel if your father talked to a parrot as Harry's does.

____

____

____

Papa's Parrot

Cynthia Rylant

Sometimes, as you grow older you become embarrassed by or dislike doing things that you enjoyed as a child. Sometimes those feelings of embarrassment or discomfort cause you to neglect important friendships and family relationships. This story is about a boy who neglects one of these relationships until he gains an important insight into his actions.

Though his father was fat and merely owned a candy and nut shop, Harry Tillian liked his papa. Harry stopped liking candy and nuts when he was around seven, but, in spite of this, he and Mr. Tillian had remained friends and were still friends the year Harry turned twelve.

For years, after school, Harry had always stopped in to see his father at work. Many of Harry's friends stopped there, too, to spend a few cents choosing penny candy from the giant bins or to sample Mr. Tillian's latest batch of roasted peanuts. Mr. Tillian looked forward to seeing his son and his son's friends every day. He liked the company.

When Harry entered junior high school, though, he didn't come by the candy and nut shop as often. Nor did his friends. They were older and they had more spending money. They went to a burger place. They played video games. They shopped for records. None of them were much interested in candy and nuts anymore.

A new group of children came to Mr. Tillian's shop now. But not Harry Tillian and his friends.

The year Harry turned twelve was also the year Mr. Tillian got a parrot. He went to a pet store one day and bought one for more money than he could really afford. He brought the parrot to his shop, set its cage near the sign for maple clusters, and named it Rocky.

Harry thought this was the strangest thing his father had ever done, and he told him so, but Mr. Tillian just ignored him.

Rocky was good company for Mr. Tillian. When business was slow, Mr. Tillian would turn on a small color television he had sitting in a corner, and he and Rocky would watch the soap operas. Rocky liked to scream when the romantic music came on, and Mr. Tillian would yell at him to shut up, but they seemed to enjoy themselves.

The more Mr. Tillian grew to like his parrot, and the more he talked to it instead of to people, the more embarrassed Harry became. Harry would stroll past the shop, on his way somewhere else, and he'd take a quick look inside to see what his dad was doing. Mr. Tillian was always talking to the bird. So Harry kept walking.

At home things were different. Harry and his father joked with each other at the dinner table as they always had—Mr. Tillian teasing Harry about his smelly socks; Harry teasing

Mr. Tillian about his blubbery stomach. At home things seemed all right.

But one day, Mr. Tillian became ill. He had been at work, unpacking boxes of caramels, when he had grabbed his chest and fallen over on top of the candy. A customer had found him, and he was taken to the hospital in an ambulance.

Mr. Tillian couldn't leave the hospital. He lay in bed, tubes in his arms, and he worried about his shop. New shipments of candy and nuts would be arriving. Rocky would be hungry. Who would take care of things?

Harry said he would. Harry told his father that he would go to the store every day after school and unpack boxes. He would sort out all the candy and nuts. He would even feed Rocky.

So, the next morning, while Mr. Tillian lay in his hospital bed, Harry took the shop key to school with him. After school he left his friends and walked to the empty shop alone. In all the days of his life, Harry had never seen the shop closed after school. Harry didn't even remember what the CLOSED sign looked like. The key stuck in the lock three times, and inside he had to search all the walls for the light switch.

The shop was as his father had left it. Even the caramels were still spilled on the floor. Harry bent down and picked them up one by one, dropping them back in the boxes. The bird in its cage watched him silently.

Harry opened the new boxes his father hadn't gotten to. Peppermints. Jawbreakers. Toffee creams. Strawberry kisses. Harry traveled from bin to bin, putting the candies where they belonged.

"Hello!"

Harry jumped, spilling a box of jawbreakers.

"Hello, Rocky!"

Harry stared at the parrot. He had forgotten it was there. The bird had been so quiet, and Harry had been thinking only of the candy.

"Hello," Harry said.

"Hello, Rocky!" answered the parrot.

Harry walked slowly over to the cage. The parrot's food cup was empty. Its water was dirty. The bottom of the cage was a mess.

Harry carried the cage into the back room.

"Hello, Rocky!"

"Is that all you can say, you dumb bird?" Harry mumbled. The bird said nothing else.

Harry cleaned the bottom of the cage, refilled the food and water cups, and then put the cage back in its place and resumed sorting the candy.

Vocabulary Development: resumed (ri zo͞omd′) *v.* began again; continued

◆ Literary Analysis

A **narrator's description** consists of details that tell about a character's appearance, thoughts, feelings, or personality traits. After reading the first bracketed passage, underline three details that describe Mr. Tillian's condition.

Mark the Text

◆ Stop to Reflect

How might Harry feel going to his father's store after his father had had a heart attack?

___

___

___

◆ Stop to Reflect

In **indirect characterization**, the writer reveals his characters' personalities through their own words, thoughts, and actions, as well as by what other characters say to or about them. List two examples of indirect characterization in the second bracketed passage and explain how they are characteristics of Harry's.

1. ___

___

___

2. ___

___

___

"Where's Harry?"

Harry looked up.

"Where's Harry?"

Harry stared at the parrot.

"Where's Harry?"

Chills ran down Harry's back. What could the bird mean? It was something from "The Twilight Zone."[1]

"Where's Harry?"

Harry swallowed and said, "I'm here. I'm here, you stupid bird."

"You stupid bird!" said the parrot.

Well, at least he's got one thing straight, thought Harry.

"Miss him! Miss him! Where's Harry? You stupid bird!"

Harry stood with a handful of peppermints.

"What?" he asked.

"Where's Harry?" said the parrot.

"I'm here, you stupid bird! I'm here!" Harry yelled. He threw the peppermints at the cage, and the bird screamed and clung to its perch.

Harry sobbed, "I'm here." The tears were coming.

Harry leaned over the glass counter.

"Papa." Harry buried his face in his arms.

"Where's Harry?" repeated the bird.

Harry sighed and wiped his face on his sleeve. He watched the parrot. He understood now: someone had been saying, for a long time, "Where's Harry? Miss him."

Harry finished his unpacking and then swept the floor of the shop. He checked the furnace so the bird wouldn't get cold. Then he left to go visit his papa.

---

1. **"The Twilight Zone"** science-fiction television series from the 1960s.

◆ Reading Check

Why does the parrot say, "Where's Harry?"

___

___

___

◆ Literary Analysis

Name two things you learn about Harry's **character** from his reaction to what Rocky says.

1. ___

___

2. ___

___

◆ Literary Analysis

Is the underlined sentence an example of **direct** or **indirect characterization**? Why?

___

___

___

◆ Reading Strategy

After reading the bracketed passage, write how you would feel if you were in Harry's shoes.

___

___

___

___

Reader's Response: Do you think Harry's behavior toward his father might change? Explain.

___

___

___

Thinking About the Skill: Why might **indirect characterization** be more challenging to read but ultimately more satisfying than **direct characterization**?

___

___

___

___

PREVIEW

Ribbons

Laurence Yep

Summary

Stacy's grandmother comes from Hong Kong to live with the family. It is difficult for the family and especially Stacy, who must give her grandmother her room. Grandmother knows some English, but she seems to favor Stacy's brother Ian, who has learned some Chinese. Then the grandmother gets upset with Stacy's riboned ballet shoes and demands the ribbons be destroyed. Stacy is very upset until she learns that her grandmother, as a child in China, was forced to bind her feet with ribbons. This painful old practice supposedly made Chinese women more beautiful. But it has left the grandmother's feet all twisted and aching. She objected to the riboned ballet shoes because she thought the custom was similar. But Stacy explains it is not and dances for her. The two finally bond.

Visual Summary

Grandmother	Grandfather
• feet bound in ribbons in China to be "beautiful" • removed ribbons created great pain • now comes to U.S. and stays in Stacy's room • reacts badly to Stacy's ballet-shoe ribbons • finally accepts Stacy's ballet dancing	• died in China
Stacy's Mother	**Stacy's Father**
• saved as baby by mother in China • tries to make mother comfortable in U.S. • takes Stacy's ballet-shoe ribbon at mother's request • has promised not to speak of mother's bad feet	• unpacks car for Grandmother • cannot afford Stacy's ballet and settling Grandmother • is not of Chinese background
Stacy	**Ian**
• gives up room and ballet lessons for Grandmother • thinks Grandmother likes Ian because he looks Chinese • doesn't understand Grandmother's reaction to her ballet-shoe ribbons • sees Grandmother's damaged feet and learns why Grandmother hated her shoe ribbons • shows the ballet she loves to Grandmother • bonds with Grandmother and realizes shared love	• younger than Stacy • bow of greeting pleases Grandmother • learns more Chinese to talk with Grandmother • looks more like Chinese mother than Stacy does

◆ Activate Prior Knowledge

Think of a time that you encountered something or someone from a culture very different from yours. Describe this experience and what you learned from it.

____

____

____

____

____

____

◆ Literary Analysis

A story's **theme** is its central message or insight into life. A story can have more than one theme, but there is usually one main theme. In the bracketed passage, see if you can figure out what a theme of the story might be.

____

____

____

____

◆ Reading Strategy

Asking questions as you read helps you understand a story and figure out its theme. After reading the bracketed passage, write three questions you might ask to help you figure out a theme of the story.

1. ______________________________

____

2. ______________________________

____

3. ______________________________

____

Ribbons

Laurence Yep

In this story, a young girl discovers that by drawing upon an older person's experiences—her grandmother's—she can learn some new ideas, gain insights, and develop empathy that she might not have learned on her own. In turn, the girl shares ideas and customs from her own culture with her grandmother and, by so doing, strengthens the bond between them.

The sunlight swept over the broad grassy square, across the street, and onto our living-room rug. In that bright, warm rectangle of light, I practiced my ballet. Ian, my little brother, giggled and dodged around me while I did my exercises.

A car stopped outside, and Ian rushed to the window. "She's here! She's here!" he shouted excitedly. "Paw-paw's here!" *Paw-paw* is Chinese for grandmother—for "mother's mother."

I squeezed in beside Ian so I could look out the window, too. Dad's head was just disappearing as he leaned into the trunk of the car. A pile of luggage and cardboard boxes wrapped in rope sat by the curb. "Is that all Grandmother's?" I said. I didn't see how it would fit into my old bedroom.

Mom laughed behind me. "We're lucky she had to leave her furniture behind in Hong Kong." Mom had been trying to get her mother to come to San Francisco for years. Grandmother had finally agreed, but only because the British were going to return the city to the Chinese Communists in 1997. Because Grandmother's airfare and legal expenses had been so high, there wasn't room in the family budget for Madame Oblomov's ballet school. I'd had to stop my daily lessons.

The rear car door opened, and a pair of carved black canes poked out like six-shooters. "Wait, Paw-paw," Dad said, and slammed the trunk shut. He looked sweaty and harassed.

Grandmother, however, was already using her canes to get to her feet. "I'm not helpless," she insisted to Dad.

Ian was relieved. "She speaks English," he said.

"She worked for a British family for years," Mom explained.

Turning, Ian ran toward the stairs. "I've got the door," he cried. Mom and I caught up with him at the front door and made him wait on the porch. "You don't want to knock her over," I said. For weeks, Mom had been rehearsing us for just this moment. Ian was supposed to wait, but in his excitement he began bowing to Grandmother as she struggled up the outside staircase.

Grandmother was a small woman in a padded silk jacket

and black slacks. Her hair was pulled back into a bun behind her head. On her small feet she wore a pair of quilted cotton slippers shaped like boots, with furred tops that hid her ankles.

"What's wrong with her feet?" I whispered to Mom.

"They've always been that way. And don't mention it," she said. "She's sensitive about them."

I was instantly curious. "But what happened to them?"

"Wise grandchildren wouldn't ask," Mom warned.

Mom bowed formally as Grandmother reached the porch. "I'm so glad you're here," she said.

Grandmother gazed past us to the stairway leading up to our second-floor apartment. "Why do you have to have so many steps?" she said.

Mom sounded as meek as a child. "I'm sorry, Mother," she said.

Dad tried to change the subject. "That's Stacy, and this little monster is Ian."

"*Joe sun, Paw-paw,*" I said. "Good morning, Grandmother." It was afternoon, but that was the only Chinese I knew, and I had been practicing it.

Mother had coached us on a proper Chinese greeting for the last two months, but I thought Grandmother also deserved an American-style bear hug. However, when I tried to put my arms around her and kiss her, she stiffened in surprise. "Nice children don't drool on people," she snapped at me.

To Ian, anything worth doing was worth repeating, so he bowed again. "*Joe sun, Paw-paw.*"

Grandmother brightened in an instant. "He has your eyes," she said to Mom.

Mom bent and hefted Ian into her arms. "Let me show you our apartment. You'll be in Stacy's room."

Grandmother didn't even thank me. Instead, she stumped up the stairs after Mom, trying to coax a smile from Ian, who was staring at her over Mom's shoulder.

Grandmother's climb was long, slow, laborious. *Thump, thump, thump.* Her canes struck the boards as she slowly mounted the steps. It sounded like the slow, steady beat of a mechanical heart.

Vocabulary Development: **sensitive** (sen´ sə tiv´) *adj.* easily hurt or irritated; touchy
meek (mēk) *adj.* timid; humble; not showing anger
coax (kōks) *v.* use gentle persuasion
laborious (la bôr´ ē əs) *adj.* taking much work or effort; difficult

◆ Reading Strategy

Mark the Text Underline the question that Stacy asks about her grandmother's feet. Then answer these **questions**: 1) Is it a question you might have asked about the story if Stacy hadn't? 2) Why do you think Stacy's mother does not answer Stacy's question? 3) Why do you think the writer does not let his readers know the answer at this time?

1. ______

2. ______

______

______

3. ______

______

______

◆ Reading Strategy

Mark the Text In the bracketed passage, underline two examples of how Stacy's grandmother treats her. Next, **ask** yourself this **question**: Will Grandmother's treatment of Stacy affect Stacy's attitude towards her? Then write what you think the answer to that question is.

______

______

______

______

◆ **Stop to Reflect**

Imagine the Grandmother's trip walking to Hong Kong with a baby strapped on her back. How does this bit of information affect what you think about the Grandmother?

◆ **Reading Check**

Why is Stacy so interested in her grandmother's belongings? What is her reaction after examining them?

◆ **Literary Analysis**

Name a theme of the story suggested in the bracketed passage.

Mom had told us her mother's story often enough. When Mom's father died, Grandmother had strapped my mother to her back and walked across China to Hong Kong to escape the Communists who had taken over her country. I had always thought her trek was heroic, but it seemed even braver when I realized how wobbly she was on her feet.

I was going to follow Grandmother, but Dad waved me down to the sidewalk. "I need you to watch your grandmother's things until I finish bringing them up," he said. He took a suitcase in either hand and set off, catching up with Grandmother at the foot of the first staircase.

While I waited for him to come back, I inspected Grandmother's pile of belongings. The boxes, webbed with tight cords, were covered with words in Chinese and English. I could almost smell their exotic scent, and in my imagination I pictured sunlit waters lapping at picturesque docks. Hong Kong was probably as exotic to me as America was to Grandmother. Almost without thinking, I began to dance.

Dad came back out, his face red from exertion. "I wish I had half your energy," he said. Crouching, he used the cords to lift a box in each hand.

I pirouetted,[1] and the world spun round and round. "Madame Oblomov said I should still practice every day." I had waited for this day not only for Grandmother's sake but for my own. "Now that Grandmother's here, can I begin my ballet lessons again?" I asked.

Dad turned toward the house. "We'll see, hon."

Disappointment made me protest. "But you said I had to give up the lessons so we could bring her from Hong Kong," I said. "Well, she's here."

Dad hesitated and then set the boxes down. "Try to understand, hon. We've got to set your grandmother up in her own apartment. That's going to take even more money. Don't you want your room back?"

Poor Dad. He looked tired and worried. I should have shut up, but I loved ballet almost as much as I loved him. "Madame put me in the fifth division even though I'm only eleven. If I'm absent much longer, she might make me start over again with the beginners."

"It'll be soon. I promise." He looked guilty as he picked up the boxes and struggled toward the stairs.

Dad had taken away the one hope that had kept me going during my exile[2] from Madame. Suddenly I felt lost, and the following weeks only made me more confused. Mom started laying down all sorts of new rules. First, we couldn't run around or make noise because Grandmother had to rest.

---

1. **pirouetted** (pir′ o͞o et′ əd) *v.* whirled around on the point of the toe.
2. **exile** (eg′ zīl′) *n.* forced absence.

Then we couldn't watch our favorite TV shows because Grandmother couldn't understand them. Instead, we had to watch Westerns on one of the cable stations because it was easier for her to figure out who was the good guy and who was the bad one.

Worst of all, Ian got all of her attention—and her candy and anything else she could bribe him with. It finally got to me on a warm Sunday afternoon a month after she had arrived. I'd just returned home from a long walk in the park with some friends. I was looking forward to something cool and sweet, when I found her giving Ian an ice cream bar I'd bought for myself. "But that was my ice cream bar," I complained as he gulped it down.

"Big sisters need to share with little brothers," Grandmother said, and she patted him on the head to encourage him to go on eating.

When I complained to Mom about how Grandmother was spoiling Ian, she only sighed. "He's a boy, Stacy. Back in China, boys are everything."

It wasn't until I saw Grandmother and Ian together the next day that I thought I really understood why she treated him so much better. She was sitting on a kitchen chair with her head bent over next to his. She had taught Ian enough Chinese so that they could hold short, simple conversations. With their faces so close, I could see how much alike they were.

Ian and I both have the same brown eyes, but his hair is black, while mine is brown, like Dad's. In fact, everything about Ian looks more Chinese. Except for the shape of my eyes, I look as Caucasian as Dad. And yet people sometimes stare at me as if I were a freak. I've always told myself that it's because they're ignorant and never learned manners, but it was really hard to have my own grandmother make me feel that way.

Even so, I kept telling myself: Grandmother is a hero. She saved my mother. She'll like me just as much as she likes Ian once she gets to know me. And, I thought in a flash, the best way to know a person is to know what she loves. For me, that was the ballet.

Ever since Grandmother had arrived, I'd been practicing my ballet privately in the room I now shared with Ian. Now I got out the special box that held my satin toe shoes. I had been so proud when Madame said I was ready to use them. I was the youngest girl on pointe[3] at Madame's school. As I lifted them out, the satin ribbons fluttered down around my wrists as if in a welcoming caress. I slipped one of the shoes

3. **on pointe** (pwant) *n.* dancing on the tip of the toe.

◆ Reading Strategy

What **question** might you ask yourself about Grandmother's treatment of Ian?

◆ Literary Analysis

How might the bracketed passage relate to a **theme** of the story?

◆ Reading Strategy

Read the underlined sentences. Then **ask a question** that relates Stacy's feelings to her grandmother's feelings.

◆ Reading Check

Underline the answer to this question: What does Stacy decide to do to get her grandmother to like her?

◆ **Reading Strategy**

What **question** might you ask about the situation in the bracketed passage?

◆ **Stop to Reflect**

In the incident of the toe-shoe ribbons, who doesn't understand whom? Who is in a position to help fix the misunderstanding?

◆ **Literary Analysis**

How does Stacy's mother's statement in the underlined sentence relate to a **theme** of the story?

◆ **Reading Check**

Underline the answer to this question: Why doesn't Stacy's mother stand up for her?

Mark the Text

onto my foot, but when I tried to tie the ribbons around my ankles, the ribbons came off in my hands.

I could have asked Mom to help me reattach them, but then I remembered that at one time Grandmother had supported her family by being a seamstress.

Grandmother was sitting in the big recliner in the living room. She stared uneasily out the window as if she were gazing not upon the broad, green lawn of the square but upon a Martian desert.

"Paw-paw," I said, "can you help me?"

Grandmother gave a start when she turned around and saw the ribbons dangling from my hand. Then she looked down at my bare feet, which were callused from three years of daily lessons. When she looked back at the satin ribbons, it was with a hate and disgust that I had never seen before. "Give those to me." She held out her hand.

I clutched the ribbons tightly against my stomach. "Why?"

"They'll ruin your feet." She lunged toward me and tried to snatch them away.

Angry and bewildered, I retreated a few steps and showed her the shoe. "No, they're for dancing!"

All Grandmother could see, though, was the ribbons. She managed to totter to her feet without the canes and almost fell forward on her face. Somehow, she regained her balance. Arms reaching out, she stumbled clumsily after me. "Lies!" she said.

"It's the truth!" I backed up so fast that I bumped into Mom as she came running from the kitchen.

Mom immediately assumed it was my fault. "Stop yelling at your grandmother!" she said.

By this point, I was in tears. "She's taken everything else. Now she wants my toe-shoe ribbons."

Grandmother panted as she leaned on Mom. "How could you do that to your own daughter?"

"It's not like you think," Mom tried to explain.

However, Grandmother was too upset to listen. "Take them away!"

Mom helped Grandmother back to her easy chair. "You don't understand," Mom said.

All Grandmother did was stare at the ribbons as she sat back down in the chair. "Take them away. Burn them. Bury them."

Mom sighed. "Yes, Mother."

As Mom came over to me, I stared at her in amazement. "Aren't you going to stand up for me?"

But she acted as if she wanted to break any ties between us. "Can't you see how worked up Paw-paw is?" she whispered. "She won't listen to reason. Give her some time. Let her cool off." She worked the ribbons away from my stunned fingers. Then she also took the shoe.

For the rest of the day, Grandmother just turned away every time Mom and I tried to raise the subject. It was as if she didn't want to even think about satin ribbons.

That evening, after the dozenth attempt, I finally said to Mom, "She's so weird. What's so bad about satin ribbons?"

"She associates them with something awful that happened to her," Mom said.

That puzzled me even more. "What was that?"

She shook her head. "I'm sorry. She made me promise never to talk about it to anyone."

The next morning, I decided that if Grandmother was going to be mean to me, then I would be mean to her. I began to ignore her. When she entered a room I was in, I would deliberately turn around and leave.

For the rest of the day, things got more and more tense. Then I happened to go into the bathroom early that evening. The door wasn't locked, so I thought it was unoccupied, but Grandmother was sitting fully clothed on the edge of the bathtub. Her slacks were rolled up to her knees and she had her feet soaking in a pan of water.

"Don't you know how to knock?" she snapped, and dropped a towel over her feet.

However, she wasn't quick enough, because I saw her bare feet for the first time. Her feet were like taffy that someone had stretched out and twisted. Each foot bent downward in a way that feet were not meant to, and her toes stuck out at odd angles, more like lumps than toes. I didn't think she had all ten of them, either.

"What happened to your feet?" I whispered in shock.

Looking ashamed, Grandmother flapped a hand in the air for me to go. "None of your business. Now get out."

She must have said something to Mom, though, because that night Mom came in and sat on my bed. Ian was outside playing with Grandmother. "Your grandmother's very upset, Stacy," Mom said.

"I didn't mean to look," I said. "It was horrible." Even when I closed my eyes, I could see her mangled feet.

I opened my eyes when I felt Mom's hand on my shoulder. "She was so ashamed of them that she didn't like even me to see them," she said.

"What happened to them?" I wondered.

Mom's forehead furrowed as if she wasn't sure how to explain things. "There was a time back in China when people thought women's feet had to be shaped a certain way to look beautiful. When a girl was about five, her mother would gradually bend her toes under the sole of her foot."

"Ugh." Just thinking about it made my own feet ache. "Her own mother did that to her?"

Mom smiled apologetically. "Her mother and father thought

◆ Reading Check

Stacy's mother gives her a clue as to why Grandmother was so upset about the ribbons. Underline it. Then circle the reason that she won't tell Stacy anything more.

Mark THE Text

◆ Reading Strategy

After reading the bracketed passage, **ask** yourself a **question** about Stacy's decision.

____

____

____

◆ Stop to Reflect

Why do you think Grandmother was so mean to Stacy when she accidentally walked in on her in the bathroom?

____

____

____

____

◆ Literary Analysis

How does Mom's explanation about Grandmother's feet relate to a **theme** of the story?

____

____

____

____

it would make their little girl attractive so she could marry a rich man. They were still doing it in some of the back areas of China long after it was outlawed in the rest of the country."

I shook my head. "There's nothing lovely about those feet."

"I know. But they were usually bound up in silk ribbons." Mom brushed some of the hair from my eyes. "Because they were a symbol of the old days, Paw-paw undid the ribbons as soon as we were free in Hong Kong—even though they kept back the pain."

I was even more puzzled now. "How did the ribbons do that?"

Mom began to brush my hair with quick, light strokes. "The ribbons kept the blood from circulating freely and bringing more feeling to her feet. Once the ribbons were gone, her feet ached. They probably still do."

I rubbed my own foot in sympathy. "But she doesn't complain."

"That's how tough she is," Mom said.

Finally the truth dawned on me. "And she mistook my toe-shoe ribbons for her old ones."

Mom lowered the brush and nodded solemnly. "And she didn't want you to go through the same pain she had."

I guess Grandmother loved me in her own way. When she came into the bedroom with Ian later that evening, I didn't leave. However, she tried to ignore me—as if I had become tainted by her secret.

When Ian demanded a story, I sighed. "All right. But only one."

Naturally, Ian chose the fattest story he could, which was my old collection of fairy tales by Hans Christian Andersen. Years of reading had cracked the spine so that the book fell open automatically in his hands to the story that had been my favorite when I was small. It was the original story of "The Little Mermaid"—not the cartoon. The picture illustrating the tale showed the mermaid posed like a ballerina in the middle of the throne room.

"This one," Ian said, and pointed to the picture of the Little Mermaid.

When Grandmother and Ian sat down on my bed, I began to read. However, when I got to the part where the Little Mermaid could walk on land, I stopped.

Ian was impatient. "Come on, read," he ordered, patting the page.

"After that," I went on, "each step hurt her as if she were walking on a knife." I couldn't help looking up at Grandmother.

This time she was the one to pat the page. "Go on. Tell me more about the mermaid."

So I went on reading to the very end, where the Little Mermaid changes into sea foam. "That's a dumb ending," Ian

◆ **Reading Check**

What truth "finally dawns" on Stacy?

____

____

____

◆ **Stop to Reflect**

Do you think Stacy's grandmother really does love her? Explain. Does her treatment of Stacy change? Why or why not?

____

____

____

____

____

◆ **Reading Strategy**

Write a **question** about Stacy and her grandmother's relationship based on the bracketed passage.

____

____

____

____

said. "Who wants to be pollution?"

"Sea foam isn't pollution. It's just bubbles," I explained. "The important thing was that she wanted to walk even though it hurt."

"I would rather have gone on swimming," Ian insisted.

"But maybe she wanted to see new places and people by going on the land," Grandmother said softly. "If she had kept her tail, the land people would have thought she was odd. They might even have made fun of her."

When she glanced at her own feet, I thought she might be talking about herself—so I seized my chance. "My satin ribbons aren't like your old silk ones. I use them to tie my toe shoes on when I dance." Setting the book down, I got out my other shoe. "Look."

Grandmother fingered the dangling ribbons and then pointed at my bare feet. "But you already have calluses there."

I began to dance before Grandmother could stop me. After a minute, I struck a pose on half-toe. "See? I can move fine."

She took my hand and patted it clumsily. I think it was the first time she had showed me any sign of affection. "When I saw those ribbons, I didn't want you feeling pain like I do."

I covered her hands with mine. "I just wanted to show you what I love best—dancing."

"And I love my children," she said. I could hear the ache in her voice. "And my grandchildren. I don't want anything bad to happen to you."

<u>Suddenly I felt as if there were an invisible ribbon binding us, tougher than silk and satin, stronger even than steel; and it joined her to Mom and Mom to me.</u>

I wanted to hug her so badly that I just did. Though she was stiff at first, she gradually softened in my arms.

"'Let me have my ribbons and my shoes," I said in a low voice. "Let me dance."

"Yes, yes," she whispered fiercely.

I felt something on my cheek and realized she was crying, and then I began crying, too.

"So much to learn," she said, and began hugging me back. "So much to learn."

Reader's Response: How might you have tried to clear up the bad feelings between Stacy and her grandmother?

____

____

Thinking About the Skill: How does pausing to **ask questions** help your comprehension of this story? Give an example.

____

____

◆ Reading Check

Answer these three questions after reading the bracketed passage. 1) Whom is Grandmother really talking about? 2) What makes you think so? 3) Why is she saying these things?

1. ______________________________

____

2. ______________________________

____

3. ______________________________

____

◆ Stop to Reflect

What was Grandmother really trying to do when she took Stacy's ribbons away? What does this say about how she feels about Stacy?

____

____

____

____

____

____

◆ Literary Analysis

How does the underlined sentence relate to a **theme** of the story?

____

____

____

____

____

PREVIEW

The Treasure of Lemon Brown

Walter Dean Myers

Summary

One night, Greg leaves home so he doesn't have to listen to his father's complaints about how badly Greg is doing in school. In an abandoned building near his home, Greg meets Lemon Brown, a homeless man who was once a noted blues musician. Brown proudly shows Greg old newspaper reviews of his performances—reviews that Brown's son was carrying when he died in the war. Greg returns home with a new respect for his own father.

Visual Summary

Greg's Attitude in the Beginning	Events That Change Greg's Attitude	Greg's Attitude in the End
• angry with father for lecturing him about schoolwork and not letting him play basketball • not interested in father's proud talk of passing test for postal service and years of hard work • tries to avoid father but ducks into empty building when rain starts	• meets Lemon Brown, who talks of his "treasure" • helps Brown frighten off troublemakers coming after Brown's treasure • looks at Brown's "treasure"—Brown's old harmonica and clippings of his successful blues career. Brown gave these to his son when son went off to war. They were returned when his son died.	• is happy to go home, even if only to his father's lecture • sees his father's hopes for him as a kind of treasure

The Treasure of Lemon Brown

Walter Dean Myers

In "The Treasure of Lemon Brown," a teenager meets a man who was once a famous blues musician. Blues, which has an African American heritage, is a style of music that has strongly influenced other forms of music, such as jazz and rock. Blues lyrics typically deal with loneliness, sorrow, sad love stories, and life's troubles. As you will discover in the story, Lemon Brown's life has certainly given him the right to sing the blues.

The dark sky, filled with angry, swirling clouds, reflected Greg Ridley's mood as he sat on the stoop of his building. His father's voice came to him again, first reading the letter the principal had sent to the house, then lecturing endlessly about his poor efforts in math.

"I had to leave school when I was thirteen," his father had said, "that's a year younger than you are now. If I'd had half the chances that you have, I'd . . ."

Greg had sat in the small, pale green kitchen listening, knowing the lecture would end with his father saying he couldn't play ball with the Scorpions. He had asked his father the week before, and his father had said it depended on his next report card. It wasn't often the Scorpions took on new players, especially fourteen-year-olds, and this was a chance of a lifetime for Greg. He hadn't been allowed to play high school ball, which he had really wanted to do, but playing for the Community Center team was the next best thing. Report cards were due in a week, and Greg had been hoping for the best. But the principal had ended the suspense early when she sent that letter saying Greg would probably fail math if he didn't spend more time studying.

"And you want to play *basketball*?" His father's brows knitted over deep brown eyes. "That must be some kind of a joke. Now you just get into your room and hit those books."

That had been two nights before. His father's words, like the distant thunder that now echoed through the streets of Harlem, still rumbled softly in his ears.

It was beginning to cool. Gusts of wind made bits of paper dance between the parked cars. There was a flash of nearby lightning, and soon large drops of rain splashed onto his jeans. He stood to go upstairs, thought of the lecture that probably awaited him if he did anything except shut himself in his room with his math book, and started walking down the street instead. Down the block there was an old tenement[1] that had been abandoned for some months. Some of

◆ Activate Prior Knowledge

In this story, a young boy learns some things about life from an older person. Think about a time when you, or someone you know, gained ideas, information, or skills from communicating with an older person. Describe your experience.

______

______

______

______

______

______

◆ Reading Strategy

What **questions** might you ask about the relationship between Greg and his father? Write two of your questions.

1. ______

______

2. ______

______

◆ Literary Analysis

How might Greg and his father's relationship be related to a **theme** of the story?

______

______

______

______

______

1. **tenement** (ten´ əh mənt) *n.* old, run-down apartment house.

◆ **Reading Strategy**

It is sometimes helpful to **ask questions** about what the writer wants you to know about something. What does the writer want you to know about Greg's neighborhood?

◆ **Literary Analysis**

Underline the sentence in the bracketed passage that you think might be related to one of the **themes** of the story. In what way might this sentence point to a theme?

Mark the Text

◆ **Stop to Reflect**

How would you feel if you were Greg in the basement of this building?

the guys had held an impromptu checker tournament there the week before, and Greg had noticed that the door, once boarded over, had been slightly ajar.

Pulling his collar up as high as he could, he checked for traffic and made a dash across the street. He reached the house just as another flash of lightning changed the night to day for an instant, then returned the graffiti-scarred building to the grim shadows. He vaulted over the outer stairs and pushed tentatively on the door. It was open, and he let himself in.

The inside of the building was dark except for the dim light that filtered through the dirty windows from the streetlamps. There was a room a few feet from the door, and from where he stood at the entrance, Greg could see a squarish patch of light on the floor. He entered the room, frowning at the musty smell. It was a large room that might have been someone's parlor at one time. Squinting, Greg could see an old table on its side against one wall, what looked like a pile of rags or a torn mattress in the corner, and a couch, with one side broken, in front of the window.

He went to the couch. The side that wasn't broken was comfortable enough, though a little creaky. From the spot he could see the blinking neon sign over the bodega[2] on the corner. He sat awhile, watching the sign blink first green then red, allowing his mind to drift to the Scorpions, then to his father. His father had been a postal worker for all Greg's life, and was proud of it, often telling Greg how hard he had worked to pass the test. Greg had heard the story too many times to be interested now.

For a moment Greg thought he heard something that sounded like a scraping against the wall. He listened carefully, but it was gone.

Outside the wind had picked up, sending the rain against the window with a force that shook the glass in its frame. A car passed, its tires hissing over the wet street and its red taillights glowing in the darkness.

Greg thought he heard the noise again. His stomach tightened as he held himself still and listened intently. There weren't any more scraping noises, but he was sure he had heard something in the darkness—something breathing!

He tried to figure out just where the breathing was coming

Vocabulary Development: **impromptu** (im prämp´ to͞o) *adj.* unscheduled; unplanned
ajar (ə jär´) *adj.* open
tentatively (ten´ tə tiv lē) *adv.* hesitantly; with uncertainty

2. **bodega** (bō dā´ gə) *n.* small grocery store serving a Latino neighborhood.

from; he knew it was in the room with him. Slowly he stood, tensing. As he turned, a flash of lightning lit up the room, frightening him with its sudden brilliance. He saw nothing, just the overturned table, the pile of rags and an old newspaper on the floor. Could he have been imagining the sounds? He continued listening, but heard nothing and thought that it might have just been rats. Still, he thought, as soon as the rain let up he would leave. He went to the window and was about to look when he heard a voice behind him.

"Don't try nothin' 'cause I got a razor here sharp enough to cut a week into nine days!"

Greg, except for an involuntary tremor[3] in his knees, stood stock still. The voice was high and brittle, like dry twigs being broken, surely not one he had ever heard before. There was a shuffling sound as the person who had been speaking moved a step closer. Greg turned, holding his breath, his eyes straining to see in the dark room.

The upper part of the figure before him was still in darkness. The lower half was in the dim rectangle of light that fell unevenly from the window. There were two feet, in cracked, dirty shoes from which rose legs that were wrapped in rags.

"Who are you?" Greg hardly recognized his own voice.

"I'm Lemon Brown," came the answer. "Who're you?"

"Greg Ridley."

"What you doing here?" The figure shuffled forward again, and Greg took a small step backward.

"It's raining," Greg said.

"I can see that," the figure said.

The person who called himself Lemon Brown peered forward, and Greg could see him clearly. He was an old man. His black, heavily wrinkled face was surrounded by a halo of crinkly white hair and whiskers that seemed to separate his head from the layers of dirty coats piled on his smallish frame. His pants were bagged to the knee, where they were met with rags that went down to the old shoes. The rags were held on with strings, and there was a rope around his middle. Greg relaxed. He had seen the man before, picking through the trash on the corner and pulling clothes out of a Salvation Army box. There was no sign of the razor that could "cut a week into nine days."

"What are you doing here?" Greg asked.

"This is where I'm staying," Lemon Brown said. "What you here for?"

"Told you it was raining out," Greg said, leaning against

3. **involuntary** (in väl′ ən ter′ ē) **tremor** (trem′ ər) *n.* automatic trembling or shaking.

◆ **Reading Strategy**

After reading the underlined sentence, what **question** might you ask about it?

____

____

____

____

◆ **Reading Check**

Underline three details that describe Lemon Brown.

Mark the Text

◆ **Reading Check**

Why does Greg relax when he sees that the owner of the voice is Lemon Brown?

____

____

____

◆ Reading Strategy

After reading the underlined passage, what **question** might you ask about it?

◆ Literary Analysis

What does Lemon Brown mean when he says, "Every man got a treasure"? How is this statement related to a **theme** of the story?

◆ Literary Analysis

In the bracketed passage, what can Greg learn about handling his anger from Lemon Brown's attitude about his poor fortunes? How is this attitude related to a theme of the story?

the back of the couch until he felt it give slightly.

"Ain't you got no home?"

"I got a home," Greg answered.

"You ain't one of them bad boys looking for my treasure, is you?" Lemon Brown cocked his head to one side and squinted one eye. "Because I told you I got me a razor."

"I'm not looking for your treasure," Greg answered, smiling. "*If* you have one."

"What you mean, *if* I have one," Lemon Brown said. "Every man got a treasure. You don't know that, you must be a fool!"

"Sure," Greg said as he sat on the sofa and put one leg over the back. "What do you have, gold coins?"

"Don't worry none about what I got," Lemon Brown said. "You know who I am?"

"You told me your name was orange or lemon or something like that."

"Lemon Brown," the old man said, pulling back his shoulders as he did so, "they used to call me Sweet Lemon Brown."

"Sweet Lemon?" Greg asked.

"Yessir. Sweet Lemon Brown. They used to say I sung the blues so sweet that if I sang at a funeral, the dead would commence to rocking with the beat. Used to travel all over Mississippi and as far as Monroe, Louisiana, and east on over to Macon, Georgia. You mean you ain't never heard of Sweet Lemon Brown?"

"Afraid not," Greg said. "What . . . what happened to you?"

"Hard times, boy. Hard times always after a poor man. One day I got tired, sat down to rest a spell and felt a tap on my shoulder. Hard times caught up with me."

"Sorry about that."

"What you doing here? How come you didn't go on home when the rain come? Rain don't bother you young folks none."

"Just didn't." Greg looked away.

"I used to have a knotty-headed boy just like you." Lemon Brown had half walked, half shuffled back to the corner and sat down against the wall. "Had them big eyes like you got, I used to call them moon eyes. Look into them moon eyes and see anything you want."

"How come you gave up singing the blues?" Greg asked.

"Didn't give it up," Lemon Brown said. "You don't give up the blues; they give you up. After a while you do good for yourself, and it ain't nothing but foolishness singing about how hard you got it. Ain't that right?"

"I guess so."

"What's that noise?" Lemon Brown asked, suddenly sitting upright.

Greg listened, and he heard a noise outside. He looked at Lemon Brown and saw the old man pointing toward the window.

Greg went to the window and saw three men, neighborhood thugs, on the stoop. One was carrying a length of pipe. Greg looked back toward Lemon Brown, who moved quietly across the room to the window. The old man looked out, then beckoned frantically for Greg to follow him. For a moment Greg couldn't move. Then he found himself following Lemon Brown into the hallway and up darkened stairs. Greg followed as closely as he could. They reached the top of the stairs, and Greg felt Lemon Brown's hand first lying on his shoulder, then probing down his arm until he finally took Greg's hand into his own as they crouched in the darkness.

"They's bad men," Lemon Brown whispered. His breath was warm against Greg's skin.

"Hey! Rag man!" A voice called. "We know you in here. What you got up under them rags? You got any money?"

Silence.

"We don't want to have to come in and hurt you, old man, but we don't mind if we have to."

Lemon Brown squeezed Greg's hand in his own hard, gnarled fist.

There was a banging downstairs and a light as the men entered. They banged around noisily, calling for the rag man.

"We heard you talking about your treasure." The voice was slurred. "We just want to see it, that's all."

"You sure he's here?" One voice seemed to come from the room with the sofa.

"Yeah, he stays here every night."

"There's another room over there; I'm going to take a look. You got that flashlight?"

"Yeah, here, take the pipe too."

Greg opened his mouth to quiet the sound of his breath as he sucked it in uneasily. A beam of light hit the wall a few feet opposite him, then went out.

"Ain't nobody in that room," a voice said. "You think he gone or something?"

"I don't know," came the answer. "All I know is that I heard him talking about some kind of treasure. You know they found that shopping bag lady with that money in her bags."

"Yeah. You think he's upstairs?"

"HEY, OLD MAN, ARE YOU UP THERE?"

Silence.

"Watch my back, I'm going up."

◆ Reading Strategy

Write two **questions** that you might ask yourself about the situation in the bracketed passage.

1. ______________________________

____

2. ______________________________

____

◆ Literary Analysis

In the underlined passage, why does Lemon Brown squeeze Greg's hand? What might this situation have to do with a **theme** of the story?

____

____

____

____

____

____

◆ Stop to Reflect

What do you think the men are planning to do with the Lemon Brown's treasure?

____

____

____

◆ **Reading Strategy**

The tense situation in the first bracketed passage might prompt you to ask what Greg and Lemon Brown will do. How would you expect to find out the answer to this **question**?

◆ **Reading Strategy**

What **question** might you ask about what happens in the underlined sentence?

◆ **Reading Check**

Underline what Greg does to try to help the situation. Why does he do this?

Mark THE Text

◆ **Literary Analysis**

How does the second bracketed passage relate to a **theme** of the story?

There was a footstep on the stairs, and the beam from the flashlight danced crazily along the peeling wallpaper. Greg held his breath. There was another step and a loud crashing noise as the man banged the pipe against the wooden banister.[4] Greg could feel his temples throb as the man slowly neared them. Greg thought about the pipe, wondering what he would do when the man reached them—what he *could* do.

Then Lemon Brown released his hand and moved toward the top of the stairs. Greg looked around and saw stairs going up to the next floor. He tried waving to Lemon Brown, hoping the old man would see him in the dim light and follow him to the next floor. Maybe, Greg thought, the man wouldn't follow them up there. Suddenly, though, Lemon Brown stood at the top of the stairs, both arms raised high above his head.

"There he is!" A voice cried from below.

"Throw down your money, old man, so I won't have to bash your head in!"

Lemon Brown didn't move. Greg felt himself near panic. The steps came closer, and still Lemon Brown didn't move. He was an eerie sight, a bundle of rags standing at the top of the stairs, his shadow on the wall looming over him. Maybe, the thought came to Greg, the scene could be even eerier.

Greg wet his lips, put his hands to his mouth and tried to make a sound. Nothing came out. He swallowed hard, wet his lips once more and howled as evenly as he could.

"What's that?"

As Greg howled, the light moved away from Lemon Brown, but not before Greg saw him hurl his body down the stairs at the men who had come to take his treasure. There was a crashing noise, and then footsteps. A rush of warm air came in as the downstairs door opened, then there was only an ominous silence.

Greg stood on the landing. He listened, and after a while there was another sound on the staircase.

"Mr. Brown?" he called.

"Yeah, it's me," came the answer. "I got their flashlight."

Greg exhaled in relief as Lemon Brown made his way slowly back up the stairs.

"You OK?"

"Few bumps and bruises," Lemon Brown said.

"I think I'd better be going," Greg said, his breath returning to normal. "You'd better leave, too, before they come back."

"They may hang around outside for a while," Lemon Brown said, "but they ain't getting their nerve up to come in here again. Not with crazy old rag men and howling spooks.

4. **banister** (ban′ is tər) *n.* railing along a staircase.

Best you stay a while till the coast is clear. I'm heading out west tomorrow, out to east St. Louis."

"They were talking about treasures," Greg said. "You really have a treasure?"

"What I tell you? Didn't I tell you every man got a treasure?" Lemon Brown said. "You want to see mine?"

"If you want to show it to me," Greg shrugged.

"Let's look out the window first, see what them scoundrels be doing," Lemon Brown said.

They followed the oval beam of the flashlight into one of the rooms and looked out the window. They saw the men who had tried to take the treasure sitting on the curb near the corner. One of them had his pants leg up, looking at his knee.

"You sure you're not hurt?" Greg asked Lemon Brown.

"Nothing that ain't been hurt before," Lemon Brown said. "When you get as old as me all you say when something hurts is, 'Howdy, Mr. Pain, sees you back again.' Then when Mr. Pain see he can't worry you none, he go on mess with somebody else."

Greg smiled.

"Here, you hold this." Lemon Brown gave Greg the flashlight.

He sat on the floor near Greg and carefully untied the strings that held the rags on his right leg. When he took the rags away, Greg saw a piece of plastic. The old man carefully took off the plastic and unfolded it. He revealed some yellowed newspaper clippings and a battered harmonica.

"There it be," he said, nodding his head. "There it be."

Greg looked at the old man, saw the distant look in his eye, then turned to the clippings. They told of Sweet Lemon Brown, a blues singer and harmonica player who was appearing at different theaters in the South. One of the clippings said he had been the hit of the show, although not the headliner. All of the clippings were reviews of shows Lemon Brown had been in more than 50 years ago. Greg looked at the harmonica. It was dented badly on one side, with the reed holes on one end nearly closed.

"I used to travel around and make money for to feed my wife and Jesse—that's my boy's name. Used to feed them good, too. Then his mama died, and he stayed with his mama's sister. He growed up to be a man, and when the war come he saw fit to go off and fight in it. I didn't have nothing to give him except these things that told him who I was, and what he come from. If you know your pappy did something, you know you can do something too.

"Anyway, he went off to war, and I went off still playing and singing. 'Course by then I wasn't as much as I used to be, not without somebody to make it worth the while. You know what I mean?"

◆ **Reading Strategy**

What does the bracketed passage teach Greg about how to handle problems like pain?

____

____

____

____

◆ **Reading Check**

Mark the Text: Underline the sentence that tells what Lemon Brown's treasure is.

◆ **Literary Analysis**

What might the details about Lemon Brown's treasure tell you about a **theme** of the story?

____

____

____

____

____

◆ **Reading Check**

Underline two sentences that explain how Lemon Brown knows that his son thought Brown's treasure was important.

Mark THE Text

◆ **Reading Strategy**

What two **questions** might you ask about the bracketed passage?

1. ______________________________

____

2. ______________________________

____

◆ **Literary Analysis**

How does the underlined passage relate to a **theme** of the story?

____

____

____

____

____

____

◆ **Stop to Reflect**

Greg asks Lemon Brown if he really thought his treasure was worth fighting for. Do you? Why?

____

____

____

____

____

"Yeah," Greg nodded, not quite really knowing.

"I traveled around, and one time I come home, and there was this letter saying Jesse got killed in the war. Broke my heart, it truly did.

"They sent back what he had with him over there, and what it was is this old mouth fiddle and these clippings. Him carrying it around with him like that told me it meant something to him. That was my treasure, and when I give it to him he treated it just like that, a treasure. Ain't that something?"

"Yeah, I guess so," Greg said.

"You *guess* so?" Lemon Brown's voice rose an octave as he started to put his treasure back into the plastic. "Well, you got to guess 'cause you sure don't know nothing. Don't know enough to get home when it's raining."

"I *guess* . . . I mean, you're right."

"You OK for a youngster," the old man said as he tied the strings around his leg, "better than those scalawags[5] what come here looking for my treasure. That's for sure."

"You really think that treasure of yours was worth fighting for?" Greg asked. "Against a pipe?"

"What else a man got 'cepting what he can pass on to his son, or his daughter, if she be his oldest?" Lemon Brown said. "For a big-headed boy you sure do ask the foolishest questions."

Lemon Brown got up after patting his rags in place and looked out the window again.

"Looks like they're gone. You get on out of here and get yourself home. I'll be watching from the window so you'll be all right."

Lemon Brown went down the stairs behind Greg. When they reached the front door the old man looked out first, saw the street was clear and told Greg to scoot on home.

"You sure you'll be OK?" Greg asked.

"Now didn't I tell you I was going to east St. Louis in the morning?" Lemon Brown asked. "Don't that sound OK to you?"

"Sure it does," Greg said. "Sure it does. And you take care of that treasure of yours."

"That I'll do," Lemon said, the wrinkles about his eyes suggesting a smile. "That I'll do."

---

5. **scalawags** (skal′ ə wagz′) *n.* people who cause trouble; scoundrels.

The night had warmed and the rain had stopped, leaving puddles at the curbs. Greg didn't even want to think how late it was. He thought ahead of what his father would say and wondered if he should tell him about Lemon Brown. He thought about it until he reached his stoop, and decided against it. Lemon Brown would be OK, Greg thought, with his memories and his treasure.

Greg pushed the button over the bell marked Ridley, thought of the lecture he knew his father would give him, and smiled.

Reader's Response: Do you think Greg's behavior will be different after this experience? What would you do if you were Greg?

Thinking About the Skill: How has thinking about the various **themes** of the story helped your understanding of the story?

◆ Reading Strategy

Write two **questions** you might ask about the bracketed passage.

1.

2.

◆ Reading Strategy

In the underlined passage, why does Greg smile when he thinks about the lecture his father will give him? How does this attitude relate to a theme of the story?

How to Enjoy Poetry

James Dickey

Summary

The author of this essay loves poetry. He wants to help others enjoy it, too. He talks about the connections that words have with our hearts. He explains how rhyme and rhythm leave lasting impressions. He suggests ways that readers can think about poetry. He even encourages them to try writing it. Reading poetry, he says, can change your life.

Visual Summary

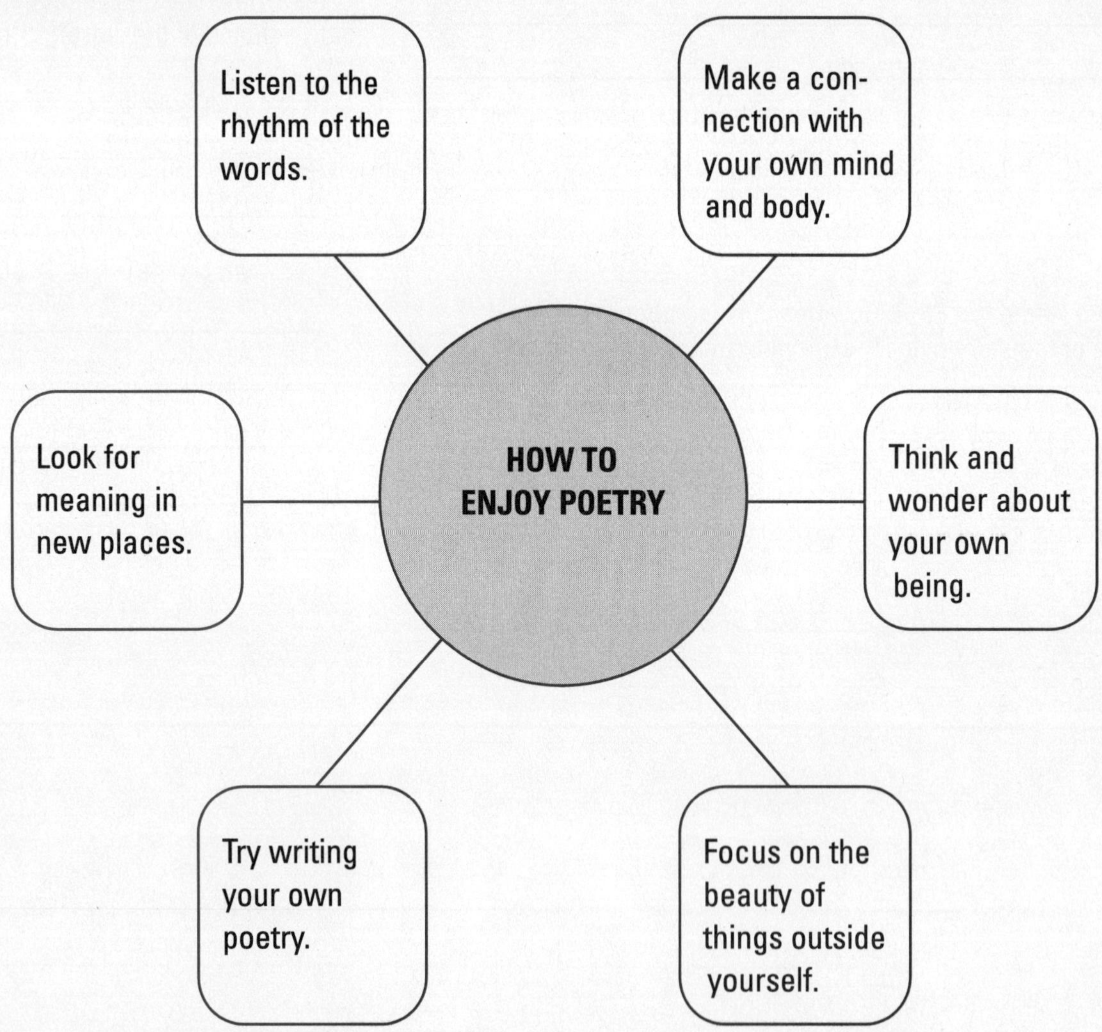

How to Enjoy Poetry

James Dickey

Poetry has existed for thousands of years. Originally, poets composed and recited long story-poems from memory. Rhythms and rhymes helped them create and remember these works.

What is poetry? And why has it been around so long? Many have suspected that it was invented as a school subject, because you have to take exams on it. But that is not what poetry is or why it is still around. That's not what it feels like, either. When you really feel it, a new part of you happens, or an old part is renewed, with surprise and delight at being what it is.

Where Poetry Is Coming From

From the beginning, people have known that words and things, words and actions, words and feelings, go together, and that they can go together in thousands of different ways, according to who is using them. Some ways go shallow, and some go deep.

Your Connection With Other Imaginations

The first thing to understand about poetry is that it comes to you from outside you, in books or in words, but that for it to live, something from within you must come to it and meet it and complete it. Your response with your own mind and body and memory and emotions gives the poem its ability to work its magic; if you give to it, it will give to you, and give plenty.

When you read, don't let the poet write down to you; read up to him. Reach for him from your gut out, and the heart and muscles will come into it, too.

Which Sun? Whose Stars?

The sun is new every day, the ancient philosopher Heraclitus[1] said. The sun of poetry is new every day, too, because it is seen in different ways by different people who have lived under it, lived with it, responded to it. Their lives are different from yours, but by means of the special spell that poetry brings to the *fact* of the sun—everybody's sun; yours, too—you can come into possession of many suns: as many as men and women have ever been able to imagine. Poetry makes possible the deepest kind of personal possession of the world.

1. **Heraclitus** (her´ ə klī´ təs) Greek philosopher who lived about 500 B.C.

◆ **Activate Prior Knowledge**

Poets describe things in new ways. Look at one of your school supplies and list three things you know about it.

1. ______________________

2. ______________________

3. ______________________

◆ **Literary Analysis**

Mark the Text

An **expository essay** is a short piece of nonfiction in which a writer explains or gives information about a subject. The main idea of an expository essay is often stated in the first paragraph. Underline the sentence in the first paragraph that states the main idea of this essay.

◆ **Reading Strategy**

This essay is **organized** logically. It is divided into sections, with a heading for each section. Each heading tells what the section is about. Write one sentence telling what each section within the bracket is about.

____

____

____

____

____

◆ **Reading Check**

What is the reader's job when reading poetry?

____

____

____

◆ **Reading Strategy**

In the bracketed section, underline the passage in which Dickey tells what to avoid in reading poetry. Then circle the advice he gives about how to approach poetry.

Mark the Text

◆ **Stop to Reflect**

Choose one of the items in Mark Van Doren's list. Write the image it calls up for you.

____

____

____

____

The most beautiful constellation in the winter sky is Orion,[2] which ancient poets thought looked like a hunter, up there, moving across heaven with his dog Sirius.[3] What is this hunter made out of stars hunting for? What does he mean? Who owns him, if anybody? The poet Aldous Huxley[4] felt that he did, and so, in Aldous Huxley's universe of personal emotion, he did.

Up from among the emblems of the
wind into its heart of power,
The Huntsman climbs, and all his
living stars
Are bright, and all are mine.

Where to Start

The beginning of your true encounter with poetry should be simple. It should bypass all classrooms, all textbooks, courses, examinations, and libraries and go straight to the things that make your own existence exist: to your body and nerves and blood and muscles. Find your own way—a secret way that just maybe you don't know yet—to open yourself as wide as you can and as deep as you can to the moment, the *now* of your own existence and the endless mystery of it, and perhaps at the same time to one other thing that is not you, but is out there: a handful of gravel is a good place to start. So is an ice cube—what more mysterious and beautiful *interior* of something has there ever been?

As for me, I like the sun, the source of all living things, and on certain days very good-feeling, too. "Start with the sun," D. H. Lawrence[5] said, "and everything will slowly, slowly happen." Good advice. And a lot *will* happen.

What is more fascinating than a rock, if you really feel it and *look* at it, or more interesting than a leaf?

Horses, I mean; butterflies, whales;
Mosses, and stars; and gravelly
Rivers, and fruit.

Oceans, I mean; black valleys; corn;
Brambles, and cliffs; rock, dirt, dust, ice . . .

Go back and read this list—it is quite a list, Mark Van Doren's[6] list!—item by item. Slowly. Let each of these things call up an image out of your own life.

2. **Orion** (ō rī´ ən)
3. **Sirius** (sir´ ē əs)
4. **Aldous Huxley** English poet, essayist, and novelist (1894–1963).
5. **D. H. Lawrence** English poet and novelist (1885–1930).
6. **Mark Van Doren** American poet, teacher, and critic (1894–1972).

Think and feel. What moss do you see? Which horse? What field of corn? What brambles are *your* brambles? Which river is most yours?

The Poem's Way of Going

Part of the spell of poetry is in the rhythm of language, used by poets who understand how powerful a factor rhythm can be, how compelling and unforgettable. Almost anything put into rhythm and rhyme is more memorable than the same thing said in prose. Why this is, no one knows completely, though the answer is surely rooted far down in the biology by means of which we exist; in the circulation of the blood that goes forth from the heart and comes back, and in the repetition of breathing. Croesus[7] was a rich Greek king, back in the sixth century before Christ, but this tombstone was not his:

No Croesus lies in the grave you see;
I was a poor laborer, and this suits me.

That is plain-spoken and definitive. You believe it, and the rhyme helps you believe it and keep it.

Some Things You'll Find Out

Writing poetry is a lot like a contest with yourself, and if you like sports and games and competitions of all kinds, you might like to try writing some. Why not?

The possibilities of rhyme are great. Some of the best fun is in making up your own limericks. There's no reason you can't invent limericks about anything that comes to your mind. No reason. Try it.

The problem is to find three words that rhyme and fit into a meaning. "There was a young man from . . ." *Where* was he from? What situation was he in? How can these things fit into the limerick form—a form everybody knows—so that the rhymes "pay off," and give that sense of completion and inevitability that is so deliciously memorable that nothing else is like it?

How It Goes With You

The more your encounter with poetry deepens, the more your experience of your own life will deepen, and you will begin to see things by means of words, and words by means of things.

Vocabulary Development: **prose** (prōz) *n.* nonpoetic language
inevitability (in evˊ ə tə bilˊ i tē) *n.* certainty

7. **Croesus** (krēˊ səs)

◆ Reading Strategy

Mark the Text

Underline the sentence that tells whether the author thinks something is more memorable if it rhymes and has rhythm.

◆ Stop to Reflect

Why do you think Dickey included this bracketed section?

____

____

____

____

____

____

◆ Reading Check

To what does Dickey compare writing poetry?

____

____

____

____

____

____

You will come to understand the world as it interacts with words, as it can be re-created by words, by rhythms and by images.

You'll understand that this condition is one charged with vital possibilities. You will pick up meaning more quickly—and you will *create* meaning, too, for yourself and for others. Connections between things will exist for you in ways that they never did before. They will shine with unexpectedness, wide-openness, and you will go toward them, on your own path. "Then . . .," as Dante[8] says, ". . . Then will your feet be filled with good desire." You will know this is happening the first time you say, of something you never would have noticed before, "Well, would you look at *that*! Who'd 'a thunk it?" (Pause, full of new light)

"*I* thunk it!"

◆ Stop to Reflect

In your own words, explain Dickey's purpose for writing this essay.

Vocabulary Development: **interacts** (in´ tər akts´) *v.* affects and is affected by
vital (vit´ əl) *adj.* essential to life; living

8. **Dante** (dän´ tā) Italian poet (1265–1321).

Reader's Response: Does reading this essay make you want to read or write poetry? Why or why not?

Thinking About the Skill: What did you find helpful about recognizing the organization of the essay?

PREVIEW

The Chase
from An American Childhood

Annie Dillard

Summary

In "The Chase," the author describes an experience from her childhood. She tells us about a winter morning, shortly after Christmas, when she and some neighborhood friends were throwing snowballs at passing cars. The driver of one car surprised the children by stopping. He got out and chased them on foot for ten blocks before finally catching up with them. Dillard is impressed that the driver chases them over such a long distance. The experience strengthens her belief that people should throw themselves into an activity with all their energy if they want to win. She wishes the excitement of the chase could last forever.

Visual Summary

The Chase

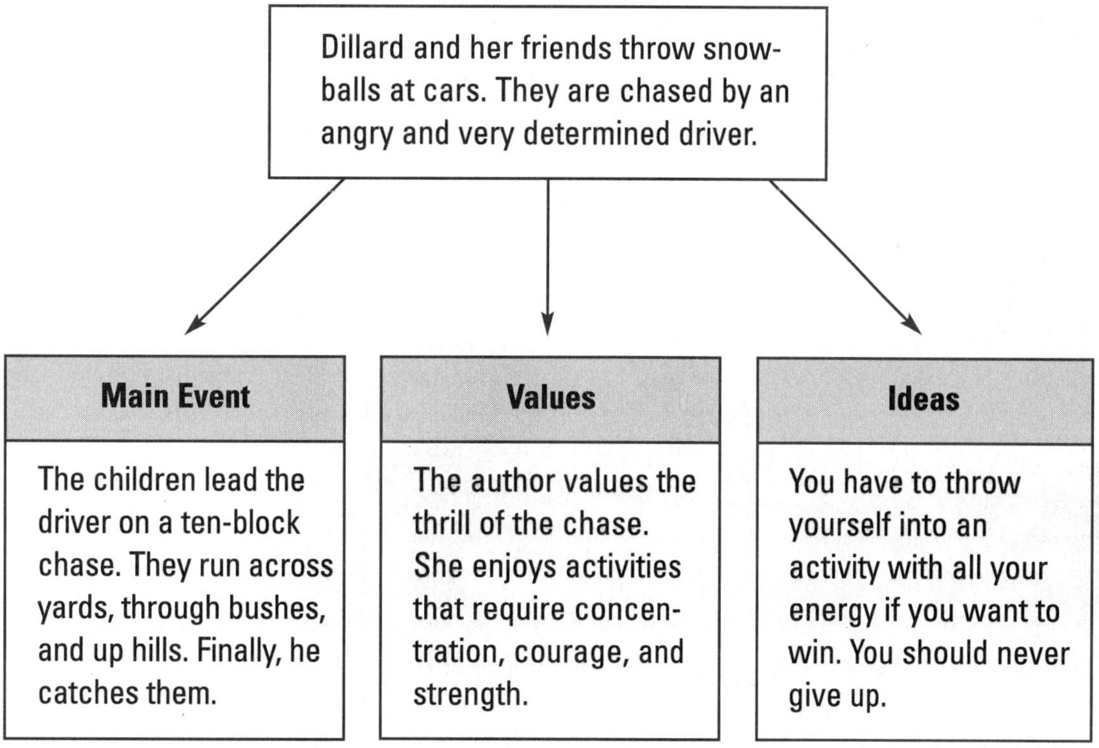

Dillard and her friends throw snowballs at cars. They are chased by an angry and very determined driver.

Main Event	Values	Ideas
The children lead the driver on a ten-block chase. They run across yards, through bushes, and up hills. Finally, he catches them.	The author values the thrill of the chase. She enjoys activities that require concentration, courage, and strength.	You have to throw yourself into an activity with all your energy if you want to win. You should never give up.

◆ Activate Prior Knowledge

Have you ever thrown yourself completely into an activity? Tell about it.

____

____

____

____

____

____

◆ Reading Strategy

An **author's purpose** is his or her reason for writing. The underlined sentence tells something Dillard believes in. Based on that sentence, what lesson do you think she learned from football?

____

____

____

____

____

◆ Reading Check

What do Dillard and the boys like to do in winter?

____

____

____

The Chase
from An American Childhood
Annie Dillard

This story retells an important event in the author's life. It reveals something of her character and what she thinks is important.

Some boys taught me to play football. This was fine sport. You thought up a new strategy for every play and whispered it to the others. You went out for a pass, fooling everyone. Best, you got to throw yourself mightily at someone's running legs. Either you brought him down or you hit the ground flat out on your chin, with your arms empty before you. It was all or nothing. If you hesitated in fear, you would miss and get hurt: you would take a hard fall while the kid got away, or you would get kicked in the face while the kid got away. But if you flung yourself wholeheartedly at the back of his knees—if you gathered and joined body and soul and pointed them diving fearlessly—then you likely wouldn't get hurt, and you'd stop the ball. Your fate, and your team's score, depended on your concentration and courage. Nothing girls did could compare with it.

Boys welcomed me at baseball, too, for I had, through enthusiastic practice, what was weirdly known as a boy's arm. In winter, in the snow, there was neither baseball nor football, so the boys and I threw snowballs at passing cars. I got in trouble throwing snowballs, and have seldom been happier since.

On one weekday morning after Christmas, six inches of new snow had just fallen. We were standing up to our boot tops in snow on a front yard on trafficked Reynolds Street, waiting for cars. The cars traveled Reynolds Street slowly and evenly; they were targets all but wrapped in red ribbons, cream puffs. We couldn't miss.

I was seven; the boys were eight, nine, and ten. The oldest two Fahey boys were there—Mikey and Peter—polite blond boys who lived near me on Lloyd Street, and who already had four brothers and sisters. My parents approved Mikey and Peter Fahey. Chickie McBride was there, a tough kid, and Billy Paul and Mackie Kean too, from across Reynolds, where the boys grew up dark and furious, grew up skinny, knowing, and skilled. We had all drifted from our houses that morning looking for action, and had found it here on Reynolds Street.

It was cloudy but cold. The cars' tires laid behind them on the snowy street a complex trail of beige chunks like crenellated castle walls.[1] I had stepped on some earlier; they

---

1. **chunks like crenellated** (kren′ əl āt′ əd) **castle walls** The snow was in rows of square clumps like the notches along the top of castle walls.

squeaked. We could have wished for more traffic. When a car came, we all popped it one. In the intervals between cars we reverted to the natural solitude of children.

I started making an iceball—a perfect iceball, from perfectly white snow, perfectly spherical, and squeezed perfectly translucent so no snow remained all the way through. (The Fahey boys and I considered it unfair actually to throw an iceball at somebody, but it had been known to happen.)

I had just embarked on the iceball project when we heard tire chains come clanking from afar. A black Buick was moving toward us down the street. We all spread out, banged together some regular snowballs, took aim, and, when the Buick drew nigh, fired.

A soft snowball hit the driver's windshield right before the driver's face. It made a smashed star with a hump in the middle.

Often, of course, we hit our target, but this time, the only time in all of life, the car pulled over and stopped. Its wide black door opened; a man got out of it, running. He didn't even close the car door.

He ran after us, and we ran away from him, up the snowy Reynolds sidewalk. At the corner, I looked back; incredibly, he was still after us. He was in city clothes: a suit and tie, street shoes. Any normal adult would have quit, having sprung us into flight and made his point. This man was gaining on us. He was a thin man, all action. All of a sudden, we were running for our lives.

Wordless, we split up. We were on our turf; we could lose ourselves in the neighborhood backyards, everyone for himself. I paused and considered. Everyone had vanished except Mikey Fahey, who was just rounding the corner of a yellow brick house. Poor Mikey, I trailed him. The driver of the Buick sensibly picked the two of us to follow. The man apparently had all day.

He chased Mikey and me around the yellow house and up a backyard path we knew by heart: under a low tree, up a bank, through a hedge, down some snowy steps, and across the grocery store's delivery driveway. We smashed through a gap in another hedge, entered a scruffy backyard and ran around its back porch and tight between houses to Edgerton Avenue; we ran across Edgerton to an alley and up our own sliding woodpile to the Halls' front yard; he kept coming. We ran up Lloyd Street and wound through mazy backyards toward the steep hilltop at Willard and Lang.

Vocabulary Development: **translucent** (trans lo͞o′ sənt) *adj.* able to transmit light but no detail of that light

◆ Reading Check

What do the underlined words "we all popped it one" mean?

◆ Reading Strategy

Why do you think Dillard describes the chase in such detail in the bracketed section?

◆ Reading Check

What makes this particular snowball-throwing episode different from all the others?

◆ **Stop to Reflect**

What important fact does the man chasing them know?

◆ **Literary Analysis**

An **autobiography** is the story of a person's life, told by that person. It usually tells important events and reveals the person's struggles, thoughts, and beliefs. Underline the sentence in the bracketed paragraph that tells how Dillard is feeling.

Mark the Text

◆ **Reading Check**

How far does the man chase them before catching them?

He chased us silently, block after block. He chased us silently over picket fences, through thorny hedges, between houses, around garbage cans, and across streets. Every time I glanced back, choking for breath, I expected he would have quit. He must have been as breathless as we were. His jacket strained over his body. It was an immense discovery, pounding into my hot head with every sliding, joyous step, that this ordinary adult evidently knew what I thought only children who trained at football knew: that you have to fling yourself at what you're doing, you have to point yourself, forget yourself, aim, dive.

Mikey and I had nowhere to go, in our own neighborhood or out of it, but away from this man who was chasing us. He impelled us forward; we compelled him to follow our route. The air was cold; every breath tore my throat. We kept running, block after block; we kept improvising, backyard after backyard, running a frantic course and choosing it simultaneously, failing always to find small places or hard places to slow him down, and discovering always, exhilarated, dismayed, that only bare speed could save us—for he would never give up, this man—and we were losing speed.

He chased us through the backyard labyrinths[2] of ten blocks before he caught us by our jackets. He caught us and we all stopped.

We three stood staggering, half blinded, coughing, in an obscure hilltop backyard: a man in his twenties, a boy, a girl. He had released our jackets, our pursuer, our captor, our hero: he knew we weren't going anywhere. We all played by the rules. Mikey and I unzipped our jackets. I pulled off my sopping mittens. Our tracks multiplied in the backyard's new snow. We had been breaking new snow all morning. We didn't look at each other. I was cherishing my excitement. The man's lower pants legs were wet; his cuffs were full of snow, and there was a prow of snow[3] beneath them on his shoes and socks. Some trees bordered the little flat backyard, some messy winter trees. There was no one around: a clearing in a grove, and we the only players.

It was a long time before he could speak. I had some difficulty at first recalling why we were there. My lips felt swollen; I couldn't see out of the sides of my eyes; I kept coughing.

Vocabulary Development: compelled (kəm peld′) *v.* forced

2. **backyard labyrinths** (lab′ ə rinths) areas behind and between the houses were like a kind of maze.
3. **prow of snow** v-shaped, like the front of a ship.

"You stupid kids," he began perfunctorily.

We listened perfunctorily indeed, if we listened at all, for the chewing out was redundant, a mere formality, and beside the point. The point was that he had chased us passionately without giving up, and so he had caught us. Now he came down to earth. I wanted the glory to last forever.

But how could the glory have lasted forever? We could have run through every backyard in North America until we got to Panama. But when he trapped us at the lip of the Panama Canal, what precisely could he have done to prolong the drama of the chase and cap its glory? I brooded about this for the next few years. He could only have fried Mikey Fahey and me in boiling oil, say, or dismembered us piecemeal, or staked us to anthills. None of which I really wanted, and none of which any adult was likely to do, even in the spirit of fun. He could only chew us out there in the Panamanian jungle, after months or years of exalting pursuit. He could only begin, "You stupid kids," and continue in his ordinary Pittsburgh accent with his normal righteous anger and the usual common sense.

If in that snowy backyard the driver of the black Buick had cut off our heads, Mikey's and mine, I would have died happy, for nothing has required so much of me since as being chased all over Pittsburgh in the middle of winter—running terrified, exhausted—by this sainted, skinny, furious red-headed man who wished to have a word with us. I don't know how he found his way back to his car.

Vocabulary Development: **perfunctorily** (pər fuŋk′ tə rə lē) *adv.* without enthusiasm; routinely

Reader's Response: Would you want the young Annie Dillard as a friend? Why or why not?

____

____

Thinking About the Skill: Part of Dillard's purpose in writing this piece was to share one of her values. What is one of her most important values?

____

____

____

◆ Literary Analysis

Mark the Text

Circle the words that tell how Dillard felt about the man's lecture.

◆ Stop to Reflect

Why does Dillard say she "would have died happy" in the bracketed passage?

____

____

____

____

____

____

I Am a Native of North America

Chief Dan George

Summary

The author of "I Am a Native of North America" remembers the culture in which he grew up. He reflects on the love that Native American people showed one another. He thinks about their great love of the earth and its precious gifts. he compares his culture with white society. He thinks that people in white society have to learn to appreciate one another. They have to learn to appreciate and respect nature. He thinks white society lacks love. In the end, he says, we all need love. He hopes that white society will take the give of love from Native American culture.

Visual Summary

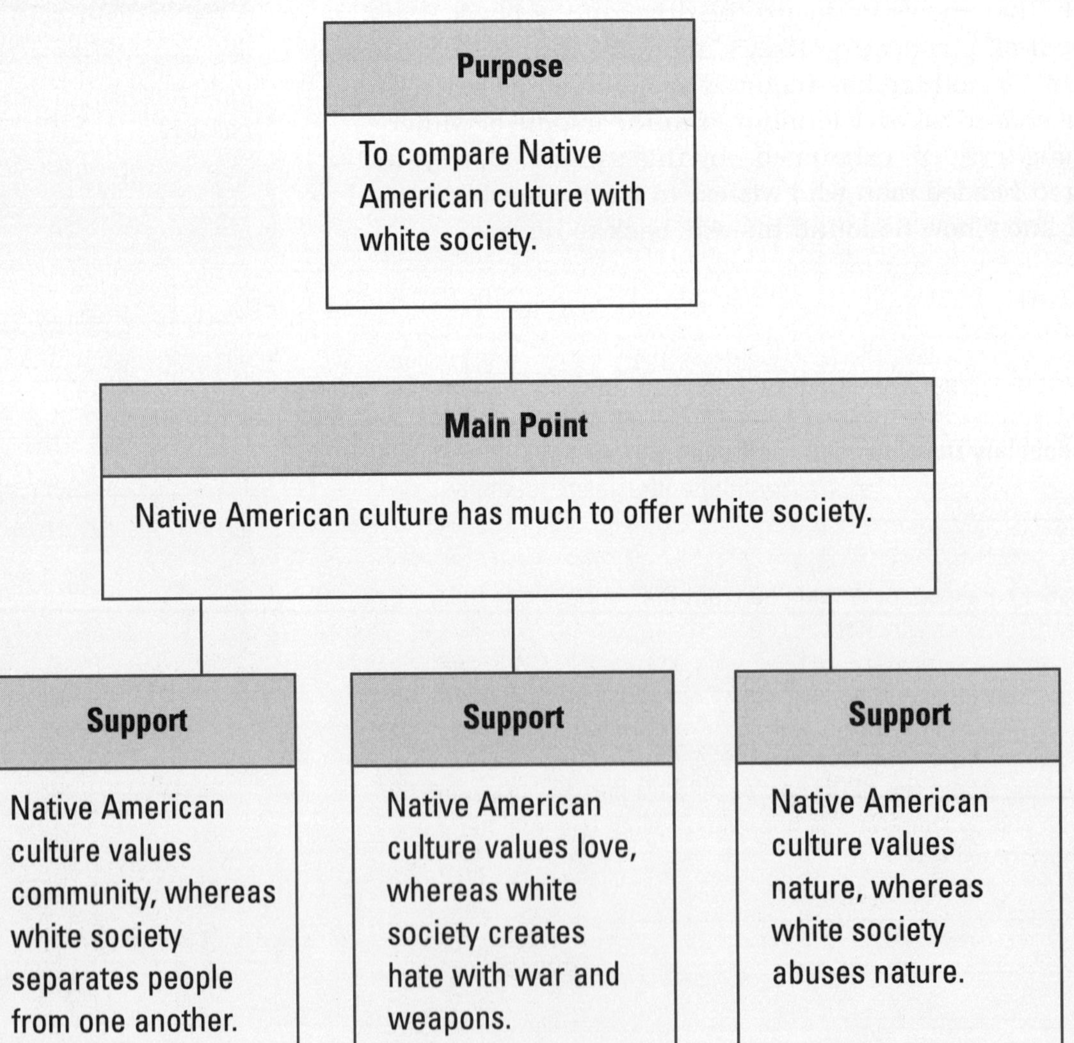

I Am a Native of North America

Chief Dan George

The first essays were written about four hundred years ago. The word essai *means "try" in French. An essay is a try at understanding something. The following essay is both reflective and persuasive—the author presents his thoughts and tries to make the reader see his point.*

In the course of my lifetime I have lived in two distinct[1] cultures. I was born into a culture that lived in communal houses. My grandfather's house was eighty feet long. It was called a smoke house, and it stood down by the beach along the inlet.[2] All my grand-father's sons and their families lived in this large dwelling. Their sleeping apartments were separated by blankets made of bull rush reeds, but one open fire in the middle served the cooking needs of all. In houses like these, throughout the tribe, people learned to live with one another; learned to serve one another; learned to respect the rights of one another. And children shared the thoughts of the adult world and found themselves surrounded by aunts and uncles and cousins who loved them and did not threaten them. My father was born in such a house and learned from infancy how to love people and be at home with them.

And beyond this acceptance of one another there was a deep respect for everything in nature that surrounded them. My father loved the earth and all its creatures. The earth was his second mother. The earth and everything it contained was a gift from See-see-am[3] . . . and the way to thank this great spirit was to use his gifts with respect.

I remember, as a little boy, fishing with him up Indian River and I can still see him as the sun rose above the mountain top in the early morning . . . I can see him standing by the water's edge with his arms raised above his head while he softly moaned . . . "Thank you, thank you." It left a deep impression on my young mind.

And I shall never forget his disappointment when once he caught me gaffing for fish[4] "just for the fun of it." "My Son," he said, "the Great Spirit gave you those fish to be your brothers, to feed you when you are hungry. You must respect them. You must not kill them just for the fun of it."

Vocabulary Development: communal (kə myo͞o′ nəl) *adj.* shared by all

1. **distinct** (di stinkt′) *adj.* separate and different.
2. **inlet** (in′ let) *n.* narrow strip of water jutting into a body of land from a river, a lake, or an ocean.
3. **See-see-am** the name of the Great Spirit, or "The Chief Above," in the Salishan language of Chief George's people.
4. **gaffing for fish** using a barbed spear to catch river fish.

◆ Activate Prior Knowledge

What do you think is an important goal for America to accomplish in the future? Write your answer below.

◆ Reading Strategy

The underlined sentence tells that people learned how to treat each other well by living together in close quarters. Circle three details in that paragraph that tell about life in Chief George's grandfather's house.

Mark the Text

◆ Reading Check

What culture was Chief George born into?

◆ **Literary Analysis**

Underline the sentence in the bracketed paragraph that indicates the author is trying to understand his experience.

Mark the Text

◆ **Reading Strategy**

An author should back up his statements with **support.** What information does the author provide to back up his claim that the white man attacks nature?

____

____

____

____

____

____

◆ **Literary Analysis**

Circle the words "need" and "must" each time they appear in the bracketed passage. Do these words suggest that this **essay** was written in part to persuade people of something? Explain.

Mark the Text

____

____

____

____

This then was the culture I was born into and for some years the only one I really knew or tasted. This is why I find it hard to accept many of the things I see around me.

I see people living in smoke houses hundreds of times bigger than the one I knew. But the people in one apartment do not even know the people in the next and care less about them.

It is also difficult for me to understand the deep hate that exists among people. It is hard to understand a culture that justifies the killing of millions in past wars, and is at this very moment preparing bombs to kill even greater numbers. It is hard for me to understand a culture that spends more on wars and weapons to kill, than it does on education and welfare to help and develop.

It is hard for me to understand a culture that not only hates and fights its brothers but even attacks nature and abuses her. I see my white brothers going about blotting out nature from his cities. I see him strip the hills bare, leaving ugly wounds on the face of mountains. I see him tearing things from the bosom of mother earth as though she were a monster, who refused to share her treasures with him. I see him throw poison in the waters, indifferent to the life he kills there; and he chokes the air with deadly fumes.

My white brother does many things well for he is more clever than my people but I wonder if he knows how to love well. I wonder if he has ever really learned to love at all. Perhaps he only loves the things that are his own but never learned to love the things that are outside and beyond him. And this is, of course, not love at all, for man must love all creation or he will love none of it. Man must love fully or he will become the lowest of the animals. It is the power to love that makes him the greatest of them all . . . for he alone of all animals is capable of love.

Love is something you and I must have. We must have it because our spirit feeds upon it. We must have it because without it we become weak and faint. Without love our self-esteem weakens. Without it our courage fails. Without love we can no longer look out confidently at the world. Instead we turn inwardly and begin to feed upon our own personalities and little by little we destroy ourselves.

You and I need the strength and joy that comes from knowing that we are loved. With it we are creative. With it we march tirelessly. With it, and with it alone, we are able to sacrifice for others.

There have been times when we all wanted so desperately to feel a reassuring hand upon us . . . there have been lonely times when we so wanted a strong arm around us . . . I cannot tell you how deeply I miss my wife's presence when I return from a trip. Her love was my greatest joy, my strength, my greatest blessing.

I am afraid my culture has little to offer yours. But my culture did prize friendship and companionship. It did not look on privacy as a thing to be clung to, for privacy builds up walls and walls promote distrust. My culture lived in big family communities, and from infancy people learned to live with others.

My culture did not prize the hoarding of private possessions; in fact, to hoard was a shameful thing to do among my people. The Indian looked on all things in nature as belonging to him and he expected to share them with others and to take only what he needed.

Everyone likes to give as well as receive. No one wishes only to receive all the time. We have taken much from your culture . . . I wish you had taken something from our culture . . . for there were some beautiful and good things in it.

Soon it will be too late to know my culture, for integration[5] is upon us and soon we will have no values but yours. Already many of our young people have forgotten the old ways. And many have been shamed of their Indian ways by scorn[6] and ridicule. My culture is like a wounded deer that has crawled away into the forest to bleed and die alone.

The only thing that can truly help us is genuine love. You must truly love us, be patient with us and share with us. And we must love you—with a genuine love that forgives and forgets . . . a love that forgives the terrible sufferings your culture brought ours when it swept over us like a wave crashing along a beach . . . with a love that forgets and lifts up its head and sees in your eyes an answering love of trust and acceptance.

This is brotherhood . . . anything less is not worthy of the name.

I have spoken.

---

5. integration (in tə grā´ shən) *n.* the mingling of different ethnic or racial groups.
6. scorn (skôrn) *n.* complete lack of respect.

Reader's Response: Do you agree that "the power to love" is the most important human quality? Why or why not?

____

____

____

____

◆ Literary Analysis

Briefly summarize Chief Dan George's thoughts in this **essay** about the cultures he has experienced.

____

____

____

____

____

____

____

____

◆ Reading Check

How does the author describe *brotherhood*?

____

____

____

____

All Together Now

Barbara Jordan

Summary

In "All Together Now," Barbara Jordan appeals to Americans to be tolerant of other races. She encourages us to make friends with people of different background. She asks us to be open to the feelings and beliefs or other cultures. She asks parents to teach tolerance to their children. She believes that by working together—at home, at school, and at work—we can make the world a more loving and peaceful place.

Visual Summary

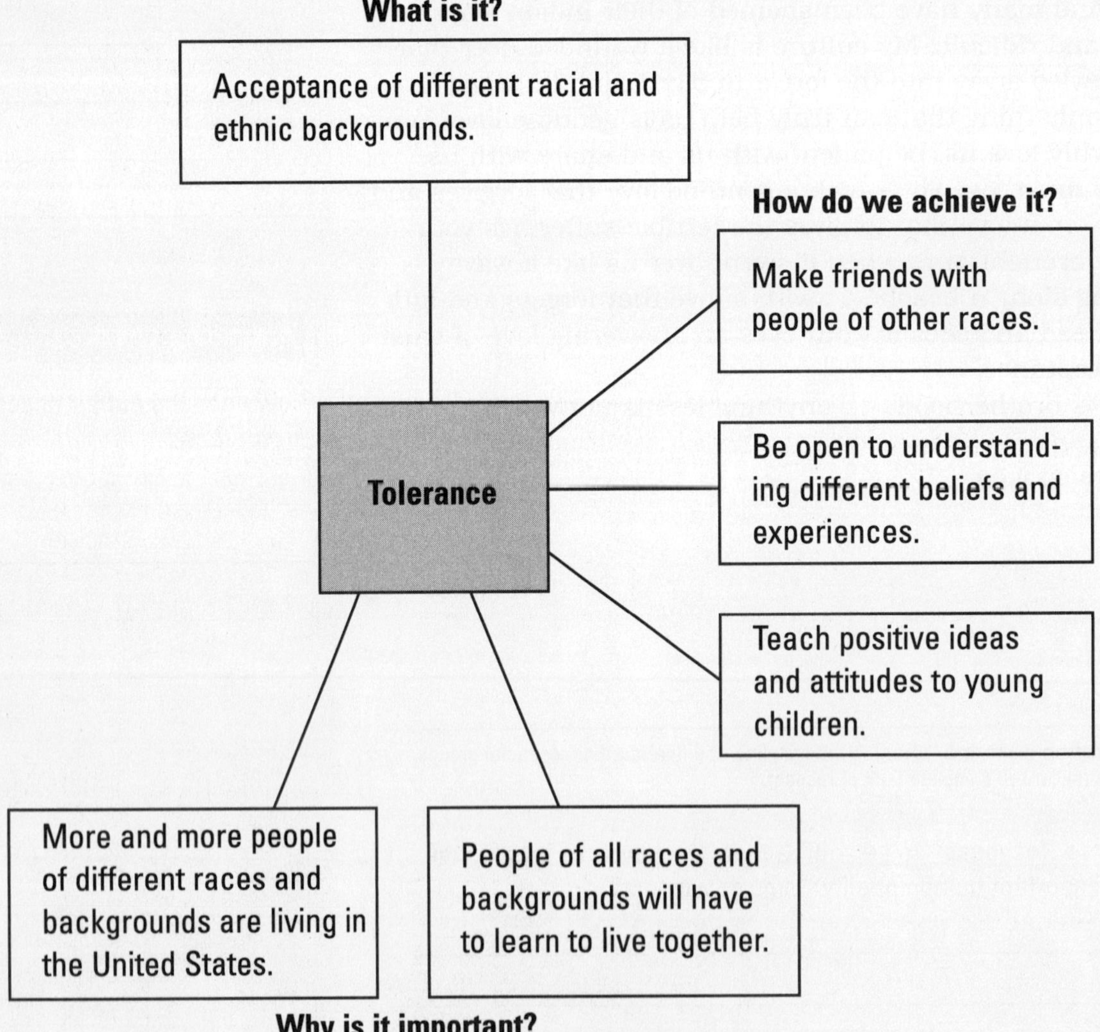

All Together Now

Barbara Jordan

Barbara Jordan, in addressing the Democratic National Convention in 1992, shares her views on the state of race relations in America. She suggests ways to bring about the American dream of tolerance and equality.

When I look at race relations today I can see that some positive changes have come about. But much remains to be done, and the answer does not lie in more legislation. We *have* the legislation we need; we have the laws. Frankly, I don't believe that the task of bringing us all together can be accomplished by government. What we need now is soul force—the efforts of people working on a small scale to build a truly tolerant, harmonious society. And parents can do a great deal to create that tolerant society.

We all know that race relations in America have had a very rocky history. Think about the 1960's when Dr. Martin Luther King, Jr., was in his heyday and there were marches and protests against segregation[1] and discrimination. The movement culminated in 1963 with the March on Washington.

Following that event, race relations reached an all-time peak. President Lyndon B. Johnson pushed through the Civil Rights Act of 1964, which remains the fundamental piece of civil rights legislation in this century. The Voting Rights Act of 1965 ensured that everyone in our country could vote. At last, black people and white people seemed ready to live together in peace.

But that is not what happened. By the 1990's the good feelings had diminished. Today the nation seems to be suffering from compassion fatigue, and issues such as race relations and civil rights have never regained momentum.

Those issues, however, remain crucial. As our society becomes more diverse, people of all races and backgrounds will have to learn to live together. If we don't think this is important, all we have to do is look at the situation in Bosnia[2] today.

How do we create a harmonious society out of so many kinds of people? The key is tolerance—the one value that is indispensable in creating community.

Vocabulary Development: tolerant (täl′ ər ənt) *adj.* free from bigotry or prejudice

1. **segregation** (seg′ rə gā′ shən) *n.* the practice of forcing racial groups to live apart from each other.
2. **Bosnia** (bäz′ nē ə) *n.* country, located on the Balkan Peninsula in Europe, that was the site of a bloody civil war between Muslims and Christians during the 1990s.

◆ Activate Prior Knowledge

Have you ever had a friend from a different background? What did you learn by knowing that person?

◆ Reading Strategy

Mark the Text

Underline the events in the first bracketed section that **support** Jordan's statement that race relations reached an all-time peak after the march in 1963.

◆ Literary Analysis

Mark the Text

A **persuasive essay** presents arguments to convince readers to believe or act in a certain way. Underline the sentence in the second bracketed passage that states the attitude that Barbara Jordan is arguing Americans should adopt.

◆ Reading Check

What is this essay about?

◆ **Literary Analysis**

Underline the suggestion Jordan makes in the bracketed paragraph about how to improve our sense of community.

Mark the Text

If we are concerned about community, if it is important to us that people not feel excluded, then we have to do something. Each of us can decide to have one friend of a different race or background in our mix of friends. If we do this, we'll be working together to push things forward.

One thing is clear to me: We, as human beings, must be willing to accept people who are different from ourselves. I must be willing to accept people who don't look as I do and don't talk as I do. It is crucial that I am open to their feelings, their inner reality.

What can parents do? We can put our faith in young people as a positive force. I have yet to find a racist baby. Babies come into the world as blank as slates and, with their beautiful innocence, see others not as different but as enjoyable companions. Children learn ideas and attitudes from the adults who nurture them. I absolutely believe that children do not adopt prejudices unless they absorb them from their parents or teachers.

◆ **Reading Check**

Why does Jordan think parents should put their faith in young children?

____

____

____

____

The best way to get this country faithful to the American dream of tolerance and equality is to start small. Parents can actively encourage their children to be in the company of people who are of other racial and ethnic backgrounds. If a child thinks, "Well, that person's color is not the same as mine, but she must be okay because she likes to play with the same things I like to play with," that child will grow up with a broader view of humanity.

I'm an incurable optimist. For the rest of the time that I have left on this planet I want to bring people together. You might think of this as a labor of love. Now, I know that love means different things to different people. But what *I* mean is this: I care about you because you are a fellow human being and I find it okay in my mind, in my heart, to simply say to you, I love you. And maybe that would encourage you to love me in return.

It is possible for all of us to work on this—at home, in our schools, at our jobs. It is possible to work on human relationships in every area of our lives.

◆ **Stop to Reflect**

This essay and the previous one "I Am a Native of North America" end with similar messages. What is that message?

____

____

____

____

____

____

____

Reader's Response: Does this essay make you think differently? Explain.

____

____

Thinking About the Skill: Do you think Jordan gives enough support to her ideas? Explain.

____

____

PREVIEW

A Christmas Carol: Scrooge and Marley, Act 1, Scenes 1 and 2

Israel Horovitz

adapted from *A Christmas Carol* by Charles Dickens

Summary

Stingy Ebenezer Scrooge is a greedy, grumpy old man. He has no friends and doesn't want any. He does not believe in the spirit of Christmas, and will not celebrate on Christmas Eve. He even refuses to visit his nephew's family or to give to charity. He barely agrees to give his clerk, Bob Cratchit, Christmas Day off! He insists that Cratchit come in earlier than usual the day after, to make up for it.

Visual Summary

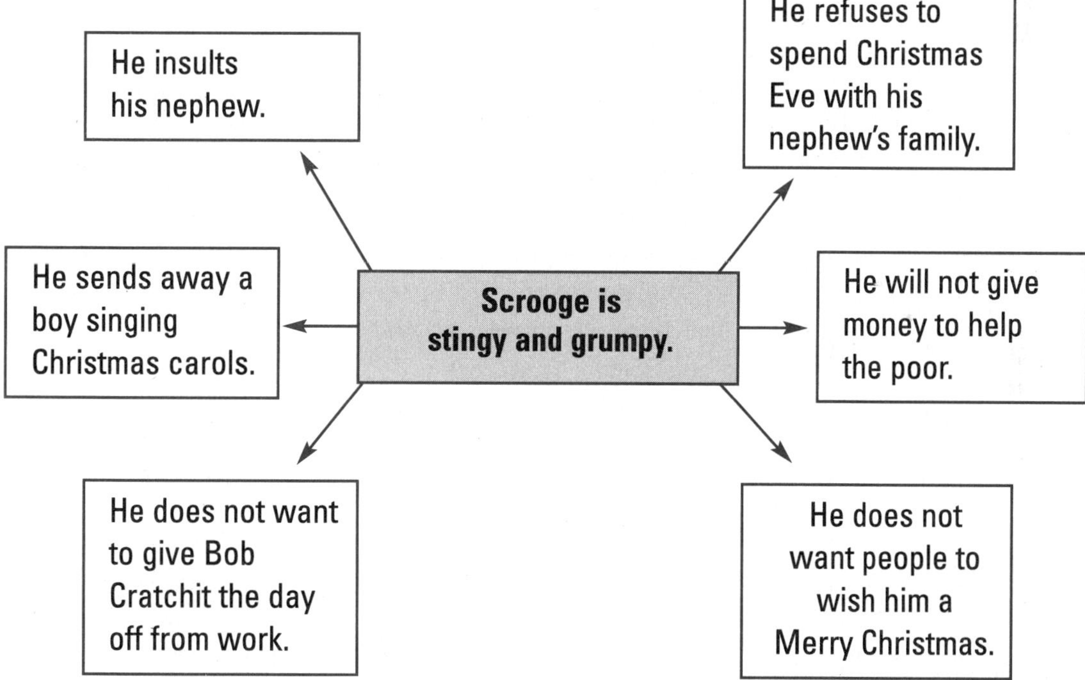

◆ Activate Prior Knowledge

Think of an experience from your past that helped make you the kind of person you are today. Describe the experience. Then explain why this experience was pivotal in your growth.

◆ Stop to Reflect

A list of characters always comes at the beginning of a play, along with information such as where and when the play takes place. Why might a list of characters be helpful to the reader?

A Christmas Carol: Scrooge and Marley

Israel Horovitz

from A Christmas Carol

by Charles Dickens

Act 1, Scenes 1 & 2

A Christmas Carol *is set in England during the 1800s. This period in English history was characterized by rapid industrial growth and a booming economy. The wealthy lived in great luxury. For the poor and the working class, however, life was hard. Factory workers put in long hours and endured brutal working conditions for low wages. Dickens had great sympathy for the poor and working classes, and you'll find this sympathy reflected in* A Christmas Carol.

THE PEOPLE OF THE PLAY

Jacob Marley, a specter
Ebenezer Scrooge, not yet dead, which is to say still alive
Bob Cratchit, Scrooge's clerk
Fred, Scrooge's nephew
Thin Do-Gooder
Portly Do-Gooder
Specters (Various), carrying money-boxes
The Ghost of Christmas Past
Four Jocund Travelers
A Band of Singers
A Band of Dancers
Little Boy Scrooge
Young Man Scrooge
Fan, Scrooge's little sister
The Schoolmaster
Schoolmates
Fezziwig, a fine and fair employer
Dick, young Scrooge's co-worker
Young Scrooge
A Fiddler
More Dancers
Scrooge's Lost Love
Scrooge's Lost Love's Daughter
Scrooge's Lost Love's Husband
The Ghost of Christmas Present
Some Bakers
Mrs. Cratchit, Bob Cratchit's wife
Belinda Cratchit, a daughter
Martha Cratchit, another daughter
Peter Cratchit, a son
Tiny Tim Cratchit, another son
Scrooge's Niece, Fred's wife
The Ghost of Christmas Future, a mute Phantom
Three Men of Business
Drunks, Scoundrels, Women of the Streets
A Charwoman
Mrs. Dilber
Joe, an old second-hand goods dealer
A Corpse, very like Scrooge
An Indebted Family
Adam, a young boy
A Poulterer
A Gentlewoman
Some More Men of Business

The Place of the Play

Various locations in and around the City of London, including Scrooge's Chambers and Offices; the Cratchit Home; Fred's Home; Scrooge's School; Fezziwig's Offices; Old Joe's Hide-a-Way.

The Time of the Play

The entire action of the play takes place on Christmas Eve, Christmas Day, and the morning after Christmas, 1843.

Scene 1

[Ghostly music in auditorium. A single spotlight on JACOB MARLEY, D.C. *He is ancient; awful, dead-eyed. He speaks straight out to auditorium.]*

MARLEY. [*Cackle-voiced*] My name is Jacob Marley and I am dead. [*He laughs.*] Oh, no, there's no doubt that I am dead. The register of my burial was signed by the clergyman, the clerk, the undertaker . . . and by my chief mourner . . . Ebenezer Scrooge . . . [*Pause; remembers*] I am dead as a doornail.

[*A spotlight fades up, Stage Right, on* SCROOGE, *in his counting-house,*[1] *counting. Lettering on the window behind* SCROOGE *reads:* "SCROOGE AND MARLEY, LTD." *The spotlight is tight on* SCROOGE'*s head and shoulders. We shall not yet see into the offices and setting. Ghostly music continues, under.* MARLEY *looks across at* SCROOGE; *pitifully. After a moment's pause*]

I present him to you: Ebenezer Scrooge . . . England's most tightfisted hand at the grindstone, Scrooge! a squeezing, wrenching, grasping, scraping, clutching, covetous, old sinner! secret, and self-contained, and solitary as an oyster. The cold within him freezes his old features, nips his pointed nose, shrivels his cheek, stiffens his gait; makes his eyes red, his thin lips blue; and speaks out shrewdly in his grating voice. Look at him. Look at him . . .

[SCROOGE *counts and mumbles.*]

SCROOGE. They owe me money and I will collect. I will have them jailed, if I have to. They owe me money and I will collect what is due me.

[MARLEY *moves towards* SCROOGE; *two steps. The spotlight stays with him.*]

MARLEY. [*Disgusted*] He and I were partners for I don't know how many years. Scrooge was my sole executor, my sole administrator, my sole assign, my sole residuary legatee,[2]

---

1. **counting-house** office for keeping financial records and writing business letters.
2. **my sole executor** (ig zek′ yə tər), **my sole administrator, my sole assign** (ə sin′), **my sole residuary legatee** (ri zij′ o͞o wer′ ē leg′ ə tē′) legal terms giving one person responsibility to carry out the wishes of another who has died.

◆ **Literary Analysis**

The **stage directions** of a play, printed here in italics and enclosed in brackets, describe the characters' actions and appearance on stage. Circle the first stage directions in this play. Why do you think they are important for the actor to have?

Mark THE Text

◆ **Reading Strategy**

To **picture in your mind** what a performance of the play might be like, use the details the playwright provides in the **stage directions** and in the **dialogue,** the words the characters in a play speak to each other. Underline three details about Scrooge that the character Marley gives in the bracketed passage that help you **picture** Scrooge **in your mind.**

Mark THE Text

◆ **Literary Analysis**

On the illustration below, circle the place that the **stage directions** tell you that Jacob Marley is standing (represented by the abbreviation *D.C.*) when the curtain goes up.

Mark THE Text

THE STAGE

Upstage Right	Upstage Center	Upstage Left
Right	Center	Left
Downstage Right	Downstage Center	Downstage Left

Curtain

Apron

Audience

◆ **Literary Analysis**

How does the **dialogue** between Scrooge and Marley reflect each character's personality?

____

____

____

____

____

____

____

◆ **Reading Check**

Rewrite the sentence in the bracketed passage in your own words.

____

____

____

____

____

____

◆ **Literary Analysis**

In the underlined **stage direction,** *N.B.* stands for "note well" in Latin, while *I.H.* stands for the author's initials. Why might the author want to suggest occasional explosions as Marley comes and goes?

____

____

____

____

____

my sole friend and my sole mourner. But Scrooge was not so cut up by the sad event of my death, but that he was an excellent man of business on the very day of my funeral, and solemnized[3] it with an undoubted bargain. [*Pauses again in disgust*] He never painted out my name from the window. There it stands, on the window and above the warehouse door: Scrooge and Marley. Sometimes people new to our business call him Scrooge and sometimes they call him Marley. He answers to both names. It's all the same to him. And it's cheaper than painting in a new sign, isn't it? [*Pauses; moves closer to* SCROOGE] Nobody has ever stopped him in the street to say, with gladsome looks, "My dear Scrooge, how are you? When will you come to see me?" No beggars implored him to bestow a trifle, no children ever ask him what it is o'clock, no man or woman now, or ever in his life, not once, inquire the way to such and such a place. [MARLEY *stands next to* SCROOGE *now. They share, so it seems, a spotlight.*] But what does Scrooge care of any of this? It is the very thing he likes! To edge his way along the crowded paths of life, warning all human sympathy to keep its distance.

[*A ghostly bell rings in the distance.* MARLEY *moves away from* SCROOGE, *now, heading* D. *again. As he does, he "takes" the light:* SCROOGE *has disappeared into the black void beyond.* MARLEY *walks* D.C., *talking directly to the audience. Pauses*]

The bell tolls and I must take my leave. You must stay a while with Scrooge and watch him play out his scroogey life. It is now the story: the once-upon-a-time. Scrooge is busy in his counting-house. Where else? Christmas eve and Scrooge is busy in his counting-house. It is cold, bleak, biting weather outside: foggy withal: and, if you listen closely, you can hear the people in the court go wheezing up and down, beating their hands upon their breasts, and stamping their feet upon the pavement stones to warm them . . .

[*The clocks outside strike three.*]

Only three! and quite dark outside already: it has not been light all day this day.

[*This ghostly bell rings in the distance again.* MARLEY *looks about him. Music in.* MARLEY *flies away.*]

[N.B. MARLEY'S *comings and goings should, from time to time, induce the explosion of the odd flash-pot. I.H.*]

Vocabulary Development: implored (im plôrd′) *v.* asked or begged earnestly

3. **solemnized** (säl′ əm nizd′) *v.* honored or remembered. Marley is being ironic.

Scene 2

[*Christmas music in, sung by a live chorus, full. At conclusion of song, sound fades under and into the distance. Lights up in set: offices of Scrooge and Marley, Ltd.* SCROOGE *sits at his desk, at work. Near him is a tiny fire. His door is open and in his line of vision, we see* SCROOGE'S *clerk,* BOB CRATCHIT, *who sits in a dismal tank of a cubicle, copying letters. Near* CRATCHIT *is a fire so tiny as to barely cast a light: perhaps it is one pitifully glowing coal?* CRATCHIT *rubs his hands together, puts on a white comforter*[4] *and tries to heat his hands around his candle.* SCROOGE'S NEPHEW *enters, unseen.*]

SCROOGE. What are you doing, Cratchit? Acting cold, are you? Next, you'll be asking to replenish your coal from my coal-box, won't you? Well, save your breath, Cratchit! Unless you're prepared to find employ elsewhere!

NEPHEW. [*Cheerfully; surprising* SCROOGE] A merry Christmas to you, Uncle! God save you!

SCROOGE. Bah! Humbug![5]

NEPHEW. Christmas a "humbug," Uncle? I'm sure you don't mean that.

SCROOGE. I do! Merry Christmas? What right do you have to be merry? What reason have you to be merry? You're poor enough!

NEPHEW. Come, then. What right have you to be dismal? What reason have you to be morose? You're rich enough.

SCROOGE. Bah! Humbug!

NEPHEW. Don't be cross, Uncle.

SCROOGE. What else can I be? Eh? When I live in a world of fools such as this? Merry Christmas? What's Christmastime to you but a time of paying bills without any money; a time for finding yourself a year older, but not an hour richer. If I could work my will, every idiot who goes about with "Merry Christmas" on his lips, should be boiled with his own pudding, and buried with a stake of holly through his heart. He should!

NEPHEW. Uncle!

SCROOGE. Nephew! You keep Christmas in your own way and let me keep it in mine.

NEPHEW. Keep it! But you don't keep it, Uncle.

SCROOGE. Let me leave it alone, then. Much good it has ever done you!

> **Vocabulary Development: morose** (mə rōs′) *adj.* gloomy; ill-tempered

4. **comforter** (kum′ fər tər) *n.* long, woolen scarf.
5. **humbug** (hum′ bug′) *interj.* nonsense.

◆ Reading Strategy

Mark the Text

Underline the stage directions that help you **picture in your mind** Scrooge's office.

◆ Literary Analysis

How does the **dialogue** on this page reveal the different attitudes of Scrooge and his nephew?

____

____

____

____

____

____

____

____

◆ Stop to Reflect

How would you describe the relationship between Scrooge and his nephew? Why do you think they have such different personalities even though they are from the same family?

____

____

____

____

____

____

____

◆ **Literary Analysis**

What does the bracketed **stage direction** tell you about Bob Cratchit's attitude?

____

____

____

____

◆ **Reading Check**

Underline the threat that Scrooge makes to Cratchit when he applauds the nephew's remark.

◆ **Stop to Reflect**

Read the second bracketed passage. What is Scrooge's attitude about love? Why do you think he feels this way?

____

____

____

____

◆ **Reading Check**

Look up the words *resolute* and *homage*. Then write in your own words what Scrooge's nephew is saying in the underlined passage.

____

____

____

____

____

NEPHEW. There are many things from which I have derived good, by which I have not profited, I daresay. Christmas among the rest. But I am sure that I always thought of Christmas time, when it has come round—as a good time: the only time I know of, when men and women seem to open their shut-up hearts freely, and to think of people below them as if they really were fellow-passengers to the grave, and not another race of creatures bound on other journeys. And therefore, Uncle, though it has never put a scrap of gold or silver in my pocket, I believe that it *has* done me good, and that it *will* do me good; and I say, God bless it!

[*The* CLERK *in the tank applauds, looks at the furious* SCROOGE *and pokes out his tiny fire, as if in exchange for the moment of impropriety.* SCROOGE *yells at him.*]

SCROOGE. [*To the* CLERK] Let me hear another sound from you and you'll keep your Christmas by losing your situation. [*To the* NEPHEW] You're quite a powerful speaker, sir. I wonder you don't go into Parliament.[6]

NEPHEW. Don't be angry, Uncle. Come! Dine with us tomorrow.

SCROOGE. I'd rather see myself dead than see myself with your family!

NEPHEW. But, why? Why?

SCROOGE. Why did you get married?

NEPHEW. Because I fell in love.

SCROOGE. That, sir, is the only thing that you have said to me in your entire lifetime which is even more ridiculous than "Merry Christmas"! [Turns from NEPHEW] Good afternoon.

NEPHEW. Nay, Uncle, you never came to see me before I married either. Why give it as a reason for not coming now?

SCROOGE. Good afternoon, Nephew!

NEPHEW. I want nothing from you; I ask nothing of you; why cannot we be friends?

SCROOGE. Good afternoon!

NEPHEW. I am sorry with all my heart, to find you so resolute. But I have made the trial in homage to Christmas, and I'll keep my Christmas humor to the last. So A Merry Christmas, Uncle!

SCROOGE. Good afternoon!

NEPHEW. And A Happy New Year!

SCROOGE. Good afternoon!

NEPHEW. [*He stands facing* SCROOGE.] Uncle, you are the most . . . [*Pauses*] No, I shan't. My Christmas humor is intact

6. **Parliament** (pär′ lə mənt) national legislative body of Great Britain, in some ways like the American Congress.

. . . [*Pause*] God bless you, Uncle . . . [NEPHEW *turns and starts for the door; he stops at* CRATCHIT'S *cage*.] Merry Christmas, Bob Cratchit . . .

CRATCHIT. Merry Christmas to you sir, and a very, very happy New Year . . .

SCROOGE. [*Calling across to them*] Oh, fine, a perfection, just fine . . . to see the perfect pair of you: husbands, with wives and children to support . . . my clerk there earning fifteen shillings a week . . . and the perfect pair of you, talking about a Merry Christmas! [*Pauses*] I'll retire to Bedlam![7]

NEPHEW. [*To* CRATCHIT] He's impossible!

CRATCHIT. Oh, mind him not, sir. He's getting on in years, and he's alone. He's noticed your visit. I'll wager your visit has warmed him.

NEPHEW. Him? Uncle Ebenezer Scrooge? *Warmed?* You are a better Christian than I am, sir.

CRATCHIT. [*Opening the door for* NEPHEW; *two* DO-GOODERS *will enter, as* NEPHEW *exits*] Good day to you, sir, and God bless.

NEPHEW. God bless . . . [*One man who enters is portly, the other is thin. Both are pleasant.*]

CRATCHIT. Can I help you, gentlemen?

THIN MAN. [*Carrying papers and books; looks around* CRATCHIT *to* SCROOGE] Scrooge and Marley's, I believe. Have I the pleasure of addressing Mr. Scroogc, or Mr. Marley?

SCROOGE. Mr. Marley has been dead these seven years. He died seven years ago this very night.

PORTLY MAN. We have no doubt his liberality[8] is well represented by his surviving partner . . . [*Offers his calling card*]

SCROOGE. [*Handing back the card; unlooked at*] . . . Good afternoon.

THIN MAN. This will take but a moment, sir . . .

PORTLY MAN. At this festive season of the year, Mr. Scrooge, it is more than usually desirable that we should make some slight provision for the poor and destitute, who suffer greatly at the present time. Many thousands are in want of common necessities; hundreds of thousands are in want of common comforts, sir.

Vocabulary Development: destitute (des′ tə to͞ot′) n. people living in complete poverty

7. **Bedlam** (bed′ ləm) hospital in London for the mentally ill.
8. **liberality** (lib′ ər al′ i tē) generosity.

◆ **Reading Check**

In the bracketed passage, why does Cratchit respond so positively to the nephew's parting holiday greeting? How does Scrooge respond?

______

◆ **Reading Strategy**

Underline **stage directions** that help you **picture in your mind** the two gentlemen that arrive as the nephew leaves.

Mark the Text

◆ **Reading Check**

In the underlined passage, what assumption can be made about Marley from what the portly man says? What assumption does the portly man mistakenly make about Scrooge?

______

◆ **Literary Analysis**

What does the section of **dialogue** in the first bracketed passage tell you about what life was like for the poor at this time in history? Explain.

◆ **Reading Check**

Underline the two sentences in the second bracketed passage that show that the portly man has misunderstood Scrooge's questions and comments.

Mark the Text

◆ **Literary Analysis**

What does the underlined **dialogue** tell you about Scrooge's attitude toward the poor?

◆ **Reading Strategy**

What expressions on the faces of the two men would you **picture in your mind** as they react to Scrooge's comments?

SCROOGE. Are there no prisons?

PORTLY MAN. Plenty of prisons.

SCROOGE. And aren't the Union workhouses still in operation?

THIN MAN. They are. Still. I wish that I could say that they are not.

SCROOGE. The Treadmill[9] and the Poor Law[10] are in full vigor, then?

THIN MAN. Both very busy, sir.

SCROOGE. Ohhh, I see. I was afraid, from what you said at first, that something had occurred to stop them from their useful course. [*Pauses*] I'm glad to hear it.

PORTLY MAN. Under the impression that they scarcely furnish Christian cheer of mind or body to the multitude, a few of us are endeavoring to raise a fund to buy the Poor some meat and drink, and means of warmth. We choose this time, because it is a time, of all others, when Want is keenly felt, and Abundance rejoices. [*Pen in hand; as well as notepad*] What shall I put you down for, sir?

SCROOGE. Nothing!

PORTLY MAN. You wish to be left anonymous?

SCROOGE. I wish to be left alone! [*Pauses; turns away; turns back to them*] Since you ask me what I wish, gentlemen, that is my answer. I help to support the establishments that I have mentioned: they cost enough: and those who are badly off must go there.

THIN MAN. Many can't go there; and many would rather die.

SCROOGE. If they would rather die, they had better do it, and decrease the surplus population. Besides—excuse me—I don't know that.

THIN MAN. But you might know it!

SCROOGE. It's not my business. It's enough for a man to understand his own business, and not to interfere with other people's. Mine occupies me constantly. Good afternoon, gentlemen! [SCROOGE *turns his back on the gentlemen and returns to his desk.*]

PORTLY MAN. But, sir, Mr. Scrooge . . . think of the poor.

SCROOGE. [*Turns suddenly to them. Pauses*] Take your leave of my offices, sirs, while I am still smiling.

[*The* THIN MAN *looks at the* PORTLY MAN. *They are undone. They shrug. They move to the door.* CRATCHIT *hops up to open it for them.*]

---

9. **the Treadmill** (tred′ mil′) kind of mill wheel turned by the weight of persons treading steps arranged around it. This device was used to punish prisoners in jails.

10. **the Poor Law** The original seventeenth-century Poor Laws called for overseers of the poor in each parish to provide relief for the needy. The New Poor Law of 1834 made the workhouses in which the poor sometimes lived and worked extremely harsh and unattractive. They became a symbol of the misery of the poor.

THIN MAN. Good day, sir . . . [*To* CRATCHIT] A merry Christmas to you, sir . . .

CRATCHIT. Yes. A Merry Christmas to both of you . . .

PORTLY MAN. Merry Christmas . . .

[CRATCHIT *silently squeezes something into the hand of the thin man.*]

THIN MAN. What's this?

CRATCHIT. Shhhh . . .

[CRATCHIT *opens the door; wind and snow whistle into the room.*]

THIN MAN. Thank you, sir, thank you.

[CRATCHIT *closes the door and returns to his workplace.* SCROOGE *is at his own counting table. He talks to* CRATCHIT *without looking up.*]

SCROOGE. It's less of a time of year for being merry, and more a time of year for being loony . . . if you ask me.

CRATCHIT. Well, I don't know, sir . . . [*The clock's bell strikes six o'clock.*] Well, there it is, eh, six?

SCROOGE. Saved by six bells, are you?

CRATCHIT. I must be going home . . . [*He snuffs out his candle and puts on his hat.*] I hope you have a . . . very very lovely day tomorrow, sir . . .

SCROOGE. Hmmm. Oh, you'll be wanting the whole day tomorrow, I suppose?

CRATCHIT. If quite convenient, sir.

SCROOGE. It's not convenient, and it's not fair. If I was to stop half-a-crown for it, you'd think yourself ill-used, I'll be bound?

[CRATCHIT *smiles faintly.*]

CRATCHIT. I don't know, sir . . .

SCROOGE. And yet, you don't think me ill-used when I pay a day's wages for no work . . .

CRATCHIT. It's only but once a year . . .

SCROOGE. A poor excuse for picking a man's pocket every 25th of December! But I suppose you must have the whole day. Be here all the earlier the next morning!

CRATCHIT. Oh, I will, sir. I will. I promise you. And, sir . . .

SCROOGE. Don't say it, Cratchit.

CRATCHIT. But let me wish you a . . .

SCROOGE. Don't say it, Cratchit. I warn you . . .

CRATCHIT. Sir!

SCROOGE. Cratchit!

[CRATCHIT *opens the door.*]

◆ Stop To Reflect

What do you think Cratchit squeezes into the hand of the thin man? What does this action tell about Cratchit?

◆ Reading Check

A crown was a unit of money in England at the time of this play. Knowing that, what do you think Scrooge is saying in the bracketed passage? Why does he use the phrase "picking a man's pocket"?

◆ Literary Analysis

How does the **dialogue** here help reveal Scrooge's personality?

CRATCHIT. All right, then, sir . . . well . . . [*Suddenly*] Merry Christmas, Mr. Scrooge!

[*And he runs out the door, shutting same behind him.* SCROOGE *moves to his desk; gathering his coat, hat, etc. A boy appears at his window. . . .*]

BOY. [*Singing*] "Away in a manger . . ."

[SCROOGE *seizes his ruler and whacks at the image of the* BOY *outside. The* BOY *leaves.*]

SCROOGE. Bah! Humbug! Christmas! Bah! Humbug! [*He shuts out the light.*]

A note on the crossover, following Scene 2:

[SCROOGE *will walk alone to his rooms from his offices. As he makes a long slow cross of the stage, the scenery should change. Christmas music will be heard, various people will cross by* SCROOGE, *often smiling happily.*

There will be occasional pleasant greetings tossed at him.

SCROOGE, *in contrast to all, will grump and mumble. He will snap at passing boys, as might a horrid old hound.*

In short, SCROOGE'S *sounds and movements will define him in contrast from all other people who cross the stage: he is the misanthrope, the malcontent, the miser. He is* SCROOGE.

This statement of SCROOGE'S *character, by contrast to all other characters, should seem comical to the audience.*

During SCROOGE'S *crossover to his rooms, snow should begin to fall. All passers-by will hold their faces to the sky, smiling, allowing snow to shower them lightly.* SCROOGE, *by contrast, will bat at the flakes with his walking-stick, as might an insomniac swat at a sleep-stopping, middle-of-the-night swarm of mosquitoes. He will comment on the blackness of the night, and, finally, reach his rooms and his encounter with the magical specter:*[11] MARLEY, *his eternal mate.*]

Vocabulary Development: misanthrope (mis´ ən thrōp´) *n.* person who hates or distrusts everyone

11. **specter** (spek´ tər) *n.* ghost.

Reader's Response: Why do you think the writer tries to make sure that the audience does not like Scrooge? Do you like anything about Scrooge, feel at all sorry for him? Why or why not?

Thinking About the Skill: How does picturing a scene in your mind seem particularly helpful as you read a play?

◆ **Stop to Reflect**

Why do you think Cratchit wishes Scrooge a Merry Christmas even though Scrooge tells him not to?

◆ **Literary Analysis**

Underline the sentence in the **stage directions** that explains what the writer thinks the audience's reaction to Scrooge ought to be. How does the writer indicate that the person playing Scrooge should do this?

Mark THE Text

◆ **Reading Strategy**

How do the **stage directions** on this page allow you to **picture** this scene **in your mind**?

A Christmas Carol: Scrooge and Marley, Act 1, Scenes 4 and 5

Israel Horovitz

adapted from *A Christmas Carol* by Charles Dickens

Summary

At home on Christmas Eve, Scrooge is visited by the ghost of his dead business partner, Jacob Marley. The ghost warns Scrooge that he must be better to other people or he will end up a miserable, chain-dragging ghost like him. He tells Scrooge that three spirits will visit him during the next three nights. Then he disappears. Later, the Ghost of Christmas Past takes Scrooge back in time. Scrooge sees himself as a young schoolboy, an older schoolboy, and a young worker. Finally, he sees himself as a young man whose sweetheart leaves him because he thinks only about money. Scrooge becomes upset. He begins to regret the choices he has made in life. The ghost disappears, and Scrooge goes to sleep.

Visual Summary

Ideas	Evidence
Scrooge was not always a stingy, greedy, cold-hearted man.	As a young boy, he loved Christmas music even though he was lonely.
	As a 12-year-old, he loved his sister.
	As a young worker, he was happy with his friends and his boss.
	As a young man, he loved a young woman and planned to marry her.
Scrooge begins to regret the choices he has made in his life.	He wishes he had given something to the boy singing Christmas carols.
	He wishes he had treated Cratchit more kindly.
	He regrets that his greed caused the woman he loved to end their engagement.

◆ Activate Prior Knowledge

Think of other famous ghosts from movies, plays, or literature. Give an example of one. From your experience, what role do ghosts usually play in stories?

____

____

____

____

◆ Literary Analysis

Name two of the things that the bracketed **stage directions** tell are happening on stage as the scene opens. Why is it important to explain this stage set-up?

1. ______________________________

2. ______________________________

◆ Literary Analysis

Underline the important piece of information that Marley reveals in his opening speech (**dialogue**) that will govern the rest of the play.

◆ Stop to Reflect

Has Scrooge changed after Marley's visit to him? Underline the sentences in Marley's opening speech that answer this question.

____

____

____

____

A Christmas Carol: Scrooge and Marley

Israel Horovitz

from A Christmas Carol

by Charles Dickens

Act 1, Scenes 4 & 5

In Scene 3, which is omitted from this version of the play, Jacob Marley's ghost, who gives the opening speech in Act I, appears and tells Scrooge that his only hope of escaping a terrible fate lies in the visits of three spirits. In Scenes 4 and 5, we see the beginning of the ghostly "cure."

Scene 4

[*Christmas music, choral, "Hark the Herald Angels Sing," sung by an onstage choir of children, spotlighted,* D.C. *Above,* SCROOGE *in his bed, dead to the world, asleep, in his darkened room. It should appear that the choir is singing somewhere outside of the house, of course, and a use of scrim*[1] *is thus suggested. When the singing is ended, the choir should fade out of view and* MARLEY *should fade into view, in their place.*]

MARLEY. [*Directly to audience*] From this point forth . . . I shall be quite visible to you, but invisible to him. [*Smiles*] He will feel my presence, nevertheless, for, unless my senses fail me completely, we are—you and I—witness to the changing of a miser: that one, my partner in life, in business, and in eternity: that one: Scrooge. [*Moves to staircase, below* SCROOGE] See him now. He endeavors to pierce the darkness with his ferret eyes.[2] [*To audience*] See him, now. He listens for the hour.

[*The bells toll.* SCROOGE *is awakened and quakes as the hour approaches one o'clock, but the bells stop their sound at the hour of twelve.*]

SCROOGE. [*Astonished*] Midnight! Why this isn't possible. It was past two when I went to bed. An icicle must have gotten into the clock's works! I couldn't have slept through the whole day and far into another night. It isn't possible that anything has happened to the sun, and this is twelve at noon! [*He runs to window; unshutters same; it is night.*] Night, still. Quiet, normal for the season, cold. It is certainly not noon. I cannot in any way afford to lose my days. Securities come due, promissory notes,[3] interest on investments: these are things that happen in the daylight! [*He returns to his bed.*] Was this a dream?

---

1. **scrim** (skrim) *n.* light, semitransparent curtain.
2. **ferret eyes** a ferret is a small, weasel-like animal used for hunting rabbits; this expression means to look persistently, the way a ferret hunts.
3. **promissory** (präm′ i sôr′ ē) **notes** written promises to pay someone a certain sum of money.

[MARLEY *appears in his room. He speaks to the audience.*]

MARLEY. You see? He does not, with faith, believe in me fully, even still! Whatever will it take to turn the faith of a miser from money to men?

SCROOGE. Another quarter and it'll be one and Marley's ghosty friends will come. [*Pauses; listens*] Where's the chime for one? [*Ding, dong*] A quarter past [*Repeats*] Half-past! [*Repeats*] A quarter to it! But where's the heavy bell of the hour one? This is a game in which I lose my senses! Perhaps, if I allowed myself another short doze . . .

MARLEY . . . Doze, Ebenezer, doze.

[*A heavy bell thuds its one ring; dull and definitely one o'clock. There is a flash of light.* SCROOGE *sits up, in a sudden. A hand draws back the curtains by his bed. He sees it.*]

SCROOGE. A hand! Who owns it! Hello!

[*Ghostly music again, but of a new nature to the play. A strange figure stands before* SCROOGE*—like a child, yet at the same time like an old man: white hair, but unwrinkled skin, long, muscular arms, but delicate legs and feet. Wears white tunic; lustrous belt cinches waist. Branch of fresh green holly in its hand, but has its dress trimmed with fresh summer flowers. Clear jets of light spring from the crown of its head. Holds cap in hand. The Spirit is called* PAST.]

Are you the Spirit, sir, whose coming was foretold to me?

PAST. I am.

MARLEY. Does he take this to be a vision of his green grocer?

SCROOGE. Who, and what are you?

PAST. I am the Ghost of Christmas Past.

SCROOGE. Long past?

PAST. Your past.

SCROOGE. May I ask, please, sir, what business you have here with me?

PAST. Your welfare.

SCROOGE. Not to sound ungrateful, sir, and really, please do understand that I am plenty obliged for your concern, but, really, kind spirit, it would have done all the better for my welfare to have been left alone altogether, to have slept peacefully through this night.

PAST. Your reclamation, then. Take heed!

SCROOGE. My what?

PAST. [*Motioning to* SCROOGE *and taking his arm*] Rise! Fly with me! [*He leads* SCROOGE *to the window.*]

SCROOGE. [*Panicked*] Fly, but I am a mortal and cannot fly!

PAST. [*Pointing to his heart*] Bear but a touch of my hand here and you shall be upheld in more than this!

◆ Reading Check

Why is Scrooge paying such close attention to the time?

◆ Literary Analysis

Why is the bracketed **stage direction** important to the understanding of the play?

◆ Stop to Reflect

If you were Scrooge, how would you feel when the ghost appeared?

◆ **Literary Analysis**

How do the bracketed **stage directions** contribute to showing what is happening in the play?

____

____

____

◆ **Stop To Reflect**

Why does the playwright have Marley speak to the audience at this point? What is Marley telling the audience (reader)?

____

____

____

____

◆ **Reading Check**

What does Scrooge mean in the underlined sentence? (Use a dictionary to find the meaning of the word *stagnant,* if necessary.)

____

____

____

◆ **Reading Strategy**

Name two ways that the stage directions and dialogue in the second bracketed passage help you **picture** the scene in your mind.

1. ______________________

____

2. ______________________

____

[SCROOGE *touches the* SPIRIT'S *heart and the lights dissolve into sparkly flickers. Lovely crystals of music are heard. The scene dissolves into another. Christmas music again*]

Scene 5

[SCROOGE *and the* GHOST OF CHRISTMAS PAST *walk together across an open stage. In the background, we see a field that is open; covered by a soft, downy snow: a country road.*]

SCROOGE. Good Heaven! I was bred in this place. I was a boy here!

[SCROOGE *freezes, staring at the field beyond.* MARLEY'S *ghost appears beside him; takes* SCROOGE'S *face in his hands, and turns his face to the audience.*]

MARLEY. You see this Scrooge: stricken by feeling. Conscious of a thousand odors floating in the air, each one connected with a thousand thoughts, and hopes, and joys, and care long, long forgotten. [*Pause*] This one—this Scrooge—before your very eyes, returns to life, among the living. [*To audience, sternly*] You'd best pay your most careful attention. I would suggest rapt.[4]

[*There is a small flash and puff of smoke and* MARLEY *is gone again.*]

PAST. Your lip is trembling, Mr. Scrooge. And what is that upon your cheek?

SCROOGE. Upon my cheek? Nothing . . . a blemish on the skin from the eating of overmuch grease . . . nothing . . . [*Suddenly*] Kind Spirit of Christmas Past, lead me where you will, but quickly! To be stagnant in this place is, for me, unbearable!

PAST. You recollect the way?

SCROOGE. Remember it! I would know it blindfolded! My bridge, my church, my winding river! [*Staggers about, trying to see it all at once. He weeps again.*]

PAST. These are but shadows of things that have been. They have no consciousness of us.

[*Four jocund travelers enter, singing a Christmas song in four-part harmony—"God Rest Ye Merry Gentlemen."*]

SCROOGE. Listen! I know these men! I know them! I remember the beauty of their song!

PAST. But, why do you remember it so happily? It is Merry Christmas that they say to one another! What is Merry Christmas to you, Mr. Scrooge? Out upon Merry Christmas, right? What good has Merry Christmas ever done you, Mr. Scrooge? . . .

4. **rapt** (rapt) *adj.* giving complete attention; totally carried away by something.

SCROOGE. [*After a long pause*] None. No good. None . . . [*He bows his head.*]

PAST. Look, you, sir, a school ahead. The schoolroom is not quite deserted. A solitary child, neglected by his friends, is left there still.

[SCROOGE *falls to the ground; sobbing as he sees, and we see, a small boy, the young* SCROOGE, *sitting and weeping, bravely, alone at his desk: alone in a vast space, a void.*]

SCROOGE. I cannot look on him!

PAST. You must, Mr. Scrooge, you must.

SCROOGE. It's me. [*Pauses; weeps*] Poor boy. He lived inside his head . . . alone . . . [*Pauses; weeps*] poor boy. [*Pauses; stops his weeping*] I wish . . . [*Dries his eyes on his cuff*] ah! it's too late!

PAST. What is the matter?

SCROOGE. There was a boy singing a Christmas Carol outside my door last night. I should like to have given him something: that's all.

PAST. [*Smiles; waves his hand to* SCROOGE] Come. Let us see another Christmas.

[*Lights out on little boy. A flash of light. A puff of smoke. Lights up on older boy*]

SCROOGE. Look! Me, again! Older now! [*Realizes*] Oh, yes . . . still alone.

[*The boy—a slightly older* SCROOGE*—sits alone in a chair, reading. The door to the room opens and a young girl enters. She is much, much younger than this slightly older* SCROOGE. *She is, say, six, and he is, say, twelve. Elder* SCROOGE *and the* GHOST OF CHRISTMAS PAST *stand watching the scene, unseen.*]

FAN. Dear, dear brother, I have come to bring you home.

BOY. Home, little Fan?

FAN. Yes! Home, for good and all! Father is so much kinder than he ever used to be, and home's like heaven! He spoke so gently to me one dear night when I was going to bed that I was not afraid to ask him once more if you might come home; and he said "yes" . . . you should; and sent me in a coach to bring you. And you're to be a man and are never to come back here, but first, we're to be together all the Christmas long, and have the merriest time in the world.

BOY. You are quite a woman, little Fan!

[*Laughing; she drags at* BOY, *causing him to stumble to the door with her. Suddenly we hear a mean and terrible voice in the hallway, Off. It is the* SCHOOLMASTER.]

SCHOOLMASTER. Bring down Master Scrooge's travel box at once! He is to travel!

FAN. Who is that, Ebenezer?

◆ **Literary Analysis**

How does the bracketed **stage direction** help you understand why Scrooge became the adult he is?

◆ **Stop to Reflect**

In the underlined passage, why does Scrooge remember the singing boy? What does this passage indicate about what's happening to him?

◆ **Reading Strategy**

What action do you picture from the second bracketed set of **stage directions**?

◆ **Reading Check**

Based on what Fan is saying, what do you think Scrooge's childhood home life was like?

BOY. O! Quiet, Fan. It is the Schoolmaster, himself!

[*The door bursts open and into the room bursts with it the* SCHOOLMASTER.]

SCHOOLMASTER. Master Scrooge?

BOY. Oh, Schoolmaster. I'd like you to meet my little sister, Fan, sir . . .

[*Two boys struggle on with* SCROOGE'S *trunk.*]

FAN. Pleased, sir . . . [*She curtsies.*]

SCHOOLMASTER. You are to travel, Master Scrooge.

SCROOGE. Yes, sir. I know sir . . .

[*All start to exit, but* FAN *grabs the coattail of the mean old* SCHOOLMASTER.]

BOY. Fan!

SCHOOLMASTER. What's this?

FAN. Pardon, sir, but I believe that you've forgotten to say your goodbye to my brother, Ebenezer, who stands still now awaiting it . . . [*She smiles, curtsies, lowers her eyes.*] Pardon, sir.

SCHOOLMASTER. [*Amazed*] I . . . uh . . . harumph . . . uhh . . . well, then . . . [*Outstretches hand*] Goodbye, Scrooge.

BOY. Uh, well, goodbye, Schoolmaster . . .

[*Lights fade out on all but* BOY *looking at* FAN*; and* SCROOGE *and* PAST *looking at them.*]

SCROOGE. Oh, my dear, dear little sister, Fan . . . how I loved her.

PAST. Always a delicate creature, whom a breath might have withered, but she had a large heart . . .

SCROOGE. So she had.

PAST. She died a woman, and had, as I think, children.

SCROOGE. One child.

PAST. True. Your nephew.

SCROOGE. Yes.

PAST. Fine, then. We move on, Mr. Scrooge. That warehouse, there? Do you know it?

SCROOGE. Know it? Wasn't I apprenticed[5] there?

PAST. We'll have a look.

[*They enter the warehouse. The lights crossfade with them, coming up on an old man in Welsh wig:* FEZZIWIG.]

SCROOGE. Why, it's old Fezziwig! Bless his heart; it's Fezziwig, alive again!

[FEZZIWIG *sits behind a large, high desk, counting. He lays down his pen; looks at the clock: seven bells sound.*]

5. **apprenticed** (ə pren´ tist) *v.* receiving financial support and instruction in a trade in return for work.

◆ Reading Check

Answer these three questions about the scene in brackets: 1) How does the Schoolmaster treat Fan? 2) What does she do in response? 3) What is evident about Scrooge's school experience from this scene?

1. ______________________________

2. ______________________________

3. ______________________________

◆ Literary Analysis

What does the **dialogue** in the bracketed passage reveal about Fan's character and her relationship to her brother?

____

◆ Reading Strategy

How do the stage directions in the bracketed passage help you to **picture** this scene **in your mind**?

____

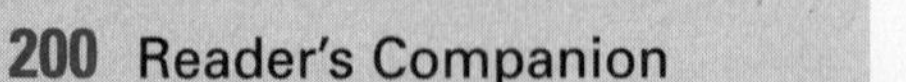

Quittin' time . . .

FEZZIWIG. Quittin' time . . . [*He takes off his waistcoat and laughs; calls off*] Yo ho, Ebenezer! Dick!

[DICK WILKINS *and* EBENEZER SCROOGE—*a young man version—enter the room.* DICK *and* EBENEZER *are* FEZZIWIG'S *apprentices.*]

SCROOGE. Dick Wilkins, to be sure! My fellow-'prentice! Bless my soul, yes. There he is. He was very much attached to me, was Dick. Poor Dick! Dear, dear!

FEZZIWIG. Yo ho, my boys. No more work tonight. Christmas Eve, Dick. Christmas, Ebenezer!

[*They stand at attention in front of* FEZZIWIG; *laughing*]

Hilli-ho! Clear away, and let's have lots of room here! Hilli-ho, Dick! Chirrup, Ebenezer!

[*The young men clear the room, sweep the floor, straighten the pictures, trim the lamps, etc. The space is clear now. A fiddler enters, fiddling.*]

Hi-ho, Matthew! Fiddle away . . . where are my daughters?

[*The* FIDDLER *plays. Three young daughters of* FEZZIWIG *enter followed by six young male suitors. They are dancing to the music. All employees come in: workers, clerks, housemaids, cousins, the baker, etc. All dance. Full number wanted here. Throughout the dance, food is brought into the feast. It is "eaten" in dance, by the dancers.* EBENEZER *dances with all three of the daughters, as does* DICK. *They compete for the daughters, happily, in the dance.* FEZZIWIG *dances with his daughters.* FEZZIWIG *dances with* DICK *and* EBENEZER. *The music changes:* MRS. FEZZIWIG *enters. She lovingly scolds her husband. They dance. She dances with* EBENEZER, *lifting him and throwing him about. She is enormously fat. When the dance is ended, they all dance off, floating away, as does the music.* SCROOGE *and the* GHOST OF CHRISTMAS PAST *stand alone now. The music is gone.*]

PAST. It was a small matter, that Fezziwig made those silly folks so full of gratitude.

SCROOGE. Small!

PAST. Shhh!

[*Lights up on* DICK *and* EBENEZER]

DICK. We are blessed, Ebenezer, truly, to have such a master as Mr. Fezziwig!

YOUNG SCROOGE. He is the best, best, the very and absolute best! If ever I own a firm of my own, I shall treat my apprentices with the same dignity and the same grace. We have learned a wonderful lesson from the master, Dick!

DICK. Ah, that's a fact, Ebenezer. That's a fact!

PAST. Was it not a small matter, really? He spent but a few pounds[6] of his mortal money on your small party. Three

6. **pounds** (poundz) *n.* common type of money used in Great Britain.

◆ Reading Strategy

Why are stage directions needed in the bracketed passage to help you **picture in your mind** what is happening?

◆ Stop to Reflect

Why do you think that the Ghost of Christmas Past showed Scrooge this scene?

◆ **Reading Check**

Underline details that explain what kind of employer Fezziwig was.

◆ **Reading Check**

What has Scrooge realized as a result of revisiting Fezziwig's warehouse?

◆ **Stop to Reflect**

In the underlined passage, what do you think the woman means when she says she has been displaced by a golden idol? (If necessary, look up the words *idol* and *displaced* in a dictionary.)

or four pounds, perhaps. Is that so much that he deserves such praise as you and Dick so lavish now?

SCROOGE. It isn't that! It isn't that, Spirit. Fezziwig had the power to make us happy or unhappy; to make our service light or burdensome; a pleasure or a toil. The happiness he gave is quite as great as if it cost him a fortune.

PAST. What is the matter?

SCROOGE. Nothing particular.

PAST. Something, I think.

SCROOGE. No, no. I should like to be able to say a word or two to my clerk just now! That's all!

[EBENEZER *enters the room and shuts down all the lamps. He stretches and yawns. The* GHOST OF CHRISTMAS PAST *turns to* SCROOGE*; all of a sudden.*]

PAST. My time grows short! Quick!

[*In a flash of light,* EBENEZER *is gone, and in his place stands an older* SCROOGE, *this one a man in the prime of his life. Beside him stands a young woman in a mourning dress. She is crying. She speaks to the man, with hostility.*]

WOMAN. It matters little . . . to you, very little. Another idol has displaced me.

MAN. What idol has displaced you?

WOMAN. A golden one.

MAN. This is an even-handed dealing of the world. There is nothing on which it is so hard as poverty; and there is nothing it professes to condemn with such severity as the pursuit of wealth!

WOMAN. You fear the world too much. Have I not seen your nobler aspirations fall off one by one, until the master-passion, Gain, engrosses you? Have I not?

SCROOGE. No!

MAN. What then? Even if I have grown so much wiser, what then? Have I changed towards you?

WOMAN. No . . .

MAN. Am I?

WOMAN. Our contract is an old one. It was made when we were both poor and content to be so. You *are* changed. When it was made, you were another man.

MAN. I was not another man: I was a boy.

WOMAN. Your own feeling tells you that you were not what you are. I am. That which promised happiness when we were one in heart is fraught with misery now that we are two . . .

SCROOGE. No!

WOMAN. How often and how keenly I have thought of this, I will not say. It is enough that I *have* thought of it, and can release you . . .

SCROOGE. [*Quietly*] Don't release me, madame . . .

MAN. Have I ever sought release?

WOMAN. In words. No. Never.

MAN. In what then?

WOMAN. In a changed nature; in an altered spirit. In everything that made my love of any worth or value in your sight. If this has never been between us, tell me, would you seek me out and try to win me now? Ah, no!

SCROOGE. Ah, yes!

MAN. You think not?

WOMAN. I would gladly think otherwise if I could, heaven knows! But if you were free today, tomorrow, yesterday, can even I believe that you would choose a dowerless girl[7]—you who in your very confidence with her weigh everything by Gain; or, choosing her, do I not know that your repentance and regret would surely follow? I do; and I release you. With a full heart, for the love of him you once were.

SCROOGE. Please, I . . . I . . .

MAN. Please, I . . . I . . .

WOMAN. Please. You may—the memory of what is past half makes me hope you will—have pain in this. A very, very brief time, and you will dismiss the memory of it, as an unprofitable dream, from which it happened well that you awoke. May you be happy in the life that you have chosen for yourself . . .

SCROOGE. No!

WOMAN. Yourself . . . alone . . .

SCROOGE. No!

WOMAN. Goodbye, Ebenezer . . .

SCROOGE. Don't let her go!

MAN. Goodbye.

SCROOGE. No!

[*She exits.* SCROOGE *goes to younger man: himself.*]

You fool! Mindless loon! You fool!

MAN. [*To exited woman*] Fool. Mindless loon. Fool . . .

SCROOGE. Don't say that! Spirit, remove me from this place.

7. **a dowerless** (dou´ ər les) **girl** a girl without a dowry, the property or wealth a woman brought to her husband at marriage.

◆ Reading Strategy

Try to **picture in your mind** this scene. What is going on between the characters?

____

____

____

____

____

____

◆ Reading Check

After reading the bracketed passage, answer these three questions: 1) What does the woman "release" the young Scrooge from? 2) Why does she do this? 3) Does she think he would ask her to marry him now? Why or why not?

1. ______________________

____

2. ______________________

____

3. ______________________

____

◆ Stop to Reflect

In the underlined passage, do you think the woman is correct in her assessment of how long Scrooge will remember her? What evidence tells you this?

____

____

____

____

____

◆ Literary Analysis

How do the actions described in the bracketed **stage directions** help show Scrooge's feelings?

◆ Stop to Reflect

What do you think the specters Christmas Present and Christmas Future, which Marley tells the audience are coming next, will show Scrooge?

PAST. I have told you these were shadows of the things that have been. They are what they are. Do not blame me, Mr. Scrooge.

SCROOGE. Remove me! I cannot bear it!

[*The faces of all who appeared in this scene are now projected for a moment around the stage: enormous, flimsy, silent.*]

Leave me! Take me back! Haunt me no longer!

[*There is a sudden flash of light: a flare. The* GHOST OF CHRISTMAS PAST *is gone.* SCROOGE *is, for the moment, alone onstage. His bed is turned down, across the stage. A small candle burns now in* SCROOGE'S *hand. There is a child's cap in his other hand. He slowly crosses the stage to his bed, to sleep.* MARLEY *appears behind* SCROOGE, *who continues his long, elderly cross to bed.* MARLEY *speaks directly to the audience.*]

MARLEY. Scrooge must sleep now. He must surrender to the irresistible drowsiness caused by the recognition of what was. [*Pauses*] The cap he carries is from ten lives past: his boyhood cap . . . donned atop a hopeful hairy head . . . askew, perhaps, or at a rakish angle. Doffed now in honor of regret.[8] Perhaps even too heavy to carry in his present state of weak remorse . . .

[SCROOGE *drops the cap. He lies atop his bed. He sleeps. To audience*]

He sleeps. For him, there's even more trouble ahead. [*Smiles*] For you? The play house tells me there's hot cider, as should be your anticipation for the specter Christmas Present and Future, for I promise you both. [*Smiles again*] So, I pray you hurry back to your seats refreshed and ready for a miser—to turn his coat of gray into a blazen Christmas holly-red.

[*A flash of lightning. A clap of thunder. Bats fly. Ghosty music.* MARLEY *is gone.*]

8. **donned . . . regret** to don and doff a hat means to put it on and take it off; askew means "crooked," and at a rakish angle means "having a dashing or jaunty look."

Reader's Response: How would you feel at this point in the play if you were Scrooge?

Thinking About the Skills: Which of the skills that you learned about while reading this play might also be useful for reading a short story or novel? Explain.

PREVIEW

The Cremation of Sam McGee

Robert Service

Summary

"The Cremation of Sam McGee" is the story of a Tennessee miner who hated the cold. Still, he joined the gold rush in northern Canada, where it is extremely cold. He knew he couldn't survive the cold, so he asked the narrator to cremate him when he died. When Sam dies from the cold, the narrator travels across the frozen landscape with Sam's corpse to find a place to cremate him. On a frozen lake, he finds an abandoned ship. He attempts to cremate Sam's body in the ship's furnace, but when the corpse is warmed by the fire, Sam comes back to life!

Visual Summary

Sequence of Events

1. →	2. →	3. →	4. →	5. →	6.
Sam McGee and miners are working in northern Canada.	McGee asks narrator to cremate him when he dies.	McGee dies.	Narrator carries the body on the sleigh to find a place to cremate him.	Narrator attempts to cremate the body.	When narrator checks on the cremation, Sam McGee is alive in the fire.

◆ Activate Prior Knowledge

Robert Service once said, "The only society I like is that which is rough and tough—and the tougher the better. That's where you get down to bedrock and meet human people." Do you agree? Explain.

____

____

____

____

◆ Literary Analysis

A **narrative poem** tells a story and has characters, a setting, and a plot. In the first two stanzas, circle details that reveal the setting, or the time and place in which the poem occurs.

Mark the Text

◆ Reading Strategy

A **figure of speech** is an expression that is not meant to be taken literally. A **simile** is a comparison of two unlike things using *like* or *as*. In the underlined sentence, the feeling of *cold* is compared to the feeling of *a driven nail*. In what way are they similar?

____

____

____

◆ Reading Check

What is Sam McGee's complaint?

____

____

____

The Cremation of Sam McGee

Robert Service

In this poem, two men prospect for gold in Canada's Yukon Territory. Located just east of Alaska, the Yukon stretches north of the Arctic Circle. Though the temperature can reach –60°F, miners have long come to the area for its mineral wealth.

There are strange things done in the midnight sun[1]
By the men who moil[2] *for gold;*
The Arctic trails have their secret tales
That would make your blood run cold;
The Northern Lights have seen queer sights,
But the queerest they ever did see
Was that night on the marge[3] *of Lake Lebarge*
I cremated Sam McGee.

Now Sam McGee was from Tennessee,
where the cotton blooms and blows.
Why he left his home in the South to roam
'round the Pole, God only knows.
He was always cold, but the land of gold
seemed to hold him like a spell;
Though he'd often say in his homely way
that "he'd sooner live in hell."

On a Christmas Day we were mushing[4] our
way over the Dawson trail.
Talk of your cold! through the parka's fold
it stabbed like a driven nail.
If our eyes we'd close, then the lashes froze
till sometimes we couldn't see;
It wasn't much fun, but the only one to
whimper was Sam McGee.

Vocabulary Development: cremated (krē′ māt id) *v.* burned to ashes
whimper (hwim′ pər) *v.* make low, crying sounds; complain

1. **the midnight sun** the sun visible at midnight in the Arctic or Antarctic regions during their summers.
2. **moil** (moil) *v.* to toil and slave.
3. **marge** (märj) *n.* poetic word for the shore of the lake.
4. **mushing** (mush′ iŋ) *v.* traveling by foot over snow, usually with a dog sled. "Mush" is a command to sled dogs to start or to go faster.

And that very night, as we lay packed tight
in our robes beneath the snow,
And the dogs were fed, and the stars o'erhead
were dancing heel and toe,
He turned to me, and "Cap," says he,
"I'll cash in[5] this trip, I guess;
And if I do, I'm asking that you
won't refuse my last request."

Well, he seemed so low that I couldn't say no;
then he says with a sort of moan:
"It's the cursed cold, and it's got right hold
till I'm chilled clean through to the bone.
Yet 'tain't being dead—it's my awful dread
of the icy grave that pains;
So I want you to swear that, foul or fair,
you'll cremate my last remains."

A pal's last need is a thing to heed,
so I swore I would not fail;
And we started on at the streak of dawn;
but God! he looked ghastly pale.
He crouched on the sleigh, and he raved all day
of his home in Tennessee;
And before nightfall a corpse was all
that was left of Sam McGee.

There wasn't a breath in that land of death,
and I hurried, horror-driven,
With a corpse half hid that I couldn't get rid,
because of a promise given;
It was lashed to the sleigh, and it seemed to say:
"You may tax your brawn[6] and brains,
But you promised true, and it's up to you
to cremate those last remains."

Now a promise made is a debt unpaid,
and the trail has its own stern code.
In the days to come, though my lips were dumb,
in my heart how I cursed that load.

◆ Reading Strategy

Hyperbole is exaggeration for a particular effect. In the bracketed section, circle the hyperbole Sam McGee uses to describe how cold he is.

Mark the Text

◆ Reading Check

What promise does the speaker make?

◆ Literary Analysis

An important part of the **plot** is a problem that must be solved. How might the speaker's promise to Sam McGee create a problem?

Vocabulary Development: **ghastly** (gast´ lē) *adv.* ghostlike; frightful
stern (stʉrn) *adj.* strict; unyielding

5. **cash in** slang expression meaning "die."
6. **brawn** (brôn) *n.* physical strength.

In the long, long night, by the lone firelight,
while the huskies,[7] round in a ring,
Howled out their woes to the homeless snows—
O God! how I loathed the thing.

And every day that quiet clay
seemed to heavy and heavier grow;
And on I went, though the dogs were spent
and the grub was getting low;
The trail was bad, and I felt half mad,
but I swore I would not give in;
And I'd often sing to the hateful thing,
and it hearkened with a grin.

Till I came to the marge of Lake Lebarge,
and a derelict[8] there lay;
It was jammed in the ice, but I saw in a trice
it was called the "Alice May."
And I looked at it, and I thought a bit,
and I looked at my frozen chum;
Then "Here," said I, with a sudden cry,
"is my cre-ma-tor-eum."

Some planks I tore from the cabin floor,
and I lit the boiler fire;
Some coal I found that was lying around,
and I heaped the fuel higher;
The flames just soared, and the furnace roared—
such a blaze you seldom see;
And I burrowed a hole in the glowing coal,
and I stuffed in Sam McGee.

Then I made a hike, for I didn't like
to hear him sizzle so;
And the heavens scowled, and the huskies howled,
and the wind began to blow.
It was icy cold, but the hot sweat rolled
down my cheeks, and I don't know why;
And the greasy smoke in an inky cloak
went streaking down the sky.

◆ Literary Analysis

Rhythm is the pattern of stresses, or beats, in language. What does the poet do in the last line of this bracketed stanza to maintain the strong rhythm of the poem?

◆ Stop to Reflect

Why do you think Cap was sweating even though it was cold?

Vocabulary Development: loathed (lōthd) *v.* hated

7. **huskies** (hus′ kēs) *n.* strong dogs used for pulling sleds over the snow.
8. **derelict** (der′ ə likt′) *n.* abandoned ship.

I do not know how long in the snow
I wrestled with grisly fear;
But the stars came out and they danced about
ere again I ventured near;
I was sick with dread, but I bravely said:
"I'll just take a peep inside.
I guess he's cooked, and it's time I looked"; . . .
then the door I opened wide.

And there sat Sam, looking cool and calm,
in the heart of the furnace roar;
And he wore a smile you could see a mile,
and he said: "Please close that door.
It's fine in here, but I greatly fear
you'll let in the cold and storm—
Since I left Plumtree, down in Tennessee,
it's the first time I've been warm."

There are strange things done in the midnight sun
By the men who moil for gold;
The Arctic trails have their secret tales
That would make your blood run cold;
The Northern Lights have seen queer sights,
But the queerest they ever did see
Was that night on the marge of Lake Lebarge
I cremated Sam McGee.

Vocabulary Development: grisly (griz′ lē) *adj.* horrible

Reader's Response: What was your reaction to the ending of the poem?

____

____

____

Thinking About the Skill: How did analyzing figures of speech deepen your understanding and enjoyment of the poem?

____

____

____

◆ **Reading Strategy**

Mark the Text

Personification is giving human characteristics to an animal or thing. Circle the human characteristic given to the stars in the bracketed section.

◆ **Literary Analysis**

How is the narrator's problem resolved at the end of the **narrative**?

____

____

____

◆ **Literary Analysis**

The last verse of this poem is the same as the first verse. Do you think this is an effective way to end a **narrative poem**? Explain.

____

____

____

____

____

____

PREVIEW

Annabel Lee

Edgar Allan Poe

Summary

The poem "Annabel Lee" tells of the deep love between the young man who tells the poem and Annabel Lee. Annabel Lee is a young woman who lives by the sea. When Annabel Lee dies from a chill, her lover grieves over her death. Still, he believes that their love is so deep that their souls are never truly separated.

Visual Summary

Setting	What Happens
• "kingdom by the sea" • "tomb by the sea"	• "The angels… / Went envying her and me" • "…the wind came out of a cloud, chilling / And killing my Annabel Lee" • "… the moon [brings] me dreams / Of the beautiful Annabel Lee" • "… I lie down by the side / Of my darling, my darling, my life and my bride… / In her tomb by the side of the sea."

Annabel Lee

Edgar Allan Poe

Poe's biographer Kenneth Silverman believes that the woman in this poem "represents all of the women he loved and lost." Poe finished the poem about a year after his wife's death and published it in a New York newspaper.

It was many and many a year ago,
  In a kingdom by the sea.
That a maiden there lived whom you may know
  By the name of Annabel Lee;—
And this maiden she lived with no other thought
  Than to love and be loved by me.

She was a child and *I* was a child,
  In this kingdom by the sea.
But we loved with a love that was more than love—
  I and my Annabel Lee—
With a love that the wingèd seraphs[1] of Heaven
  Coveted her and me.

And this was the reason that, long ago,
  In this kingdom by the sea,
A wind blew out of a cloud by night
  Chilling my Annabel Lee;
So that her highborn kinsmen[2] came
  And bore her away from me,
To shut her up in a sepulcher[3]
  In this kingdom by the sea.

The angels, not half so happy in Heaven,
  Went envying her and me:—
Yes! that was the reason (as all men know,
  In this kingdom by the sea)
That the wind came out of a cloud, chilling
  And killing my Annabel Lee.

Vocabulary Development: coveted (kuv′ it id) *v.* wanted greatly

1. **seraphs** (ser′ əfs) *n.* angels.
2. **highborn kinsmen** relatives of noble birth.
3. **sepulcher** (sep′ əl kər) *n.* vault for burial; grave; tomb.

◆ Activate Prior Knowledge

Who is someone you feel close to? Describe what makes him or her special to you.

◆ Literary Analysis

Mark the Text

Rhyme is the repetition of a sound at the ends of nearby words. In the first two stanzas of this poem, circle all of the words at the ends of lines that rhyme with *tree.*

Is the pattern of rhymed words regular or irregular?

◆ Reading Check

What has happened to Annabel Lee?

◆ **Reading Strategy**

You can **paraphrase,** or restate, part or all of a poem in order to get to the heart of the meaning. Use your own words to paraphrase the bracketed stanza.

____

____

____

____

____

____

◆ **Literary Analysis**

Read the underlined section of the poem to yourself and notice the **rhythm** of the lines. Some syllables are more strongly stressed than others. Circle those syllables.

Mark the Text

Is the rhythm regular or irregular?

____

____

____

But our love it was stronger by far than the love
 Of those who were older than we—
 Of many far wiser than we—
And neither the angels in Heaven above
 Nor the demons down under the sea,
Can ever dissever[4] my soul from the soul
 Of the beautiful Annabel Lee:—

For the moon never beams without bringing
 me dreams
Of the beautiful Annabel Lee;
And the stars never rise but I see the bright eyes
 Of the beautiful Annabel Lee;
And so, all the nighttide,[5] I lie down by the side
Of my darling, my darling, my life and my bride,
 In her sepulcher there by the sea—
 In her tomb by the side of the sea.

4. **dissever** (di sev′ ər) *v.* separate.
5. **nighttide** (nīt′ tīd′) *n.* an old-fashioned way of saying nighttime.

Reader's Response: Do you think this poem would make a good song? Why or why not?

____

____

Thinking About the Skill: What was the effect of the repeated rhymes?

____

____

PREVIEW

Maestro

Pat Mora

Summary

In "Maestro," a great musician plays the violin in concert. As he bows before an audience, he recalls the sound of his mother's voice and his father's guitar. When the audience applauds, he hears the music he and his parents played together at home.

Visual Summary

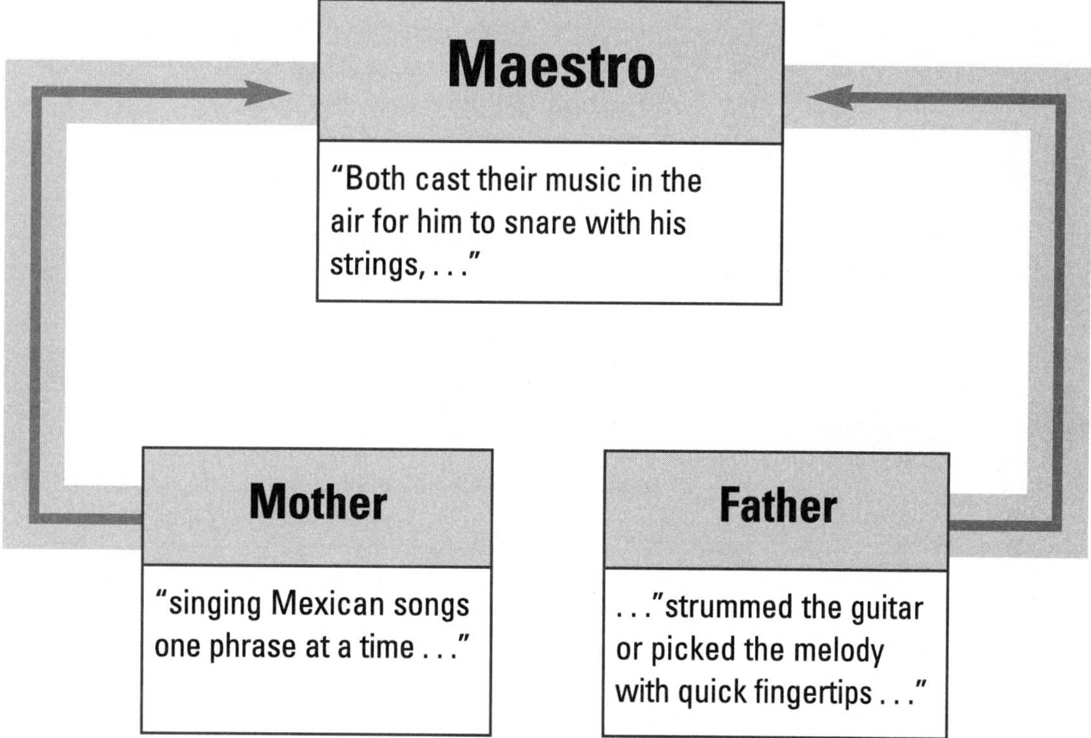

Maestro

Pat Mora

Sound is very important to poetry. The words in this poem were chosen both for their musical effect and for their meaning.

He hears her
when he bows.
Rows of hands clap
again and again he bows
to stage lights and upturned faces
but he hears only his mother's voice

years ago in their small home
singing Mexican songs
one phrase at a time
while his father strummed the guitar
or picked the melody with quick fingertips.
Both cast their music in the air
for him to snare with his strings,
songs of *lunas*[1] and *amor*[2]
learned bit by bit.
She'd nod, smile, as his bow slid
note to note, then the trio
voz,[3] *guitarra*,[4] *violín*[5]
would blend again and again
to the last pure note
sweet on the tongue.

Vocabulary Development: maestro (mīs´ trō) *n.* great musician
snare (snar) *v.* catch or trap

1. ***lunas*** (lo͞o´ näs) *n.* Spanish for "moons."
2. ***amor*** (ä môr´) *n.* Spanish for "love."
3. ***voz*** (vōs) *n.* Spanish for "voice."
4. ***guitarra*** (gē tär´ rä) *n.* Spanish for "guitar."
5. ***violín*** (vē ō lēn´) *n.* Spanish for "violin."

Reader's Response: Would you like to know the family described in this poem? Why or why not?

____

____

Thinking About the Skill: In what way does understanding onomatopoeia add to your enjoyment of poetry?

____

____

◆ Activate Prior Knowledge

Do you have a happy memory you like to replay in your mind? Describe it briefly.

____

____

____

____

◆ Literary Analysis

Sound devices make a poem pleasing to listen to. **Onomatopoeia** is the use of words whose sounds suggest their meaning. Circle the word in the underlined sentence that sounds like the action it describes.

Mark the Text

◆ Reading Check

Whom does the violinist hear when the audience applauds?

____

____

____

The Village Blacksmith

Henry Wadsworth Longfellow

Summary

"The Village Blacksmith," a strong, muscular man, works at his forge under a chestnut tree. He is a hard and honest worker. The children pass by on their way home from school. They like to look in at the fire. On Sundays, the blacksmith goes to church with his children. He thinks of his children's mother, who has died, and he sheds a tear. His life is a lesson to all: Life should be forged by working hard and setting good examples.

Visual Summary

The Blacksmith's Life		
He works hard at his forge every day.	Children like to look in at the fire as they pass by.	He goes to church on Sundays. He feels sad that his children's mother has died.
Lesson		
Live life well, and shape your fortune by your deeds and thoughts.		

◆ **Activate Prior Knowledge**

Is there someone in your life whom you admire? List three qualities you admire in the person.

1. ______________________________

____

2. ______________________________

____

3. ______________________________

____

◆ **Literary Analysis**

Poetry often includes **figurative language**, words that are not meant to be taken literally. A **simile** is a comparison using *like* or *as*. The underlined sentence compares the sound of the smith swinging his sledge to something else. Circle the line that tells what this sound is being compared to.

Mark the Text

◆ **Reading Check**

What does the blacksmith look like?

____

____

____

____

The Village Blacksmith

Henry Wadsworth Longfellow

The speaker of this poem describes the life of a strong, simple, hard-working blacksmith. The blacksmith leads a worthy life filled with honest attitudes and a deep love of family and community.

Under a spreading chestnut tree
  The village smithy[1] stands;
The smith, a mighty man is he,
  With large and sinewy[2] hands;
And the muscles of his brawny arms
  Are strong as iron bands.

His hair is crisp,[3] and black, and long,
  His face is like the tan;
His brow is wet with honest sweat,
  He earns whate'er he can,
And looks the whole world in the face,
  For he owes not any man.

Week in, week out, from morn till night,
  You can hear his bellows[4] blow;
You can hear him swing his heavy sledge,[5]
  With measured beat and slow,
Like a sexton[6] ringing the village bell,
  When the evening sun is low.

And children coming home from school
  Look in at the open door;
They love to see the flaming forge,
  And hear the bellows roar,
And catch the burning sparks that fly
  Like chaff from a threshing floor.

Vocabulary Development: brawny (brôn´ ē) *adj.* strong and muscular

1. **smithy** (smith´ ē) *n.* workshop of a blacksmith.
2. **sinewy** (sin´ yo͞o wē) *adj.* tough and strong.
3. **crisp** (krisp) *adj.* closely curled and wiry.
4. **bellows** (bel´ ōz) *n.* device for quickening the fire by blowing air on it.
5. **sledge** (slej) *n.* sledgehammer; a long, heavy hammer, usually held with both hands.
6. **sexton** (seks´ tən) *n.* person who cares for church property and rings church bells.

He goes on Sunday to the church,
  And sits among his boys;
He hears the parson pray and preach,
  He hears his daughter's voice,
Singing in the village choir,
And it makes his heart rejoice.

It sounds to him like her mother's voice,
  Singing in Paradise!
He needs must think of her once more,
  How in the grave she lies;
And with his hard, rough hand he wipes
  A tear out of his eyes.

Toiling—rejoicing—sorrowing,
  Onward through life he goes;
Each morning sees some task begin,
  Each evening sees it close;
Something attempted, something done,
  Has earned a night's repose.

Thanks, thanks to thee, my worthy friend,
  For the lesson thou hast taught!
Thus at the flaming forge of life
  Our fortunes must be wrought;
Thus on its sounding anvil shaped
  Each burning deed and thought.

◆ Reading Strategy

You can experience a poem more fully if you **use your senses.** What sense is the blacksmith using in lines 28 and 29?

____

____

◆ Stop to Reflect

What lesson do you think the speaker has learned?

____

____

____

____

Reader's Response: Do you admire the blacksmith? Explain.

____

____

Thinking About the Skill: Give three details from the poem that appeal to your senses, and tell what sense they appeal to.

1. ____

2. ____

3. ____

Popocatepetl and Ixtlaccihuatl

Juliet Piggott

Summary

"Popocatepetl and Ixtlaccihuatl" is a legend that explains the origin of two volcanoes near present-day Mexico City. A powerful emperor in the Aztec capital of Tenochtitlan forbids his daughter, the beautiful princess Ixtla, to marry Popo, the brave warrior she loves. Eventually, the aging emperor offers his daughter's hand to the warrior who will defeat his enemies. After a lengthy war, the emperor's men prevail. Most soldiers agree that Popo has fought hard and is responsible for the victory. But a few jealous warriors hurry back to the city and report that Popo has been killed. This news causes Ixtla to fall ill and die. Popo returns and responds by killing the guilty soldiers and refusing to become emperor. He then has two stone pyramids built outside the city. He buries Ixtla near the peak of one and then takes his place atop the taller of the two. He holds a lighted torch and watches over Ixtla's body for the rest of his days. The two volcanoes stand as reminders of the two lovers who dreamed of always being together.

Visual Summary

Elements of Legend

Larger-than-life characters	Exaggerated details
Popo, brandishing his club and shield, leads the warriors to victory.	Popo stands on top of stone pyramid for the rest of his life, holding the torch in memory of Ixtla.

Reveals values of culture	Fantastic details
Legend reflects Aztec belief in loyalty and bravery.	Two stone pyramids built by Popo turn into two volcanoes.

Popocatepetl and Ixtlaccihuatl

Juliet Piggott

This legend comes from the Aztec Indians, who controlled a great empire in Mexico 500 years ago. Great builders and engineers, the Aztecs built their capital city, Tenochtitlan (te nôch' tē tlän'), on a lake. The city contained an incredible system of canals for transportation and floating gardens for crops. The Spanish conquered the Aztec empire in 1521.

Before the Spaniards came to Mexico and marched on the Aztec capital of Tenochtitlan[1] there were two volcanoes to the southeast of that city. The Spaniards destroyed much of Tenochtitlan and built another city in its place and called it Mexico City. It is known by that name still, and the pass through which the Spaniards came to the ancient Tenochtitlan is still there, as are the volcanoes on each side of that pass. Their names have not been changed. The one to the north is Ixtlaccihuatl (ēs' tä sē' wät' əl), and the one on the south of the pass is Popocatepetl (pô pô kä tē' pet' əl). Both are snowcapped and beautiful, Popocatepetl being the taller of the two. That name means Smoking Mountain. In Aztec days it gushed forth smoke and, on occasion, it does so still. It erupted too in Aztec days and has done so again since the Spaniards came. Ixtlaccihuatl means The White Woman, for its peak was, and still is, white.

Perhaps Ixtlaccihuatl and Popocatepetl were there in the highest part of the Valley of Mexico in the days when the earth was very young, in the days when the new people were just learning to eat and grow corn. The Aztecs claimed the volcanoes as their own, for they possessed a legend about them and their creation, and they believed that legend to be true.

There was once an Aztec Emperor in Tenochtitlan. He was very powerful. Some thought he was wise as well, whilst others doubted his wisdom. He was both a ruler and a warrior and he kept at bay those tribes living in and beyond the mountains surrounding the Valley of Mexico, with its huge lake called Texcoco (tā skō' kō), in which Tenochtitlan was built. His power was absolute and the splendor in which he lived was very great.

It is not known for how many years the Emperor ruled in Tenochtitlan, but it is known that he lived to a great age. However, it was not until he was in his middle years that his wife gave him an heir, a girl. The Emperor and Empress loved the princess very much and she was their only child. She was a dutiful daughter and learned all she could from her father about the art of ruling, for she knew that when he died she would reign in his stead in Tenochtitlan.

1. **Tenochtitlan** (te nôch' tē tlän') Aztec capital, conquered by the Spanish in 1521.

◆ Activate Prior Knowledge

Think of a story you know that gives a fantastical version of how a natural feature came to be. Describe it briefly.

◆ Reading Strategy

Often, a word or idea is clarified when you **read ahead**. Read the underlined sentence. Then, read ahead to determine why some people thought the emperor was unwise.

◆ Reading Check

What are the Ixtlaccihuatl and Popocatepetl?

◆ Reading Check

What bears the same name as the princess?

◆ Reading Strategy

In the bracketed paragraph, underline the answer to the question, "Why did some people think the emperor was unwise?"

Mark the Text

◆ Reading Strategy

If you do not understand a passage, **reread** it to look for connections among words and sentences. Reread to find out why Ixtla and Popo cannot marry.

Her name was Ixtlaccihuatl. Her parents and her friends called her Ixtla. She had a pleasant disposition and, as a result, she had many friends. The great palace where she lived with the Emperor and Empress rang with their laughter when they came to the parties her parents gave for her. As well as being a delightful companion Ixtla was also very pretty, even beautiful.

Her childhood was happy and she was content enough when she became a young woman. But by then she was fully aware of the great responsibilities which would be hers when her father died and she became serious and studious and did not enjoy parties as much as she had done when younger.

Another reason for her being so serious was that she was in love. This in itself was a joyous thing, but the Emperor forbade her to marry. He wanted her to reign and rule alone when he died, for he trusted no one, not even his wife, to rule as he did except his much loved only child, Ixtla. This was why there were some who doubted the wisdom of the Emperor for, by not allowing his heiress to marry, he showed a selfishness and shortsightedness towards his daughter and his empire which many considered was not truly wise. An emperor, they felt, who was not truly wise could not also be truly great. Or even truly powerful.

The man with whom Ixtla was in love was also in love with her. Had they been allowed to marry their state could have been doubly joyous. His name was Popocatepetl and Ixtla and his friends all called him Popo. He was a warrior in the service of the Emperor, tall and strong, with a capacity for gentleness, and very brave. He and Ixtla loved each other very much and while they were content and even happy when they were together, true joy was not theirs because the Emperor continued to insist that Ixtla should not be married when the time came for her to take on her father's responsibilities.

This unfortunate but moderately happy relationship between Ixtla and Popo continued for several years, the couple pleading with the Emperor at regular intervals and the Emperor remaining constantly adamant. Popo loved Ixtla no less for her father's stubbornness and she loved him no less while she studied, as her father demanded she should do, the art of ruling in preparation for her reign.

When the Emperor became very old he also became ill. In his feebleness he channeled all his failing energies towards instructing Ixtla in statecraft, for he was no longer able to exercise that craft himself. So it was that his enemies, the tribes who lived in the mountains and beyond, realized that the great Emperor in Tenochtitlan was great no longer, for he was only teaching his daughter to rule and not ruling himself.

The tribesmen came nearer and nearer to Tenochtitlan

until the city was besieged. At last the Emperor realized himself that he was great no longer, that his power was nearly gone and that his domain was in dire peril.

Warrior though he long had been, he was now too old and too ill to lead his fighting men into battle. At last he understood that, unless his enemies were frustrated in their efforts to enter and lay waste to Tenochtitlan, not only would he no longer be Emperor but his daughter would never be Empress.

Instead of appointing one of his warriors to lead the rest into battle on his behalf, he offered a bribe to all of them. Perhaps it was that his wisdom, if wisdom he had, had forsaken him, or perhaps he acted from fear. Or perhaps he simply changed his mind. But the bribe he offered to whichever warrior succeeded in lifting the siege of Tenochtitlan and defeating the enemies in and around the Valley of Mexico was both the hand of his daughter and the equal right to reign and rule, with her, in Tenochtitlan. Furthermore, he decreed that directly he learned that his enemies had been defeated he would instantly cease to be Emperor himself. Ixtla would not have to wait until her father died to become Empress and, if her father should die of his illness or old age before his enemies were vanquished, he further decreed that he who overcame the surrounding enemies should marry the princess whether he, the Emperor, lived or not.

Ixtla was fearful when she heard of her father's bribe to his warriors, for the only one whom she had any wish to marry was Popo and she wanted to marry him, and only him, very much indeed.

The warriors, however, were glad when they heard of the decree: there was not one of them who would not have been glad to have the princess as his wife and they all relished the chance of becoming Emperor.

And so the warriors went to war at their ruler's behest, and each fought trebly[2] hard for each was fighting not only for the safety of Tenochtitlan and the surrounding valley, but for the delightful bride and for the right to be the Emperor himself.

Even though the warriors fought with great skill and even though each one exhibited a courage he did not know he possessed, the war was a long one. The Emperor's enemies were firmly entrenched around Lake Texcoco and Tenochtitlan by the time the warriors were sent to war, and as battle followed battle the final outcome was uncertain.

Vocabulary Development: besieged (bi sējd′) *adj.* surrounded by enemies
decreed (di krēd′) *v.* officially ordered
relished (rel′ isht) *v.* especially enjoyed

2. **trebly** (tre′ blē) *adv.* three times as much; triply.

◆ Reading Check

Mark the Text

Underline two sentences that tell what realizations the Emperor comes to.

◆ Reading Strategy

If you did not understand the emperor's decree, **reread** the bracketed passage. Then answer these questions: 1) What bribe does the emperor offer? 2) What will happen to the emperor when his enemies are defeated?

1. ______________________

____

____

2. ______________________

____

____

◆ Stop to Reflect

What do you think about the emperor's decision to reverse his decree about his daughter getting married?

____

____

____

____

____

____

____

◆ **Literary Analysis**

Legends are stories passed down from generation to generation by word of mouth. They often reflect the culture and the values of the people from which they come. What can you tell about the Aztec culture from the bracketed paragraph?

____

____

____

____

◆ **Stop to Reflect**

Why do you think some of the men are jealous of Popo?

____

____

____

____

◆ **Reading Check**

Underline the lie that the jealous soldiers tell the king.

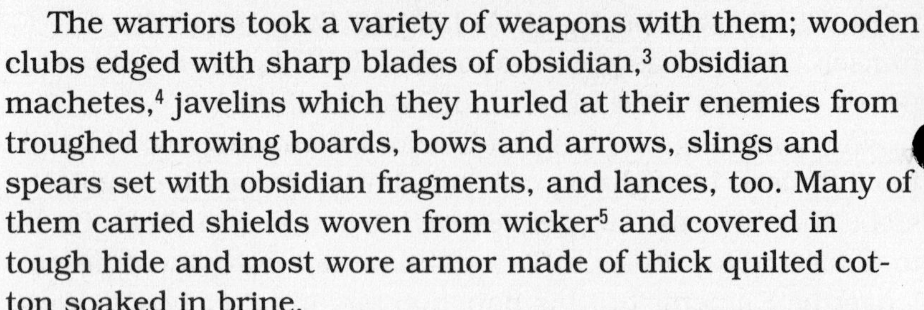

The warriors took a variety of weapons with them; wooden clubs edged with sharp blades of obsidian,[3] obsidian machetes,[4] javelins which they hurled at their enemies from troughed throwing boards, bows and arrows, slings and spears set with obsidian fragments, and lances, too. Many of them carried shields woven from wicker[5] and covered in tough hide and most wore armor made of thick quilted cotton soaked in brine.

The war was long and fierce. Most of the warriors fought together and in unison, but some fought alone. As time went on natural leaders emerged and, of these, undoubtedly Popo was the best. Finally it was he, brandishing his club and shield, who led the great charge of running warriors across the valley, with their enemies fleeing before them to the safety of the coastal plains and jungles beyond the mountains.

The warriors acclaimed Popo as the man most responsible for the victory and, weary though they all were, they set off for Tenochtitlan to report to the Emperor and for Popo to claim Ixtla as his wife at last.

But a few of those warriors were jealous of Popo. Since they knew none of them could rightly claim the victory for himself (the decision among the Emperor's fighting men that Popo was responsible for the victory had been unanimous), they wanted to spoil for him and for Ixtla the delights which the Emperor had promised.

These few men slipped away from the rest at night and made their way to Tenochtitlan ahead of all the others. They reached the capital two days later, having traveled without sleep all the way, and quickly let it be known that, although the Emperor's warriors had been successful against his enemies, the warrior Popo had been killed in battle.

It was a foolish and cruel lie which those warriors told their Emperor, and they told it for no reason other than that they were jealous of Popo.

When the Emperor heard this he demanded that Popo's body be brought to him so that he might arrange a fitting burial. He knew the man his daughter had loved would have died courageously. The jealous warriors looked at one another and said nothing. Then one of them told the Emperor that Popo had been killed on the edge of Lake Texcoco and that

Vocabulary Development: brandishing (bran´ dish iŋ) *adj.* waving in a menacing way
unanimous (yo͞o nan´ ə məs) *adj.* based on complete agreement

3. **obsidian** (əb sid´ ē ən) *n.* hard, usually dark-colored or black, volcanic glass.
4. **machetes** (mə shet´ ēs) *n.* large, heavy-bladed knives.
5. **wicker** (wik´ ər) *n.* thin, flexible twig.

his body had fallen into the water and no man had been able to retrieve it. The Emperor was saddened to hear this.

After a little while he demanded to be told which of his warriors had been responsible for the victory but none of the fighting men before him dared claim the successful outcome of the war for himself, for each knew the others would refute him. So they were silent. This puzzled the Emperor and he decided to wait for the main body of his warriors to return and not to press the few who had brought the news of the victory and of Popo's death.

Then the Emperor sent for his wife and his daughter and told them their enemies had been overcome. The Empress was thoroughly excited and relieved at the news. Ixtla was only apprehensive. The Emperor, seeing her anxious face, told her quickly that Popo was dead. He went on to say that the warrior's body had been lost in the waters of Lake Texcoco, and again it was as though his wisdom had left him, for he spoke at some length of his not being able to tell Ixtla who her husband would be and who would become Emperor when the main body of warriors returned to Tenochtitlan.

But Ixtla heard nothing of what he told her, only that her beloved Popo was dead. She went to her room and lay down. Her mother followed her and saw at once she was very ill. Witch doctors were sent for, but they could not help the princess, and neither could her parents. Her illness had no name, unless it was the illness of a broken heart. Princess Ixtlaccihuatl did not wish to live if Popocatepetl was dead, and so she died herself.

The day after her death Popo returned to Tenochtitlan with all the other surviving warriors. They went straight to the palace and, with much cheering, told the Emperor that his enemies had been routed and that Popo was the undoubted victor of the conflict.

The Emperor praised his warriors and pronounced Popo to be the new Emperor in his place. When the young man asked first to see Ixtla, begging that they should be married at once before being jointly proclaimed Emperor and Empress, the Emperor had to tell Popo of Ixtla's death, and how it had happened.

Popo spoke not a word.

He gestured the assembled warriors to follow him and together they sought out the few jealous men who had given the false news of his death to the Emperor. With the army of warriors watching, Popo killed each one of them in single combat with his obsidian studded club. No one tried to stop him.

That task accomplished Popo returned to the palace and,

Vocabulary Development: refute (ri fyo͞ot´) *v.* prove someone wrong
routed (rout´ əd) *v.* completely defeated

◆ Stop to Reflect

Why is it unwise of the Emperor to talk to Ixtla as he does in the bracketed passage?

◆ Reading Strategy

Reread the description of Ixtla and Popo's relationship on page 220. How does it help explain Ixtla's illness?

◆ Literary Analysis

In the underlined passage what does the fate of the warriors who lied tell you about the Aztec culture?

◆ Literary Analysis

Because you already know that this is a **legend** about two volcanoes, what do you think happens to the two pyramids? Explain.

◆ Reading Strategy

Reread the description of the volcanoes at the beginning of the story. Which details of the volcanoes' description have parallels here at the end of the story?

still without speaking and still wearing his stiff cotton armor, went to Ixtla's room. He gently lifted her body and carried it out of the palace and out of the city, and no one tried to stop him doing that either. All the warriors followed him in silence.

When he had walked some miles he gestured to them again and they built a huge pile of stones in the shape of a pyramid. They all worked together and they worked fast while Popo stood and watched, holding the body of the princess in his arms. By sunset the mighty edifice was finished. Popo climbed it alone, carrying Ixtla's corpse with him. There, at the very top, under a heap of stones, he buried the young woman he had loved so well and for so long, and who had died for the love of him.

That night Popo slept alone at the top of the pyramid by Ixtla's grave. In the morning he came down and spoke for the first time since the Emperor had told him the princess was dead. He told the warriors to build another pyramid, a little to the southeast of the one which held Ixtla's body and to build it higher than the other.

He told them too to tell the Emperor on his behalf that he, Popocatepetl, would never reign and rule in Tenochtitlan. He would keep watch over the grave of the Princess Ixtlaccihuatl for the rest of his life.

The messages to the Emperor were the last words Popo ever spoke. Well before the evening the second mighty pile of stones was built. Popo climbed it and stood at the top, taking a torch of resinous pine wood with him.

And when he reached the top he lit the torch and the warriors below saw the white smoke rise against the blue sky, and they watched as the sun began to set and the smoke turned pink and then a deep red, the color of blood.

So Popocatepetl stood there, holding the torch in memory of Ixtlaccihuatl, for the rest of his days.

The snows came and, as the years went by, the pyramids of stone became high whitecapped mountains. Even now the one called Popocatepetl emits smoke in memory of the princess whose body lies in the mountain which bears her name.

Vocabulary Development: edifice (ed´ ə fis) *n.* large structure

Reader's Response: If you had loved Ixtla as Popo did, would you have spent the rest of your life guarding her grave? What do you think of his decision?

The People Could Fly

Virginia Hamilton

Summary

In "The People Could Fly," the story is told that long ago in Africa people knew how to fly. When they were captured and sent away in slave ships, it was too crowded and the people who knew how to fly lost their wings. As the enslaved African Americans labored in the fields, they had to work very hard and were often mistreated. An old man, Toby, helps the people to fly away from their misery by whispering magic words that help them remember how to fly. He finally flies himself, leaving those who cannot fly to tell the tale to others.

Visual Summary

Details of Cultural Context

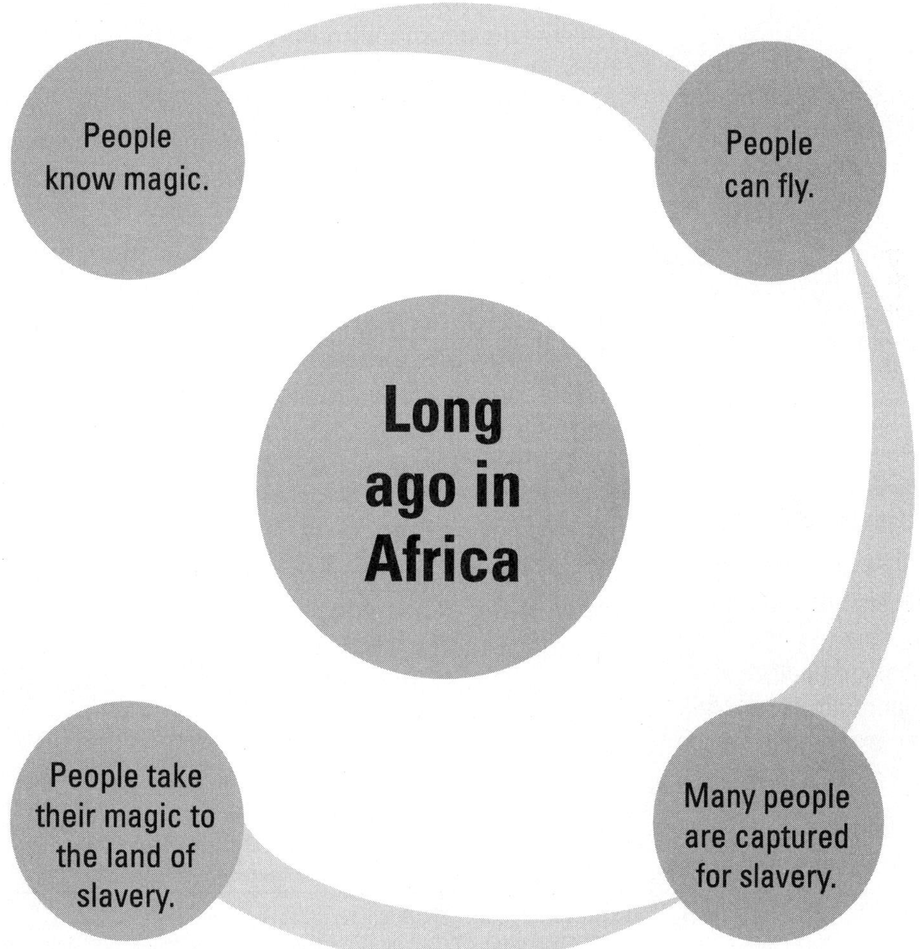

The People Could Fly

African American Folk Tale

Virginia Hamilton

One way that enslaved Africans kept their hopes alive despite the tremendous hardships they faced was to tell freedom tales—folk tales about the fight for freedom. These tales helped people to believe that they would eventually find freedom from slavery and injustice. As you'll notice in this folk tale, these stories are full of references to the storytellers' native Africa.

They say the people could fly. Say that long ago in Africa, some of the people knew magic. And they would walk up on the air like climbin up on a gate. And they flew like blackbirds over the fields. Black, shiny wings flappin against the blue up there.

Then, many of the people were captured for Slavery. The ones that could fly shed their wings. They couldn't take their wings across the water on the slave ships. Too crowded, don't you know.

The folks were full of misery, then. Got sick with the up and down of the sea. So they forgot about flyin when they could no longer breathe the sweet scent of Africa.

Say the people who could fly kept their power, although they shed their wings. They kept their secret magic in the land of slavery. They looked the same as the other people from Africa who had been coming over, who had dark skin. Say you couldn't tell anymore one who could fly from one who couldn't.

One such who could was an old man, call him Toby. And standin tall, yet afraid, was a young woman who once had wings. Call her Sarah. Now Sarah carried a babe tied to her back. She trembled to be so hard worked and scorned.

The slaves labored in the fields from sunup to sundown. The owner of the slaves callin himself their Master. Say he was a hard lump of clay. A hard, glinty[1] coal. A hard rock pile, wouldn't be moved. His Overseer[2] on horseback pointed out the slaves who were slowin down. So the one called Driver[3] cracked his whip over the slow ones to make them move faster. That whip was a slice-open cut of pain. So they did move faster. Had to.

Sarah hoed and chopped the row as the babe on her back slept.

◆ Activate Prior Knowledge

Think of a tale, story, or song about freedom. Retell it.

____

____

____

____

____

____

____

____

◆ Literary Analysis

A **folk tale** is a story that was passed from person to person by word of mouth. Circle a word in the bracketed passage that is spelled unusually to show how it would be spoken.

Mark THE Text

◆ Reading Strategy

Recognizing the **cultural context**—the background, history, customs, and beliefs of the people from the time the story was originally told—can help your appreciation of a folk tale. Name one thing that the people in this culture believed in.

____

____

1. **glinty** (glint′ ē) *adj.* shiny; reflecting light.
2. **Overseer** (ō′ vər sir′) *n.* someone who watches over and directs the work of others.
3. **Driver** *n.* someone who forced (drove) the slaves to work harder.

Say the child grew hungry. That babe started up bawling too loud. Sarah couldn't stop to feed it. Couldn't stop to soothe and quiet it down. She let it cry. She didn't want to. She had no heart to croon to it.

"Keep that thing quiet," called the Overseer. He pointed his finger at the babe. The woman scrunched low. The Driver cracked his whip across the babe anyhow. The babe hollered like any hurt child, and the woman fell to the earth.

The old man that was there, Toby, came and helped her to her feet.

"I must go soon," she told him.

"Soon," he said.

Sarah couldn't stand up straight any longer. She was too weak. The sun burned her face. The babe cried and cried, "Pity me, oh, pity me," say it sounded like. Sarah was so sad and starvin, she sat down in the row.

"Get up, you black cow," called the Overseer. He pointed his hand, and the Driver's whip snarled around Sarah's legs. Her sack dress tore into rags. Her legs bled onto the earth. She couldn't get up.

Toby was there where there was no one to help her and the babe.

"Now, before it's too late," panted Sarah. "Now, Father!"

"Yes, Daughter, the time is come," Toby answered. "Go, as you know how to go!"

He raised his arms, holding them out to her. *"Kum . . . yali, kum buba tambe,"* and more magic words, said so quickly, they sounded like whispers and sighs.

The young woman lifted one foot on the air. Then the other. She flew clumsily at first, with the child now held tightly in her arms. Then she felt the magic, the African mystery. Say she rose just as free as a bird. As light as a feather.

The Overseer rode after her, hollerin. Sarah flew over the fences. She flew over the woods. Tall trees could not snag her. Nor could the Overseer. She flew like an eagle now, until she was gone from sight. No one dared speak about it. Couldn't believe it. But it was, because they that was there saw that it was.

Say the next day was dead hot in the fields. A young man slave fell from the heat. The Driver come and whipped him. Toby come over and spoke words to the fallen one. The words of ancient Africa once heard are never remembered

Vocabulary Development: croon (kro͞on) *v.* sing or hum quietly, soothingly

◆ Stop to Reflect

How would you feel if you were the people in the first bracketed passage? Why do you think the Driver is so cruel?

◆ Literary Analysis

In the second bracketed passage, underline two examples of magic in this **folk tale**.

Mark the Text

◆ Reading Check

Underline the answer to this question: Where does Sarah go? Then circle the answer to this question: What proof does the writer offer to verify her story?

Mark the Text

◆ **Reading Check**

Circle the words Toby says to make someone fly.

Mark THE Text

◆ **Reading Strategy**

In the bracketed passage, why does Toby laugh when the owner threatens him with a gun?

____

____

____

____

____

____

____

____

◆ **Reading Strategy**

How does the underlined sentence relate to the slaves' values?

____

____

completely. The young man forgot them as soon as he heard them. They went way inside him. He got up and rolled over on the air. He rode it awhile. And he flew away.

Another and another fell from the heat. Toby was there. He cried out to the fallen and reached his arms out to them. *"Kum kunka yali, kum . . . tambe!"* Whispers and sighs. And they too rose on the air. They rode the hot breezes. The ones flyin were black and shinin sticks, wheelin above the head of the Overseer. They crossed the rows, the fields, the fences, the streams, and were away.

"Seize the old man!" cried the Overseer. "I heard him say the magic words. Seize him!"

The one callin himself Master come runnin. The Driver got his whip ready to curl around old Toby and tie him up. The slaveowner took his hip gun from its place. He meant to kill old, black Toby.

But Toby just laughed. Say he threw back his head and said, "Hee, hee! Don't you know who I am? Don't you know some of us in this field?" He said it to their faces. "We are ones who fly!"

And he sighed the ancient words that were a dark promise. He said them all around to the others in the field under the whip,

". . . buba yali . . . buba tambe. . . ."

There was a great outcryin. The bent backs straightened up. Old and young who were called slaves and could fly joined hands. Say like they would ring-sing.[4] But they didn't shuffle in a circle. They didn't sing. They rose on the air. They flew in a flock that was black against the heavenly blue. Black crows or black shadows. It didn't matter, they went so high. Way above the plantation, way over the slavery land. Say they flew away to *Free-dom.*

And the old man, old Toby, flew behind them, takin care of them. He wasn't cryin. He wasn't laughin. He was the seer.[5] His gaze fell on the plantation where the slaves who could not fly waited.

"Take us with you!" Their looks spoke it but they were afraid to shout it. Toby couldn't take them with him. Hadn't the time to teach them to fly. They must wait for a chance to run.

"Goodie-bye!" The old man called Toby spoke to them, poor souls! And he was flyin gone.

Vocabulary Development: shuffle (shuf´ əl) *v.* walk with dragging feet

4. **ring-sing** joining hands in a circle to sing and dance.
5. **seer** (sē´ ər) *n.* one who has supposed power to see the future; prophet.

So they say. The Overseer told it. The one called Master said it was a lie, a trick of the light. The Driver kept his mouth shut.

The slaves who could not fly told about the people who could fly to their children. When they were free. When they sat close before the fire in the free land, they told it. They did so love firelight and *Free-dom*, and tellin.

They say that the children of the ones who could not fly told their children. And now, me, I have told it to you.

Reader's Response: 1) How would you feel if you were one of the people who could fly? 2) How would you feel if you were one of the ones left behind?

1. ______________________________

____

____

2. ______________________________

____

____

Thinking About the Skill: How does thinking about the values and beliefs of the people in this culture help you understand the story and why it was important to the people?

____

____

____

____

____

◆ **Literary Analysis**

Mark the Text In the bracketed passage, underline the sentences that tell how this story was passed down in the oral tradition.

◆ **Literary Analysis**

The **theme** of a **folk tale**—the message or lesson it suggests—often reflects the culture of the people. What do you think the message of this story was to enslaved Africans?

____

____

____

____

____

____

Demeter and Persephone

Anne Terry White

Summary

"Demeter and Persephone" explains the Earth's seasons. When Pluto, king of the underworld, appears on Earth, Eros causes him to fall in love with Persephone. Pluto kidnaps Persephone and carries her away. When she is unable to find her daughter, Demeter, goddess of the harvest, becomes angry and makes the Earth infertile. Because humankind is threatened with starvation, Zeus asks for Persephone's release—upon the condition that she has not tasted food in the underworld. Pluto reluctantly agrees. Unfortunately, Persephone has tasted four pomegranate seeds, so she must return to Pluto for four months of every year while her mother grieves. These months are known as winter. During the months she is home, the soil is fertile and productive.

Visual Summary

Prediction Chart

CLUE		PREDICTION
• Eros shoots an arrow into Pluto's heart.	→	• Pluto will fall in love with Persephone.
• Pluto kidnaps Persephone.	→	• Demeter will be angry.
• Demeter blames the land for Persephone's disappearance.	→	• Demeter will not let anything grow on earth.
• Zeus knows where Persephone is.	→	• Zeus will send Hermes to bring Persephone back home.

Demeter and Persephone

Anne Terry White

The ancient Greeks believed in a complex collection of gods and goddesses, all ruled by Zeus, who lived on Mt. Olympus. Beneath Zeus in rank were many lesser gods and goddesses, each linked to different ideas or qualities. For example, Aphrodite was the goddess of love and Pluto was the god of the underworld.

Deep under Mt. Aetna, the gods had buried alive a number of fearful, fire-breathing giants. The monsters heaved and struggled to get free. And so mightily did they shake the earth that Pluto, the king of the underworld, was alarmed.

"They may tear the rocks asunder and leave the realm of the dead open to the light of day," he thought. And mounting his golden chariot, he went up to see what damage had been done.

Now the goddess of love and beauty, fair Aphrodite (af′ rə dit′ ē), was sitting on a mountainside playing with her son, Eros.[1] She saw Pluto as he drove around with his coal-black horses and she said:

"My son, there is one who defies your power and mine. Quick! Take up your darts! Send an arrow into the breast of that dark monarch. Let him, too, feel the pangs of love. Why should he alone escape them?"

At his mother's words, Eros leaped lightly to his feet. He chose from his quiver[2] his sharpest and truest arrow, fitted it to his bow, drew the string, and shot straight into Pluto's heart.

The grim King had seen fair maids enough in the gloomy underworld over which he ruled. But never had his heart been touched. Now an unaccustomed warmth stole through his veins. His stern eyes softened. Before him was a blossoming valley, and along its edge a charming girl was gathering flowers. She was Persephone (pər sef′ ə nē), daughter of Demeter (di mēt′ ər), goddess of the harvest. She had strayed from her companions, and now that her basket overflowed with blossoms, she was filling her apron with lilies and violets. The god looked at Persephone and loved her at once. With one sweep of his arm he caught her up and drove swiftly away.

"Mother!" she screamed, while the flowers fell from her apron and strewed the ground. "Mother!"

And she called on her companions by name. But already they were out of sight, so fast did Pluto urge the horses on.

1. **Eros** (er′ äs) in Greek mythology, the god of love. identified by the Romans with Cupid.
2. **quiver** (kwiv′ ər) *n.* case for arrows.

◆ Activate Prior Knowledge

Think of another myth—from Greece or another culture—and tell what phenomenon of nature it describes.

____

____

◆ Literary Analysis

Mark the Text

A **myth** is a story created by ancient people to explain phenomena in nature. Myths usually revolve around the magical powers of the gods and godesses of that culture. Underline the elements in the first paragraph that tell you right away that this is a myth.

◆ Literary Analysis

Through **characterization**, a writer describes a character's traits.

Mark the Text

Underline two words the author uses to describe Pluto before he falls in love.

◆ Reading Strategy

A prediction is an educated guess, based on clues, about what will happen in the story. In the underlined passage, the author mentions that Persephone strayed. **Predict** what will happen as a result.

____

____

____

____

◆ **Literary Analysis**

Name two elements of a **myth** found in the bracketed passage.

1. ____________________

____

2. ____________________

____

◆ **Reading Strategy**

Predict the revenge Demeter might take on the land based on the underlined passage.

____

____

____

____

◆ **Reading Strategy**

Was your prediction correct? Underline three things that happen to the land as a result of Demeter's revenge.

Mark the Text

◆ **Reading Check**

Whom does Zeus send to plead with Demeter?

____

____

____

In a few moments they were at the River Cyane.[3] Persephone struggled, her loosened girdle[4] fell to the ground, but the god held her tight. He struck the bank with his trident.[5] The earth opened, and darkness swallowed them all—horses, chariot, Pluto, and weeping Persephone.

From end to end of the earth Demeter sought her daughter. But none could tell her where Persephone was. At last, worn out and despairing, the goddess returned to Sicily. She stood by the River Cyane, where Pluto had cleft[6] the earth and gone down into his own dominions.

Now a river nymph[7] had seen him carry off his prize. She wanted to tell Demeter where her daughter was, but fear of Pluto kept her dumb. Yet she had picked up the girdle Persephone had dropped, and this the nymph wafted[8] on the waves to the feet of Demeter.

The goddess knew then that her daughter was gone indeed, but she did not suspect Pluto of carrying her off. She laid the blame on the innocent land.

"Ungrateful soil!" she said. "I made you fertile. I clothed you in grass and nourishing grain, and this is how you reward me. No more shall you enjoy my favors!"

That year was the most cruel mankind had ever known. Nothing prospered, nothing grew. The cattle died, the seed would not come up, men and oxen toiled in vain. There was too much sun. There was too much rain. Thistles[9] and weeds were the only things that grew. It seemed that all mankind would die of hunger.

"This cannot go on," said mighty Zeus. "I see that I must intervene." And one by one he sent the gods and goddesses to plead with Demeter.

But she had the same answer for all: "Not till I see my daughter shall the earth bear fruit again."

Zeus, of course, knew well where Persephone was. He did not like to take from his brother the one joyful thing in his life, but he saw that he must if the race of man was to be preserved. So he called Hermes[10] to him and said:

"Descend to the underworld, my son. Bid Pluto release his bride. Provided she has not tasted food in the realm of the dead, she may return to her mother forever."

Vocabulary Development: dominions (də min´ yənz) *n.* regions over which someone rules

3. **River Cyane** (sī´ an) a river in Sicily, an island just south of Italy.
4. **girdle** (gər´ dəl) *n.* belt or sash for the waist.
5. **trident** (trīd´ ənt) *n.* spear with three points.
6. **cleft** (kleft) *v.* split or opened.
7. **river nymph** (nimf) goddess living in a river.
8. **wafted** (wäft´ əd) *v.* carried.
9. **thistles** (this´ əlz) *n.* stubborn, weedy plants with sharp leaves and usually purplish flowers.
10. **Hermes** (hur´ mēz) a god who served as a messenger.

Down sped Hermes on his winged feet, and there in the dim palace of the king, he found Persephone by Pluto's side. She was pale and joyless. Not all the glittering treasures of the underworld could bring a smile to her lips.

"You have no flowers here," she would say to her husband when he pressed gems upon her. "Jewels have no fragrance. I do not want them."

When she saw Hermes and heard his message, her heart leaped within her. Her cheeks grew rosy and her eyes sparkled, for she knew that Pluto would not dare to disobey his brother's command. She sprang up, ready to go at once. Only one thing troubled her—that she could not leave the underworld forever. For she had accepted a pomegranate[11] from Pluto and sucked the sweet pulp from four of the seeds. With a heavy heart Pluto made ready his golden car.[12] He helped Persephone in while Hermes took up the reins.

"Dear wife," said the King, and his voice trembled as he spoke, "think kindly of me, I pray you. For indeed I love you truly. It will be lonely here these eight months you are away. And if you think mine is a gloomy palace to return to, at least remember that your husband is great among the immortals. So fare you well—and get your fill of flowers!"

Straight to the temple of Demeter at Eleusis, Hermes drove the black horses. The goddess heard the chariot wheels and, as a deer bounds over the hills, she ran out swiftly to meet her daughter. Persephone flew to her mother's arms. And the sad tale of each turned into joy in the telling.

So it is to this day. One third of the year Persephone spends in the gloomy abode of Pluto—one month for each seed that she tasted. Then Nature dies, the leaves fall, the earth stops bringing forth. In spring Persephone returns, and with her come the flowers, followed by summer's fruitfulness and the rich harvest of fall.

---

11. pomegranate (päm′ gran′ it) *n.* round fruit with a red leathery rind and many seeds.
12. car *n.* chariot.

Reader's Response: If you were Demeter, would you have done what she did? Explain.

____

____

Thinking About the Skill: How did predicting help your understanding of the story?

____

____

◆ Reading Check

Mark the Text

Circle the words that tell what Persephone dislikes about the underworld.

◆ Reading Strategy

Based on the underlined passage, **predict** the results of Persephone's eating the pomegranate seeds.

____

____

____

◆ Stop to Reflect

Do you think it is fair that Persephone has to live in the underworld as Pluto's wife? Explain.

____

____

____

____

____

____

◆ Literary Analysis

What phenomenon does this **myth** explain?

____

____

____

____

____

PREVIEW

Icarus and Daedalus

Josephine Preston Peabody

Summary

In the myth of "Icarus and Daedalus," a boy's impulsive nature brings about a terrible punishment. Daedalus, once the master architect for King Minos of Crete, finds himself imprisoned on that island along with his son, Icarus. In order to escape, Daedalus puts his inventive mind to work and creates wings from feathers, thread, and wax. As he attaches the wings to Icarus' back, he warns his son not to fly too close to the sun. However, all Icarus can think about is the wonder and excitement of being able to fly. He barely hears his father's warning. Predictably, he soars too close to the sun, melts his wings, and crashes into the sea.

Visual Summary

Prediction Chart

CLUE		PREDICTION
• Daedalus is looking for a way to escape from Crete. He observes the flight of sea-gulls.	→	• Daedalus will make wings with which he and Icarus can fly to freedom. 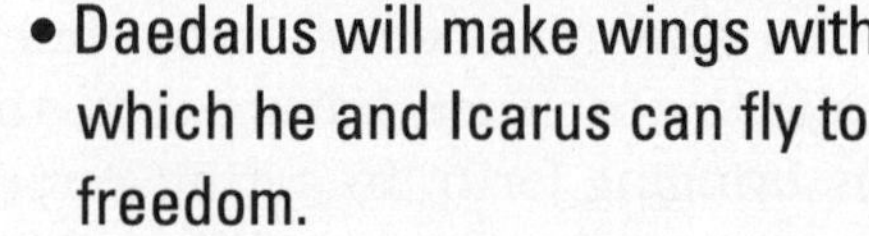
• Daedalus warns Icarus not to fly too high or too low, but Icarus doesn't pay attention.	→	• Icarus is going to have trouble when he attempts to fly. 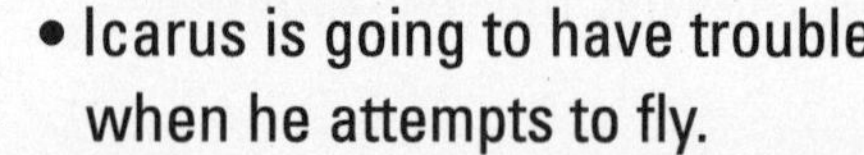
• Icarus flies too close to the sun.	→	• Icarus' wings will melt and he will fall into the sea and drown. 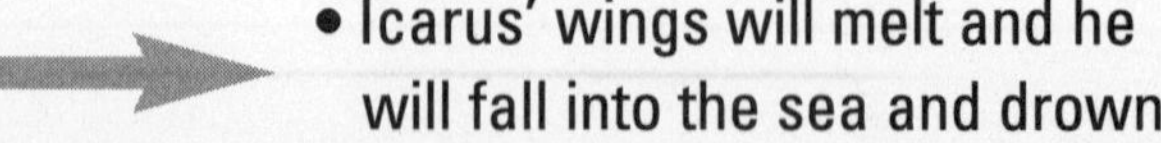

Icarus and Daedalus

Josephine Preston Peabody

Besides telling stories about what causes natural phenomena, myths express a culture's beliefs about right and wrong. The ancient Greeks believed that a person who tried to do something beyond his or her own natural human power—tried to assume godlike powers—would be punished for being overly proud and arrogant.

Among all those mortals who grew so wise that they learned the secrets of the gods, none was more cunning[1] than Daedalus (ded′ əl əs).

He once built, for King Minos of Crete,[2] a wonderful Labyrinth[3] of winding ways so cunningly tangled up and twisted around that, once inside, you could never find your way out again without a magic clue. But the king's favor veered[4] with the wind, and one day he had his master architect imprisoned in a tower. Daedalus managed to escape from his cell; but it seemed impossible to leave the island, since every ship that came or went was well guarded by order of the king.

At length, watching the sea-gulls in the air—the only creatures that were sure of liberty—he thought of a plan for himself and his young son Icarus (ik′ ə rəs), who was captive with him.

Little by little, he gathered a store of feathers great and small. He fastened these together with thread, molded them in with wax, and so fashioned two great wings like those of a bird. When they were done, Daedalus fitted them to his own shoulders, and after one or two efforts, he found that by waving his arms he could winnow[5] the air and cleave it, as a swimmer does the sea. He held himself aloft, wavered this way and that with the wind, and at last, like a great fledgling,[6] he learned to fly.

Without delay, he fell to work on a pair of wings for the boy Icarus, and taught him carefully how to use them, bidding him beware of rash adventures among the stars. "Remember," said the father, "never to fly very low or very high, for the fogs about the earth would weigh you down, but the blaze of the sun will surely melt your feathers apart if you go too near."

For Icarus, these cautions went in at one ear and out by the other. Who could remember to be careful when he was to fly for the first time? Are birds careful? Not they! And not an idea remained in the boy's head but the one joy of escape.

1. **cunning** (kun′ iŋ) *adj.* skillful; clever.
2. **King Minos** (mī′ nəs) **of Crete** King Minos was a son of the god Zeus. Crete is a Greek island in the eastern Mediterranean Sea, southeast of Greece.
3. **Labyrinth** (lab′ ə rinth′) *n.* maze.
4. **veered** (vird) *v.* changed directions.
5. **winnow** (win′ ō) *v.* beat as with wings.
6. **fledgling** (flej′ liŋ) *n.* young bird.

◆ Activate Prior Knowledge

Think about a time when you tried to do something beyond your ability. Briefly describe the incident.

◆ Literary Analysis

Mark the Text

In the bracketed passage, circle the words the writer uses to **characterize** Daedalus.

◆ Reading Strategy

After reading the underlined passage, **predict** what Daedalus's plan might be. What hint helped you with your prediction?

◆ Stop to Reflect

Would Daedalus's plan really have worked? Explain.

The day came, and the fair wind that was to set them free. The father bird put on his wings, and, while the light urged them to be gone, he waited to see that all was well with Icarus, for the two could not fly hand in hand. Up they rose, the boy after his father. The hateful ground of Crete sank beneath them; and the country folk, who caught a glimpse of them when they were high above the treetops, took it for a vision of the gods—Apollo, perhaps, with Cupid after him.

At first there was a terror in the joy. The wide vacancy of the air dazed them—a glance downward made their brains reel.

But when a great wind filled their wings, and Icarus felt himself sustained, like a halcyon bird[7] in the hollow of a wave, like a child uplifted by his mother, he forgot everything in the world but joy. He forgot Crete and the other islands that he had passed over: he saw but vaguely that wingèd thing in the distance before him that was his father Daedalus. He longed for one draft of flight to quench the thirst of his captivity: he stretched out his arms to the sky and made towards the highest heavens.

Alas for him! Warmer and warmer grew the air. Those arms, that had seemed to uphold him, relaxed. His wings wavered, drooped. He fluttered his young hands vainly—he was falling—and in that terror he remembered. The heat of the sun had melted the wax from his wings; the feathers were falling, one by one, like snowflakes; and there was none to help.

He fell like a leaf tossed down the wind, down, down, with one cry that overtook Daedalus far away. When he returned, and sought high and low for his poor boy, he saw nothing but the birdlike feathers afloat on the water, and he knew that Icarus was drowned.

The nearest island he named Icaria, in memory of the child; but he, in heavy grief, went to the temple of Apollo in Sicily, and there hung up his wings as an offering. Never again did he attempt to fly.

Vocabulary Development: vacancy (vā´ kən sē) *n.* emptiness
sustained (sə stānd´) *adj.* supported

7. **halcyon** (hal´ sē ən) **bird** *n.* legendary bird, identified with the kingfisher, that could calm the sea by resting on it.

◆ Reading Strategy

After reading the underlined sentence, **predict** what might happen next in the story. What clue makes you think this?

______

______

______

______

◆ Literary Analysis

Answer these questions about the end of the **myth**: 1) What does Daedalus do after his flight? 2) What lesson has he learned?

1. ______

______

2. ______

______

Reader's Response: How would you feel if you were Daedalus at the end of the story?

______

______

______

Part 2

Selection Summaries With Alternative Reading Strategies

Part 2 contains summaries of all selections in *Prentice Hall Literature: Timeless Voices, Timeless Themes*. An alternative reading strategy follows each summary.

- Use the selection summaries in Part 2 to preview what you will read in *Prentice Hall Literature: Timeless Voices, Timeless Themes.*
- Read the selection in *Prentice Hall Literature: Timeless Voices, Timeless Themes.*
- Use the alternative reading strategies in Part 2 to guide your reading or to check your understanding of the selection.

Name ____ Date __________________

"The Cat Who Thought She Was a Dog and the Dog Who Thought He Was a Cat"
by Isaac Bashevis Singer

Summary Jan Skiba, a poor peasant, lives a simple life with his wife, his daughters, a cat, and a dog in a small hut. The family does not own a mirror, and they have rarely seen their images. Because the dog and cat have never seen other dogs and cats, the dog thinks he is a cat and the cat thinks she is a dog. One day the family buys a mirror from a peddler. The mirror causes a stir. Each girl is upset about her looks and fears she'll never make a good marriage. The dog and cat, disturbed by their images, fight. Skiba decides that having a mirror is troublesome and that the family would be better off admiring the world around them than themselves. He exchanges the mirror for other goods. Life returns to normal for the family and its pets.

Use Context Clues While you are reading, you may come across a word whose meaning you don't know. The context, or the words before and after the unfamiliar word, can provide clues to help you understand the meaning of the word. Context clues may be in the same sentence in which the unfamiliar word appears or in sentences before or after the word. Notice the word *gulden* in the following sentence from the story.

> They asked the peddler his price and he said a half gulden, which was a lot of money.

You probably don't know the meaning of the word *gulden*, but you do know that the peddler was giving a price. The sentence also includes the word money. From these context clues, you can figure out that a gulden is probably an amount of money.

Directions: Read the sentences below from the selection. Use context clues to determine the meaning of each underlined word. Find the meaning of the word in the following list. Write its letter in the blank.

a. one of several payments
b. very interested
c. proposal
d. faults or flaws

____ 1. After a while, Jan Skiba's wife, Marianna, made a <u>proposition</u> to the peddler. She would pay him five groshen a month for the mirror.

____ 2. Now they could see themselves clearly and they began to find <u>defects</u> in their faces, defects they had never noticed before. Marianna was pretty but she had a tooth missing in front and she felt that this made her ugly.

____ 3. That day the women became so <u>absorbed</u> in the mirror they didn't cook supper, didn't make up the bed, and neglected all the other household tasks.

____ 4. When the peddler came for his monthly <u>installment</u>, Jan Skiba gave him back the mirror and, in its stead, bought kerchiefs and slippers for the women.

Name ______________________________ Date ______________

"Two Kinds" by Amy Tan

Summary A Chinese immigrant who has started life over in the United States wants her American-born daughter to be a famous prodigy. To that end, she pushes the reluctant girl first to be an actress like Shirley Temple, then a musician like a young pianist she saw performing on TV. Despite the girl's fiasco at a talent show, her mother expects her to continue piano lessons and eventually become a famous musician. The girl balks. She asserts in a forceful and hurtful way that she's not the obedient daughter her mother wants. In conflict with her mother's expectations, the daughter says that she can only be herself. Years later, she realizes that she is two kinds of daughter—one who follows her own mind and one who is obedient.

Apply Word Identification Strategies "Two Kinds" includes a number of compound words, or words that are made up of two or more words put together. Here are two examples from the story.

hair + cut = haircut   bath + room = bathroom

A compound word may seem long and completely unfamiliar. However, if you break it into the words that make it up, you will often find that you know the meaning of one or more of the shorter words. For example, in the selection, Jing-mei finds some *handwritten* scales. Suppose you do not know the word *handwritten*. You probably recognize the word *hand*, and the word *written*. You can figure out that *handwritten* means "written by hand." Some compound words, such as *speed-reading*, have a hyphen between the words that make them up.

Directions: Examine each of the following compound words from "Two Kinds." Beside each word, write the two words that make it up. If you do not know the meaning of the compound word, try to figure it out from the two smaller words. If necessary, use a dictionary for help. Write the meaning of the compound word on the line provided

1. tiptoes ______________ ______________
   meaning: ______________________________
2. housecleaning ______________ ______________
   meaning: ______________________________
3. high-pitched ______________ ______________
   meaning: ______________________________
4. earsplitting ______________ ______________
   meaning; ______________________________
5. daydreamed ______________ ______________
   meaning: ______________________________
6. showpiece ______________ ______________
   meaning: ______________________________

Name ______________________________ Date ______________

from "Song of Myself" by Walt Whitman
"I'm Nobody" by Emily Dickinson
"Me" by Walter de la Mare

Summary These three poems discuss the idea of identity—who we are, what makes each of us different, and how we are viewed by others. The speakers in these poems accept and like themselves just as they are. In "Song of Myself," the speaker celebrates himself and all selves as equally important. In "I'm Nobody," the speaker is proud of being a "Nobody" because, she says, a "Somebody" needs the praise of other people to feel worthwhile. In "Me," the speaker compares himself to trees and flowers. Like the things in nature, he says, he will always be who he is and no other.

Read Poetry According to Punctuation Reading poetry aloud helps you hear the speaker's voice, and helps you understand the meaning of the poem.

Directions: Listen to the audiocassette recordings of the poems as you follow along in your textbook. Listen carefully for the places where the reader pauses and stops. Then, with a partner, take turns reading the poems aloud. Practice pausing briefly at commas, ellipsis points (three dots), and dashes and longer at end marks. Don't stop at the ends of lines if there is no punctuation. You may use the following chart to note the various places in the poems where you should pause.

Poems	**Pausing Points**
from "Song of Myself"	
"I'm Nobody"	
"Me"	

Name ______________________________ Date ______________

"**My Furthest-Back Person**" by Alex Haley

Summary In this essay, Alex Haley describes how he traced his ancestors. Remembering family names he had heard from his grandmother, he began his search by examining old census reports. He recalled stories about the family's "furthest-back person"—an African kidnapped from his native land and sold into slavery in the United States. He thought the strange "k" sounds his grandmother had muttered over the years might be words from an African language. He discovered that one of the sounds, Kin-tay (Kinte) is the name of an old African clan. He flew to Gambia and, after traveling on foot and by boat deep into the back country, he finally found his distant relatives. An old man told him the clan's history, confirming that Haley's "furthest-back person" was a Kinte, kidnapped in Africa and sold into slavery in Annapolis, Maryland, in 1767.

Break Down Long Sentences Many of the sentences in this story are three lines long—or even longer. To help understand the long sentences, break them down into parts. Use the punctuation marks (commas, dots, dashes, colons, and semicolons) to find appropriate places to break. You may need to add a word or two to have the part make sense. Study the following example.

Sentence: I was beginning to tire, when in utter astonishment I looked upon the names of Grandma's parents: Tom Murray, Irene Murray … older sisters of Grandma's as well—every one of them a name that I'd heard countless times on her front porch.

Sentence broken into parts: I was beginning to tire. In utter astonishment I looked upon the names of Grandma's parents. [Their names were] Tom Murray, Irene Murray. [The names included] older sisters of Grandma's as well. Every one of them [was] a name that I'd heard countless times on her front porch.

Directions: Find at least four more sentences in the essay that are three or more lines long. Break them into parts. Compare your sentences with those of your classmates.

Name ______________________________ Date ______________

"The Third Level" by Jack Finney

Summary Grand Central Station is supposed to have two levels. Yet Charlie finds a tunnel that takes him down to a third level, where he finds himself in the year 1894. Charlie wants to buy himself and his wife train tickets for a small town called Galesburg as it was in 1894. However, the ticket clerk will not take his modern money. Charlie later buys old-style money and tries without success to find the third level. His psychiatrist friend, Sam, says that Charlie must have imagined the third level to escape from pressures of the present. Sam later disappears. Charlie finds a letter in his grandfather's stamp collection. It is dated 1894 and addressed to Charlie. It is from Sam, who says he found the third level and has a hay and feed business in Galesburg.

Use Context to Determine Meaning When you come across a name, word, or phrase you don't know, use its context—the words, phrases, and sentences around it—to figure out its meaning. To help you identify context clues, look for words and phrases that define, compare, contrast, describe, provide examples, or offer information about the unfamiliar word or phrase.

Directions: Practice identifying context clues. On the lines provided, write the context clues for each underlined word or phrase.

1. That made my wife kind of mad, but he explained that he meant the modern world is full of <u>insecurity</u>, fear, war, worry and all the rest of it, and that I just want to escape.

   insecurity ______________________________

2. I am just an <u>ordinary</u> guy named Charley, thirty-one years old...; I passed a dozen men who looked just like me.

   ordinary ______________________________

3. Sometimes I think Grand Central is <u>growing like a tree</u>, pushing out new corridors and staircases like roots.

   growing like a tree: ______________________________

4. It's a wonderful town still, with big old frame houses, huge lawns and tremendous trees whose branches meet overhead and <u>roof the streets</u>.

   roof the streets ______________________________

Name ____________________ Date __________

"A Day's Wait" by Ernest Hemingway

Summary When Schatz has the flu, his father calls the doctor. The doctor says Schatz's temperature is 102 degrees. A few hours later, Schatz asks about his temperature. He is very quiet and worried, and his father cannot understand why. Finally, Schatz asks when he is going to die. His father says he is not that ill, and will not die. Schatz says boys at school in France told him a person could not live with a temperature of 44 degrees. His father then realizes Schatz has been waiting to die all day. He explains to Schatz that the French use a different kind of thermometer. On that thermometer, a normal temperature is 37 degrees. On Schatz's thermometer, normal is 98. Schatz is relieved by the explanation and becomes visibly relaxed.

Reread When you read a story, you may be puzzled at first by the way a character behaves. By the end of the story, your questions may be answered. If they are not, you can read part or all of the story again. The second time, look for specific details that will answer your questions about the character's behavior.

Directions: Use a Character Behavior Chart like the following to describe Schatz's actions. As you read the story the first time, list details that tell how Schatz behaves. If you understand why he behaves that way, check the box under "Read." If you don't understand, read the story a second time to find the answer. Then check the box under "Reread." The first action is listed for you.

BEHAVIOR	READ	REREAD
Schatz enters his father's room and closes the window.		

Name ______________________ Date ______________

"Was Tarzan a Three-Bandage Man?" by Bill Cosby
"Oranges" by Gary Soto

Summary These selections deal with childhood memories. "Was Tarzan a Three-Bandage Man?" recalls a time when the author and his friends tried to act cool by imitating their heroes. Bill's mother scolds him for walking funny to imitate a famous baseball player and putting bandages on his face like a prizefighter. In the end, Bill realizes it might have been better to admire the injurer rather than the injured. In "Oranges," a boy of twelve walks with a girl for the first time. He has two oranges and a nickel in his pocket. When he asks what she wants from a store, the girl chooses a ten-cent chocolate. He puts his nickel and an orange on the counter. Silently, the clerk accepts them.

Context Clues This article may contain some words that you don't know. You could look up each word in a dictionary. But you also may be able to figure out the meaning by using **context clues**. Look at the words and phrases that are near the word you don't know. The familiar words and phrases can help you guess the meaning of the unfamiliar word.

Directions: In each sentence below, read the word in **boldface print**. Then find another word or phrase in the sentence that can help you guess the word's meaning. Underline your clues. Write what you think the word means. You may check a dictionary if necessary. The first one has been done for you.

1. We **imitated** their walk. When they walked bowlegged, we did it too.
   Meaning: did the same thing as someone else
2. People with **acne** walked that way too, but it wasn't their bad skin that we admired.
   Meaning: ______________________
3. Tough guys wore bandages over their eye, but really tough guys wore **tourniquets** around their necks.
   Meaning: ______________________
4. Trying to be like the injured was ridiculous, since we should have been **emulating** those who caused the injuries.
   Meaning: ______________________
5. (Supply your own sentence from the selection here.)
   ____
   ____
   Meaning: ______________________

Name ____ Date ____________________

from *In Search of Our Mothers' Gardens* by Alice Walker

Summary In this moving and solemn tribute, the author praises her mother and other black women like her for their hard work, dedication, and inspiration. Walker views her mother as an artist whose creative spirit inspired her own life as a writer. Her mother shared herself as an artist through the stories she told and through the beautiful flower gardens she grew, despite the family's poverty. Walker admires how black women of her mother's generation managed to "hold on," despite the exhausting labors placed upon them. As a result, Walker inherited a respect for strength as well as a love of beauty in life.

Ask Questions A good way to better understand the selection is to ask yourself questions as you read. As you read, think of what you already know about the subject, and then think of what questions you would like answered.

Directions: Think about people you know who work tirelessly. Remembering how you feel about them will help you develop a deeper understanding of the woman Alice Walker describes in "In Search of Our Mothers' Gardens." Discuss your ideas with a small group. Then begin a KWL chart like the one shown to record interesting ideas and details you know and questions you have.

- Start the chart by filling in what you know about people who work hard.
- Add questions about what you want to know.
- As you read "In Search of Our Mothers' Gardens," continue the KWL chart with what you Learn, and add new questions that come up.

What I **K**now	What I **W**ant to Know	What I've **L**earned
________	________	________
________	________	________
________	________	________
________	________	________
________	________	________
________	________	________
________	________	________
________	________	________

Name ______________________________ Date ______________

"Seventh Grade" by Gary Soto
"Melting Pot" by Anna Quindlen

Summary These two selections examine, in different ways, how people relate to each other. In "Seventh Grade," Victor goes through the first day of school trying to impress Teresa, who he hopes will be his girlfriend. Though Victor embarrasses himself in class by pretending to speak French, Teresa is fooled and impressed, much to Victor's surprise and pleasure. In "Melting Pot," the author describes how her New York neighborhood is a mixture of different ethnic groups. She sees the concept of the American melting pot existing where she lives, but only on a person-to-person basis. In groups, the neighbors are enemies, but as individuals, they are friends.

Relate to Your Own Experience One way to get more enjoyment out of what you read is to relate the characters' experiences to your own. To help you link your experience with a character's, form a mental picture of the scenes described by the author. As you read "Seventh Grade," pause from time to time. Picture each scene in your mind. Use this page to jot down notes to describe what you imagine. Then work with a partner to draw sketches of what Gary Soto describes in each of the following scenes. If you prefer, choose some scenes from "Melting Pot" and write notes about them. Then draw sketches of the scenes you imagined.

Victor and Michael exchanging greetings on the first day of school

Victor practicing his scowling as a girl looks at him

Victor lingering in homeroom after the bell rang, hoping to bump into Teresa as she left

Victor sitting at a table outside, near where Teresa is sitting under a plum tree

Victor pretending to know how to speak French

Mr. Bueller shuffling papers in the classroom as Victor and Teresa talk about French

____

____

____

____

____

____

____

____

____

____

____

____

____

____

Name ______________________________ Date ______________

"Fable" by Ralph Waldo Emerson
"If—" by Rudyard Kipling
"Thumbprint" by Eve Merriam

Summary These three poems focus on the ideas of individuality and wholeness. In "Fable," a squirrel resents that a mountain has called it a "little prig." The squirrel responds by saying that although a mountain is big, it is not as lively as a squirrel and it cannot crack a nut. In other words, individuals possess their own special talents that make them no better or worse than other individuals. In "If—," the speaker details the positive qualities that a person must possess to be considered a successful and complete individual. In "Thumbprint," the speaker celebrates her singularity through the special design of curved lines that make up her unique thumbprint.

Paraphrase Sometimes the language of poetry is different from familiar, everyday language. The words themselves might be unfamiliar, or the order of the words might be unusual. As you read these poems, identify and list examples of poetic language. Then write more familiar words or word order for the phrases you list. Create a chart like the one below. A few phrases from Rudyard Kipling's poem have been modeled for you. Choose more from his poem, and choose some from Ralph Waldo Emerson's and Eve Merriam's poems as well.

Poetic Language	**More Familiar Language**
If you can keep your head when all about you / Are losing theirs and blaming it on you	If you can stay calm when others cannot
If you can force your heart and nerve and sinew / To serve your turn long after they are gone	If you can keep on going when your body feels worn out

Name ______________________________ Date ______________

"Mother to Son" by Langston Hughes

"The Courage That My Mother Had" by Edna St. Vincent Millay

"The Hummingbird That Lived Through Winter" by William Saroyan

Summary These three selections focus on the themes of courage and persistence. In "Mother to Son," the speaker talks of the hardships she has endured. She uses her own experiences to warn her son not to give up when he faces similar obstacles. In "The Courage That My Mother Had," the poet praises the courage her deceased mother showed when she was living. Though her mother left her a golden brooch, the poet would prefer the treasure of her mother's courage for herself because she needs it now. "The Hummingbird That Lived Through Winter" tells about an elderly, sight-impaired man lovingly nursing an ailing hummingbird back to life, exhibiting a love for all living creatures.

Question: After reading a selection, you need to determine what you understand and don't understand about it. You can write down questions that you may have, and then seek help from your teacher or a classmate.

Directions: Use the chart below to record what you do and do not understand about each selection. Then discuss your questions with another person.

Selection	What I Understand	What I Do Not Understand

Name ______________________ Date ______________

"The Third Wish" by Joan Aiken

Summary Mr. Peters discovers a swan tangled in thorns. He frees the swan, which turns into a little man—the King of the Forest. Mr. Peters requests three wishes as a reward. The King obliges, giving him three leaves to wish upon, but warns that wishes often leave people worse off than before. Mr. Peters wishes for a beautiful wife and receives Leita, a former swan. Over time, Leita grows unhappy because she misses her sister, who is still a swan. Mr. Peters uses his second wish to turn Leita back into a swan. He and the two swans remain close. One morning, old Mr. Peters is found dead in bed, smiling, with a leaf and feather in his hands.

Clarify Sometimes when you read, the meaning of a passage may not be clear. To help you understand it better, you can write down questions that you have about the passage. Then try reading the section again. As you read, look for details that will answer your questions. Also, use a dictionary to look up words you do not understand.

Use a chart like the one below to help clarify the meaning of passages in "The Third Wish." First record your questions about each passage. Then reread the passage and tell what you now understand that you did not understand before.

Questions (What I Don't Understand)	**Answers** (What I Now Understand)

Name ______________________ Date ______________

"A Boy and a Man" by James Ramsey Ullman
from *Into Thin Air* by Jon Krakauer

Summary Both selections deal with the drama of mountain climbing. In "A Boy and a Man," Rudi Matt risks his life to save a man who has fallen in an icy crevasse, or deep crack, in the Alps. The man, renowned mountaineer Captain John Winter, is surprised to discover that Rudi is only sixteen. He seeks Rudi's advice on climbing the Citadel, a peak upon which Rudi's father died while climbing. Rudi makes Winter promise not to tell his mother that he was mountain climbing. In the second selection, Jon Krakauer describes his dangerous trek up the Icefall on Mt. Everest, detailing how the ice made the climb an uncertainty. Krakauer's experience leaves him awestruck at the task of reaching Everest's peak.

Predict As you read a story, you can be an active reader by trying to **predict**, or guess, what will happen next. Your predictions should not be wild guesses, however. Good story predictions are always based on details and hints that the author gives you along the way.

Use the chart below to predict events from "A Boy and a Man" and from *Into Thin Air*. After each prediction, record the details and hints that led you to make that prediction.

My Prediction	Details and Hints
"A Boy and a Man"	
from *Into Thin Air*	

Name ______________________________ Date ______________

"The Charge of the Light Brigade" by Alfred, Lord Tennyson
from *Henry V*, "St. Crispian's Day Speech" by William Shakespeare
"The Enemy" by Alice Walker

Summary All of these poems deal with war. In "The Charge of the Light Brigade," a brigade of six hundred cavalry soldiers charges into an enemy position heavily fortified with cannon. Many of the soldiers are killed, but their bravery will be honored always. In the excerpt from *Henry V*, King Henry speaks of the glory that will come to soldiers who fight in a battle to be fought on St. Crispian's Day. Those who survive the battle and live to old age will proudly tell battle stories to their sons. In "The Enemy," the tiny fist of a dead child holds the "crumpled heads / of pink and yellow flowers." This is a harsh reminder that when a country goes to war, the children suffer.

Reading Poetic Contractions A contraction is a shortened form of a word or words. For example, the contraction *aren't* is short for the words *are not.* Notice that an apostrophe (') takes the place of the missing *o* in the contraction. Often in poetry, you find special contractions, called **poetic contractions,** that you do not find in ordinary writing. For example, in "The Charge of the Light Brigade," the author uses the contraction *sab'ring*, a shortened form of the word *sabering.* When you come across such a contraction, look at it closely to figure out what letter or letters are missing. Then read the word as if all the letters were there.

Use the chart below to record the word or words that are shortened in each poetic contraction. The first one is done for you.

Contraction	Missing Letter or Letters	Full Word or Words
sab'ring	e	sabering
call'd		
rememb'red		
ne'er		
accurs'd		

Name ______________________________ Date ______________

"The Californian's Tale" by Mark Twain
"Valediction" by Seamus Heaney

Summary Both selections deal with the effect a woman's absence has on a home. In "The Californian's Tale," a California gold prospector comes to the well-kept home of Henry, who invites the traveler in. Henry credits the niceness of his home to his young wife, who is away until Saturday night. He urges his guest to stay until she returns. Henry's friends come over on Saturday and give Henry a drink with a drug that puts him to sleep. They explain that Henry's wife has been dead for nineteen years. They go through the annual act of pretending she's returning, so that Henry won't go wild. In "Valediction," the speaker mourns the absence of the lady who once brightened his home but for whom he now grieves.

Summarize When you read a story, you can check your understanding along the way by summarizing different sections as you complete them. To summarize, first jot down all the important events and details that appear in a section of the story you are reading. Then, write a brief summary based on your notes.

Use the chart below to summarize sections of "The Californian's Tale." Record the main events and details in each section. Then use them to summarize the section. The beginning of the story has been done for you.

Main Events and Details	Summary
Thirty-five years ago Twain prospected on the Stanislaus. Once heavily populated, the area was now empty.	Mark Twain prospected on the Stanislaus, an area once heavily populated. Now the region has few people.

Name ______________________________ Date ______________

"Stopping by Woods on a Snowy Evening" by Robert Frost
"Four Skinny Trees" by Sandra Cisneros
"Miracles" by Walt Whitman

Summary These three selections celebrate the wonders of nature, each in a different way. In "Stopping by Woods on a Snowy Evening," a traveler pauses to watch snow fall in woods that belong to someone else. The traveler cannot stay, however, because of promises to keep and miles yet to be traveled. In "Four Skinny Trees," the narrator admires the determination of four scrawny trees outside her window that possess the secret strength to keep growing and going on. The trees inspire the narrator to continue going on, too. In "Miracles," the speaker celebrates all aspects of nature—both indoors and outdoors—which some people might consider ordinary, but which he sees as miracles.

Respond to Levels of Meaning Often when you read a piece of literature, you can find several meanings in it. You may find one meaning that other readers find as well. But you may also find a personal meaning that other readers don't necessarily experience.

Work with a partner. First, read the three selections together. Then, discuss what each selection means to each of you personally. How do you both feel about the work? Use the chart to record your individual feelings, and then see how similar or different they are.

Selection	What It Means to Me	What It Means to My Partner
"Stopping by Woods …"		
"Four Skinny Trees"		
"Miracles"		

Name ______________________________ Date ______________

"The Night the Bed Fell" by James Thurber

Summary In this hilarious story, James Thurber recalls the chain of events that led to chaos one night when he was a youth. His father had gone to the attic to sleep, despite his mother's protests that the wobbly bed might collapse. During the night, young James accidentally tipped over his own cot. The noise caused his mother to scream, which woke up a visiting cousin, Briggs, who immediately poured camphor—a strong-smelling medicine—on himself, thinking he had stopped breathing. The camphor made the room smell so foul that Briggs broke a window to get air. James's mother, still thinking her husband had fallen, went to the attic. The father was puzzled by all the commotion. Eventually the confusion was sorted out.

Identify Causes and Effects In many stories, there is a pattern of causes and effects. A **cause** is the reason something happens. An **effect** is what happens as a result of the cause. For example, in Thurber's story, Father wants to be away where he can think. Therefore, he goes to the attic to sleep. His desire to be alone is the cause; sleeping in the attic is the effect.

Think about the things that happen in "The Night the Bed Fell." Record each important cause and the effect that it leads to.

Cause		Effect
	>	
	>	
	>	
	>	
	>	
	>	
	>	
	>	
	>	
	>	
	>	
	>	
	>	
	>	
	>	
	>	

Name ______________________________ Date ______________

"All Summer in a Day" by Ray Bradbury

Summary A class of nine-year-old children living on the planet Venus looks forward to seeing the sun for the very first time. A seemingly endless seven-year rainfall is predicted to stop for a short time. The children taunt a frail classmate, Margot, who came from Earth and had seen the sun from there. They don't believe her reports about what the sun is like. As a cruel joke, the children lock Margot in a closet before going out to play in the sun for the only hour of sunshine in seven years. When the rain resumes, and the children sadly return indoors, they realize that Margot has missed the sunshine. Knowing how cruel they have been, they slowly go to the closet to let Margot out.

Picture Setting and Actions When you **Picture a setting and actions,** you picture what is happening and where it is happening. As you read, pay close attention to story details that describe the setting. If you were standing in that setting, what would you see? Hear? Touch? Smell? Taste? Also pay attention to details that describe the action. Picture everything that is happening around you.

Record details about "All Summer in a Day" in the chart below.

"All Summer in a Day"

What I see ______________________________

____

What I hear ______________________________

____

What I feel ______________________________

____

What I smell ______________________________

____

Name ______________________________ Date ______________

"The Highwayman" by Alfred Noyes

"The Real Story of a Cowboy's Life" by Geoffrey C. Ward

Summary In "The Highwayman," a dashing highwayman tells Bess, his beloved, that he'll return to her after a short while. Tim, the horse keeper, overhears the conversation and informs authorities who then tie Bess with a musket aimed at her heart. When the highwayman returns, Bess pulls the trigger, to warn him of danger, and is killed. The highwayman comes back to avenge her death, but is shot and killed. "The Real Story of a Cowboy's Life" describes the dirty and dangerous work of a cattle drive. Among numerous difficulties are settlers angered over cattle crossing their land and nighttime stampedes that sometimes cause cowboys' deaths. However, a cowboy's life is also full of small pleasures like the beauty of the animals crossing the plains and the songs of the other cowboys.

Identify Cause and Effect In many stories, there is a pattern of causes and effects. A **cause** is the reason something happens. An **effect** is what happens as a result of the cause. Think about the things that happen in each of the three selections. Record each important cause and the effect that follows.

"The Highwayman"

Cause		Effect
______________________	>	______________________
______________________	>	______________________
______________________	>	______________________

"The Real Story of a Cowboy's Life"

Cause		Effect
______________________	>	______________________
______________________	>	______________________
______________________	>	______________________

Name ______________________________ Date ______________

"**Amigo Brothers**" by Piri Thomas
"**The Walk**" by Thomas Hardy
"**Justin Lebo**" by Phillip Hoose
"**The Rider**" by Naomi Shihab Nye

Summary Finding a way around a problem is a central theme of these selections. The "Amigo Brothers" are best friends who must fight against each other for a championship. They train separately and they worry about hurting each other. In the ring, they throw their toughest punches, learning that their friendship will endure no matter who wins. The speaker in "The Walk" finds a way to appreciate a walk to a hilltop even without the company of a special companion. Justin Lebo overcomes difficulties while making bikes to give to less fortunate boys. He learns to collaborate with his parents and others who can help him with money, know-how, and bike parts. He tolerates publicity because it helps him meet his goal, giving joy to others. The speaker in "The Rider" learns to leave loneliness behind while riding around the neighborhood on a bicycle.

Make Inferences When you **make an inference,** you take a guess about something not stated directly in the story. For example, in "The Rider," the speaker never says that she feels lonely. However, you could make that inference for two reasons: She wonders if riding a bicycle can rid a person of loneliness, and she is riding a bicycle. From those two clues you infer that she may feel loneliness herself.

Make an inference about a character or event in each selection. Give the reasons that lead you to make each inference.

"Amigo Brothers"

Inference	Reasons
______________________	______________________
______________________	______________________

"The Walk"

Inference	Reasons
______________________	______________________
______________________	______________________

"Justin Lebo"

Inference	Reasons
______________________	______________________
______________________	______________________

"The Rider"

Inference	Reasons
______________________	______________________
______________________	______________________

Name ______________________________ Date ______________

"Our Finest Hour" by Charles Osgood

Summary In this humorous essay, journalist Charles Osgood describes the series of mistakes that occurred the night he was a substitute anchor on the *CBS Evening News* telecast. First, the lead story that Osgood introduced did not appear on the monitor; a different story ran instead. The next report didn't appear on the monitor, either. Then, a cue for a commercial brought no commercial. Later, a news story that no one had pre-screened was abruptly cut during its broadcast. After another mishap, a worker's cursing was picked up by a microphone. To top off Osgood's embarrassment, that night journalists from China visited the studio to observe the broadcast.

Distinguish Fact From Opinion As you read, it is important to recognize when writers are stating facts and when they are stating opinions. A **fact** is a statement that can be proven true. An **opinion** is a statement that expresses someone's personal feelings or taste, and cannot be proven true or false.

Read each statement from "Our Finest Hour." Tell whether it is a fact or an opinion. If it is a fact, tell how you could prove it. If it is an opinion, tell what word or words in the statement express a personal feeling.

1. Anchoring is easy enough, most of the time.
   Fact or opinion? Why?

   ____

   ____

2. A reporter was beginning a story.
   Fact or opinion? Why?

   ____

   ____

3. When the commercial was over, I introduced a piece from Washington.
   Fact or opinion? Why?

   ____

   ____

4. All in all, it was not the finest broadcast CBS News had ever done.
   Fact or opinion? Why?

   ____

   ____

5. They must have had a really great impression of American electronic journalism.
   Fact or opinion? Why?

   ____

   ____

Name ______________________________ Date ______________

"Cat on the Go" by James Herriot

Summary Veterinarian James Herriot relates his experiences with an unusual cat. Herriot and his assistant perform surgery to save the stray cat after it is brought near death to his office. Herriot and his wife Helen then nurture the cat in their home. One evening the cat disappears, and is found later at a church meeting. Another night, the cat is found at a darts championship. After a third incident, the Herriots realize that the cat enjoys visiting places at night before returning home. They are devastated, however, when the cat's real owners unexpectedly show up one day to reclaim it. After giving up the pet, the Herriots visit it about a month later, and are thrilled that it recognizes them.

Understand Bias In their writings, writers show bias—the knowledge and interest that they have in their subject. You can see bias in the details they use, such as descriptions of characters and their actions. For example, when James Herriot says of the cat Oscar, "He was a warm and cherished part of our home life," you can tell the writer really loves and enjoys animals.

Explain what you can tell about writer James Herriot from each of his statements below from "Cat on the Go."

1. I had no more desire to pour ether onto that comradely purring than he had.
   What it tells about Herriot:

   ____

   ____

2. I am fond of cats but we already had a dog in our cramped quarters and I could see difficulties.
   What it tells about Herriot:

   ____

   ____

3. This time Helen and I scoured the marketplace and side alleys in vain and when we returned at half past nine we were both despondent.
   What it tells about Herriot:

   ____

   ____

4. Ever since our cat had started his excursions there had been the gnawing fear that we would lose him, and now we felt secure.
   What it tells about Herriot:

   ____

   ____

5. Feeling helpless and inadequate, I could only sit close to her and stroke the back of her head.
   What it tells about Herriot:

   ____

   ____

Name ______________________________ Date ______________

"The Luckiest Time of All" by Lucille Clifton

"in Just-" by E. E. Cummings

"The Microscope" by Maxine Kumin

"Sarah Cynthia Sylvia Stout Would Not Take the Garbage Out" by Shel Silverstein

"Father William" by Lewis Carroll

Summary These selections celebrate unusual personalities. In "The Luckiest Time of All," a woman tells how she met her husband by running off to see the circus when she was young. She was chased by a dog and rescued by her future husband. "In Just-" describes different individuals who are out enjoying a spring day. "The Microscope" describes how Anton Leeuwenhoek invented the microscope, despite people's sneers at him and his odd pursuit. In "Sarah Cynthia...," the title character refuses to take out the garbage and, as a result, winds up with a pile of garbage from coast to coast. In "Father William," an elderly yet lively father offers humorous answers to his son's questions about how he has managed to stay fit all these years.

Recognize Author's Purpose Authors usually write with a specific purpose in mind. Sometimes they want to *amuse* or *entertain* you. Sometimes they wish to *inform* or *educate* you about a topic. Sometimes they want to *reflect* or *reminisce* about an experience. Sometimes they wish to *persuade* you to accept their opinion or to *take action* on an issue.

The author's purpose in all of the selections in this grouping is to amuse and entertain readers.

Below each selection title, write a passage that demonstrates the purpose of amusing and entertaining readers. The first one has been done for you.

1. "The Luckiest Time of All"

   But the stone was gone from my hand and Lord, it hit that dancin dog right on his nose!

2. "In Just-"

   ____

   ____

   ____

3. "The Microscope"

   ____

   ____

   ____

4. "Sarah Cynthia Sylvia Stout Would Not Take the Garbage Out"

   ____

   ____

5. "Father William"

   ____

   ____

   ____

Name ______________________________ Date ______________

"Zoo" by Edward Hoch
"The Hippopotamus" by Ogden Nash
"How the Snake Got Poison" by Zora Neale Hurston

Summary These three selections look humorously at the world through the eyes of animals. In "Zoo," a professor comes to Earth bringing a spaceship full of animals from other planets. Humans pay to see the creatures. Ironically, the animals believe that they are visiting a zoo of odd creatures on Earth, and pay the professor as well! In "The Hippopotamus," the speaker suggests that though a hippo looks strange to us, we probably look equally strange to the hippo. "How the Snake Got Poison" explains how snakes were given poison as a means of protection against other creatures. But the snake starts using the poison too often, so he is given a rattle to warn creatures that the snake is there.

Evaluate an Author's Message Most authors have a message that they convey in their writing. As a responsible reader, you must decide what that message is. What is the author trying to teach you about people, or about life in general, through the characters and events in the writing?

Read each passage below. Identify the author's message. The first one has been done for you.

"Zoo"

1. "There are bars to protect us from them .... Next time you must come with us. It is well worth the nineteen commocs it costs .... It was the very best Zoo ever ...."

   Author's message: Feelings of superiority are often the result of an individual's perspective, or how one views others.

"Zoo"

2. "And the crowd slowly filed by, at once horrified and fascinated by these strange creatures that looked like horses but ran up the walls of their cages like spiders. 'This is certainly worth a dollar,' one man remarked, hurrying away."

"The Hippopotamus"

3. We laugh at how he looks to us / And yet in moments dank and grim / I wonder how we look to him.

   Author's message: ______________________________

   ____

"How the Snake Got Poison"

4. "When you hear feets comin' you ring yo' bell and if it's yo' friend, he'll be keerful. If it's yo' enemy, it's you and him."

   Author's message: ______________________________

   ____

Name ______________________________ Date ______________

"After Twenty Years" by O. Henry

Summary A New York police officer walking his beat one night comes upon a man, Bob, who says he's waiting to meet a friend, Jimmy Wells, whom he hasn't seen in twenty years. Bob, who left New York twenty years ago to make a fortune out West, is confident that loyal, honest Jimmy will honor their appointment. Once the officer leaves, another man arrives and greets Bob. After talking briefly, Bob realizes that the other man is not Jimmy. He is a plainclothes officer, who arrests Bob for suspicion of a crime commited in Chicago. He hands Bob a letter from Jimmy, the first officer, who explains that he didn't have the heart to arrest Bob himself.

What Happens Next? We all like to predict what will happen next, whether it is in a movie, in real life, or in stories that we read.

Directions: As you read "After Twenty Years," pause from time to time to ask yourself what will happen next. Keep track of your predictions in this chart. When you find out what actually does happen, record that information on the chart, too. A sample entry has been given.

Event	My Prediction	What Actually Happens
The policeman walks his beat.	He will see someone.	He sees a man in a darkened doorway.

Name ______________________________ Date ______________

"Rikki-tikki-tavi" by Rudyard Kipling

Summary In India, a mongoose named Rikki-tikki-tavi is washed from his burrow by a flood. He is adopted by the family of a young boy named Teddy. Exploring the garden of his new home, Rikki meets Nag and Nagaina, two deadly cobras. Rikki instinctively recognizes the snakes as enemies who are meant to be killed. Later that day, Rikki rescues Teddy by killing a small poisonous snake. That night, Rikki overhears the cobras' plot to enter the house and kill Teddy's family. Rikki attacks Nag in the bathroom, fighting until Teddy's father shoots the cobra dead. The next day, Rikki finds Nagaina's eggs and begins crushing them. When the cobra threatens to kill Teddy, Rikki chases her into the rat hole in which she lives and kills her. Teddy's family and the garden animals hail Rikki as a hero.

Predict Trying to figure out what will happen next is one way to stay interested in a story. You can use prior knowledge, or what you already know before you start reading, to help yourself make predictions. For example, if you find out that a cobra is one of the characters in a story, you can use what you already know about cobras to predict what will happen. You can also use clues from the story to help predict the outcome.

Directions: As you read "Rikki-tikki-tavi," stop occasionally and think about what might happen next. Record your predictions and your reasons for making them in this chart. In the last column, keep track of whether you were right. A sample entry has been made.

What I Predict	Why I Predict It	Was I Right?
The mongoose will survive the flood that washed him from his burrow.	The opening paragraph says that "Rikki-tikki did the real fighting," so he must have survived.	Yes.

Name ______________________________ Date ______________

"**Papa's Parrot**" by Cynthia Rylant

Summary This touching story examines the relationship between a father and his son. A boy named Harry once enjoyed visiting and helping at his father's candy store, but as he grows older, he goes there less often. In Harry's absence, the father keeps a parrot in the shop, talking to the parrot instead of his son. Harry is embarrassed by his father's behavior, and continues to stay away from the shop. When his father falls ill, Harry goes to the store to help out. To his astonishment, he hears the parrot repeatedly say, "Where's Harry? Miss him." Harry realizes the bird is echoing his father's words. Understanding that his father misses their time together in the shop, Harry goes to visit him in the hospital.

Identify with a Character The characters you read about in stories are not much different from characters you meet in real life. In fact, as you read a story, you might even recognize some attitudes, feelings, or qualities of your own in the characters of the story.

Directions: Choose one of the characters in "Papa's Parrot." Then choose one of the story events. Put yourself in that character's place as the event took place. Think about how you would have felt if you had been there. Write a diary entry based on the event, from the point of view of the character. Use the lines provided to make notes and to write your diary entry.

Character: ______________________________

Story Event: ______________________________

How You Feel: ______________________________

____

____

____

Dear Diary,

____

____

____

____

____

____

____

____

____

____

____

Name ______________________________ Date ______________

"Suzy and Leah" by Jane Yolen

Summary This story is told through a series of diary entries written by two girls during World War II. Leah, a German-Jewish refugee of World War II, has been sent to America with her brother. The rest of her family has been killed in Germany. Suzy, an American girl, visits the refugee shelter and brings treats and clothing to the refugees. But she does not try to understand what the refugees have suffered. She is puzzled and offended by Leah's shyness and distrust of others. When Leah goes to the hospital with appendicitis, Suzy visits her. After secretly reading Leah's diary, Suzy understands her better, and offers her own diary for her new friend to read.

Make Inferences It wouldn't be much fun to read a story in which the author told you everything straight out. It's more fun to put the clues together and figure out what the author is telling you about the characters or the setting. For example, if an author says, "Bob was very poor," that doesn't give you much to figure out. However, the author might say, "Bob's shoes were so full of holes that Bob had to stuff newspaper inside them so his feet wouldn't touch the ground." This gives you the chance to infer that Bob was poor.

Directions: Choose two paragraphs from "Suzy and Leah." List three details from each paragraph. For each detail, tell what it suggests about the character or the setting.

Paragraph 1

Paragraph beginning with the words ______________________________

Detail #1: ______________________________

What it suggests: ______________________________

Detail #2: ______________________________

What it suggests: ______________________________

Detail #3: ______________________________

What it suggests: ______________________________

Paragraph 2

Paragraph beginning with the words ______________________________

Detail #1: ______________________________

What it suggests: ______________________________

Detail #2: ______________________________

What it suggests: ______________________________

Detail #3: ______________________________

What it suggests: ______________________________

Name ______________________________ Date ______________

"Ribbons" by Laurence Yep
"The Treasure of Lemon Brown" by Walter Dean Myers

Summary In "Ribbons," Stacy, a Chinese-American girl, is offended when her grandmother, a recent immigrant from Hong Kong, disapproves of her ribboned ballet shoes. Later Stacy learns that, as a child, her grandmother had been forced to bind her feet with ribbons, a Chinese tradition believed to enhance a woman's beauty. Stacy explains to her grandmother the purpose of ballet shoes, dances for her, and bonds with her. In "The Treasure of Lemon Brown," Greg, a teenager, leaves home one night to avoid his father's lecture on the importance of school. In an abandoned building, Greg meets Lemon Brown, a homeless man who was once a noted musician. Brown proudly shows Greg old newspaper reviews of his performances, which his son had been carrying when he died in the war. Greg returns home with a new respect for his father.

Ask Questions Sometimes it is difficult to understand what you are reading. One way to make it easier is to ask yourself questions as you read. When you come across a difficult passage, ask yourself why the author is including it. Does it tell you more about the setting, the characters, or the theme? Does it give a hint about what might happen next? How does this part relate to what has happened before?

Directions: As you read "Ribbons" and "The Treasure of Lemon Brown," practice this reading strategy by writing questions and answers in the ovals below. One sample has been given.

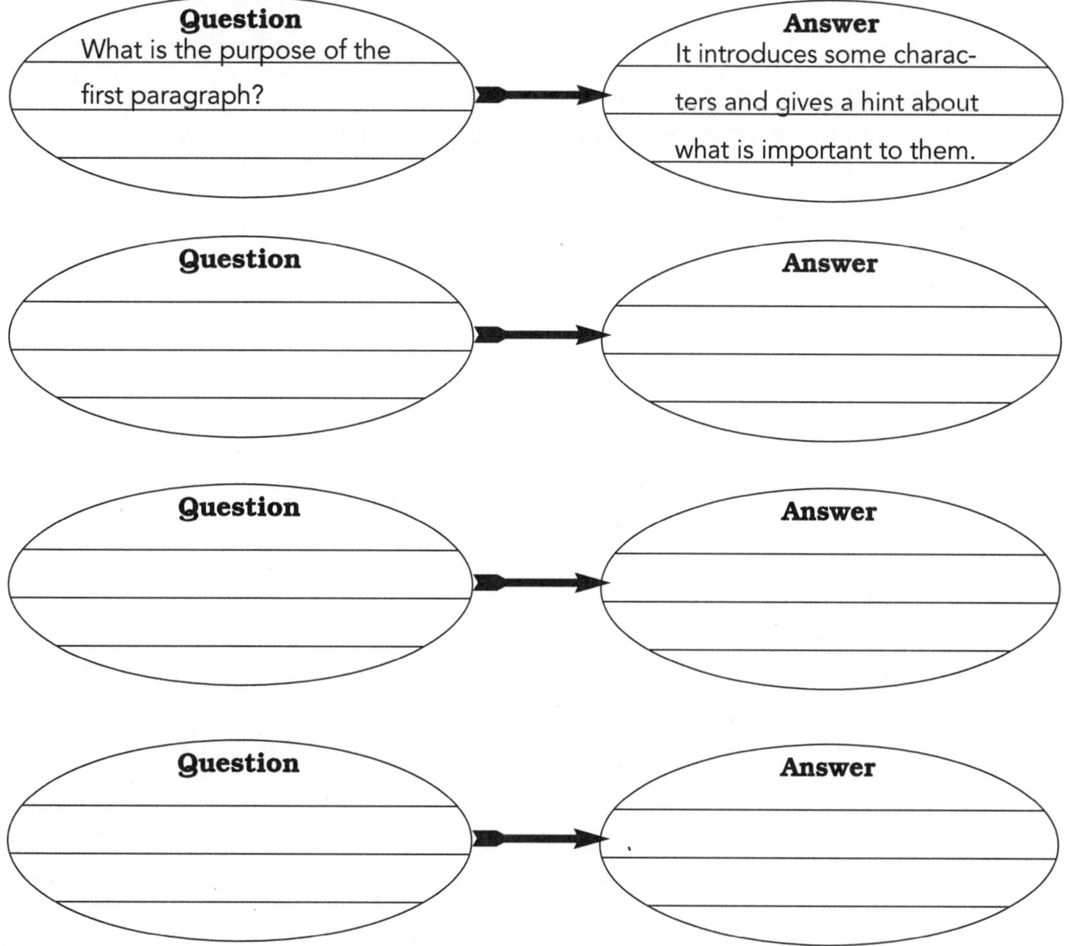

Name ______________________________ Date ______________

"Stolen Day" by Sherwood Anderson

Summary This story looks at the relationship of a parent and child, particularly a son's need to feel his mother's love. The boy is fascinated and frightened by a neighbor's disease of inflammatory rheumatism. Imagining he also has it, the boy is scared and leaves school to go home. Once home, however, his mother does not treat him as if he has a serious disease. The boy is sure that he will die and is bothered by his mother's busyness and seeming lack of pity. He recalls how she had once show great compassion for a drowned child, and aches for the same show of compassion for himself.

Identify with the Characters: Identifying with characters can help you appreciate their stories and the themes or ideas the story conveys. When you identify with a character, you put yourself in the character's place and think about how you would act.

Think about the boy from the story "Stolen Day." Try to identify with him by answering these questions on the lines provided.

1. How is the boy's situation in life similar to your own or to that of someone you know?

____

____

2. In what ways, if any, are his problems similar to any that you or a friend or relative might have faced?

____

____

3. When have you felt joy, sorrow, and other emotions similar to those that the character experiences?

____

____

4. Which, if any, of the boy's values and interests do you share?

____

____

5. Do you identify with any of the other characters in the story (Walter, the mother, the siblings)?

____

____

Name ______________________________ Date ______________

"How to Enjoy Poetry" by James Dickey

Summary This touching story examines the relationship between a father and his son. A boy named Harry once enjoyed visiting and helping at his father's candy store, but as he grows older, he goes there less often. In Harry's absence, the father keeps a parrot in the shop, talking to the parrot instead of his son. Harry is embarrassed by his father's behavior, and continues to stay away from the shop. When his father falls ill, Harry goes to the store to help out. To his astonishment, he hears the parrot repeatedly say, "Where's Harry? Miss him." Harry realizes the bird is echoing his father's words. Understanding that his father misses their time together in the shop, Harry goes to visit him in the hospital.

Recognize the Organization One way to read and understand nonfiction more effectively is by noting how the information is organized. In "How to Enjoy Poetry," author James Dickey chooses to list his advice for reading poetry in chronological order. That is, he tells you what you should do first, next, and so on. Notice how, early in his essay, he writes, "The first thing to understand about poetry is ...." That phrase is a clue that Dickey is presenting his suggestions in chronological order.

Copy the chart below. As you read Dickey's essay, jot down in chronological order his tips for enjoying poetry. Start with the advice that he offers first.

"How to Enjoy Poetry"
Tip #1:
Tip #2:
Tip #3:
Tip #4:
Tip #5:
Tip #6:
Tip #7:
Tip #8:
Tip #9:
Tip #10:

Name ______________________________ Date ______________

"No Gumption" by Russell Baker
"The Chase" from *An American Childhood* by Anne Dillard

Summary In these autobiographical pieces, the authors recall memorable childhood experiences. In "No Gumption," Baker describes how, in 1932 during the Depression, his mother was concerned with his laziness. She encouraged him, at age eight, to sell magazines in town, first on the streets, and then door to door. Unable to sell any, Russell was then shown up by his younger sister, whose determination enabled her to sell all Russell's magazines. Later, an A grade on a school composition inspired Russell to choose a writing career, which he saw as requiring no gumption. In "The Chase," the author describes how she and friends, as children, threw a snowball at a passing car. The driver chased the children on foot for ten blocks until finally catching up with them. While Dillard was unimpressed by the driver's scolding words, she was astonished that he had chased them over such a long distance.

Understand the Author's Purpose Authors write for different purposes, or reasons. Some wish to *inform*, some wish to *entertain*, and others wish to *persuade*. Sometimes a writer has more than one purpose in mind when writing. Russell Baker and Anne Dillard each manage to inform, entertain, and persuade at various points in their essays.

Answer these questions about the two essays.

1. Where does Baker *entertain* you with a humorous description of himself?

____

____

2. Where does he *inform* you about the kind of town he lived in as a boy?

____

____

3. Where does he try to *persuade* you that he had no gumption?

____

____

4. Where does Dillard *entertain* you with a humorous description of the chase?

____

____

5. Where does she *inform* you about the children in her neighborhood?

____

____

6. Where does she try to *persuade* you that she is as tough as the boys?

____

____

Name ______________________________ Date ______________

"**Nolan Ryan: Texas Treasure**" by William W. Lace

Summary This selection looks at the habits and balanced lifestyle of major-league baseball pitcher Nolan Ryan. Ryan continues the good habits he learned in early life: eating only wholesome, low-fat foods and working out daily even in the off-season. Ryan takes care of his mental health, as well, by keeping up his interests in other things. His family and his commitment to the community are a big part of his life. He raises cattle on several different ranches and participates in charity work whenever he can. He has a generosity of spirit until he's on the mound and his drive to win takes over, making him a fierce competitor. Ryan's character makes him an exciting person to watch, on or off the baseball field.

Set a Purpose for Reading Before you read a selection, it is helpful to know why you are reading it. You can decide that for yourself by setting a purpose for reading. First, learn the topic of the selection. Next, think of specific questions you would like answered by reading the selection. Then, as you read, look for details that will help you answer your questions.

For the selection, list four questions you have about the topic. Then, as you read the selection, see if you can answer each question.

Question 1: ______________________________

Question 2: ______________________________

Question 3: ______________________________

Question 4: ______________________________

Answer 1: ______________________________

Answer 2: ______________________________

Answer 3: ______________________________

Answer 4: ______________________________

Name ______________________________ Date ______________

from *Barrio Boy* by Ernesto Galarza
"I Am a Native of North America" by Chief Dan George
"Rattlesnake Hunt" by Marjorie Kinnan Rawlings
"All Together Now" by Barbara Jordan

Summary In the excerpt from *Barrio Boy,* the author tells of his entrance into first grade as a fearful Mexican boy trying to learn English. Thanks to a dedicated teacher, he ultimately triumphs. In "I Am a Native of North America," the author recalls his father's great love of the earth and its precious gifts, contrasting his culture with that of white society, which he sees as lacking love. In "Rattlesnake Hunt," the author describes how she overcame her fear of snakes by joining a snake expert on a rattlesnake hunt. In "All Together Now," Barbara Jordan appeals to American parents to teach their children to tolerate racial and ethnic differences in order to cultivate a love for all humanity.

Identify the Author's Main Points In an essay, an author usually makes several main points. A main point is a general and important idea. It is supported by specific details such as facts, statistics, stories, and examples.

For each selection below, list one main point that the author makes. Then cite at least two details that help support the main point.

from *Barrio Boy*

(a) Main Point ______________________________

(b) Supporting Details ______________________________

"I Am a Native of North America"

(a) Main Point ______________________________

(b) Supporting Details ______________________________

"Rattlesnake Hunt"

(a) Main Point ______________________________

(b) Supporting Details ______________________________

"All Together Now"

(a) Main Point ______________________________

(b) Supporting Details ______________________________

Name ______________________________ Date ______________

"A Christmas Carol: Scrooge and Marley" Act I by Charles Dickens
dramatized by Israel Horovitz

Summary On Christmas Eve, stingy Ebenezer Scrooge rejects all holiday celebration. He refuses to visit his nephew's family or to give to charity. He even chases away a caroler, and only reluctantly agrees to give his clerk, Bob Cratchit, the next day off. That night at home, Scrooge is visited by the ghost of his dead business partner, Jacob Marley. The ghost warns Scrooge to open his heart to humanity or suffer serious consequences. After telling Scrooge that three spirits will visit him on successive nights, Marley disappears. Later, the first spirit, the Ghost of Christmas Past, comes and takes Scrooge back in time. Scrooge is upset to see himself first as a lonely schoolboy, and then as a young man whose fiancee leaves him because of his obsession with money. The ghost then disappears, and Scrooge goes to sleep.

Picture As you read a play, it helps if you picture the production in your mind. You can do that with the help of stage directions, which appear in italic type enclosed in brackets. Always read stage directions carefully. Use details about the setting to imagine what the stage looks like in each scene. Use details about the characters to imagine how the actors move and speak on stage.

Use the chart below to record important stage directions in Act I. Tell how each direction helps you envision the play. The first one has been done for you.

Stage Direction	How It Helps Me Picture the Play
Ghostly music in the auditorium. A single spotlight on JACOB MARLEY, D.C. He is ancient; awful, dead-eyed	The scene is eerie, and Jacob Marley is frightening.

Name ______________________________ Date ______________

"A Christmas Carol: Scrooge and Marley" Act II by Charles Dickens
dramatized by Israel Horovitz

Summary In Act I, Ebenezer Scrooge revisited the Christmases of his past, where he recalled a lonely childhood and a young adulthood in which he benefited from the kindness of a generous supervisor. In Act II, he visits first his Christmas Present—and sees how poorly he is regarded by his nephew and his wife and by the family of his clerk, Bob Cratchit. He moves on to the Christmas of his future. There, he looks in on three vagrants who have made off with the trappings of his deathbed, including even the shirt on his back. Determined to change both present and future, Scrooge awakens on Christmas day and sets off to provide richly for family, friends, and strangers alike.

Question As you read a play, you may have questions about the characters or their actions. You might wonder what a character meant by a particular comment. You might not understand why a character behaved as he or she did. When you have questions, it is best to write them down. Then, as you read on, see if you can find the answers.

Use the left column of the chart below to record questions about things you don't understand as you read Act II. Then, as you find answers, record them in the right column.

What I Don't Understand	What I Now Understand

Name ______________________________ Date ______________

"The Monsters Are Due on Maple Street" by Rod Serling

Summary It is an ordinary day in an ordinary town. Suddenly, a flash of light appears overhead and all electrical devices in town stop working or go on and off haphazardly. The townspeople, in their panic, look for someone to blame. They accuse one another of being the alien behind the strange happenings. One particularly disturbed man even shoots another. The blaming and confusion continue and increase. No one is safe from the mob that is seeking answers. While all this happens on Maple Street, two aliens watch from their spacecraft, which is sitting atop a nearby hill. They discuss how the most dangerous enemy humans confront is themselves.

Predict As you read a play, it can be fun to predict, or guess, what will happen next. The most reliable predictions are those based on story details you've already read. Before you make a prediction, ask yourself: What has each character done so far? What type of person is each character? If I were a character in the story, what might I do next?

Use the chart below to record your predictions in the story. For each prediction, explain why you think it will happen.

What I Predict Will Happen	Why I Think It Will Happen

Name ______________________________ Date ____________

"The Cremation of Sam McGee" by Robert Service
"Washed in Silver" by James Stephens
"Winter" by Nikki Giovanni

Summary These three poems demonstrate the impact that nature has on our lives. "The Cremation of Sam McGee," is the story of the Tennessee miner who died of the cold during the Gold Rush in the Yukon. The narrator tells the tale of the final trip across the frozen landscape with Sam's corpse. But when the corpse is warmed by the fire, Sam comes back to life! In "Washed in Silver," poet James Stephens describes the transforming power of the moonlight that shines on the landscape, and how he himself blends into the silvery light. The poem "Winter" describes how creatures large and small, including humans, have the natural instinct to prepare for the cold months.

Identify the Speaker The **speaker** in a narrative poem is the person telling the story. Sometimes the speaker is a character who takes part in the story's action. At other times he or she may be an observer who merely reports the action. Either way, you can learn about the speaker from the way he or she tells the story. The things the speaker says, and the way the speaker says them, are important clues to the speaker's personality and to the meaning of the poem.

Read each statement below made by the speaker in "The Cremation of Sam McGee." Then explain what the comment seems to indicate about the speaker's personality. The first one has been done for you.

1. Why he left his home in the South to roam 'round the Pole, God only knows.

   What it indicates about the speaker: He doesn't think that traveling to the Pole is an activity meant for everyone.

2. Well, he seemed so low that I couldn't say no.

   What it indicates about the speaker: ______________________________

3. A pal's last need is a thing to heed, so I swore I would not fail.

   What it indicates about the speaker: ______________________________

4. In the days to come, though my lips were dumb, in my heart how I cursed that load.

   What it indicates about the speaker: ______________________________

5. The trail was bad, and I felt half mad, but I swore I would not give in.

   What it indicates about the speaker: ______________________________

6. Then I made a hike, for I didn't like to hear him sizzle so.

   What it indicates about the speaker: ______________________________

Name ______________________________ Date ____________

Name ______________________________ Date ______________

"Seal" by William Jay Smith
"The Pasture" by Robert Frost
"Three Haiku" by Matsuo Bashō, translated by Daniel C. Buchanan

Summary These descriptive poems paint pictures with words. "Seal"—a poem whose words are arranged in the shape of a seal—describes the actions of a seal. The animal dives with a zoom and swims "Quicksilver-quick," past sting ray and shark. Soon, the seal resurfaces and "…plops at your side / With a mouthful of fish!" In "The Pasture," the poet states in a conversational tone that he is going to the pasture. He's going "to rake the leaves away" or to fetch a calf that's young and still totters on its legs when the mother licks it. He invites the reader also to come to the pasture. The poems that make up the selection "Three Haiku" describe the beauty of nature. One of the poems describes sunrise. Another depicts spring, and the third one reflects upon an evening graced by the fragrance of blossoms.

Read According to Punctuation Punctuation marks are like traffic lights. They tell you when to stop and go. In poetry, it is not always obvious from the structure of the lines where you should pause and stop as you read. You should not necessarily stop at the end of a line. To help you read, pay close attention to the **punctuation**. Stop at a period, even if it's in the middle of a line. Pause at a comma or a dash. Read with emphasis at an exclamation point.

Read each of the three poems. Find places where punctuation helps you understand how to read the passage. Record each example in its proper place in the chart. One example has been done for you.

Punctuation Signals and Passages

Stop at a Period
____
____
____
____
Pause at a Comma or Hyphen
____
____
____
____
Read with Emphasis at an Exclamation Point
See how he dives from the rocks with a zoom!
____
____
____

Name ______________________________ Date ______________

"Martin Luther King" by Raymond Richard Patterson
"Annabel Lee" by Edgar Allan Poe

Summary These poems use words designed to call up intense, often vivid feelings, about someone who has died. In his poem about the late civil rights leader Martin Luther King, Jr., Patterson's choice of words shows how the passion of King's beliefs made him admirable and keeps him memorable, even after his death. "He showed what Man can be/Before death sets him free." The poem "Annabel Lee" tells of the deep love between the young woman Annabel Lee, who lived by the sea, and a young man. When Annabel Lee dies from a chill, her lover grieves her death. But he believes that their love is so profound that their souls are never truly separated.

Paraphrase When you **paraphrase** the lines of a poem, you restate the ideas in your own words. Paraphrasing can help you discover how well you understand the passage. When you paraphrase, you change the poetic language into language you might use in prose writing or conversation. A paraphrase does not have to rhyme, even if the original lines of the poem do. Above all, remember not to change the meaning of the lines when you paraphrase them.

Read each passage below from the three poems. Restate the same idea in your own words. The first one has been done for you.

Original Passage	Paraphrase
1. His love so deep, so wide, He could not turn aside.	He had too much love in him to ignore the problems of others.
2. His passion, so profound, He would not turn around.	
3. He taught this suffering Earth, The measure of Man's worth.	
4. So that her highborn kinsmen came / And bore her away from me.	
5. With a love that the wingèd seraphs of Heaven / Coveted her and me.	
6. ... The stars never rise but I see the bright eyes / Of the beautiful Annabel Lee.	

Name ______________________________ Date ______________

"Full Fathom Five" by William Shakespeare
"Onomatopoeia" by Eve Merriam
"Maestro" by Pat Mora

Summary The focus in these poems is on different types of music, real or imagined. In "Full Fathom Five," a son is told that his father lies dead beneath the sea. However, the father is transformed into the beautiful pearls and coral of the depths; and sea nymphs, or goddesses, ring bells in his honor. "Onomatopoeia" is about the sounds water makes when it flows from a rusty spigot. There is a stream of noise that becomes its own symphony. In the poem by Pat Mora, the maestro plays the violin in concert. As he bows before an audience he recalls the lyrical sound of his mother's voice. Each time the audience applauds, instead of hearing the clapping he hears in his mind the music that he and his parents played together at home.

Listen as You Read Poetry Poems are meant to be read, but even more so, they are meant to be heard. When you read a poem, read it out loud in order to **listen** to the musical language. Listen for rhyme, rhythm, and repetition of sounds and words. Don't just silently read a passage such as, "Full fathom five thy father lies." Say the line aloud, and hear the effective repetition of the *f* sound four times.

Read each passage below aloud. Describe the special or unusual sounds you hear. The first one has been done for you.

Passage	What I Hear
1. Full fathom five thy father lies.	the repetition of the *f* sound four times
2. "Hark! Now I hear them—ding-dong, bell."	
3. slash, / splatters, / scatters, / spurts, / finally stops sputtering / and plash!	
4. gushes rushes splashes / clear water dashes.	
5. while his father strummed the guitar / or picked the melody with quick fingertips.	
6. *voz, guitarra, violin* / would blend again and again	

Name ______________________________ Date ______________

"Fog" by Carl Sandburg
"Life" by Naomi Long Madgett
"Loo-Wit" by Wendy Rose
"The Village Blacksmith" by Henry Wadsworth Longfellow

Summary Each of these poems makes a comparison. In "Fog," Carl Sandburg compares fog to a cat, giving fog the cat's quiet, stealth-like qualities. In "Life," Naomi Madgett shows how a watch is like a life. She demonstrates the passage of time by characterizing the watch as a lively toy used to amuse an infant. As time goes by and the end of life draws near, the watch runs down, unwinding. In "Loo-Wit," a volcano takes on the characteristics of an old woman. The land surrounding the volcano's crater, or the woman's throat, is described as patches of her skin. "The Village Blacksmith" compares life to the blacksmith's forge, where everything we do works to shape us into who we are.

Respond to Poetry When poets speak to you in their work, they do not want you merely to read or listen. They also want you to **respond**. When you respond to a poem, you consider how its ideas relate to your own life and experiences. You think about whether or not you agree with the poet's ideas. You allow the poem to inspire you to ask questions, and then you try to answer those questions.

Complete the outline below with your responses to each poem.

I. "Fog"

How I feel about the poet's ideas:

____

II. "Life"

How I feel about the poet's ideas:

____

III. "Loo-Wit"

How I feel about the poet's ideas:

____

IV. "The Village Blacksmith"

How I feel about the poet's ideas:

____

Name ______________________________ Date ______________

"Popocatepetl and Ixtlaccihuatl" by Juliet Piggott

Summary This Mexican legend explains the origin of the volcanoes Popocatepetl and Ixtlaccihuatl. An aging Aztec emperor plans for his daughter, Ixtla, to succeed him as ruler. She loves the warrior Popo, but her father forbids her to marry anyone. However, when his empire is threatened by enemy tribes, he changes his mind. He decrees that Ixtla will marry the warrior who can defeat his enemies. All the warriors wish to marry the princess, but Popo is the one who defeats the enemy. After the battle, some jealous warriors run ahead to tell the emperor that Popo is dead. Hearing the news, Ixtla dies. A mournful Popo has a giant pyramid of stones built and buries Ixtla at the top. Then, from atop a second pyramid, he watches over her grave for the rest of his life.

Predict As you read a legend, you may be able to guess, or **predict**, things that will happen in the story. To make a good prediction, pay close attention to story details. Think about everything that has happened so far in the legend. Think what you have learned about the characters so far. By doing so, you will be better able to predict what characters may do next or what may happen to them.

As you read "Popocatepetl and Ixtlaccihuatl," make predictions about future events. Tell why you think each event will occur. Then, once you finish the story, record what actually happens.

My Prediction:

____

Why It May Happen:

____

What Actually Happens:

____

My Prediction:

____

Why It May Happen:

____

What Actually Happens:

____

My Prediction:

____

Why It May Happen:

____

What Actually Happens:

____

Name ______________________________ Date ______________

"The People Could Fly" by Virginia Hamilton
"All Stories Are Anansi's" by Harold Courlander
"The Lion and the Statue" by Aesop
"The Fox and the Crow" by Aesop

Summary Folk tales and fables demonstrate how stories are used to explain ideas and teach lessons. In "The People Could Fly," African slaves escape plantations by floating into air and flying to freedom. "All Stories are Anansi's" tells how a clever spider gained ownership of all stories by capturing the hornets, the great python, and the leopard for the Sky God. "The Lion and the Statue" shows a lion and man arguing their strength. Readers learn that people often see things only as they want them to be. In "The Fox and the Crow," a hungry fox plays upon a crow's vanity by flattering the crow into singing. The crow opens its mouth to sing, and drops a piece of cheese right to the fox!

Recognize Storyteller's Purpose When you **recognize a storyteller's purpose,** you understand why the story was written. Some tales are told in order to entertain or amuse the audience. Others are told to inform or educate listeners. Still others are told to persuade the audience to accept an opinion, or to teach listeners a lesson about life.

For each of the selections below, identify the storyteller's purpose, and tell what you learned from the story.

1. **"The People Could Fly"**
   Storyteller's purpose:
   ____
   What I learned:
   ____

2. **"All Stories are Anansi's"**
   Storyteller's purpose:
   ____
   What I learned:
   ____

3. **"The Lion and the Statue"**
   Storyteller's purpose:
   ____
   What I learned:
   ____

4. **"The Fox and the Crow"**
   Storyteller's purpose:
   ____
   What I learned:
   ____

Name ______________________________ Date ______________

"Phaëthon, Son of Apollo" by Olivia Coolidge
"Demeter and Persephone" by Anne Terry White
"Icarus and Daedalus" by Josephine Preston Peabody

Summary These three selections relate Greek myths. In "Phaëthon, Son of Apollo," the sun god Apollo grants Phaëthon's request to drive his chariot across the sky so that the boy can prove he is Apollo's son. Phaëthon loses control, and is killed after Zeus destroys the carriage to save the earth. In "Demeter and Persephone," Persephone, daughter of the harvest goddess Demeter, is rescued from the underworld. Because she has eaten food there, Persephone can stay on earth for only eight months a year. The myth explains why nothing grows there just before spring. In "Icarus and Daedalus," Daedalus builds wings for himself and his son to escape the king. When Icarus flies too close to the sun, he dies.

Predict As you read a myth, you may be able to guess, or **predict**, things that will happen in the story. To make a good prediction, pay close attention to story details. Think about everything that has happened so far in the myth. By doing so, you will be better able to predict what will happen next.

As you read the three myths, make predictions about future events. Tell why you think each event will occur.

1. "Phaëthon, Son of Apollo"

My Prediction: ______________________________

Why It May Happen: ______________________________

____

2. "Demeter and Persephone"

My Prediction: ______________________________

Why It May Happen: ______________________________

____

3. "Icarus and Daedalus"

My Prediction: ______________________________

Why It May Happen: ______________________________

____

(Acknowledgments continued from page ii)

Helmut Hirnschall
"I Am a Native of North America" by Chief Dan George, from *My Heart Soars.* Copyright © 1974 by Clarke Irwin.

International Paper Company
"How to Enjoy Poetry" by James Dickey from *The Power of the Printed Word Program.*

Alfred A. Knopf Children's Books, a division of Random House, Inc.
"People Could Fly" from *The People Could Fly: American Black Folktales* by Virginia Hamilton, copyright © 1985 by Virginia Hamilton.

Charles Neider
Excerpt from "The Californian's Tale" by Mark Twain, from *The Complete Short Stories of Mark Twain.* Copyright © 1957 by Charles Neider.

Hugh Noyes, on behalf of the Trustees of Alfred Noyes
"The Highwayman" from *Collected Poems* by Alfred Noyes (J.B. Lippincott).

Random House, Inc.
"Melting Pot" from *Living Out Loud* by Anna Quindlen, copyright © 1987 by Anna Quindlen.

William Saroyan Foundation for the Trustees of Leland Stanford Junior University
"The Hummingbird That Lived Through Winter" by William Saroyan, from *Dear Baby.* Copyright © 1935, 1936, 1939, 1941, 1942, 1943, 1944 by William Saroyan.

St. Martin's Press, Inc., and Harold Ober Associates, Inc.
"Cat on the Go" from *All Things Wise and Wonderful* by James Herriot. Copyright © 1976, 1977 by James Herriot.

Scribner, a division of Simon & Schuster Inc.
"A Day's Wait" from *Winner Take Nothing* by Ernest Hemingway. Copyright © 1933 Charles Scribner's Sons. Copyright renewed © 1961 by Mary Hemingway.

Simon & Schuster Books for Young Readers, an imprint of Simon & Schuster Children's Publishing Division
"Papa's Parrot" by Cynthia Rylant from *Every Living Thing* by Cynthia Rylant. Copyright © 1985 Cynthia Rylant.

Piri Thomas
"Amigo Brothers" by Piri Thomas from *El Barrio.* Copyright © 1978 by Piri Thomas.

Rosemary A. Thurber and The Barbara Hogensen Agency
"The Night The Bed Fell" by James Thurber. Copyright © 1933, 1961, James Thurber, from *My Life and Hard Times,* published by Harper & Row.

Viking Penguin, a division of Penguin Putnam
"Was Tarzan a Three-Bandage Man?" from *Childhood* by Bill Cosby. Copyright © 1991 by William H. Cosby. Reprinted by permission of Viking Penguin, a divison of Penguin Putnam Inc.

Note: Every effort has been made to locate the copyright owner of material reprinted in this book. Omissions brought to our attention will be corrected in subsequent editions.